Introduction to Law in the Republic of Ireland

Its History, Principles, Administration & Substance

WITH SUPPLEMENT 1988

Richard H. Grimes, LL.B., M.A., Solr.

and

Patrick T. Horgan, B.C.L., LL.B., LL.M. (Osgoode)

WOLFHOUND PRESS

WOLFHOUND PRESS
68 Mountjoy Square,
Dublin 1.

British Library Cataloguing in Publication Data
Grimes, Richard H.
Introduction to Law in the Republic of Ireland
1. Law — Ireland
2. Justices, Administration of — Ireland
I. Title II. Horgan, Patrick T.
340'.09417 KDK172

ISBN 0 86327 218 5 pbk

Typeset by Redsetter Ltd.
Printed in the Republic of Ireland by Leinster Leader Ltd., Naas.

PREFACE

Our common experiences in teaching 'introductory law' type courses were the chief motivation in writing this book. The absence of a general introductory text on Irish law caused many problems for our students and, indeed, for us as teachers. But unlike most substantive courses, such as contract and tort, introductory type courses can vary as much as the personalities and interests of those who teach them. We have attempted to provide sufficient material to support various types of introductory courses, from the traditional black letter type to the more modern courses which lay greater emphasis on method and concepts. It has been our intention, also, to present the material in a manner which illustrates not only the rules themselves but the values and assumptions (social, political and economic) upon which the law is based.

While we ourselves are solely responsible for any shortcomings in the following pages, there are many who have helped us in the completion of this work. First, we must express our thanks to University College Cork for providing us with the facilities and opportunity to produce this book. We would like to acknowledge the assistance of our colleagues in the Law Department at U.C.C. and in particular the help of Professor Bryan McMahon, David Morgan and David Tomkin each of whom offered welcome advice on parts of the work during preparation. We are particularly grateful to Professor Donnacha Ó Corráin for his assistance on the topic of the Brehon Laws. Finally we acknowledge a special debt to Lisa Murray and Mary Henchion, secretaries in the Law Department who painstakingly typed and retyped various drafts of this work.

We are indebted to Mr. Seamus Cashman of Wolfhound Press whose keen interest in this venture has been a great inspiration.

Finally our thanks to our respective families. Gillian deserves special mention for her assistance with typing and administration and Mary for preparation of the tables of cases and statutes. We have attempted to state the law as of 1st January, 1981. (See also The Supplement to the 1988 reprint pp. 327-332).

Contents

PART II: THE ADMINISTRATION OF JUSTICE

INTRODUCTION

As the title suggests, this text contains an introduction to law as it is found in the Republic. It is as such aimed primarily at the reader who is encountering legal study for the first time. If others find the material useful or enlightening, this will be an added bonus.

Even though the development of the common law has moved from detail to doctrine, it has been our experience that the law is best understood if generalisation precedes rather than follows specialisation. Despite the attention given to the detail of the law in educational institutions, the decisions of the courts can largely be explained by reference to principles. Thus it is vital to understand on what basis the legal system works, as well as the individual rules that may be applicable to a case in hand.

The law is seen as an animal of some mystery. It is complex as well as abstract. While the letter of the law may be traced to a written and declaratory form this tells us little about its nature or application. The writers are concerned to provide information as well as critical material. In many texts the nature of the law is either ignored entirely or is mentioned as a preface to the substantive work. We consider an appreciation of the foundation or ideology of the law to be vital to a rewarding study of the overall legal system. Consequently a chapter is devoted to the wider implications of, and reasons for, the legal system. It was felt that this would be best understood in conclusion to, rather than prefacing, the text and so the chapter appears at the end of the book.

The law appears to the public in general, and law students in particular, as a strange and often intimidating form. While writing the text we have had in mind those who would encounter this obstacle. Wherever we were faced with the decision to include or omit certain detail, we have asked ourselves whether the reader would need the information in question in order to obtain a general overview or idea of the topic under discussion. As a result we have, it is hoped, inspired the legally uninformed to identify the legal dimension to his or her problems, which might otherwise go unnoticed. Hence, to complement this in sufficient detail to be useful in application, the text includes the basic principles of legal study, the traditional areas of substantive material and the more recently evolved rules affecting what lawyers have previously considered 'fringe areas'.

The bulk of this book, however, is concerned with the study of law in relation to its content rather than philosophy. Three general divisions are drawn:

(a) Basic legal principles
(b) Administration of the law
(c) Substance of the law

The first section describes the fundamental principles of the Irish legal system. The reader is given an overview of *Irish legal history,* looking at the development of law and its administration. Then the *sources* of law are examined. Here reference is made to the forms of law, namely, custom, judicial precedent and legislation. That such sources may be English as well as Irish in origin is explained. In understanding the operation of the law attention must be given to those subject to the law. Therefore the *personality* or capacity of such subjects is revealed. Finally, as the law works through a number of devices and techniques, these are explained under the heading of *legal method.*

The second section is concerned with the framework responsible for administering the law. The *courts, legal personnel, legal procedure* and *access* to the law are discussed. With this information assimilated the reader should know, at least in outline, the basis upon which the law works and how the machinery for implementing the law operates.

In conclusion, the reader is left to consider the 'letter' of the law and some of the more important of the legal rules and regulations are explained.

The actual rules of the law can be set out in a number of ways. For instance, a traditional distinction is made between *public* and *private* law. Public law regulates relationships between State and State, or State and the individual. Private law regulates relationships between individual and individual. Alternatively, a distinction can be made between the *criminal* and *civil* law. Criminal law is a set of regulations imposed by a society upon its individual members, breaches of which incur sanctions aimed at prohibiting certain behaviour and punishing the offender. The civil law in this context compensates a person for losses incurred and is not essentially punitive. Individual rather than societal interests are at stake.

Whatever model is used it will become apparent that the rules can also be classified according to the subject matter involved. Thus law regulating for example, holdings in land, relationships within the family, and anti-social behaviour are labelled land law, family law and criminal law respectively. These are merely titles used to identify the collections of rules relating to each of these topics. In many instances, however, a number of legal topics may be relevant in any one case; for example, a labour law dispute may involve issues of contract, tort and criminal law, as well as industrial relations legislation.

As far as possible we have attempted to describe the laws by reference to defined subject areas, with those affecting the State and the individual appearing first and the remainder second. Where overlaps in subject occur, this is explained. It would seem that the State's position under the law is one of growing importance in the political and, consequentially, legal context.

The table of contents enumerates those subjects examined.

It must be stressed that this information, while giving the student a general and sometimes detailed picture of law in Ireland, should not be regarded as in any way autonomous. The law does not operate independently of political, social or market forces. Law is only one way in which society makes certain decisions. This can be clearly illustrated by reference to the role, in civil litigation, of the insurance company. A claim resulting from a road traffic accident may be pursued under the law, but the matter is often settled out of court by the parties' respective insurance companies. While having no *locus standi* the insurance company has a significant say in the outcome of legal proceedings, for it is the insurance company who may ultimately foot the bill for losses incurred. Similarly the function of the Gardai illustrates the issue. This agency has the task of law enforcement and largely controls the reference of cases to court by selection and investigation. The law is but one aspect of the social structure and is also one aspect of one legal system. To regard the law in any other way would be unrealistic and artificial.

For readers wanting more detailed explanations reference is given in the notes to further material on the relevant issues.

If questioned about the structure and content of the law, the reader will at least be equipped to answer, and this text will serve a valuable purpose. Law, in common with other primary services such as health and education, is an institution to which all should have access and the facility to study and comprehend, and where necessary utilise.

One note of explanation in conclusion here. As the title suggests, the text is concerned with law as it is found in the Republic of Ireland. For political and constitutional reasons it would be unsatisfactory to disregard the six counties of Northern Ireland. The reader will appreciate, notwithstanding the provisions of the 1937 Constitution, that Northern Ireland, as part of the United Kingdom, is subject to laws of British origin and is under the *de jure* control of the British Parliament. The historical connections and geographical proximity of the North to the Republic, however, make it inevitable that law in both areas has enjoyed considerable overlap in a practical sense.

In order to describe law as it is found in the Republic, the North is effectively ignored, except where the jurisdiction of the Irish courts extends to matters over the border. Where overlap does occur, it is duly noted.

The purpose of this book is to present a clear, simplified, and questioning analysis of the law. It is hoped that readers will include law students and those working alongside of the law (e.g. social workers) as well as members of the general public, each using the text as a broad base from which to pursue further objectives.

The law is stated as at 1st January, 1981. The 'Supplement' on p. 327 below outlines significant developments since this book was first published.

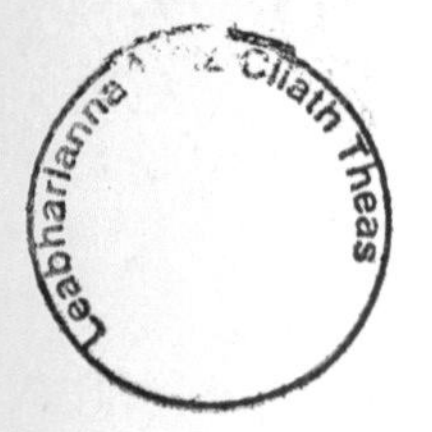

PART I

BASIC LEGAL PRINCIPLES

Chapter 1

HISTORY OF IRISH LAW

This chapter is devoted to a study of the growth of law and its administration in Ireland.

Two problems are encountered when unfolding the details of such development. First, the Irish legal system is rooted in a variety of sources, from supposed tribal origins, through the intervention of the common law, to the written constitutions of the 20th century. Each has a particular relevance to Irish legal history and, indeed, the extent to which the influence of each outweighs or complements the other is a matter for speculation. It is perhaps a common failing to explain Irish law either with nationalistic fervour or to lapse into generalisations, overplaying the role of the English law in this process of development. What *should* be assessed are the distinct regional and national differences peculiar to Ireland.

The second problem is that traditional explanations of legal history tend to be essentially descriptive, stressing dates, statutes, kings and queens. While there is much to be learnt from this 'factual' exposition it really avoids the fundamental issues that contextualise the study of law. To understand the meaning and relevance of law (if this is to be an objective) reference must be made to the political, economic and social structures within which that law operates. For example, many texts deal with the history of law in two separate categories, namely, the courts and the body of law (i.e. the rules). It is suggested in the following pages that by dealing chronologically with the development of the legal system (i.e. law and administration) emphasis can be placed on significant characteristics of law rather than on a description of content, as if it were autonomous.

Consequently, the history of Irish law herein is divided into the following periods:

(i) Law in Ireland before 1171
(ii) The growth of the common law, 1171-1800
(iii) The 19th century reforms

(iv) The Constitutional upheavals of 1922-37

Although these divisions span enormous periods of time it is felt that they highlight the salient features of Irish legal history. In the following brief and general summary it is hoped that certain characteristics as well as 'facts' emerge in the account of the shaping of the law in Ireland as it is found today.

LAW IN IRELAND BEFORE THE NORMANS

The Law of Kingdoms

Before the Norman invasions of 1066 and 1171 both England and Ireland were regionally administered. National identities were still largely unassumed and the law was that of the kingdom rather than the country. It is, however, there that the similarities end.

Unlike England, Ireland had experienced a history free from significant foreign intervention. Before the 12th century (excepting Viking interruptions) Irish social and legal institutions evolved from their basis in early secular custom and native canon law without serious interruption from outside.

While both countries were in this way upholding *local customary law*, their means of doing so were different. By the 11th century England had a system of local courts administering law in the county, towns and villages with a crude but recognisable court procedure. The laws enforced did not carry the criminal/civil distinction of modern jurisprudence but rather were aimed at preserving the social relationship of lord and commoner and maintaining the local peace. Given the power of local magnates and the lack of communication within the country, it is hardly surprising to find a local concept of law and order, and a lack of national unity.

In Ireland, however, while sharing the characteristic of no central administrative force, the law assumed the form of tribal ritual and preserved, so far as one can tell, a wide variety of concepts of ownership and possession. Land was owned in severalty by extended families (the deirbfini) and divided among those who were *sui juris* (i.e. adult males of the derbfine) *per capita*. Individuals could not alienate or encumber their rights without the prior consent of the members of the derbfine itself. The important point to stress is that this tribal legality is to be found in a recognisable form by the 7th century, even though it was a changeable and mobile corpus.

The Sources of the Brehon Laws

What were these rules and how were they administered?

Before answering this question a particular difficulty must be explained. There is a distinct lack of coherent material to assist study. The law tracts, being texts and commentaries of Irish law, are diverse in origin and are riddled with problems for the Old and Middle Irish linguist. Understanding this vital material is therefore problematic. Its interpretation and collation necessitates the combined skills of philology, law and a detailed knowledge of the Irish language in particular. The writers do not intend to do more than to paint a rudimentary picture of the Brehon Laws as they are thought to have existed at the time of Henry II's invasion of Ireland in 1171. While doing so, we acknowledge that few, if any, could satisfactorily paint such a picture, even today, in any comprehensive sense. However, the main characteristics can be presented.

The extent of tribal settlement in pre-Norman Ireland is a matter of some scholastic disagreement. It would be an oversimplification to describe the Brehon Laws merely as the customary behaviour of a number of different tribes. The law tracts made no distinction between law of one area or another but expressed such rules as law of Ireland. It is how these laws were *administered* that provides the clue to their nature. The laws were essentially customary to the extent that they reflected socially acceptable behaviour relating to the *structure* of each territory or *tuath.* There appears to be no legislative function exercised by either King or Assembly and the laws were therefore behaviours that were adhered to from area to area. The laws appear to have evolved from oral expositions to written documentation through the activities of scholarly institutions referred to in modern texts as 'law schools'. The earliest prose texts (excluding legal aphorisms perhaps) are, it is suggested, to be found in the 7th century. Material, principally in verse, however, is attributed to the previous century.

The professional scribes who assumed the task of collating the laws are generally known as Brehons and their authority stemmed from a social acceptance of their learned qualities and religious powers. Gathered in their respective schools, these legal commentators compiled the tracts acting in the capacity of guardians of the law. Much of the initial documentation was in verse and, once recited, the works appear to have assumed a sacrosanct authority. The tract known as *Senchas Már,* for example, has been described as 'Patrick's law, and no moral jurist among the Irish is competent to rescind anything he shall find in the Senchas Már'.[1]

The earliest stratum of Irish law can be traced to the 6th century and by the 8th century some eight recognisable tracts had emerged. The evidence that tracts lack consistency on similar issues does perhaps show the recognition of changing customs and usages from place to place and the way in which the absolute authority of the texts could be altered.

The law therefore in medieval Ireland grew from orally expressed customs, recognisable legal maxims and aphorisms to the legal tracts. One similarity that this particular structure shares with its contemporary counterpart is that the law 'in gaelic Ireland remained . . . a secret science.'[2] That is, the domain of the professional.

The Brehon Law in Practice

The administration of these ancient laws in the particular tuath was essentially a matter for the family unit. Unlike the present-day concept of the nuclear family (that is parents and offspring) the Irish then had a wider perception of family definition and attached to this were particular rights and duties. It was the legal status of persons and groups that was to affect the operation of the Brehon Laws. The scholars went to great lengths to divide the populus into two sections, the free and the unfree. In passing, it is necessary to amplify this rather simplistic analysis. The concept of free and unfree arose from the terms *sóer* and *dóer*. The former included the aristocrats and nobility, and the latter the ignoble or commoners. To each, the respective tags of free and unfree were applied. However, this categorisation is too rigid, for not only were the unfree so by virtue of their economic and class base (i.e. status), but also they included those who were alien to the community in question, because they were not members of the community or because of outlawry. The distinction between sóer and dóer is apparently important but, in addition, and it is suggested of primary significance, the distinction for the bulk of the pre-Norman Irish lay in the distinction between those *sui juris* and those not.

Professor Binchy suggests that such divisions were fictions of uniformity and were artificial. They expose, he says, 'unreal schematism and passion for classification'.[3]

There were, however, recognised and practised social divisions between:

(i) Those who held property in land.
(ii) Men of learning.
(iii) Liberal (skilled) craftsmen.
(iv) Others not falling into the above categories, who were either strangers to the tuath or who had been deprived of their status by the law, or who were unfree.

The first three categories were *free*, and as such they held local political power. The remainder were in a similar position to the serfs under the feudal system.

An additional feature of this complex structure involves the concept of *clientship*. The free could, by giving their possessions to other members of the local society, create a bond of allegiance that had both pecuniary and cultural advantages. The *patron*, in return for giving possessions to the *client*, received support and power from the relationship. This was recognised as a personal 'contract' rather than a feudal inheritance. Once a person had acquired ten clients a particular capacity was achieved known as *flaith* and a status of *noble* was attained. The noble then had representative functions at the local assemblies that administered both the day-to-day functioning of the area as well as quasi-judicial powers. Clientship was the socio-economic underpinning of the aristocracy. It was technically contractual but effectively the client could dissolve the agreement even if at a great if not prohibitive loss.

Of the families themselves, while members would be of a particular status, it was the concept of the family unit that gave rise to most of the relevant law of the period. The family or *fine* had both a narrow and wide meaning. The narrow definition of *derbfine* consisted of, say, X and the male descendants of X for four generations. By the early 7th century the derbfine was the principal family unit for all legal purposes. The functions of the wider kin groups were contingent on the extinction or insolvency of the derbfine. Thus tribes, houses and septs were structured accordingly. The wide definition or *indfine* related further to the fourth cousins. The immediate and separate family was therefore not the basic unit of society but rather part of a larger or joint family to which potential legal responsibility attached. The rights and duties of the derbfine and its individual members were paramount in the operation of the Brehon Laws. The wider family definitions structured the 'tribes', giving leadership to a king, houses or clans of collective importance, *septs* (combinations of families) and the derbfine. While accurate definitions are perhaps impossible to achieve and for our purposes unimportant, it is significant to stress the lineal structure of the tuath and its representatives.

Given the family or lineal bases to the social order, that had the same function in customary law elsewhere, what were the laws therefore aimed at? Judging from the tracts, laws were vague even if sacrosanct but were aimed at preserving the status of the free and unfree, protecting the social hierarchy with the concept of inheritance and succession, and recognising the possibility of individual and joint ownership and possession of property.

There was no public enforcement of such private obligations, though remedies such as they existed were customary. They relied for implementation on the tribal structure with the arbitrative efforts of the jurists. This is not to suggest that sanctions were not effectively administered, for the arbitration was shaped by notions of equity and precedent, and affected by the elaborate pledge-system allied to the arbitrative process. It might also be noted that a concept of royal enforcement also existed through the intervention of the regional kingships. By the 8th century a 'law of neighbourhood' had been documented and a comprehensive 'law of person' was also in existence.[4]

In summary, therefore, the Brehon Laws were complex and ritualised rules, gathered in the voluminous works known as tracts. They protected, as in any subsequent age, the factors essential to the maintenance of the *status quo* in the given social order. By their nature, they were conservative and technical in theory and probably more liberally construed. As Professor MacNeill has noted:

> 'Irish Law tracts arose not as a kind of phonographic record of primitive customary law nor as the practice of assemblies but from schools of law and from a long tradition of teaching under a class of men who claimed to be and were recognised to be the authentic expositers of all high knowledge.'[5]

This in simple terms was therefore the law that the Normans were to encounter and largely ignore over the following centuries.

The Nature of Change

It has been seen that by the 12th century Ireland had both law and administration in a form unrecognisable against its modern successor. The next six hundred years were to lay the foundations for both the law and legal system known today. While a span of six centuries in so few pages will hardly do credit to the historical detail involved, it is demarcated for two reasons.

The Norman invasion brought a system of *centralised* administration that attempted to turn away from the whims of local magnates and the complex rituals of tribal society. This led the way not only to legal uniformity but to a consolidation of political power.

Secondly, and of paramount importance, a totally different social and economic base was given to the law. In the case of the Normans it was to be *feudalism.* This was vitally important in the context of legal history as it was to dictate both the structure of the administration as well as the type and extent of the substantive law itself. Feudalism gave way to capitalism and by the time the 19th century reforms took place the law was a highly technical civil (commercial) body of rules and a harsh and rigorous form of social control (criminal law). The whole period can be identified with the arrival and growth of the common law but, of course, legislation was to gradually increase in importance at the end of the period in question.

For reasons of historical importance it is necessary to deal briefly with the effect of the Norman invasion in England before turning to events in and after 1171.

The Norman Invasion

William I arrived in England in 1066 and had no claim as of right to a crown. He had been a military leader and owed much to his fighting forces. In order therefore to assume and maintain power William had to impose a rigid system of control on the Anglo-Saxons while eliciting continued support from his followers. This was achieved gradually by the imposition of the *feudal system.* It was impractical for this control to be imposed by legislative order, for the country was lacking in both political unity and communication. In addition, with a mere 6000 invaders William could not hope to sanction his wishes. The origins of the feudal system lay in the creation of the relationship of lord and serf, and it was through this delegated authority that William was gradually to assume control of the country.

The operation was commenced by the granting of land to Norman followers and Anglo-Saxons who had co-operated after William's arrival. By giving *estates* in land to selected persons, William was able to both reward their loyalty and in effect buy their allegiance. The allegiance itself was in the form of recognition of William as head of state and *overlord.* Both influential Norman warriors and native magnates had little to lose by complying with this scheme as, individually, they stood negligible chance of gathering support to overthrow William, and as lords of their domains, they were secure and potentially wealthy. There were technical 'rents' to pay for such grants and these were either in the form of goods or services. The units of land held were made subject in the grant either to provision of military assistance with material goods or, in the form of spiritual services, to grants to the church. As will be noted in Chapter 14, the feudal system was to herald the arrival of the basic real property principles of rights, obligations and duties appertaining to the ownership and possession of land. The *tenure*, that is the condition of grant, was termed in accordance with the obligation (e.g. a grant of knights service obliged the grantee to provide military power).

Most importantly feudalism was to develop by the further granting of lands within the original holding to tenants below the status of the *tenant-in-chief,* that is the person to whom William made the initial grant. The process continued until a complex hierarchy of holdings had been created, each involving subdivisions of original grants and each subject to a 'rent' in support or kind. The whole is termed *subinfeudation.*

The law, therefore, apart from controlling public order (criminal law), now began to represent land-holding interests. Coupled with this growth came the concept of *inheritance,* for on the death of any tenant that person's holding could be taken by the family heir on payment of a fee to the appropriate lord. The feudal system was to endorse a rigid distinction between the *free* and the *unfree.* Basically all Normans, and those Anglo-Saxons who were in favour, were free, and as such were capable of holding land as tenants and were at liberty to move around the country. In addition, the courts and the law served to settle any disputes arising within this privileged social order. By contrast, any other person, that is, the bulk of the population, was unfree, capable of having *possession* only of land on the lord's estate, with no mobility of labour (unlike the labour force in the 19th century, as will be seen) and limited access to the courts, mainly in the form of the criminal law which regulated their behaviour.

In order to implement this scheme William, in addition to gathering help from his tenants-in-chief, made full use of the existing *court system* inherited on the invasion. Regional courts did exist prior to 1066 and these were three-tiered in structure. The *Shire* court under the Reeve controlled administration of law in the county area; the *hundred* court represented the towns and areas within the county; and the *vill* court was a local tribunal. The jurisdiction of the courts was largely undefined, with much overlap between the judicial and administrative functions. Also a system of procedure had been developed that was known as the *writ system.* This dictated a particular form of letter from the king to the parties involved, to come and present their case before him. As will be seen later, the writ system was to develop the content of civil law and procedure throughout the next three centuries.

William also introduced a system of feudal courts that were to sit regionally under the names *seignorial, baronial* and *manorial.* These courts were primarily concerned with the disputes arising out of the feudal relationship and heard matters, of diminishing importance in that order, so that the seignorial court was concerned with inter-landlord disputes, and the manorial with disputes between the serfs.

Finally, as the centre of both judicial and non-judicial business, William had his own court known as the *Curia Regis.* This originated in the Witan Moot of pre-Norman England and comprised himself and his counsellors, later termed King's justices. This tribunal is of vital importance to the development of both courts and law for over the next three or four hundred years it was to consume all the major civil litigation in the country, with regional courts administering only criminal law and seemingly trivial civil disputes. The ascendancy of the Royal Courts will be examined shortly. The consequential demise or growth of certain courts remains a matter for speculation but for present purposes it is sufficient to note that the Royal Courts which grew from the origins of the Witan Moot were to gather greater importance as time went on, and the regional courts less, except for the administration of the criminal law and a limited civil jurisdiction.

At this stage it may be worth noting the sources of law as operated by the proliferation of English courts during the 11th and 12th centuries. The laws upheld were of customary origin, that is, stemming from standards of behaviour originating either locally, or in fact practised nationally. The local customs related especially to matters of inheritance and trade, while nationally accepted customs form the origins of, for example, the criminal law, recognising essential rules for an organised society valuing both life, liberty and possessions. That, however, is somewhat ironic when one considers the number of crimes carrying capital punishment, of which more later.

Coupled with these customary practices the law also stemmed from the dictates of the king and his council, which took the form of decrees and proclamations. Confusingly they are often referred to as *statutes,* and these must be distinguished from legislation enacted by *democratic* Parliament of the 17th century and after. In addition, the Church in its expositions wielded considerable influence in the shaping of the law on a basis of *moral* dictates.

The subject matter of the law was concerned with maintaining social control, with upholding the rights of ownership and occupation of land, with complicated rules of inheritance and with a rudimentary concept of trading.

Feudalism at Work

Within a hundred years of the English being invaded, the seeds of a number of important legal developments had been sown. First, a rigid and clear-cut social order had been established with the recognition of rights and duties appertaining to the feudal relationship. The population of the country was increasingly subject to central administration that not only unified the political structure but gave the law, in theory at least, greater consistency. In addition, taxes could be levied to pay for the administration and the waging of war. The Domesday Book of 1086 was a remarkable monitor of the populus at this time.

The regional control of the population was ingeniously brought about through the creation of the *tithing.* This was an imposed unit of 12 persons who had to account for themselves and each other to the local sittings of the courts. Thus, if any of them misbehaved, they could be punished jointly and severally – policing by the people themselves.

One major development in this context was the recognition of a difference between civil and criminal disputes. A categorical distinction was not apparent for some years, but criminal disputes were remedied with the use of *punishment* and civil disputes with the use of *compensation.* The courts sat to hear particular disputes of the same nature and a separate *procedural process* was consequently to evolve.

While William allowed local lords and barons to operate the regional courts, he appointed a *sheriff* to act as a link between the Crown and the local magnates in judicial matters. There is insufficient space here to discuss the important features of this office, but it must be noted that the sheriff by the mid-13th century, was to be responsible for the administration of local criminal matters and limited civil disputes. It is in connection with the sheriff's criminal jurisdiction that a significant proclamation was made in 1166 known as the *Assize of Clarendon,* whereby 12 men were ordered to produce all persons in breach of the law for trial by the sheriff at the sitting of the hundred or, as it became known, the *Assize Court.* Mention of the criminal jurisdiction to develop over the next 250 years will follow. While the sheriff effected the criminal law regionally, with the intervention of the *King's justices,* the civil law was increasingly being pushed towards London.

The monarch's court was soon to prove far more a judicial than administrative body and by the 12th century handled the three facets of power, i.e. the executive, legislative and judicial. Owing to the demands on its time, in both quality and quantity, the *Curia Regis* recognised the necessity for specialisation and it was this that was to divide the *Curia Regis* into the recognisable courts of the modern law. In principle all courts of common law (i.e. not created by legislation) derived their power from the monarch (prerogative power), but the separation of executive and judicial functions through the Royal Courts was to manifest itself clearly endorsed by the Parliamentary upheavals during the English Civil War of the 17th century. By contrast with the swift and impressive imposition of the feudal system on England (and, later, Ireland), the growth of the common law was to be slow and gradual.

At the time of the accession of Henry II in 1154, the *Curia Regis* had established a division known as the *Court of Exchequer.* As the name implies, this court dealt with the collection and distribution of royal revenue. The judges of the court in these fiscal matters were known as *Barons,* and within a hundred years disputes in all such financial matters fell within the court's domain. The Court of Exchequer was only abolished in the 19th century. The second division to handle more specialised business arose in 1180 when five judges were appointed by the monarch to handle civil disputes, not specifically concerning the Crown, and here both financial matters and disputes over land were litigated. This court took the name of *Common Pleas.* The last of the common law courts to appear was that of *King's Bench,* which followed closely behind the creation of Common Pleas and dealt with a wide jurisdiction in civil law excluding financial matters. There was in fact considerable poaching of business between the two courts of King's Bench and Common Pleas. The main characteristic of the King's Bench was its close association with the monarch in the granting of prerogative orders, restraining excesses and abuses of jurisdiction by both courts and officials. The details of these courts and the fourth court known as *Chancery* will be examined at a later stage.

This description of the origins of the individual courts stemming from the *Curia Regis,* however, warrants further comment. The nature of this division and the new emphasis on a specialised jurisdiction can be clearly illustrated. As mentioned, the treasury officials within the *Curia Regis* were the impetus behind the origins of the Court of Exchequer. The *Barons* were, in service of their particular interest (i.e. revenue raising) able to rationalise and extend their jurisdiction through elevation of their function to that of legal adjudicator, or judge. This was largely made possible through a fiction known as *Quominus.* Apart from its individual significance the nature of this change is vital to the common law system. The law and courts were to respond to social demand time and time again by analogy and fiction.

Quominus was a writ, or cause of action, that involved an allegation by X, who was owed money by Y, that X needed payment of this debt to settle the revenue account owed to the king.

Consequently the Court of Exchequer had become involved not only as a revenue collector but as a royal debt-collecting agency.

While a detailed analysis of the origins of all of the Royal Courts is not possible here, for present purposes it must be stressed that they were able to rise and expand in direct (and often fictional) response to the commercial demands of medieval England.

The administration of justice by the Royal Courts developed rapidly and during the reign of Henry II it was felt desirable to increase their scope by sending out itinerant justices to represent the Crown in the provinces. The body of judges so appointed was termed the *General Eyre* and, as a royal deputation, had limitless jurisdictional powers in both civil and criminal matters. With hindsight it may be said that the General Eyre was to enable law to be seen to be done throughout the country. For convenience the country was divided into *circuits,* and the towns entertained this travelling body in rotation. The Eyre also, once every seven years, carried out a revision of the administration of justice, and therefore kept the provincial situation under review. In name the Eyre was to be abolished in the 14th century, but the principle of circuits still remains a feature of the modern law. A division therefore grew not only between civil and criminal disputes but between inferior and superior courts. This was an important issue for administrative reasons (reference will shortly be made to the role of the Justices of the Peace, who pre-empted long-drawn-out criminal trials), and also in terms of a hierarchy of judicial authority. In later years it was to give rise to the principle of *stare decisis.*[6]

Before turning to the imposition of feudalism in Ireland it may now be appropriate to consider how the courts outlined above did function, i.e. what was the mode of trial? Three factors probably influenced the way in which the early courts set about deciding the cases before them: Firstly, even the most educated classes were highly superstitious and depended on prevailing religious doctrines. These stressed the classical division between good and evil, or God and the Devil. Consequently the outcome of disputes, both civil and criminal, were often resolved by recourse to primitive encounters that left as much as possible to supposed divine intervention. As a result *trial by ordeal* was common, involving, for example, an accused person holding a red-hot bar, walking a number of paces with the bar in his or her grasp, and then seeing if blisters resulted after a certain lapse of time! The outcome of these trials were presumed to indicate guilt or innocence, depending on the rules of the ritual. In addition to trial by ordeal, disputes were also resolved by battle on the basis that the virtuous would win.

Slightly more sophisticated trials were later developed involving the reciting of particular words and incantations, which if spoken by relevant party and witnesses would excuse liability. This was known as *compurgation.* The oath taken was of course felt to be of great religious significance. It might be noted at this stage that if convicted in such a trial a person would not only stand to be punished but would, for the major offences, stand to lose his or her property by way of confiscation. This often led to a refusal on the part of the accused to agree to come to trial by entering a plea of guilt or innocence, and consequently an equally primitive method of persuasion was introduced to elicit a plea. This was carried out by placing weights on a person's chest until he or she be made to plea. If a person did not plead guilty but died as a result of the torture imposed, their property could not be confiscated. These modes of trial were therefore both primitive and unmitigating.

Secondly, particularly at a local level, a rough justice was probably achieved by the knowledge of the trustworthiness of the parties by the local populus. That is to say, in the absence of formal rules of evidence and procedure, a 'rogue' was well known and a virtuous man likewise. This informed guesswork must have accounted for much of the working of the inferior courts.

Finally, the adjudication of the courts was greatly affected, at least in potential, by *The Grand Assize of 1189* which allowed, though it did not compel, the use of trial by a selection of members of the community, i.e. trial by *jury.* This only applied to the Royal Courts. The *Petty Assizes* of the time were merely administrative processes avoiding the technicality of Royal Court procedure, of which mention will be made later.

Feudalism Comes to Ireland

The claim of the Normans to Ireland can be traced to 1155 when Pope Adrian IV, an Englishman, granted feudal lordship of Ireland to Henry II. The authority for such a grant is believed to date back to the Roman Empire and the donation of *Constantine.* The extent to which this was accepted by Henry in a *de jure* sense must be speculated. It was at least an excuse for invasion.

Acting on the basis of legal and constitutional entitlement, Henry II decided to conquer this previously ignored territory, thus extending the common law to Brehon Ireland. In 1166 the Earl of Pembroke, referred to as 'Strongbow', undertook to restore one Diarmuid, a lord in Leinster, who had been dispossessed of land. This followed the Irish lord's pledged allegiance to Henry II as feudal lord. Pembroke apparently married one of the lord's daughters and under feudal law claimed inheritance rights on her father's death. To reinforce these claims and to lend legitimacy to the feudal law, Henry arrived on Irish shores in 1171.

Surprisingly he met no opposition for, in return for allegiance, Henry left the Irish kings to their own ways. Henry's immediate contribution to Irish legal history was to establish a settlement, as overlord, in Dublin. Apparently *Ruaidhn* of Connacht was the only king who resisted this move and after a treaty and a series of double-dealings Ireland was assumed to be totally the property of the English monarch. By 1226 a *justiciar* called De Mansio had been appointed to act as the King's Representative in Ireland and to rule in the monarch's name. The succession of the English monarchy to Ireland had, for present purposes, two relevances.

First, as in England, the base for a political and social economy was created with vast tracts of land being granted and subinfeudation promoted. Secondly, two distinct and irreconcilable legal systems were ostensibly in force in one country, the Brehon Laws and the common law. As a reflection of both this incompatible difference and the energies and priorities of the invaders, the common law in Ireland had, despite the function of the justiciar, little more than symbolic effect on Ireland as a whole.

It is perhaps worthwhile to note that the common law, centred in Dublin and its environs, worked to promote the interests of the feudal lords and their vassals. Of the native Irish only those within this relationship, inside the Pale (i.e. Dublin and the surrounding area), were afforded the right to use such law. They were known as *Betaghs.* The remaining indigenous population (the majority) had no right to use, and were not considered by, the common law. Their only recourse to law was in the *Brehon* tradition. Indeed it was only in 1331 that the common laws extended to the Irish in principle and as late as 1558 the Brehon Laws were still referred to as being applicable to certain litigants.[7] That the Norman law was *personal* rather than territorial perhaps accounts for the slow process of its application.

From a Framework to a System

How did the law grow in response to the economic structure bequeathed by the Normans?

The development, essentially, was in two complementary directions. The inferior courts (that is all except the Royal Courts) were regularised and more closely defined over the next three centuries. The superior courts were to expand the civil law, reflecting the growth of trade and commerce that arose with a unified and stable nation entering into both domestic and European trade.

The Inferior Courts: The inferior courts were, as previously mentioned, primarily concerned with the application of most of the criminal law, and the regulation of local trade and fairs. While attention is attracted to the prestigious and financially important cases of the day decided by the Royal Courts, it must be stressed that the daily administration for the bulk of the population was carried out in the inferior courts. For reasons of both convenience and expense, a development took place in the 14th century that was to shape inferior court administration up to the present day. This was the creation of the *Justice of the Peace.* Although it is possible to trace the assistant peace keeper back to 1195,[8] the J.P. took office in a recognisable form by royal proclamations in 1327/61. Their function was twofold: to administer local affairs (e.g. to set wage levels and food prices), and to assist the sheriff in the trial of criminal offences. It was not until 1496, however, that the exclusive domain of the magistrate or J.P. was recognised. In passing it might be relevant to note that, judicial function apart, the J.P. was to be the centre of political activity in the 18th and 19th centuries in issuing orders to keep the peace.[9] The magistracy, by virtue of the sheer number of cases heard before it, was to assume a vital role in the administration of justice.

By the turn of the 16th century criminal procedure was well defined, with a three-tiered court structure. The *assize* remained the principle court of trial, the *quarter sessions* tried less serious matters and met four times a year, and *petty sessions* tried the minor offences and met as necessary. The distinction, however, between major and minor offences is really a superfluous one, for most offences, certainly in medieval times, attracted capital punishment. The distinction between the *felony* and *misdemeanour* was to lead to the concept of the *indictable* and *summary* offences, the latter being the Magistrate's domain and the former the superior court's. The process of bringing the accused to trial varied in accordance with the gravity of the offence in question. The serious offences were dealt with under the term *Oyer and Terminer,* and the less serious matters were handled by *General Goal Delivery.* It is also worth noting that despite the increasing professionalism of the law, the sessional courts were staffed by lay persons rather than trained lawyers. In England this is still largely the case, but in Ireland the district justice, replacing the magistrate, has formal legal qualifications.

The inferior civil courts were also important for their widespread effect, if not for their impact, on the development of the law. The feudal and communal courts had generally fallen into disuse by the 14th century as the result of a number of factors. The Statute of Gloucester, 1278, was passed to curb the jurisdiction of the common law courts. This specified that in an action for less than 40s, a matter could not be brought before the Royal Courts. This was presumably intended to limit the action in the Royal Courts, which were already overworked. However, judges interpreted this as meaning that the inferior courts could not try matters of more than 40s, which effectively made the Sheriff's Court a criminal tribunal only and reduced this *Shire* or *County Court* to a form for resolving minor civil disputes. This directed the business towards the Royal Courts and limited the likely development of the substantive law to decisions by the superior tribunals. The discussion, for example, on the growth of the law of trespass will shortly illustrate this point.

The transition therefore from a plethora of inferior courts to a clear-cut jurisdiction for most criminal and some civil disputes was both gradual and accountable in terms of current *social* practice. Several particular inferior courts, however, did assume civil importance, mainly the *mercantile courts,* known as Courts of *Pie Powder* and *Staple,* the maritime courts at the principal ports and the Ecclesiastical Tribunals. The jurisdiction of each court reflected a particular need in a locality, or represented a jurisdiction that common law did not recognise. By the end of the Middle Ages the jurisdiction of these courts, with the exception of the Ecclesiastical Courts, had largely been absorbed into the common law, although in name the court still sat, e.g. the Liverpool Court of Passage. Most were abolished either in the Judicature Acts, 1873/75 and 1877 (Ireland), and in England in the Courts Act, 1971. Irish reform in the 1922/37 Constitution and the 1924/61 court legislation ended such anomalies. Brief mention will be made of the Ecclesiastical Courts when considering the miscellaneous courts in the following section on the administration of justice.

The Royal Courts: It has been stressed that the inferior courts were numerically significant in terms of cases handled but perhaps were less important in developing substantive areas of law. The Royal Courts, however, were not only to develop along the specialised lines indicated above but were to increase the scope of the common law by the use of a technical process known as the *Writ System.*

Even before the feudal innovations, a system of writs was recognised in the Communal Courts. With increased specialisation not only did an action have to be commenced in the correct court but also the appropriate writ had to be issued that covered the particular dispute in hand. The *King's Writ* or *Breve* was the first formal document to commence litigation issued directly by the king, either in the form of a letter of enquiry asking the parties to attend court or in the form of a command and remedy rectifying a dispute. Crudely put, the writ was a device for conducting proceedings by way of a Royal

Favour. A contemporary maxim of the day echoes the sentiment behind this concept, namely, *ubi jus ibi remedium,* or where there is a right there is a remedy. If a litigant could convince the king (court) that he had a legal right, the writ that provided the remedy reinforced the law. Consequently once a right was recognised it created a precedent for future cases.

Initially disputes were concerned with rights to land and the first recorded writs dealt with this matter.

The writ of Right is clearly documented by the 13th century and ordered the overlord of the two parties in dispute to resolve the case, failing which the king would hear the matter in the Royal Courts; it was a general writ for most such disputes.

The writ of *Praecipes* was similar in nature and asked the local sheriff or lord to investigate and resolve the issue, but by the end of the 12th century it took on a new form that was of particular significance, as now the defendant (against whom the writ was issued) had to explain why he did a particular act. No longer was it purely a matter for local investigation but the *onus* was on the parties to establish their case.

While these general writs existed the system was able to administer them without undue difficulty, but increased pressure on the early courts for specific remedies upholding particular rights questioned exactly the extent to which the courts had the appropriate jurisdiction, i.e. was the court able to issue the writ? Henry II, with a decree permitting the possessory assizes, recognised the importance of possession of land and created the method by which a particular procedure could be adopted to regain land without any undue delay. These processes were known as *Novel Disseisin* and *Mort d'Ancestor.* The former applied to a person dispossessed of freehold land and the latter when land was wrongly taken on the death of the owner. Such was the demand for these writs that, subject to a technical restriction within the Magna Carta (not allowing a person to be deprived of a right to hold a feudal court), the Royal Courts began exclusively to invent writs in a piece-meal fashion, to create in effect new areas of law. By the mid- 12th century two types of writs had emerged – a *writ for real action* and a *writ for personal action.* This distinction is one of the fundamental concepts of modern property law. The real actions related to *land* and the *personal actions* to *money* or *possessions.*

In order to curb the development of such writs the Provisions of Oxford, 1258, were enacted that restricted the issue of a new, that is novel, writ by making royal consent a prerequisite to the issue of the writ in question.

Writs in existence by 1258 were unaffected, and the Statute of Marlborough, 1267, extended the speedier processes of the Petty or Possessory Assize to develop those actions already in existence. By 1285 the real actions included the previously mentioned writs together with the writ of *entry* (to regain land). The personal actions covered a wide ambit from writs of *debt* (money owed), *detinue* (wrongful detention of goods), *covenant* (failure to perform an obligation) and *account.* Additionally a writ of *trespass* was recognised. Its origins are obscure but it is of vital importance, for it is centred on the breach of the king's peace rather than personal deprivation of goods, land or money. The concept of *vi et armis* is relevant here as this was the essence of the civil wrong, meaning direct interference with force and arms with a person's property against the king's peace. The writ of trespass perhaps marks the turning point from traditional writs of land and property to wider ideas of the general and undefined civil wrongs. It should be noted that when the law of tort is considered, trespass will be such as to be an underlying principle of this civil wrong, and this was therefore a new dimension of civil law.

Because of the limitations of 1258 injustices resulted whereby unrecognised legal rights had no remedy. This was altered in 1285 when the Statute of Westminster was enacted, which provided that new writs could be created if a writ exists in like *case*. This was termed in *Consimili Casu*.

Briefly, this provision led the way for an introduction of writs which filled the spaces left by the real and personal writs and the writ of trespass that existed prior to the limitations of the Provisions of Oxford. It is to this area that the modern law of tort and contract can be traced. One of the most important developments to stem from these *actions on the case* was the writ of *assumpsit* that recognised an enforceable agreement between parties, or what would now be termed *contractual law*. The wider implications therefore of the writ of trespass in suggesting the concept of civil wrong led the way to the growth of the civil law as it is known today. Other examples of 'action on the case' include *defamation, deceit* and *nuisance*. That the law provided a remedy was carefully noted by the Chief Justice *Willes* when he said, 'A special action on the case was introduced for this reason, that the law will never suffer an injury and a damage without a remedy.'[10]

This was perhaps an overstatement in so far as the correct writ was still a prerequisite to success, but 'actions on the case' were available to supplement the shortcomings of the original real and personal writs.

By the late 16th century, therefore, a clear distinction had arisen, first in the type of action available at law (as shown by the appropriate writ) and secondly in the specialised tribunals that developed to adjudicate in such matters, i.e., the divisions of the *Curia Regis*. The missing link between this structure and that known today as law are the 19th-century reforms, particularly legislative influence in the Industrial Revolution, to which reference will shortly be made.

The actual division of the old *Curia Regis* was to manifest itself as early as the 12th century with the courts of Exchequer, Common Pleas and King's Bench emerging. Each had a distinct, if sometimes overlapping, jurisdiction. While the substantive matters of each has been referred to above, it is relevant to stress here, in terms of the development of the common law, the additional jurisdiction of the Court of King's Bench. All of the Royal Courts had a remedial jurisdiction, that is, arbitrating in a dispute and awarding a judgement. King's Bench, with its close association with the monarch (who could sit at the court hearings), acquired a jurisdiction to issue *prerogative orders,* i.e. controlling the administration of governmental and judicial functions. This is an important concept, as it permeates the present administration of justice, with such reviewing powers vested in the present High Court.

It may be noted that prerogative orders, or writs as they are known in Ireland, consist of *Mandamus, prohibition and certiorari. Mandamus* would lie to order a particular person or court to carry out a function, *prohibition* would be in reverse to prevent such being carried out, and *certiorari* would require an issue to be transferred to the court for an order to be reviewed by the court and if necessary to be quashed if, for example, the order was made *ultra vires* to the court's power. Also, as a result of the monarch's close link with the court, King's Bench had the power to grant the writ of Habeas Corpus. This is especially important in Irish Constitutional law as it is contained in the written Constitution and, when granted, secures the release of a person who is wrongfully detained. Habeas Corpus means, literally, delivery of the body. The function of prerogative orders will be noted in greater detail when considering the concept of judicial review in Chapter 4.

Common Law and Equity

It is important at this stage to stress that medieval England and Ireland had by the 13th century a firmly established common law system with negligible influence from organised legislation. The law was therefore declaratory of custom and judicial interpretation. Ireland of course had the added complication of the Brehon Laws.

The common law, however, did not enjoy exclusive jurisdiction as the above descriptions might lead one to believe. To understand the operation of the law in England prior to the 19th-century reforms and to comprehend legal concepts currently in operation it is necessary to consider the rise of an additional court known as the *Court of Chancery,* and the meaning of *equity.*

The Royal Courts were busy evolving technical rules and procedures that enshrined private common law rights and duties. Petitions were being made to the monarch to intervene in matters which were either not capable of being resolved by the common law courts, or, if they were resolved, the remedy given was not appropriate. The origins of equity are not clear, except that the role of the *Chancellor* was vital to the development of *Chancery* and equity was *supplemental* rather than *competitive* in its relationship with the common law. Simply put, equity grew in response to the inadequacies of the common law and established itself as an additional legal procedure not supposedly bound by formal rules and limitations. The Chancellor, historically, came from an ecclesiastical background and it was his function to assist the monarch and Council in matters of conscience. Hence the Chancellor has been known as the 'keeper of the king's conscience'.

The number of petitions or 'bills' referred to the monarch for his intervention rapidly increased as the litigants before the royal common law courts became increasingly dissatisfied with the function of these courts. In brief, the king expected the Chancellor to remedy such defects by examining the facts in dispute and awarding a remedy as appropriate, without necessarily depending on the formal rules of the common law. Likewise, while retaining control over the jurisdiction of equity and the consequential Court of Chancery, the Chancellor delegated responsibility to *masters* of the Court of Chancery to hear disputes. The Chancellor and chief Master (*Master of the Rolls*) were in fact to be the two judges of the court. It was, however, by the end of the 15th century that a distinct Court of Chancery emerged. There is therefore an important additional dimension being added to the Royal Courts. Given that the origins of equity were supplemental, how did this potential rival to the common law operate? The function of equity works on three presumptions.

First, it presumes the extent of the common law and, unless there is good reason to, it would not divert from the course of the common law. It was for this reason that equity did not assume a conflicting role for many centuries and it was only in the early 17th century that conflict came to a head. Consequently the common law grew and equity backed it, only developing additional areas of law hitherto ignored by the common law.

The second presumption of equity was that the truth was obtainable, and it was sought, at any expense. While the common law method involved establishing technical merit, equity intended the righteous to succeed. References are made to cases being litigated literally for years, regardless of delay and cost. So, while the aim of equity was 'justice', its ambit was perhaps even more limiting than that of the Royal Courts, as only those with considerable wealth could afford access – this is of course, not to suggest that the Royal Court of the common law provided a service for anyone other than the propertied classes.

The final basis for equitable jurisdiction was that it assumed a *personal* adjudication. This can be a rather confusing concept. The common law acts *in rem,* i.e. under the common law, although a dispute is between two parties, the judgement is good against the whole world. Equity acts *in personam.* Perhaps a useful illustration of this distinction can be found in the following example. If A went to fight in the crusades abroad and left B his property to hold for him pending A's return and A died while overseas, the common law would recognise the property as being vested in B. B's right would be a right in the property, a right *in rem,* against all. Equity may force B, however, to surrender the property to A's next of kin as B may have held the property on *trust* for A and his successors. This was a personal right not in the property itself but in the relationship between A and his successors and B.

In the absence of formal rules the nature of this personal justice has been enshrined in what are known as *maxims of equity.* Consequently a number of sayings have been recorded as describing the function of equity. Such expressions include the following:

'Equity does not suffer a wrong to be without a remedy.'
'Equity is equality.'
'Equity looks on matters done that ought to be done.'
'He who comes to equity must come with clean hands.'
'He who wants equity must do equity.' . . . and so on.[11]

While it may be felt that such sayings are anachronistic and without contemporary relevance, they serve as examples of the nature of its origins. Equity therefore grew with response to demands for greater flexibility and remedial powers in supplement to the common law.

It is perhaps safe to say that equity remained a vague set of informal principles until the 18th and 19th centuries, when law reporting and greater legislative influence created more uniformity in the law. Ironically, from its undefined and virtually unrestricted beginnings, equity gradually developed its own forms of procedure and while the nature of the remedy was discretionary rather than mandatory, the use of precedent did develop. This was assisted from the 16th century onwards by the appointment of lawyers rather than ecclesiastics to the office of Chancellor. Perhaps with greater weight than the leading figures in the common law courts, the Chancellor shaped equity with his own personality. While such may have assisted the growth and increased dominance of equity, it lay the court open to numerous allegations of corruption and nepotism. This came to a head in the early 18th century when Lord Maccelesfield was heavily fined and impeached for corruption.

Before turning to the relevance of this development to Ireland in particular, it is appropriate to consider the subject matter of equity. It has been stated that equity is a gloss on the law.[12] Its subject matter was threefold. First, it provided additional remedies where the common law was deficient. For example, the basic remedies at common law were either possessory, i.e. regaining physical possession of land or goods, or pecuniary, i.e. receiving financial damages for loss incurred. Equity, however, provided additional remedies that were more appropriate to a particular case. The remedy of *specific performance* (compelling the performance of an agreement) and the *injunction* (ordering or forbidding a particular activity) are perhaps the best-used and known examples. The exact extent of these remedies will be revealed.

Secondly, equity, albeit with a lack of formality, developed rules of procedure that altered the style of hearings. For example, a writ of *subpoena* could be issued, compelling the attendance of a witness. The justification was presumably that such would result in the discovery of truth.

Finally, and most importantly, equity recognised new law. The previous example of the crusader leaving for foreign lands illustrates the point well. Equity recognised interests on land and property that had no basis at common law. The example most relevant to modern practice would be that of the *trust* or *use,* that is, legal title (ownership) may lay with A but as equity looks 'to the intent and not to the form'. If it can be shown that A held land by virtue of some agreement for the benefit of others, then those rights must be upheld. Consequently a law of *trusts* grew that enforced and upheld the beneficial interest of persons in property, both real and personal. This was based on the express (i.e. agreed) or implied (i.e. where the court would uphold a trust despite lack of agreement) trusteeship recognised or imposed by the courts. The relationship of trustee and beneficiary has had far-reaching effect not only in land law but also in succession (inheritance), family law and commerce.

Equity had, in particular, effect in land law, attention to which will be given in Chapter 14. This involved the recognition of *equitable interests.* While the common law recognised the right of occupation and ownership in land, equity promoted the use of land other than by direct ownership and occupation, for example, in this context it would be interest that might arise in the future. Mention should also be made at this juncture of the relevance of equity to *mortgages.* Under the common law, if land was subject to a mortgage, i.e. a security for a loan of money, unless repayment was made by a certain date the person lending the money could take the property from the borrower. Equity imposed conditions whereby if the loan was repaid then the property must be surrendered to the purchaser accordingly. The law of real property has to a certain extent been greatly simplified in England since 1925, but in Ireland there has been no such legislation. The relevance of this will be examined later.

It must come as no surprise to learn that this supplemental jurisdiction of equity was to conflict with the common law, but the clash was in fact not apparent, at least in the court's decisions, until the 17th century. When equity effectively reversed a common law decision by granting relief it began to give this judgement force by coupling with the decision a device called a *common injunction* that forbade the unsuccessful party from carrying out any other remedy, that is, compelling a submission to equity. Conflicts were avoided politically by dismissing certain court officials in the endeavour to harmonise these two aspects of law. By 1615, however, the basis of conflict was laid when in the case of *Courtney* v. *Glanvil*[13] Coke C. J. held that the Court of Chancery had no power to intervene in matters decided by the common law courts. Further, he declared that parties who petitioned the Court of Chancery aggrieved at a decision of the Common Law Court should be imprisoned. At this time Lord Ellesmere, the Lord Chancellor, had occasion in the *Earl of Oxford's Case*[14] to decide that Chancery did have the prerogative to set common law judgement aside in the name of conscience. While conflict prior to this time had been avoided through political juggling and the playing down of differences, now an issue of principle as well as practice was involved. Did equity have the superior 'appelate' function?

It was James I who had to resolve such a problem and after consultation with Sir Francis Bacon (destined to be the next Lord Chancellor) the common injunction was upheld and equity recognised as supreme *where conflict arose.* As will shortly be seen, this was to be endorsed by legislation in the Judicature Acts, 1873/75/77. Attempts made to challenge this were in vain.

Perhaps the growth and success of equity can be traced to other elements away from the judicial personalities. What law was being upheld by the 18th century? Clearly, with the exception of a rigorous criminal law, the law was concerned with encouraging commercial growth and in maintaining ownership of property. Of all the factors to influence the preservation of the *status quo* inheritance must stand to the fore, and it was in this area that equity specialised. Equity provided the machinery by which property could be tied up in the future to secure family prosperity and the trust provided the means by which wealth could be preserved. It is hardly surprising that the wealthy did not object to the growth of equity, despite the protestations of the common law, for their interests were served by devices available for the transfer of property. That is not to say that the common law did not serve the same interests, but it was extremely technical and did not recognise the trust as a means of avoiding such technicality. However, these devices were met with initial opposition, especially owing to the innovatory nature of their use (e.g. deprivation of fees). The extent of the use had still to be realised.

Common law and equity therefore served to provide a system which, as a whole, was complementary to social demands of the propertied classes. Both the subject matter of the Royal Courts and Chancery as well as the expense of litigation made them the forum for dispute of a privileged few.

The Appeal – Myth or Reality?

The reader might understandably ask whether it was possible to use equity as a form of appealing against an unjust decision of the common law and if so did this pre-empt appeals from one common law court to another? In practice the fact that A asks equity to offset a common law decision that was given in B's favour is, of course, in the nature of an appeal. What briefly must be examined is whether if A is aggrieved with the decision of, say, the local County Court, could an appeal be made to the Royal Courts? The answer under today's structure would clearly be 'yes', provided certain criteria are satisfied. However, under the common law system prior to the 19th-century reforms, there was no possibility of questioning the virtue of a prior decision. There were, however, three exceptions to this statement. First, the 'backdoor' of equity could be used enabling a decision to be challenged in a *de facto* sense. Secondly, however, a writ of error could be issued alleging some inconsistency or mistake on the record of the court, for example, a defect in pleading or omission of notice to all parties to the trial. The Royal Courts would then re-hear the matter. Under exceptional circumstances a new trial could be requested by an aggrieved party, though this was not available until the 17th century.

Finally, a party could attempt to obtain a prerogative order from King's

Bench, alleging that a court would not hear the matter or had exceeded its jurisdiction or had breached principles of natural justice.

The question of appeal was greatly to influence the drafters of the 19th-century legislation when the court structure was given a recognisable hierarchy.

The Irish Experience

An attempt has been made in the previous pages to identify the main characteristics of law as it was practised prior to the legislative reforms that gave the legal system its modern form. How, therefore, did the common law system and equitable principles affect the administration of justice in pre-19th-century Ireland?

In a text of this length it is difficult to marry the political wrangling peculiar to Ireland's historical relationship with England with an account of the development of law and its administration; for this reason the writers have chosen an essentially descriptive rendering in the section that follows.

As has been explained, two particular problems appertain to Ireland's legal system by the turn of the 18th century. First, how far did the Brehon Laws still operate and, secondly, to what extent did the English legal institutions control legal history in Ireland? Delaney notes that:

> Finally in the 17th century, due mainly to the energies of the Irish Attorney General, Sir John Davies, the Common Law came to be extended to the whole country. Two decisions of the King's Bench in the reign of James 1st practically destroyed the whole of the customary system of land tenure. . . [but that] . . . as late as the beginning of the 17th century there are occasional references in state papers to the native 'regions' which show the survival of the old law there.[15]

While the court structure, under the justiciar, assumed divisions in common with its London 'parent', i.e. with the Exchequer, Common Pleas and King's Bench and Chancery, the Irish Royal Courts also included two additional courts, namely Prerogative and Faculties and, much later, the High Court of Admiralty, but reference will be made to these in detail shortly.

Where, however, controversy did arise was not in the structure of law in courts, but in the relevance of statutes, passed by the English Parliament, to Ireland. In spite of platitudes mouthed as early as King John's visit in the 13th century, there was considerable resistance to the adoption without question of the English legislation. Repeated attempts were made to assert English legislative authority and Poyning's Act, 1494/95, passed by the English, declared to remove every doubt that all statutes previously made by the English were binding on Ireland and future statutes were so binding unless excepted. Apparently this did not end controversy which continued until a clearer proposition was included in the Irish Parliament Act, 1781/82 (Yelvertons Act) and, finally the Act of Union, 1800. Poyning's Act, however, was far more significant than might be indicated above, for the old Irish Parliament, hitherto enjoying a local and largely uninterrupted exercise of power, was dissolved by this Act. Parliament was only to be convened on instruction from Westminster.[16]

Similar problems arose as to the scope of the English House of Lords and its power to act as final appellate court for Ireland. In fact the whole of the 17th and 18th centuries saw a fluctuating struggle for both legal and political supremacy that was eventually mediated ostensibly in Ireland's favour, as will be seen, in the Constitutional changes of the 1920s.

The Act of Union of 1800 conveniently brings the examination to the threshold of social, economic and political reform. What was the law in Ireland at this time?

The feudal system, that had so clearly favoured the settlers with grants of land and the subservience of the masses, had outgrown its own subsistence economy and, as in the English example, it was trade that provided the initiative for legal growth. Despite violent nationalism, insurrection and rebellion of the 16th and 17th centuries, there seemed little formal opposition to the justiciar's law, for up to the 16th century it was the *Brehon* system that perhaps operated as a safety valve outside of the *Pale.* Land disputes and commercial transactions formed the basis of law with the predominance of the Ecclesiastical Court in assuming what would now be described as probate and family matters. To appreciate the legal system in Ireland by 1800, however, mention should be made, at least in passing, to additional social pressures that were to both arise from and change the law. Three issues appear pertinent: famine, absentee landlordism and religious discrimination.

Nothing emphasises the extent of imperialist domination more clearly than these issues which were to provide fuel for revolutionary fire, ballast for the politicians and, above all, were to underlie law in Ireland.

The Catholics were effectively excluded from wealth and power and, as has been noted:

> In 1641 59 percent of the land in Ireland remained in Catholic hands; in 1703 the corresponding figure was 14 percent . . . . 'Protestant Ascendancy' over a landless Catholic majority was to be the established pattern of the next two centuries.[17]

Catholics were to be enfranchised only in 1793, and even then economic barriers existed.

Although the Catholic bourgeoisie managed to extract a steady flow of concessions the active discrimination against the Catholic faith, current in law until the late 19th century, continued.

It is again beyond the scope of this text to examine the civil and penal restrictions implicit here except to emphasise the importance of the discrimination in terms of the origins of reform of law in Ireland. Likewise one can note the effects of famine and the system of landholding in Ireland by the turn of the 19th century; how the law was to cause and gradually remedy, at least in part, the resulting social disasters, is another subject. Suffice it to say for the present that an overview of Irish legal history would be incomplete if it ignored the relevance of domestic pressures in 17th and

18th century Ireland.

The legislation of 1800 enacted by both the English and Irish Parliaments recognised that:

> . . . all laws enforced at the time of the Union, and all the courts of civil and ecclesiastical jurisdiction within the respective Kingdoms, shall remain as now by law established within the same, subject only to such alterations as regulations from time to time as circumstance may appear to the Parliament of the United Kingdom to require.[18]

thus ensuring a continuity of law in both pre- and post-Union legislation.

It is suggested that the characteristics of the law were little different from the English tradition, but local demands were reflected both in the substance and structure of the administration. Rules that centred on property and trading, rather than on developed commerce and industry (especially labour), were the foundation of Irish law. In addition, succession and inheritance were issues of principal concern to the Irish courts by 1800. The complexity of the local customs must also be acknowledged though it is elsewhere suggested that such customs were restricted by the Irish court's adherence to the common law and definitions adopted by the English judiciary.[19]

It remains to describe briefly the courts in existence in Ireland up to the turn of the 19th century.

The superior courts were divided in the same way as at Westminster with the exception of two additional courts, the Court of Prerogative and Faculties, which dealt with inheritance, family and religious matters (owing its jurisdiction to 16th-century legislation), and the Court of Admiralty (created by statute in 1784), dealing with maritime disputes.[20] In addition to these courts, from the mid-14th century the Court of Exchequer Chamber heard writs of error from the Court of Exchequer, and this court was reformulated under the Act of Union of 1800 to hear all writs of error. The assize also met, with five circuits established by the early 17th century. Dublin had a permanent assize sitting. To supplement this jurisdiction the J.P.s first appearance in Irish legal history was in 1351, and a similar system of quarter and petty sessions was in operation by 1600. It would appear, however, that, unlike in England, the Magistrate's Courts did not function smoothly and legislation was to follow in the early 19th century attempting to regulate discrepancies. One of the significant changes not carried out in England, however, and brought into effect in Ireland, was the appointment of the stipendiary magistrate, i.e. a full-time J.P., to administer and adjudicate in these sessional courts. Dublin appears to have received such an appointment in 1795.[21] These appointments were to continue until 1924.

An interesting development in the inferior court structure arose in Ireland in the 16th to 17th century. While in England civil trials primarily commenced by writ, the Irish system used an ancient process known as the *civil bill*. This was a simple method of commencing proceedings without recourse to the technical writ system and assizes were granted power to try disputes on circuit either by writ or civil bill, and in 1796 in each county a lawyer was appointed to act as an assistant to the quarter sessions to hear civil bills. This figure became known as the *assistant barrister* and the 19th century saw this office assume increased importance until the County Court judge replaced the post in 1877. It will be recalled that the English Shire (County) Court also heard minor civil actions, but owing to the lack of express alternative procedures these actions did not appear to have been so readily commenced as they were in Ireland. In other words, *via* the civil bill minor actions were encouraged.

Many other local courts existed but as these mainly owe their origins to 19th-century legislation they will be ignored in this section.

Finally, reference can be made to the relationship between English and Irish courts prior to the Judicature Acts. It will be recalled that a petition to equity, prerogative orders and writs of error were essentially the only devices available to question a common law decision. So far as Ireland is concerned this caused particular problems, for at various stages of their legal history the English courts claimed, and were often denied, the final 'appellate' function in Irish disputes. Once an appellate hierarchy was created in the Judicature Acts, the question was resolved, with limited internal appellate jurisdiction in Ireland coupled with the function of the English House of Lords.

Because of its legal connections writs of error lay not from the Irish Common Pleas Court to the Irish King's Bench but from the Irish King's Bench to the English King's Bench. The Irish House of Lords claimed to act as final arbitrator but this was not accepted by the English House of Lords and conflict was finally reached in the case of *Annesley* v. *Sherlock.* The case involved two 'appeals' to the respective House of Lords, both giving conflicting judgements from which neither would retreat. This was followed by a Statute of 1719 (English) declaring the Irish House of Lords incompetent to determine Irish appeals. A further enactment in 1782 confused the situation by reversing this in effect by excluding English jurisdiction.[22] The Act of Union resolved the matter by reverting to the English courts' jurisdiction and establishing the House of Lords in Westminster as the lawful forum for final appeals from Ireland.

Confusion is also caused by the proliferation of other courts exercising domestic appellate functions, including the Privy Council and the Court of Appeal in Chancery, but again these owe their origin to the 19th century.

It is to this most significant century in legal history that we may at last now turn.

THE 19th CENTURY: PERIOD OF CHANGE

While it has taken some seven or eight hundred years for the basis of a legal system to evolve, the years of the 19th century were to organise and rationalise a legal system that, despite constitutional changes, forms the corner-stone for the present administration of law in Ireland. It is possible to enumerate such reforms as follows:

(i) Reform of the administration of justice.
(ii) Substantive changes in the civil law.
(iii) A new philosophy of crime and punishment.
(iv) The mechanics of the law.

The changes were caused by an upsurge of legislative energy and interest which Dicey has explained as follows:

> Whence this sudden outburst of legislative activity? The answer may be given in one sentence: the English people had at last come to perceive the intolerable incongruity between a rapidly changing social condition and the practical unchangelessness of the law.[23]

The change arose for a combination of reasons. The law was clearly unable to cope with the numerical burden and changing demands placed on it by a rapidly growing industrial society. Certainly the Industrial Revolution in England was the most important single influence prompting this change. This social and economic upheaval brought a division between *capital* and *labour,* which as will be seen called for, with varying degrees of success, fresh fields of law. It brought with it a rapid increase of population in England and, more importantly, a shift in lifestyle from an essentially rural one to the urban existence of *factory workers.* This, it can be argued, was not the case in Ireland except for the docks and factories of Dublin and Belfast, but once the avalanche of legislative reform began to flow, the English handed out provisions without meaningful reference to their Celtic neighbours. Ireland was to experience the changes of an Industrial Revolution without the goods.

Coupled with an immense social change the legislature had to balance the need for progress with the demand for internal stability. Civil revolution in the U.S.A. and France served as a bloody reminder of potential dangers. In short, the 19th century changed the face of Western society and consequently its law.

The first point to note therefore when considering the nature of the change is the rising importance of legislation and Parliamentary supremacy. This is not to say that custom and judicial precedence were not still instrumental in shaping the law, but legislation was the main tool of reform.

The law, as a result of the pressures mentioned above, was open to considerable criticism from all quarters. It will be remembered that the common law and equity still operated independently and, while *de facto* conflict had been avoided, the dual jurisdictions were both costly in time and money. The appellate system (via the writ of error) was both complex and inappropriate, and required a final system of review. Procedures were anachronistic, pleadings cumbersome and errors fatal to an action.

In addition, a large number of courts had developed jurisdictions that did not fit comprehensively into a uniform court structure. A consolidation of the law was essential if the law was to be administered satisfactorily.

Above all perhaps, a political consciousness developed that no longer put the law above question. It is not suggested that the reforms were socialist in nature, far from it, but they were conscious attempts to adapt the law to social change.

It is suggested elsewhere that:

> The reformers were, therefore, faced with a threefold problem. First the system of courts required to be simplified. Secondly, the administration of law and equity need to be harmonised. Finally the system of procedure was ripe for recasting.[24]

It is these areas that are considered in the next section.

Administration of Justice

Blackstone's *Commentaries on the Laws of England* (1765) epitomise the stagnant optimism of the turn of the 19th century, a system that according to these commentaries required only renovation and repair. Consequently changes in the administration of justice in the early 19th century were ill-considered and piecemeal. The machinery that had been grinding to a halt for centuries was only lightly oiled and, of course, such adjustments did little to resolve the problems inherent in the system. Examples of such minor reforms are numerous and include the Uniformity of Process Act, 1832, the Civil Procedure Acts, 1833, and the Common Law Procedure Acts, 1852-60. However, despite there being no wholesome reform as yet, certain statutes were to have a wider effect than may be hinted at above, namely, the creation of the *County Courts* in 1846 and the introduction of the Chancery Amendment Act, 1858, the latter allowing Chancery to award damages in lieu of equitable remedies.

While Ireland was similarly affected it is worthwhile to take note of administrative changes in the first half of the 19th century, such as the Court of Appeal in Chancery created in 1856 which heard writ of error from Chancery and Admiralty. A number of specialised courts including the Encumbered Estates Court of 1849, the Landed Estates Court of 1858, the Court for the Release of Insolvent Debtors of 1818, the Court of Bankruptcy 1857 and the Court of Crown Cases Reserved of 1848 were introduced. The Court of Probate was created in 1857 to take over from the Court of Prerogative and Faculties.

Although these provisions did alter the course of administration, Judicature Acts laid the foundation for the modern court structure, at least, in Ireland's case, until the 1924/61 court legislation.

The Acts of 1873-75, which came into effect in November 1875, altered the court structure in England and the Act of 1877 applied to the Irish administration of justice.

The main change in both pieces of legislation was to create a new Supreme Court of Judicature divided into two, the High Court and the Court of Appeal. The English High Court was separated into *five divisions,* namely, Chancery, Probate, Divorce and Admiralty, Queen's Bench, Common Pleas and Exchequer, and by 1880 the latter two had merged with Queen's Bench to leave three divisions. More importantly, however, the jurisdiction of the judges was to merge, that is, each had the same powers limited only by statute and the action before the court. Thus the specialised powers of a judge of a particular division was not limited to that division. Of course, this had greatest effect in the relationship of common law and equity, for by virtue of section 25 of the Judicature Act, 1873, the administration of common law and equity was fused in England. Section 28 of the 1877 Act had the same effect in Ireland.

While a particular division would still specialise in, say, revenue, trusts or succession, the power to consider equitable principles was available to all the divisions of the High Court. In England further changes were made in 1970,[25] creating a family division in place of Divorce, Probate and Admiralty, but the structure is otherwise unaltered.

The Court of Appeal was now to hear appeals from the High Court (later in certain cases the County Court) without the necessity to prove an error in record. In other words the appeal could be based on law (or occasionally fact), if the aggrieved party could show good reason to doubt the court in the particular decision.

The English House of Lords was open to much criticism at this time for it was staffed by non-judicial peers and was, in the words of the Judicature Act, to be abolished. But this section was repealed before the Act came into force, and by convention and statute since 1876 with the appointment of salaried lawyers, its function has been that of final appeal court in the United Kingdom. The House of Lords in Ireland saw its function largely usurped during the centuries before independence.

Finally, the supremacy of equity was confirmed in the 1873 Act, and in case of conflict equity was to prevail.

The equivalent statute for Ireland was passed in the Judicature (Ireland) Act, 1877, and this created a similar structure to that in England, based on the Supreme Court of Judicature. Similar provisions were enacted to fuse common law and equity, reserving equity's supremacy in matters of conflict. The actual courts were, by name, a little different with Chancery, Queen's Bench, Common Pleas, Exchequer, Probate, Matrimonial causes and matters and Landed Estates comprising the High Court. A Court of Appeal was also created.

Admiralty, Common Pleas and Exchequer were to merge with Queen's Bench by the end of the century. In addition, an appellate structure was created again on English lines, with final appeal to the English House of Lords.

The inferior courts, with the exception of the rise of the County Courts and the stipendiary magistrate, remained unaltered and appeals lay to the High Court and the Court of Appeal in Ireland.

In terms of the administration of justice, therefore, these reforms were to shape the English courts with only recent, minor alterations, and formed the model upon which Irish Law was based until the Constitutional reform of the 1920s.

The Civil Law

Whilst the courts were being restructured, however, equally significant reforms were occurring in the civil law, again directly reflecting the social demand of a rapidly changing industrial society. Despite not experiencing the full Industrial Revolution, Ireland was to inherit the form of its substantive changes.

Space limits a detailed examination of the growth of civil law here, but the principal areas of such growth can be identified. The civil law responded to the industrialisation of England, and consequently Ireland, by recognising new *classes* and their interests. Consequently the law recognised the *labour force* and throughout the 19th century a battle raged as this force struggled to obtain legal and political identity. The industrial workers enjoyed a variety of fortunes during these years, from the repression of the Combination Acts in which organised labour was made illegal, through the militant charitism of the 1830s to the eventual recognition of the right of organised labour contained in the Trade Union Act, 1871. Coupled with this see-saw history came a number of judicial devices, especially the wide-reaching introduction of the crime of conspiracy that eroded away some of the protection that labourers had achieved. Just as the law gave a status to employees, the class of the capitalist arose. The law provided not only legislation to regulate labour relations (e.g., the J.P.s role in controlling workers' activities), but the means by which business could be conducted. Legislation of the 19th century was to allow commercial growth, including the recognition of the *company* and the *partnership* as being essential commercial units. Consequently the Companies Act, 1862, the Partnership Act, 1890, and the Sale of Goods Act, 1893, are such important developments in the commercial law. The management of money became the concern of the law, with sterling providing an international monetary standard. The growth of marketing stocks, shares and money therefore thrived in hitherto-unexploited fields of both domestic and international markets.

While the areas of most pertinent change in the 19th century relate to industry and commercial growth, there were dramatic spin-offs as a result of the industrialisation of the country that brought a number of problems that the law had previously not had to face. Basically a rural economy meant a widespread and diverse population, but industrialisation caused huge concentrations of people in cities and towns. This observation is legislatively significant, even though Ireland's cities and towns were by contrast few in number. The law, which was to develop a 'charitable' guise in the form of social security, was then in step with the philosophy of the period, i.e. based on merit rather than need. The State therefore was to assume responsibility in a number of ways for the masses. The notorious Poor Law of the 1830s was to provide rudimentary provision for those deemed unable to assist themselves. It was 70 years later that the State assumed fuller financial responsibility. Housing was also the subject of legislation. In Acts of 1884 and 1890 the working environment similarly became the subject of scrutiny, with law affecting both hours and capacities, especially in the employment of children.

Likewise, education was an important area affected by 19th-century legislation, particularly by the Education Act, 1870. Women were recognised as a distinct social group, with supposed equality in voting rights and property ownership. This seems to warrant qualification, as recent legislation (1977) has drawn attention to current practices of discrimination. The Married Women's Property Act, 1882, was to provide such property reform, giving the woman the right, if not the means, to own property in her own name and independently of her family and spouse.

Civil liability at law, of course, responded to the new and often acute demands. From the aged principles of land law and trespass came the concept of negligence, that is, a duty to take reasonable care not to injure people with whom one came into contact. A concept of strict liability arose, i.e. responsibility for an action without fault, on grounds of public policy, and a principle of vicarious liability were enforced, i.e. liability of, for example, an employer for the acts of the employee. Much of this law owes its origins to the rise of transport in the country and the operation of factories bringing people into physical contact with each other, and machinery resulting in personal injury. The law in respect of these general *tortious* duties was, however, extended by way of judicial precedent and case-law rather than legislative intervention.

Such were the 19th-century developments in the civil law.

The Criminal Law

While legislative fervour was to strike at criminal law as well as other fields of reform, it is perhaps appropriate to note the particular demands for changes affecting this field.

The criminal law, prior to the 19th century, was a bloody code rigorously enforced and unmitigatingly harsh. By the end of the 18th century Romilly noted the existence of approximately two hundred capital offences, though according to contemporary but unreliable statistics, only one in five of those sentenced to death were actually executed.[26] Clearly the philosophy of the 19th century was veering towards a more liberal standpoint under the leadership of Jeremy Bentham. A balance had to be drawn between crimes of great seriousness to the social order and lesser offences. An English commission of 1827 recognised that the severest penalties were for property offences and that public exaggeration made the situation worse than it really was. In other words if property could be protected in a more humanitarian and efficient manner, the rigours of the law could more accurately reflect the seriousness of the crime and not the extent of public outcry.

The reforms were reflected in a statutory redrafting of many offences, especially against the person (e.g. The Offences Against the Person Act, 1861), a reduction in capital offences (murder, piracy and treason remaining) and a review of policies of incarceration. Prisons were built on utilitarian principles, encouraging reform and setting an example by way of deterrence.

In addition, in England a police force was to be created in the early 19th century, only made national and mandatory in 1856. In Ireland the policing of the country owes its origin to an enactment of 1836.[27]

The increased population and urbanisation led to the need to redefine crime, and theft in particular assumed a new relevance. Significantly attempts were made to suppress not only deviance (attention can be drawn to the Riot Acts and the control of civil unrest) but to examine the causes of criminal behaviour.

This led to an attempt to regulate the supposed causes of crime, and efforts were made at this time to make provision for the poor, to limit the sale of alcohol, and generally to improve the standard of education. As previously mentioned, these attempts were, however, qualified by the presumption that to be assisted a person must show both need and merit and that a certain category termed the criminal classes would invariably exist. All that could be done with these people was to imprison them and hope they would see the error of their ways.

The criminal law therefore became largely rationalised in statutory form as policies developed with regard to crime prevention, detection and punishment. The 19th century brought with it a clearly defined criminal jurisdiction, but increased the role of the Justice of the Peace in both judicial and administrative functions, and introduced the policing of towns and countryside.

Finally, however, it must be pointed out that the criminal law was *not* codified in a complete sense, despite legislative interference. This was partly because of the sheer bulk of law involved in its many diverse forms and origins, and partly because the consideration of the legislative was directed towards many other areas of reform. Thus a complete reshaping of the law was not achieved.

Mechanics of the Law

It has been seen how the 19th century brought changes in structure and in substance. It is appropriate now to consider the changes in the operation of the law, that is, in the cogs of its machinery. Primarily, the 19th century saw the creation of a legal profession in the modern sense. Without dwelling on the history of lawyers it is safe to say that the function of the professional advocate and draughtsman (remembering that it was vital to have correct pleadings and writs) can be recognised as early as the 13th century. A description of the present functions of barristers and solicitors will follow in a later chapter, but for present purposes we can briefly look at the origins of the two branches of the legal profession.

Barristers, or counsel, came from the only 'law schools' available, known as the *Inns of Court.* The four Inns in London were the centre of training, regulating both the knowledge, skill and discipline of advocates. Two grades of advocates were recognised, the *junior* and the *King's Counsel.* The Irish were actively discriminated against at *the Bar* for it would appear that in judicial preferment the English were virtually the only race considered, that is to say it was (and is) from the Bar that the judiciary were recruited. In consequence Ireland broke away and formed the *Kings Inn* but training requirements still meant that a barrister had to train partially at one of the four Inns in London. The first of the 19th-century reforms to affect the profession occurred in 1839 with the establishment of the *Dublin Law Institute* to provide education and training for all lawyers, but after a report of a select committee on legal education in 1846, the Bar began in conjunction with Trinity College, Dublin, to train its own branch of the profession. The four Inns remain in London the institution for the training of English barristers under the auspices of the *Bar Council.*

As for solicitors, they started as draftsmen or attorneys. The first organisational move was linked with the Bar when in Ireland, in 1797, the Honourable Society of Kings Inn was given supervisory power over both barristers and solicitors. In England this was not the case, as solicitors were self-organised, albeit under the eye of the judiciary, (a solicitor being an officer of the court), from 1739, and later in 1845 with the incorporation of *The Law Society.*

The link with the Kings Inn existed in Dublin until 1866 when, after negotiation, the newly formed Law Society of Ireland (1830) obtained independence from the Bar. Full disciplinary control followed by the end of the century. Therefore, the 19th century both separated and organised the professionals into two distinct and expanding branches, with clear functions and recognised training.

The practitioners of the law, however, were not the only mechanics to be shaped by the 19th century reforms. As will be seen in the following chapter the growth of the law was, outside of legislation, to be made by the judges based on the principle of *Stare decisis* or judicial precedent. This source of law was to a certain extent required as a prerequisite to uniformity of decision making. One of the mechanical devices relevant to this was Law Reporting. Many of the superior courts had kept rudimentary records of proceedings as early as the 13th century and from the time of Edward I commentaries and notes were prepared on cases, highlighting the legal, as well as factual, arguments involved. The earliest records of formal reports of cases can be found in the *Year Books* that were kept during the years 1283-1500. These however were not compiled with any consistency and the earliest were often recorded in the formal court language of Anglo-French. For the next two hundred years or so private reports were written mainly by the judges and barristers in particular courts. The English Chief Justice Coke of the 17th century issued such private reports that began to be quoted as *authoritative* in subsequent hearings. Many of the early English private reports have now been collected and reported in 126 volumes called the *English Reports.* Law reporting in Ireland was following a similar line to that in England though never reaching the same authoritative status until the reforms of the 1800s.

In England the General Council of Law Reporting was created in 1865 and from that date reports that were approved and authorised, i.e. checked and corrected by the judges, were issued and known as the *Law Reports.* Private reporting ceased after this date, as a commercial concern had arisen, being recognised as *the* source of case reporting. Since this development other commercial enterprises have arisen in England, the most noticeable being the *All England Law Reports* (since 1936) and the *Weekly Law Reports.* The *Irish Reports* formed the basis of law reporting in Ireland and date from 1922. The 19th-century was, therefore, to be the period during which precedent grew to its present strength with the formalisation and standardisation of law reports. The extent to which, however, precedent is binding on the Irish courts will be examined in the following chapter.

REVOLUTIONS AND CONSTITUTIONS

While it may be acceptable to describe Irish legal history in terms of the English experience, coupled with particular local details, a line must be drawn at the beginning of the 20th century. In the Constitutional changes of 1921 to 1924 Ireland was to totally restructure its legal system and give a new framework upon which the law was to be based. As will be seen, law was to derive its origin from two separate but inter-related sources, that is, the pre-1922 common law and legislation (unless such was repugnant to the Constitution) and the post-1922 legislation by the Irish Parliament or *Oireachtas.*

The Last Attempt at Unity

Recognising the rapidly diminishing chances of reconciling Ireland within the United Kingdom, the English Parliament enacted the Government of Ireland Act in 1920, which was to be of little relevance except for its application in the North. This legislation divided the country into two quasi-autonomous political units called Northern and Southern Ireland, with the Supreme Court of Judicature structure, created in 1875, being established in both areas, with a bicameral legislature. The English Parliament, however, was to retain legislative jurisdiction in major matters. It was anticipated that such political demarcation was to remain in force until both North and South could be united within the United Kingdom. Whilst North and South now each had the High Court and Court of Appeal, a joint appellate court known as the High Court of Appeal was created for both jurisdictions. The court was later abolished in 1922 after proving itself totally unworkable. As will be seen the formal British court structure remained largely symbolic in Southern

Ireland, as the administration of justice was to a great extent conducted by courts of the new revolutionary Government. The 1920 legislation, however, still forms the basis of law in Northern Ireland's judicial administration.

The imposition of the units of Northern and Southern Ireland came into force on the 1st October, 1921, and officially the Supreme Court of Judicature created by Judicature (Ireland) Act, 1877, was duly superseded. However, by 1921 the Republican Government had already set up its own administrative machinery.

The Rise of the Republic

To fix a date upon which Ireland assumed legal sovereignty of its own territory and, consequently, its administration of justice, is difficult, as much depends on one's interpretation of the events of 1919-22. It may be of academic interest only, for it is easy to confuse *de facto* control with *de jure* authority, that is to say, Ireland by 1921 clearly had both a governmental organ and a basic court structure in opposition and in addition to the British system. To what extent this was able to operate with legal authority depends on one's view of the subsequent events. The *de facto* control, especially in the south and west of Ireland, cannot be denied and the Republican Government meeting in January 1919 assumed for itself *de jure* authority. Whether this did or did not correspond with the English law seems of little practical relevance.

The Republican view of the legality of the origins of the Irish Free State and consequently of its derived law and administration is clear. The first meeting of the Dail in January 1919, which had been elected in the previous year, affirmed the Easter Rising Proclamation of 1916 and the State accordingly existed as from that date. This was only recognised by the United Kingdom in the Anglo-Irish Treaty of December 1921. The Treaty of course recognised the partition of Northern Ireland in so far as that area did not 'wish' to be included in the Free State. The second meeting of the Dail ratified this Treaty and the third drafted the Constitution in 1922.

The Constitution of the Irish Free State (Saorstat Eireann) Act, 1922, was the legislative form enacted by the Irish Parliament giving force to the provisions of the Constitution. This document recognised the history as explained and for present purposes set out the means by which a court structure was to be established and, as importantly, declared that British law was only valid in so far as it had existed in Ireland *prior* to 1922 and was not repugnant to the Constitutional provisions. The process by which new law was to be made was clearly established through the Acts of the Oireachtas.

Prior to the Constitutional provisions affecting the validity of law in Ireland, the Dail had proclaimed that English law was no longer to be considered, pending the enactment of law by the Dail, and in the meantime that *Irish legal codes* or commentaries, *continental codes* and *Roman law* were to form the basis of Irish law. But clearly this would not have ensured continuity of law for the new administration and in the Constitution of 1922, pre-1922 law that had operated in Ireland prior to the Republican victory was upheld as being valid, and it was left to the Oireachtas to legislate for the future.

The Courts of Justice Act, 1924, as will be seen, gave formal force to a new administrative structure.

The British view of events, though unimportant, for reasons stressed above, should be mentioned by way of completeness. They regarded the first Dail as illegal and treasonous. As a result of negotiations the Treaty was agreed between the United Kingdom and members of the Parliament itself in Ireland, i.e. based on the 1920 legislation. British recognition of the Treaty was included in the Irish Free State (Agreement) Act, 1922, and at no time was the Dail recognised as existing in any sense. The British allowed in the 1922 Act the provisional Government (*de facto,* the Dail) to draft its Constitution, which was enacted by Britain in the Irish Free State (Constitution) Act, 1922, and the Irish legislation was merely scheduled to this enactment. Therefore the British argue that they created the Irish Free State. Certainly for present purposes there seems little point in examining such Constitutional details, recognising that from 1919 a *de facto* control existed that was the foundation of the modern Irish legal system.

The Supplanting of the Common Law

From 1919 the English common law days were numbered in so far as the Supreme Court of Judicature existed in name until 1924 and exercised certainly a hampered jurisdiction during these five years or so. Likewise, in perhaps nationalistic over-reaction, English authorities were increasingly frowned upon and were resisted, especially in the Republican courts. The preservation of pre-1922 English law in the Constitution ensured continuity of law, a law that reflected similar social and commercial demands even if less intense in form. The task of law-making as has been noted was given to the Oireachtas ensuring the independence of the legislative function in the future from the common law.

Although the revolutionary courts established during the 1919-21 period acted only for a few years they were to have a long-term effect in the shaping of the Irish administration of justice. By September of 1920 a three-tiered court structure had been created in addition to the British legacy. Parish Courts were created as a local forum for the cheap and speedy administration of law. They consisted of three members and dealt with the minor civil and criminal disputes. District Courts were created with five members to meet monthly to hear the more important matters and appeals from the Parish Court. The Court sat occasionally under the title of 'Circuit Court', with unlimited jurisdiction on specific dates throughout the year. Finally, a Supreme Court was created with not less than three members hearing matters at both first instance and on appeal. In these courts, for principally political reasons, English authorities were avoided, with law cited from the Republican and Constitutional systems, as well as local customs and codes.

It is estimated that by 1921 over 900 Parish Courts and 70 District Courts were functioning respectively.[28] The Dail courts were important for the Republican Government as they lent credibility to their claims of sovereignty, and promoted public confidence in the *de jure* claim of authority.

With the compromises of the 1922 Treaty the provisional Government was faced with the problem of coping with a dual system of courts. It was decided to abolish the Republican courts, perhaps in line with the collaboratory nature of the 1922 legislation; after all, these courts, despite being originally British, were now controlled by the Free State. The Dail courts were abolished finally in October 1922, although the judgements of matters pending in these courts had to be arbitrated where appropriate, and a Commissioner was appointed in the following year to settle outstanding disputes. Legal continuity was hence preserved by endorsing the authority of one system of law that had, since the Norman invasion, existed in Ireland.

The Irish Legal System As It Is Now Found

Bridging briefly the following gap of 50 years or so one can trace the present outline of Irish administration and law that will be examined in detail in later chapters. To ensure continuity of law, officials and courts, the 1922 Constitution made provision for the creation of a court structure, a judiciary and a law-making machinery. The Constitution dictated what should exist in outline and left due process of law to describe the details. Before the 1924 court legislation, as the old system of the Supreme Court of Judicature and the inferior court had been retained, the Government had to deal with the existence of judicial power of 'undesirable' persons, who perhaps were too closely aligned with the pre-1922 situation. The District Justices were appointed under the power of the legislation of 1836 to run the petty and quarter session. This kept the machinery oiled until the committee could sit to work out from the terms of reference contained in the Constitution a court structure. The Constitution in Article 63 allowed for the creation of 'courts of first instance and a Court of Final Appeal to be called the Supreme Court . . . the Courts of First Instance shall include a High Court'.

The Courts of Justice Act, 1924, had abolished all existing courts including the Supreme Court of Judicature, petty sessions and County Courts, and the following tribunals were created:

(a) The District Court presided over by a full-time lawyer, the district justice, with limited civil and criminal jurisdiction. Peace Commissioners (the old Justice of the Peace) were to be retained and appointed to carry out the administrative functions, e.g. issuing warrants and taking oaths.

(b) The Circuit Court of Justice replacing the County Courts, with a Circuit Court judge dealing with wider but still limited powers of civil and criminal jurisdiction.

(c) The High Court, with six judges including the President, and the jurisdiction of the Old High Court was transferred to this new court. The High Court was, in addition to its civil jurisdiction, to sit as a criminal tribunal under the name of the Central Criminal Court in Dublin for serious crimes and was in particular to assume prerogative powers.

(d) The Supreme Court, with three judges, with the jurisdiction of the old Court of Appeal and the additional powers granted by the Constitution.

(e) The Court of High Court Circuit to travel on circuit. This provision was not enacted.

Amendments were made in 1936 but this basic structure remained unaltered for a decade until the abolition of the Free State in 1937 and the Constitution of that year. This Constitution came into force in December 1937 and laid down the framework for law and its administration. Article 34 deals with the administration of justice and the judiciary, and in effect ratified the court structure created in 1924. One anomaly must be mentioned at this stage: no ratifying legislation formally creating a court structure was enacted for almost 25 years, and in 1961 the Courts (Establishment and Constitution) Act and the Courts (Supplemental Provision) Act were passed to give effect to the framework spelt out in the Constitution. This gives rise to certain Constitutional questions. Article 34 of the 1937 Constitution allows for the law to be administered in courts established by law, and by judges appointed in accordance with the provisions of the Constitution. This would appear to mean that the courts in existence prior to the 1937 Constitution, as they had been created by law (1924 legislation), were Constitutional, despite the lack of legislation specifically creating a court structure until 1961. However, Article 35 dictates that the judiciary should be appointed by the President and it is arguable, although perhaps somewhat academic, that the courts between 1937 and 1961 were unconstitutional to the extent that they were staffed by judges who had not been appointed under the Constitution.

The details of this legislation and the description of the present function and jurisdiction of the courts will follow later.

CONCLUSION

Irish legal history dates back over at least ten centuries. The vague and undefined origins and forms of the Brehon Laws mingle with the gradual domination of the common law and both Anglo-Saxon and Norman influences. The Constitutional changes brought about in recent years have to a certain extent clarified the position, in so far as the basis for law and its administration had now a written and authoritative form. To study such, however, in isolation would be a serious error. Not only do the previous centuries complete a chronological history, but the very nature of the system as it works today, the presumptions upon which it is based, and the institutions it attempts to preserve, are thus more clearly revealed.

Speculation is not the purpose of this text, but it is interesting to take note of the direction in which law and administration in Ireland is heading *vis-à-vis* historical evolution. While the formal court structure operates as described, additional forms of judicial and quasi-judicial tribunals have emerged to cope with the adjudicative demands of modern society. For example, the Employment Appeals Tribunal has recently been formulated to deal exclusively with labour law disputes and is specifically geared to hearing these specialised matters. Similarly tribunals have been created to handle other reaches of law and administration that the courts are traditionally unfamiliar with. In this area the example of disputes concerning the award of welfare benefits would appear particularly relevant, although in Ireland there is as yet an undeveloped tribunal system to administer such disputes, unlike its English neighbour. This seems to be an important direction in terms of modern legal history.

The following pages will attempt to highlight the characteristics of a system inherited from the history of events portrayed, to draw attention to the machinery for the operation of that system and briefly, to sketch the most important of its laws.

Chapter 2

THE SOURCES OF IRISH LAW

One of the more significant differences between a lawyer and his client is not, strictly speaking, that the lawyer knows more law, but rather that the lawyer knows more *about* the law. Indeed when one considers the vast bulk of principles and rules of which any modern system is comprised, lawyers actually *know* very little law. A lawyer's value or contribution to his client is based essentially on two skills: first, his ability *to find* the appropriate legal rules or principles and, secondly, his ability *to predict the effect* of such rules or principles upon the problem presented by a client. There are of course many other skills which a competent lawyer must possess, for example, the ability to employ the legal process to the best advantage of his client, but they all presuppose the ability to select properly and apply the appropriate rules. In this chapter we are concerned with these two important skills.

To explain what we mean by a 'source of law' in this context we could do much worse than adopt the following words of Sir Rupert Cross, as expressed in his excellent work *Precedent in English Law*:

> In this sense 'source' means, not a causal origin, direct or remote, but that from which a rule derives its validity as a rule of law. The inquiry is not 'How do you account for the content of a particular legal rule?' but, 'Why do you say that certain rules are rules of law?'[1]

In one sense, then, the chief source of Irish law is the Constitution of 1937 which lends validity or legitimacy to all rules and principles. The authority of the Oireachtas and of the courts, as well as all the previous law, derives validity from the Constitution of 1937. But this hardly solves the issue since we are concerned to find the actual rule of principle itself, rather than with just determining its validity.

In a very small and simple society all the necessary rules or principles might be found in one book, though even here it is unlikely that it would be possible to provide for all contingencies in advance. Alternatively, or additionally, such a society could appoint one of its members to resolve all disputes, guided only by his own sense of justice and the generally accepted customs of the society. As such a society grew in numbers and complexity, two further problems would be likely to emerge. First, there would probably be a need to appoint more judges, with the consequential need to ensure consistency and uniformity of decision from one judge to another. Secondly, a developing society is likely to require new rules on matters, and at a rate which the judges could not efficiently deal with. In addition, people may require to know what the law is when planning even the simplest of transactions, in order to avoid a subsequent dispute. Only after much time and energy could these latter needs be met by a system which depended solely on disputes to produce new rules. The main sources of Irish law are derived from both of these approaches, namely, the authority of the judges and the authority of the people as expressed through Parliament.

The two major sources of Irish law are judge-made law (or case-law) and legislation (or statutes). In the early days of the common law there was very little legislation and thus the chief source of law was the decisions of the courts in particular cases. It has only been in the last two hundred years or so that legislation has emerged as an important source of legal rules and principles. In addition to these two major sources there are a number of minor sources such as custom and authoritative texts. We intend to deal with each source separately but it should be emphasised that the principles which govern any particular issue may have to be derived from several different sources. Thus if we wished to discover the law which governs the rights of a consumer against the seller or manufacturer of a defective article, we would have to refer to principles of contract and tort as developed by the courts, to legislation such as the Sale of Goods Act, 1893 and 1980, and The Consumer Information Act, 1978, various directives and regulations emanating from the institutions of the European Communities and possibly even to some recent decisions of foreign courts. In other words it would be necessary to check through all the sources in order to select the relevant principles.

I CASE-LAW OR PRECEDENT

We have already dealt with the vital role played by the Royal Justices and the Royal Courts in the development of our law. The common law judges were clearly aware of the need for consistency and uniformity in their decisions and attempted to achieve this by following previous decisions wherever possible. Such a practice has much to recommend it and it is a feature not only of all legal systems but also of most forms of collective (and even individual) behaviour. In the early stages of the common law it was in this general sense that precedent was employed. It is clear that, even as early as the 12th century, cases were being cited before the courts, but at this time, and indeed for long thereafter, there was no suggestion the courts were *bound* to follow such precedents. This was a much later development and could only occur when there had been established a settled hierarchy of courts and when reliable and accurate law reports were made available. The peculiarity of the common law, then, lies not in its use of precedent but rather in the special way in which the doctrine has been applied since about the middle of the last century when these two latter conditions were satisfied. In referring to the special manner in which our law employs precedent we refer to the doctrine of *stare decisis.*

According to this doctrine not only will courts follow previous decisions but in certain cases they are bound to do so. To put the matter another way previous decisions create law which must be followed or applied by subsequent courts when dealing with similar cases. Each court in the judicial hierarchy is, strictly speaking, bound by its own previous decisions and by the decisions of courts superior to it in the hierarchy. But this apparently simple description raises two crucial matters: first, what part of a judge's decision is law and therefore binding on subsequent courts and, secondly, when are cases considered 'similar' in this context.

RATIO DECIDENDI AND OBITER DICTA

It is not everything which a judge says in his judgement which constitutes 'law', or is binding on subsequent courts. It is only the principle of law, based on the material facts of the case, which the judge considers necessary for his decision which is given this status. Lawyers refer to this principle as the *ratio decidendi* of the case. Statements or pronouncements on legal principle which are not essential to the decision are referred to as *obiter dicta.* Statements of legal principle which are *obiter* may be highly *persuasive,* particularly when made by eminent judges of the superior courts, but they are never binding on subsequent courts. Though such statements are frequently followed or applied by subsequent courts there can be no question of a later court being bound to do so. On the other hand the *ratio decidendi* of a decision must be followed or applied by a later court of equal or inferior jurisdiction when the material facts are similar in both cases.

Students sometimes experience considerable difficulty, not in understanding these rules, but in applying them. 'I know what ratio decidendi is,' the student will say, 'but how do I find it in a written judgement of anything from ten lines to one hundred pages?' It is cold comfort to such a student to be informed that his question raises a problem of technique or skill which he will surely acquire after sufficient dealing with the law reports. Fortunately it is possible to offer some guide-lines on the matter of finding or extracting the ratio decidendi of a decision, but there is more than a grain of truth in the advice that the best way to acquire a skill is through prolonged (and sometimes painful) practice.

While there is no standard form to which judges must conform when presenting or writing their judgements, it is usual for most judges to follow a common pattern. A judge will usually divide his judgement into three parts. First, he will set out the facts as agreed or proven, secondly, he will review a number of applicable principles and select the appropriate one(s) and, finally, he will apply the latter to the former and give his decision. The judge himself will not point to the *ratio decidendi,* and it is extremely rare to be able to point to a particular section or extract from the judgement as constituting the *ratio.* More frequently the *ratio* must be constructed, i.e. it will be necessary, after a careful reading of the entire judgement, to formulate the *ratio decidendi* by combining the appropriate ingredients. The process, therefore, is usually one of formulation or construction rather than one of extraction or identification of a particular part of the judgement.

The starting-point will, of course, be the judge's pronouncements on the law, since what we are searching for is the legal principle underlying the decision. But such statements must be qualified in view of the particular facts of the case. The point was well illustrated by Lord Halsbury in *Quinn* v. *Leathem* when he said:

> Every judgement must be read as applicable to the particular facts proved, since the generality of the expressions which may be found there are not intended to be expositions of the whole law but govern and are qualified by the particular facts of the case in which such expressions are to be found.[2]

The first task, therefore, is to determine the principles which 'govern and are qualified' by the particular or material facts of the case. One method which can assist in this process is the Inversion Test or, as it is sometimes called, Wambough's Test. This test involves the following steps:

(i) Frame carefully the proposed principle.

(ii) Insert a word which reverses the meaning of this principle.

(iii) Consider the following question: 'If the court had this new proposition in mind when reaching its decision and had accepted it as good law, could the court have reached the same decision?'

(iv) If the answer in (iii) is in the affirmative then the original proposition cannot be the correct principle.

An example will help to illustrate the point. Let us suppose that we are dealing with a case in which the consumer of a bottle of beer is suing the manufacturer because the contents of the bottle contained some poisonous substance which caused serious injury to the consumer. Let us further suppose that the consumer was successful in his action. In searching for the ratio of the case we come across a statement by the judge that 'motorists owe a duty of care to pedestrians'. In order to determine whether this principle forms part of the ratio we could proceed in the following way:

(i) Motorists owe a duty of care to pedestrians.

(ii) Motorists *do not* owe a duty of care to pedestrians.

(iii) If the judge had treated the proposition in (b) as a correct statement of the law, could he nonetheless have decided that a manufacturer owes a duty of care to a consumer?

(iv) Clearly the answer is in the affirmative; there is nothing contradictory in stating the motorists do not owe a duty to pedestrians while manufacturers do owe a duty to consumers. These propositions are not mutually exclusive.

Our conclusion therefore would be that, irrespective of how accurate the original proposition might be, it did not form part of the *ratio decidendi* of the case. This example also helps to illustrate the impossibility of attempting to select the appropriate proposition without regard to the facts of the case. In the final analysis we rejected the original proposition because it was not sufficiently related to those facts. This is the sense in which the statements of principle must govern the facts.

Usually the most difficult problem in formulating the ratio is not in selecting the appropriate principle but rather in determining how far that principle as enunciated by the judge must be qualified by the particular facts of the case. The first point to note is that the proposition or statement of principle is not governed by *all* the facts of the case but only by those treated as *material* by the judge. Let us return to our example and amplify the facts. The bottle of beer was produced by a Cork firm and sold in Dublin at 3 a.m. to a Wexford man. The beer was purchased for 50p. It was consumed the same day and the consumer was removed to hospital with severe stomach pains later that evening. His illness was diagnosed as food poisoning and he was released after two weeks hospitalisation. His loss of salary was £200 during this period and his doctor's fees and hospital expenses amounted to a further £150. It was established in the course of the trial that the consumer could not have detected the poisonous substance in the beer without exceptional precaution which he could not have been expected to take. It was also established that the manufacturer intended the product to reach the consumer in the form in which it left him.

How do we determine the facts treated as material by the judge? Common sense and normal powers of perception should take us very close to a solution. First, the geographical information is clearly not material, secondly, the time of purchase and the price must also be excluded, as must the details of the injury (though not the fact of the injury) to the plaintiff. We are then left with the following facts. A manufacturer produced a product which he intended to reach the ultimate consumer in the form in which it left him and which contained a defect which no reasonable examination could reveal. The plaintiff consumed the product and suffered injury. The plaintiff was awarded damages.

Returning to the question of statements of legal principle let us assume that the judge had said 'all manufacturers owe a duty of care to protect consumers just as a man owes a duty of care to his neighbour'. We can now see that while the principle obviously contains the germ or basis of the *ratio* it is much too wide and does not pay sufficient attention to the material facts. As it stands it could be classed as *obiter dicta,* but to find the *ratio* we must qualify it by the material facts. Because the *ratio decidendi* is a rule of law, we would frame it as a rule in the following way:

> Where a manufacturer produces a product which he intends to reach the ultimate consumer in the form in which they left him and without any reasonable possibility of an examination, then the manufacturer owes a duty of care to the consumer and will be liable to the consumer who is injured as a result of a breach of that duty.

Here we have identified the appropriate principle by general reference to the facts and then qualified the broad manner in which the judge stated that principle by reference to the material facts.

FOLLOWING AND DISTINGUISHING

We have already indicated that previous decisions (more correctly, the *ratio decidendi* of previous decisions) are binding upon subsequent courts which are faced with cases containing the same material facts. As Professor Goodhart points out:

> Any court bound by the case must come to a similar conclusion unless there is a further fact in the case before it which it is prepared to treat as material, or unless some fact treated as material in the previous case, is absent.[3]

Thus in a case which arose subsequent to our example, in a court bound by that decision, the subsequent court would be bound to reach the same conclusion unless there was a difference in the material facts of the cases. If the second case dealt with a poisonous can of beans but was otherwise identical, then that would not amount to a difference in the material facts. A case in which a reasonable examination would have revealed the defect, however, would probably amount to a material difference. The problem, therefore, is in identifying the material facts of both cases; if they are the same then the previous decision is binding on the subsequent court; if they are not the same, the subsequent court is not bound by that decision though it may, of course, be bound by others. Some legal scholars have long been suspicious of this technique, suggesting that because of the possibility of distinguishing a previous case, the rule of *stare decisis* is more mythical than real.

Nor has such scepticism been confined to academics for even the judges themselves have sometimes expressed similar sentiments. Thus, Asquith J. once quoted the following remark:

> The rule is quite simple: if you agree with the other bloke you say its part of the *ratio*; if you don't you say its *obiter dictim,* with the implication that he is a congenital idiot and this may well, as a matter of pure psychological fact, have more underlying truth than we know, or care to avow.[4]

While it is clear that the decision on the similarity of the material facts of both cases rests in the first instance with the judge of the latter court, that is by no means the end of the matter. The issue may well arise again in even later cases and the views of judges in such cases are also very pertinent in determining the material facts, and hence the *ratio*, of the original decision. A stage is finally reached when the issue of the material facts of the original decision becomes so well settled that it would be almost impossible for a later court to raise the issue again. Unfortunately this process may be a very slow and arduous one and, in the meantime, it is possible for judges to draw very arbitrary and artificial distinctions between the material facts of the original case and those of the case before it in order to avoid being bound to follow the previous decision. Even when the issue of the material facts of a previous decision has been finally settled a judge will always have the possibility of distinguishing by selecting different material facts in the case before him.

The real issue raised by the quotation from Lord Asquith, however, is whether judges draw artificial distinctions in order to avoid following a previous decision and, if so, whether they do this on a scale which renders the doctrine of stare decisis mythical or fictitious. It is suggested that while the answer to the first question must be a qualified 'yes', that the answer to the second and more important question must be 'no'. It is not possible in a work of this nature to explore the matter more fully but the short discussion will have sufficed if the reader is now aware of two things. First, the application of the doctrine of stare decisis is not a mechanical operation but one in which the judge enjoys a certain latitude in distinguishing a previous authority from the case before him. Secondly, that the existence of such latitude does not result in artificial or arbitrary distinguishing on such a scale by judges who wish to avoid following a previous decision as to render the entire doctrine mythical or artificial.

THE DOCTRINE OF STARE DECISIS IN IRELAND

The Supreme Court

Until 1964 the Irish Supreme Court had always followed its own previous decisions and also the decisions of those courts which had preceded it as the court of ultimate jurisdiction. In the *State (Quinn)* v. *Ryan*[5], however, the Supreme Court broke with this tradition in declaring unconstitutional a statutory provision which it had previously declared constitutional in the earlier case of the *State (Duggan)* v. *Tapley*[6]. In the course of his judgement (in which the other members of the court concurred) Walsh J. rejected the proposition that the Supreme Court, in interpreting the Constitution of 1937, would be bound to follow previous decisions. He said:

> . . . this Court is the creation of the Constitution and is not in any sense the successor in Ireland of the House of Lords . . . I reject the submission that because upon the foundation of the State our Courts took over an English Legal system and the common law that the Courts must be deemed to have adopted and should now adopt an approach to Constitutional questions conditioned by English judicial methods and English legal training which despite their undoubted excellence were not fashioned

> for interpreting written constitutions or reviewing the constitutionality of legislation.[7]

Walsh J., however, was not advocating abandoning entirely the doctrine of stare decisis. He qualified his remarks in this way:

> This is not to say, however, that the Court would depart from an earlier decision for any but the most compelling reasons. The advantages of stare decisis are many and obvious so long as it is remembered that it is a policy and not a binding unalterable rule.[8]

The matter was further developed soon afterwards by Kingsmill Moore J. in *A. G. and Another* v. *Ryan's Car Hire Co. Ltd.* Delivering judgement for a unanimous court he said:

> This Court is a new court, set up by the Courts (Establishment and Constitution) Act, 1961, pursuant to the Constitution and is free to consider whether it should adopt the rule which prevails in the House of Lords or any of the less restrictive rules which have found favour in other jurisdictions. It seems clear that there can be no legal obligation on this court to accept "stare decisis" as a rule binding upon it just because the House of Lords accepted it . . . . A decision which only purported to affect the House of Lords could not, by virtue of Article 73 of the Constitution of 1922 have been carried over into our law so as to bind the Supreme Court set up by that Constitution: and if that Supreme Court in fact adopted the rule (as it would seem to have done . . .) any such determination could only bind that Court and would not under Article 50 of our present Constitution be binding on the new Supreme Court created by Article 34, 4, of our present Constitution and the Courts (Establishment and Constitution) Act, 1961.[9]

The learned judge was of opinion that an approach less rigid than that of the House of Lords was more appropriate for the Irish Supreme Court:

> In my opinion, the rigid rule of stare decisis must in a court of ultimate resort give place to a more elastic formula. Where such a court is clearly of opinion that an earlier decision was erroneous it should be at liberty to refuse to follow it, at all events in exceptional cases.[10]

The decision in *Ryan's Car Hire* had the effect, therefore, of extending the more liberal approach beyond the confines of Constitutional issues which a strict interpretation of the *State (Quinn)* v. *Ryan* suggested. But Kingsmill Moore J., like Walsh J. in the former case, made it clear that he was not heralding the complete rejection of stare decisis. He refuted such a possibility in the following terms:

> . . . there can be no question of abandoning the principle of following precedent as the normal, indeed almost universal, procedure. To do so would be to introduce into our law an intolerable uncertainty. But where the Supreme Court is of the opinion that there is a compelling reason why it should not follow an earlier decision of its own, or the Courts of ultimate jurisdiction which preceded it, where it appears to be clearly wrong, is it to be bound to perpetuate the error?

He continued:

> If it could safely be assumed that all members of the Supreme Court were perfectly endowed with wisdom and completely familiar with all branches of law to treat their judgements as infallible would need but little justification. Judicial modesty has refrained from putting forward such a claim and to most jurists such a court appears a Platonic rather than ideal.

The effect of these two decisions may be briefly summarized. The Supreme Court will, as a general rule, follow its own previous decisions. Where it appears to the court, however, that the earlier decision is 'clearly erroneous', it may refuse to follow it where there are 'exceptional' or 'compelling' reasons. Two recent decisions from the Supreme Court give some indication of when such conditions will be satisfied. In *McNamara* vs. *E.S.B.*[12] the Supreme Court departed from a long line of previous decisions which had essentially held that the only duty owed by an occupier of property to a trespasser was not to set a trap for such a trespasser. In our context the judgement of Henchy J. is particularly instructive. He began by reiterating the principle established in the *State (Quinn)* vs. *Ryan* and *Ryans Car Hire Co. Ltd.* in the following terms:

> The degree of certainty, continuity and predictability that judicial decisions should have . . . would normally dictate that this Court should follow its own decisions . . . But there are exceptional and compelling reasons for not doing so.[13]

The exceptional and compelling reasons in *McNamara* were essentially threefold:

(i) Modern decisions in various jurisdictions had all shown a desire to escape from the old rule on the grounds of its unsuitability to modern social conditions.

(ii) The rule ran counter to the more modern and widely accepted rule in negligence as propounded in *Donoghue* vs. *Stephenson*[14] and it was inconsistent with the broad application which the more modern rule had received.

(iii) The old rule was initially formulated by the House of Lords in *Addie* v. *Dumbeck,*[15] a decision which was overruled by their Lordships in *Herrington's Case.*[16]

Also of assistance is the judgement of the same learned judge in *Mogul of Ireland Ltd.* v. *Tipperary (N.R.) County Council,*[17] where the court refused to depart from a Supreme Court decision of 1949. In the course of his judgement, Henchy J. (Walsh J. concurring) set out clearly his reasons for refusing to depart. He said:

> The [1949] case was argued before a full court, whose jurisdiction to declare the law authoritatively was no less comprehensive than that of this

Court. No point of substance seems to have been advanced in arguments at this hearing that was not then brought to the Court's attention. The Court was fully aware that its task was to decide authoritatively and conclusively a point on which there had been a divergence of judicial opinion in previous cases. The Court took time to consider its opinion and then decided . . . The decision has stood unquestioned in the Courts of this State from 1949 to now.

Referring to *Ryan's Car Hire Co. Ltd.* he said:

> It is implicit from the use in that judgement of expressions such as 'convinced', 'for compelling reasons' and 'clearly of opinion that the earlier decision was erroneous', that the mere fact that a later court, particularly a majority of the members of a later court, might prefer a different conclusion, is not in itself sufficient to justify overruling the earlier decision. Even if the later court is clearly of opinion that the earlier decision was wrong, it may decide in the interests of justice not to overrule it if it has become inveterate and if in a widespread and fundamental way people have acted on the basis of its correctness, to such an extent that greater harm would result from overruling it than from allowing it to stand. In such cases the maxim *communis error facit jus* applies.

Nor did it make any difference that the earlier decision was that of a former Supreme Court. According to Henchy J. the principles applicable were the same:

> A decision of the full Supreme Court – be it the pre-1961 Court or the post-1961 Court – given in a fully argued case and on consideration of all the relevant materials, should not normally be overruled because a later court inclines to a different conclusion.[18]

These two decisions serve to emphasise the fact that the Supreme Court will not overrule a previous decision lightly and that such departure will only occur where there is substantial agreement among the members of the court that there are compelling reasons for doing so. In *Ryan's Car Hire Co. Ltd.* Kingsmill Moore J. indicated that an earlier decision which was given in ignorance of the existence of some statutory provision, or in reliance of some statutory provision which was subsequently discovered to have been repealed, would not be a binding authority. The same reasoning would be applicable if the decision was given in ignorance of an earlier authority of compelling validity and, where a point had been entirely overlooked or conceded without argument, the authority of a decision might be weakened 'to vanishing point'. To these guide-lines must now be added the more recent remarks of Henchy J. in *McNamara* v. *E.S.B.*, and *Mogul of Ireland Ltd.* v. *Tipperary (N.R.) County Council.*

Overruling and Reversing

It is convenient to draw a distinction between overruling and reversing at this stage. When an appeal from an inferior court is upheld by a superior court, the decision of the former is said to be 'reversed' by the decision of the latter.

Reversal in itself only affects the parties to the action and may occur for any number of reasons. When a superior court (either dismissing or upholding an appeal) rejects a previous decision which hitherto had been binding upon the inferior court (or in some cases, the appellate court itself), the court is said to have 'overruled' the previous decision. Such overruling, unlike reversal, affects all citizens since it amounts to a change in the law. Though it is more usual to find a court overruling and reversing or reversing without overruling, it is also possible for a court to overrule without reversing, as occurred in *Davis* v. *Johnson*[19] where the House of Lords upheld the decision of the Court of Appeal and overruled earlier decisions of that court which the Court of Appeal itself had (wrongly in the view of the House of Lords) attempted to overrule.

THE HIGH COURT

There are a number of special problems relating to the operation of the doctrine in this court. Clearly the High Court is bound by the decisions of the Supreme Court and this point has recently been emphasised by the latter court in *McDonnell* v. *Byrne Engineering Co. Ltd.*[20] In directing the jury at the trial of an action in the High Court, Murnaghan J. had declined to follow the guide-lines laid down by the Supreme Court in *Carroll* v. *Clare County Council.*[21] and had also indicated his intention of so declining in the future. The Supreme Court, in allowing the appeal and ordering a new trial, was adamant that the High Court must follow the decisions of the Supreme Court. In the course of his judgement O'Higgins C. J. said that, under the Constitution, the Supreme Court was the final Court of Appeal. As such it had the duty, when necessary, to declare what legal principles should apply to cases that were reviewed by the court. Where necessary it had the duty to lay down guidelines for all courts and all judges as to the manner in which such cases were to be tried. It was equally the duty of all courts and judges to follow directions as to law and procedures as given by the Supreme Court. He went on:

> It is with real concern that this court notes that despite being asked by counsel to leave the question . . . in accordance with the directions of this court, the trial judge . . . expressly refused to do so. Not only did he refuse to do so, but he has indicated it is his intention to disregard this in other cases . . . This court will not permit this situation to continue and will insist that its directions be respected and obeyed.[22]

A reader may be slightly surprised to find the court of ultimate resort being obliged to reprimand an inferior tribunal for disregarding the former's directions on the law, but it is not unique to this jurisdiction and is even more commonly seen on the other side of the Irish sea where, on a number of occasions, the House of Lords has found it necessary to express similar concern with regard to the activities of some members of the Court of Appeal.

A much more complex issue with regard to the High Court relates to how far that court is bound by its own decisions. The difficulty is accentuated by the fact that, in practice, the High Court may adopt a more or less rigid approach depending on how the previous case came before it. As we will see in more detail in Chapter 5, the High Court may hear cases in one of three, if not four different ways:

(i) As a court of first instance sitting permanently in Dublin.

(ii) As an appellate court, hearing appeals from the Circuit Court (or District Court) and again sitting in Dublin.

(iii) As the High Court on circuit, hearing cases at first instance or on appeal at a number of different centres throughout the country.

(iv) As a divisional court, with three judges.

Addressing a meeting at Trinity College, Dublin, in the early 1950s Black J., a former member of the High (1939-1942) and Supreme (1942-1951) Courts, indicated that the strictness with which the doctrine applied in the High Court varied in each of these circumstances. After referring to the rule under which the English Court of Appeal is bound by its own previous decisions, the learned judge felt that the same rule would apply when the High Court was sitting as a divisional court with three judges. The circumstances in which the High Court may sit with three judges are set out in Article 40.4.4., of the Constitution of 1937 and are dealt with in greater detail elsewhere. It suffices here to say that they are all essentially related to State-side applications of a Habeas Corpus nature. Moreover such a court is summoned at the discretion of the President of the High Court and the tendency in recent years has been for a single judge to deal with these matters. The occasions on which the High Court sits as a divisional court are now much less frequent than formerly and the sheer weight of business is likely to ensure that this trend continues. The English rule to which the learned judge referred arises from the decision of the Court of Appeal in that country in *Young* v. *Bristol Aeroplane Co.*[23] In that case the court held itself bound by its own previous decisions except in the following situations:

(i) Where there are two previous decisions which are in conflict, the court may choose between them.

(ii) Where the previous decision is inconsistent with a subsequent decision of the House of Lords.

(iii) Where the previous decision was given *per incuriam,* i.e. in ignorance of an important legal principle of a statute.

The view of Black J., therefore, was that a decision of the High Court, sitting as a divisional court, could only be departed from in these three exceptional circumstances.

With regard to decisions of the High Court when comprising only one judge, Black J. indicated that a more flexible attitude prevails. He said:

> If I were confronted with a decision of a court of co-ordinate jurisdiction, which appeared to me of merely doubtful soundness, I nonetheless applied the rule of comity and followed it, leaving it for an appellate court to settle the matter, and the longer the other decision had remained unchallenged, the more ready I was to follow it. But if I were presented with a decision of a court of co-ordinate jurisdiction, my dislike of which went beyond mere doubt, and amounted to a firm conviction that if it was wrong, then I declined to follow it.[24]

The learned judge went on to give an example of this approach which occurred during his tenure of office. He explained:

> Thus, in the important case of charities, *Re Nolan* [1939] I. R. 388, the late Mr. Justice Gavan Duffy refused to follow a decision of Mr. Justice Barton in *Dwyer (deceased)* (1908) 46 I.L.T.R. 147; but later in *Re Clancy* [1943] I.R. 23, I refused to follow the last mentioned decision of Mr. Justice Gavan Duffy. My example was followed by Mr. Justice Overend in *Re Morrissey* [1944] I.R. 361 and our view was eventually upheld by the Supreme Court in *Re Solomons* [1949] I.R. 3.[25]

More recently, however, another member of the High Court has suggested that there should be a greater reluctance among High Court judges to depart from the previous decisions of courts of co-ordinate jurisdiction. In *Irish Trust Bank Ltd.* v. *Central Bank of Ireland*[26] Parke J. did not exhibit the same flexibility as the remarks of Black J. above. Parke J. put the matter thus:

> Whatever may be the case in Courts of final, appellate jurisdiction, a Court of first instance should be very slow . . . [to depart from one of its own previous decisions] unless the arguments in favour of it were coercive.
>
> If a decision of a Court of first instance is to be challenged I consider that the appellate Court is the proper tribunal to declare the law unless the decision in question manifestly displays some one or more of the infirmities to which I have referred.[27]

Earlier in his judgement Parke J. had stated that he considered the occasions to be extremely rare when the High Court could depart from one of its own previous decisions. He then indicated that these exceptional circumstances might arise:

> A court may depart . . . if it appears that such a decision was given in a case in which either insufficient authority was cited or incorrect submissions advanced or in which the nature and wording of the judgement itself reveals that the judge disregarded or misunderstood an important element in the case or the arguments submitted to him or the authority

cited or in some other way departed from the proper standard to be adopted in judicial determination.[28]

Though it is clear that there is not total agreement between the two learned judges, the difference between them is largely one of degree or emphasis. As a general rule the High Court should follow its own previous decision, one indicating a greater reluctance to depart than the other.

It is suggested that decisions of the High Court on circuit would not be considered as binding as those given when the court is sitting in Dublin. Since most of the cases dealt with on circuit do not raise questions of law but are merely disputes of fact, this is not a serious issue. It also should be noted that any suggestion that decisions given shortly before 1922 would not bind post-1922 courts of co-ordinate jurisdiction now appears to be without foundation.

Finally, references must be made to the influence of decisions from other jurisdictions upon Irish courts. It is inevitable that jurisdictions which share a common tradition and which face similar social and economic problems should on occasion influence each other in selecting the appropriate solution. This is just as much the case with regard to judicial law-making as it is with regard to political action. Because of the close historical links between Ireland and England, judically as well as politically, it is not surprising to find that our courts continue to pay particular respect to the decisions emanating from at least the superior English courts. But such respect must not be confused with blind adherence. The Supreme Court has, on more than one occasion (perhaps most notably in *State (Quinn)* v. *Ryan, supra*), insisted that as the court of a sovereign independent State it will not blindly follow the decisions of foreign courts. Of course in recent years the courts have had to deal with problems arising under a written Constitution and on this point there was no relevant authority in English law. On such matters the courts have not been without assistance, however, for they have turned to another common law neighbour, namely the United States, for inspiration and the practice of citing decisions from that jurisdiction (and in particular from the U.S. Supreme Court) in Constitutional matters seems to be growing. Because of the differences in legal tradition (and problems of language) it would be unusual for a decision of a French, German or other continental court to be cited in an Irish court, but membership of the European Communities may result in a greater approximation or harmonisation of laws among the member states and we may yet witness the occasion when the citation of a decision from the French *Conseil d'État* or the Federal Supreme Court of the German Democratic Republic is as common (and raises as few eyebrows) as the citation of English or U.S. decisions.

We can now consider the role of legislation as a source of law.

II LEGISLATION

Legislation is law enacted by the sovereign body. In Ireland legislation is enacted by the Oireachtas. Prior to receiving the Presidential assent, which is the final stage in the legislative process, an inchoate Act does not have the force of law and is known as a 'Bill'. Bills are divided into two main classes:

(i) *Public* bills: these alter the general law or affect the community at large.

(ii) *Private* bills: these deal with matters relating to a particular locality or individual(s).

Public bills are far more numerous than private ones. They usually originate in the Dail or the Seanad but certain classes of bills, e.g. Finance bills, must, under the Constitution, originate in the Dail. Those introduced by a minister with the support of the Government are called Government bills; those introduced by private or ordinary members, without the guaranteed support of the government, are called *private members' bills,* and must not be confused with *private bills* already mentioned.

Bills normally pass through a number of stages or 'readings'. The first 'reading', which may take place in either the Dail or Seanad, consists of placing the title of the bill before the House. After this the bill is printed but if it does not pass this stage (as might happen with a private member's bill which is considered inconsistent with Government policy) then the bill is defeated. Assuming this does not occur, the printed bill is circulated and given a second reading. At this stage the minister responsible for conducting the bill through the Oireachtas usually explains the nature of his intended legislation and often goes through the bill section by section. The third stage is the committee stage. Except where a bill is highly technical, the 'committee' is the entire House. Next follows the report stage at which further amendments may be made and then the bill is referred to the other House where a similar process may be followed. The bill then receives its final reading and the Presidential assent normally follows as a matter of course. It should not be overlooked that at any reading a bill may be defeated. Thus in the case of private members' bills the usual practice has been for them to receive a first reading (thus permitting them to be printed) but to be defeated after a second reading. Since the Government usually has a majority in both Houses, Government bills normally go through all stages without any danger of defeat. In these cases the opposition may succeed in introducing some amendments but then only with the support of the Government.

The Form of Legislation

Today statutes are usually drafted in a uniform way, with a short title and a number for reference purposes, e.g. the Companies Act, 1963 (No. 33 of 1963). They may also have a long title which recites the general purpose of the Act. In the case of the Companies Act, 1963, this is as follows: 'An Act to Consolidate with Amendments certain Enactments relating to the

Companies and for purposes connected with that matter [23rd December, 1963].'

The date after the long title is the date upon which the Act was signed by the President, but this is not necessarily the date upon which all or any part of the Act came into force. It is not usual for a Minister to be given power in the Act itself to determine when all or any provision of the Act shall come into operation. At common law a statute came into operation on the first day of the parliamentary session in which it was enacted, unless there was a provision to the contrary.

In many of the older statutes there is a long preamble which sets out the reasons for the legislation and the objects which it was intended to achieve, but modern statutes rarely contain such a preamble.

The actual text of an Act, unless it is extremely short, is arranged into sections. Each section deals with one subject and may be subdivided into several subsections, which in turn may be divided into several paragraphs. Thus 's.4, ss.2(b)' refers to paragraph (b) of subsection 2, section 4.

In the longer statutes various related sections are collected into 'parts'. Thus, in the Companies Act, 1963, there are 15 parts, each dealing with a particular matter. Part I, as is usually the case, is entitled 'Preliminary' (sometimes 'Preliminary and General') and contains, *inter alia,* a definitional section. Such a section attempts to define certain words which appear in the Act but usually stipulates that such definition is to yield to a contrary intention in the Act itself. Other 'parts' of the Companies Act are entitled 'Incorporation of Companies and matters incidental thereto' (Part II), 'Share Capital and Debentures' (Part III), 'Management and Administration' (Part V) and 'Winding Up' (Part VI). In addition, many statutes contain schedules which are used to list matters of detail such as fees and matters of procedure. Very often, however, this is done by the use of regulations, the statute containing a section empowering someone, usually a Minister, to make such regulations.

Different Species of Legislation

A distinction must be drawn between a consolidating and codifying statute. A consolidating Act is one which attempts to collect all of the *statutory provisions* on a particular topic and embody them in one Act. This becomes necessary because over a period of time several Acts may be enacted on the same topic, each making some amendment to its predecessor. For example, at present there are four statutes regulating adoption in the Republic. They are collectively cited as the Adoption Acts, 1952 to 1976, and include Acts passed in 1952, 1964, 1974 and 1976. A consolidating adoption statute would incorporate all of these Acts into one, making only minor amendments or improvements. A codifying statute is one which attempts to collect the *whole law* on a particular topic (common law as well as the statutory provisions). An example of a codifying statute is not easy to find in our legal system but two notable ones are the Sale of Goods Act, 1893, and the Bills of Exchange Act, 1882. The importance of the distinction between a consolidating and a codifying statute lies in the presumption that the former, though not the latter, does not change the previous law. As one writer has put it:

> The authorities on previous statutory provisions consolidated in a later enactment retain their force as precedents, whereas recourse should only be had to the previous authorities of a codifying statute in cases in which construction is doubtful or in order to settle a dispute about the state of the previous law. There would be little point in codifying the common law if previous cases could be invoked to cast doubt on the clear words of the code.[29]

Finally there is legislation which, though enacted under the authority of the Oireachtas, is not actually enacted by the Oireachtas itself. To that vast body of ever-increasing rules we give the term 'delegated legislation'. Delegated legislation consists mainly of statutory instruments prepared by government departments. They are laid before (or on the table of) the House for a specified number of days (usually 60) and in the absence of a negative ruling become law at the end of that period. By-laws made by local authorities, borough councils and harbour commissioners are further examples of delegated legislation. All of these bodies, as well as the powers they exercise, are statutory in origin and when exercising their powers they must comply strictly with the terms of the appropriate Act. The various regulations, directives and decisions emanating from the European Communities are sometimes classed as delegated legislation, but because of their relative volume and importance when compared with other forms of delegated legislation we have decided to deal with them as a separate source of law.

Territorial Extent

The general rule is that our legislation applies to conduct and transactions within Ireland and not to those which occur outside. A statute may provide, however, that certain conduct is prescribed wherever it is committed, e.g. the Offences Against the Person Act, 1861, s.9 (murder) and s.57 (bigamy). In the *State (Devine)* v. *Larkin*[30] it was argued on behalf of the defendant that Article 3 of the 1937 Constitution limited the powers of the Oireachtas to enact laws having extra-territorial effect and that an Act of 1952, which attempted to create an offence for acts or omissions in that part of the Foyle area which lies outside the jurisdiction of the State, was unconstitutional. McMahon J. rejected this argument holding that Article 3 of the Constitution could not be construed in this way:

> No reason has been suggested for limiting the power of the State by reference to the extent to which Saorstát Éireann had exercised the power to make laws having extra-territorial effect. In my opinion Article 3 of the Constitution, in providing that the laws enacted by parliament shall have the like extra-territorial effect as the laws of Saorstát Éireann, means that the laws of the Oireachtas shall have the like extra-territorial effect as

the laws of Saorstát Éireann were capable of having. Under Article 3 . . . laws having a purely domestic import do not extend to Northern Ireland; but laws which are expressed to operate extra-territorially can bind those who are subjects of the State in regard to their conduct in Northern Ireland.[31]

In *In re The Criminal Law Jurisdiction Bill, 1975,*[32] the Supreme Court adopted a similar view to McMahon J. Section 2 of the bill of 1975 (now the Criminal Law (Jurisdiction) Act, 1976) provided that where a person in Northern Ireland does an act that, if done in the State would constitute an indictable offence specified in the schedule to the bill, he should be guilty of an offence. The bill was passed by both Houses of the Oireachtas on the 3rd March, 1976, but on the 10th March, 1976, the President referred the bill to the Supreme Court. One of the arguments put forward in that court was that section 2 was repugnant to the provisions of Article 3 of the Constitution. The Supreme Court rejected that argument.

Statutory Interpretation

In what is arguably the leading modern work on the subject Sir Rupert Cross defined the word 'interpretation' as 'the process by which the courts determine the meaning of a statutory provision for the purpose of applying it to the situation before them', and it is in this sense that we use the term here. The reader should not overlook, however, that, in a general sense, much statutory interpretation by lawyers and others takes place outside the courts. Lawyers are frequently called upon to apply statutory provisions to situations presented by their clients without seeking assistance from the judiciary. The courts themselves frequently are involved in a similar process. In the words of Sir Rupert Cross:

Courts spend more of their time applying words of undisputed meaning to facts which have been disputed than in interpreting statutory words of disputed meaning. . . . It simply shows that, if the word is construed sufficiently broadly, 'interpretation' is a many-sided process.[33]

It is useful to emphasise this point with reference to a highly litigated area. Until relatively recently there existed a special code of rules relating to injuries sustained by persons while engaged in employment. Essentially, compensation was payable by an employer to his employee provided the latter sustained his loss 'arising out of and in the course of' his employment. In *Reid* v. *Hutchinson*[34] a workman cycling from his home to the first of two places where he was required to work on the same day, fell from his bicycle and was injured. It was held that the workman was not running any further risk than that of an ordinary road user and, accordingly, the accident did not arise 'out of and in the course of' his employment. In *Redmond* v. *Bolger*[35], however, a domestic servant sustained injuries after falling from her bicycle on her night out when doing an errand for her employer. The court held that, as the applicant was on the particular road where the accident happened solely for her employer's business, the accident arose out of and in the course of her employment.

In these cases the court was not concerned with any dispute as to the meaning of the words 'out of and in the course of employment'. In each it was simply a question whether the conduct of the plaintiff came within the terms of a provision which, in itself, was plain and unambiguous.

We are here concerned with more the difficult process of explaining the techniques or devices which the courts employ to ascertain the meaning of disputed words.

The approach adopted by the courts to the problem of interpreting statutes has varied over the centuries. Up to the 18th century the courts exercised considerable flexibility in interpreting statutes. Thus in *Stradling* v. *Morgan*[36] a provision relating to receivers and treasurers without any qualifying words was held to be confined to such officials appointed by the King and not to cover those appointed by private persons. During this period the Barons of the Exchequer enunciated the famous *Mischief Rule* of interpretation to which we shall refer later.

During the 18th and 19th centuries a more restrictive or literal approach became popular. For example, in *R.* v. *Harris*[37] it was held that an accused who bit off the end of his victim's ear was not guilty under a provision which rendered it unlawful to 'stab, cut or wound any person'.

The modern approach is a combination of, or compromise between, these two extremes, though it is not uncommon to find judges going to either one. At the outset it should be said that there are no binding rules which judges must employ but rather are there a number of guides or aids upon which they may call. Among these, the following are the most important:

The Literal Rule: Sometimes referred to as the cardinal rule of interpretation, it means that the words of a statute must *prima facie* be interpreted in their ordinary, literal and grammatical sense. In *Duffy* v. *Dublin Corporation*[38] the question was whether a statute which provided that 'it shall be lawful' for the defendants to carry on a cattle market imposed upon them the duty of doing so. In the Supreme Court, Henchy J. referred with approval to the following remarks of Cairns L. C. in *Julius* v. *Bishop of Oxford*:

> The question has been argued . . . as if the words 'it shall be lawful' might have a different meaning, and might be differently interpreted in different statutes, or in different parts of the same statute. I cannot think that this is correct. The words . . . are not equivocal. They are plain and unambiguous. They are merely making that legal and possible which there would otherwise be no right or authority to do. They confer a faculty or power, and they do not of themselves do more . . .[39]

The Lord Chancellor went on to say, however, that the context and other circumstances of the Act might impose a duty to exercise such power but, *prima facie*, no such obligation arose. In the *Duffy* case, the Supreme Court reached the same conclusion.

In *Lonergan* v. *Morrissey*[40] the issue was whether the applicant for an affiliation order was bound to enter into recognizances within the prescribed period, if she wished to appeal the decision of a District Justice dismissing her application. The appropriate provision was as follows: 'In the event of an appellant failing to enter into such recognizance *he* shall be deemed to have abandoned his right to appeal'[41] (emphasis added).

It is provided by the Interpretation Act, 1937, s.11(a) that the use of the masculine gender in a statute is to include the feminine gender unless a contrary intention appears. This is a necessary provision since otherwise substantial duplication, e.g. 'he and she' or 'his or hers', would have to be necessary when drafting legislation. In *Lonergan* v. *Morrissey,* Sealy J. refused to depart for this literal interpretation.

> I must construe the rule according to the Interpretation Act. As drafted, the rule applies to the masculine gender only but I am entitled to substitute the feminine gender for the masculine. I do not see any contrary intention and thus the applicant's appeal fails.

The Golden Rule: If the literal interpretation leads to some absurdity, some repugnancy or inconsistency with the rest of the statute then the grammatical sense of the words may be modified to avoid such absurdity or inconsistency, but no further.

It is clear that to employ the strict grammatical meaning of words on all occasions could lead to manifest absurdity. When such absurdity arises courts will usually attempt to modify their meaning in order to avoid such a result. But there is a limit to how far the courts may modify, and certain matters may be used in this process. The court may review the entire statute and may derive particular assistance from the long title of the act or, if there is one, from the preamble. The court may not refer, however, to the marginal notes for assistance nor may it rely on punctuation. The history of the statute may also be of assistance but there are certain limitations. If the statute forms part of a series of statutes dealing with the same subject, recourse may be had to the earlier statutes and to the manner in which they have been interpreted by the courts. In particular the words in question may have already been construed by the courts when dealing with one of the earlier statutes. In this situation a strong presumption arises in favour of adhering to the previous interpretation. James L. J. put the matter as follows:

> Where once certain words in an Act of Parliament have received a judicial construction in one of the superior courts, and the legislature has repeated them without alteration in a subsequent statute, I conceive that the legislature must be taken to have used them according to the meaning which a court of competent jurisdiction has given to them.[42]

This statement must be qualified in view of the more recent remarks of Denning L. J. in *Royal Court Derby Porcelain Ltd.* v. *Raymond Russell,* where he said:

> The true view is that the court will be slow to overrule a previous decision on the interpretation of a statute when it has long been acted upon, and

> it will be more than usually slow to do so when Parliament has, since the decision, re-enacted the statute in the same terms.[43]

The reader will have noted that the issue here is the rigidity or flexibility with which the doctrine of stare decisis is applied to the interpretation of statutes. First, where the facts in both cases are substantially the same it would appear that the earlier interpretation must be followed in the later case. Secondly, the ratio decidendi of the earlier decision is only a guide where the facts are substantially different. Finally, where the words under consideration have been re-enacted without alteration from a previous statute which has been interpreted by the courts, there is a strong presumption that the earlier interpretation should be followed.

In examining the history of the statute, reports of the Parliamentary debates have, in the past, been excluded in Ireland and in England, though they are commonly employed in other jurisdictions. Recently, however, a number of English decisions has led one writer to conclude that '. . . in cases to which the literal or plain meaning rule in its modern form is inapplicable, the ban of Parliamentary materials is (possibly) not quite as absolute as it is usually supposed to be'.[44] In any event the rule prohibits using such reports *as the basis for decision* but does not prohibit *any* reference to such materials.

The term 'pre-parliamentary materials' is usually employed to refer to advisory reports (such as those of the Law Reform Commission) upon which the legislation is founded. Should such material be admissible? There are two possible views, the first summarised in the following quotation from Lord Halsbury, and the other in a quotation from Lord Wright.

Lord Halsbury in *Eastman Photographic Materials Co. Ltd.* v. *Controller General of Patents* was in favour of admitting such material:

> I think no more accurate source of information as to what the evil or defect which the Act of Parliament now under consideration was intended to be remedied could be imagined than the report of that commission (in consequence of which the statute was enacted)![45]

In *Assam Railways and Trading Co. Ltd.* v. *Inland Revenue Commissioners* Lord Wright was not prepared to admit such material as evidence of the intention of Parliament:

> But on principle no such evidence for the purpose of showing the intention that is the purpose and object of an Act is admissible; the intention of the legislature must be ascertained from the words of the statute with such extraneous matter as is legitimate . . . . It is clear that the language of a minister . . . in proposing to Parliament a measure which eventually becomes law is inadmissible and the report of Commissioners is even more removed from value as evidence of intention, because it does not follow that their recommendations were accepted.[46]

With regard to the use of treaties and international conventions, recently the Supreme Court referred extensively, not only to a Convention, but also to the *travaux preparatoires* upon which the Convention was based. In *In re Bourke*[47] the court was called upon to interpret section 50 in Part III of the

Extradition Act, 1965 (No. 17). Though not identical in terms, there was a close similarity between section 50 in Part III and section II in Part II. The latter section was acknowledged to be derived from Article 3 of the European Convention on Extradition. O'Dálaigh C. J. in the course of his judgement said:

> . . . we have been invited as a means of throwing light on the interpretation of s.50 to look at the *travaux preparatoires* for the Convention. I accept that this is a valid and proper approach. Section II and s.50 speak of the same things. As the Convention may be examined to discover the meaning of s.11, it is no less legitimate for the Court to look at Article 3 and the *travaux preparatoires* in interpreting section 50.[48]

It is important to note, however, that resort was made to the Convention and *travaux preparatoires* because an ambiguity had arisen. If the words were plain and unambiguous the court may not have been prepared to resort to these materials. This was the approach adopted by the House of Lords in *Ellerman Lines* v. *Murray*[49] where, because the court held the words in question to be plain and unambiguous, they refused to give them the meaning which they were intended to bear by an international convention mentioned in the long and short title to the Act, the preamble and partially set out in the schedule.

The Mischief Rule: It has already been indicated that the early approach of the courts to statutory interpretation was a most flexible one. During this period the courts, more specifically the Barons of the Court of Exchequer, developed this rule which is also sometimes referred to as the Rule in Haydon's Case. Because legislation at this period was dealing with matters with which the common law was familiar, the rule was adequate. It involves proceeding through the following four stages: (i) What was the common law before the Act? (ii) What was the mischief and defect for which the common law did not provide? (iii) What remedy did Parliament resolve to solve the mischief? (iv) What is the true reason of the remedy?

The most off-cited example of the application of this rule in the case of *Gorris* v. *Scott*[50] where the plaintiff claimed damages in respect of the loss of his sheep which were washed overboard and drowned while the defendant was engaged in transporting them at sea. There was a statutory duty on the defendant to provide pens for the sheep and the loss of the sheep would have been avoided had such pens been provided. It was held, however, that the plaintiff was not entitled to recover for breach of this particular statutory duty (today he might recover in negligence) because the purpose of the particular provision was to prevent the spread of disease rather than prevent sheep being lost overboard.

Other Guides to Statutory Interpretation

In addition to the 'rules' just mentioned, the courts have developed various other maxims and presumptions to assist them in their task. Some of the more important or commonly used presumptions and maxims are as follows:

Presumption of Constitutionality: It is presumed that legislation enacted by the Oireachtas is constitutional until the contrary is shown. A corollary of this is that where the court is faced with two possible interpretations, one of which renders the statute repugnant to the Constitution and the other which does not, the court will select the latter interpretation. In *McDonald* v. *Bord na gCon* Walsh J. put the matter as follows:

> One practical effect of this presumption is that if in respect of any provision or provisions of the Act two or more constructions are reasonably open, one of which is constitutional and the other or others are unconstitutional, it must be presumed that the Oireachtas intended only the constitutional construction. . . .[51]

Moreover there is also a presumption that legislation enacted between 1922 and 1937 was in accord with the 1922 Constitution of the Irish Free State, though legislation enacted before that time enjoys no such presumption.

Ejusdem Generis Rule: This rule means that general words which follow particular words must be cut down to meanings similar to those of the particular words.

In *Meskell* v. *Coras Iompair Eireann*[52] the plaintiff was dismissed by the defendant company because of his refusal to join a trade union. The union had entered into an agreement with the defendant company to the effect that all employees should be trade union members. The plaintiff claimed that this constituted an actionable conspiracy to deprive him of his constitutional right of freedom of association. One of the arguments raised by the defence was that such an agreement was expressly provided for by statute and thus could not constitute such a conspiracy. They relied upon s.10 of the Railways Act, 1933, as applied by S.46 of the Transport Act, 1950. These sections provided that the rates of pay, the hours of duty and *other conditions of service* should be regulated by agreement between the defendant company and the trade union representatives. Walsh J. denied that this was a valid argument. He said:

> I do not think that s.10 of the Act of 1933 is capable of any such interpretation. On the ordinary rules of construction the reference to other conditions of service, being preceded by the express reference to rates of pay and hours of duty, could not be held to include matters so different in kind from the ones mentioned as compulsory membership of trade unions . . .[53]

It is important to realise, however, that the provision in question was one in which general words followed particular words. In *In re Quinn*[54] the issue was whether particular words which followed general words had the effect of limiting the meaning of the general words. Section 2 (2) of the Public Dance Halls Act, 1935 (No. 2), provides that, in considering an application under that section for a public dance hall licence, a District Justice shall 'in addition to any other matter which may appear to him to be relevant' have regard to certain specified matters. The Supreme Court rejected the contention that the particular words had the effect of limiting the general words. Henchy J. dealt with the point as follows:

> On the basis of the maxim *noscitur a sociis* or the application of the *ejusdem generis* rule, counsel for the applicant contends that the [general] words . . . must be read restrictively so as to confine their scope to matters allied to or within the same classification as the specific matters . . . I do not consider that such a restrictive interpretation is the correct one and I look upon the decision of the Privy Council in *Canadian National Railways* v. *Canada Steamship Lines Ltd.* [1945] A.C. 204, as good authority for so holding. That case followed *Ambatielos* v. *Anton Jurgens Margarine Works* [1923] A.C. 175, in holding that, where a discretion is given in general words followed by particular instances, the generality of the discretion is in no way cut down by the particular words.[55]

Expressio unius est exclusio alterius: (If something is expressed, it must be taken to exclude something else) : Thus, where an Act imposed rates upon 'houses, buildings, works, tenements and hereditaments', but expressly exempted 'land', it was held that the word 'land', which normally includes houses and buildings attached to it, must here mean land alone.

Ut res magis valeat quam pereat (Let the word stand rather than fall): It must be presumed that the draftsman intended every word to bear a meaning or, in other words, to contribute to the meaning of the other words with which it is found. Hence there is a presumption that no word is redundant or merely repetitious, and if a particular word or clause appears on the face of it to be either of these then the court must seek to give it an interpretation which avoids such a conclusion.

Other Presumptions: At common law it was presumed that all legislation was in accord with international law. Hence if two possible interpretations were available, one which accorded with international law and one which did not, the court applied the former interpretation. To some extent this presumption has now been subsumed into the presumption of constitutionality since by Article 15 of the Constitution of 1937 Ireland has undertaken to comply with 'the generally recognised principles of international law'. In so far as there may be a distinction between the 'generally recognised principles of international law' and international law (derived from a treaty of limited effect to which Ireland is a party), the presumption retains some relevance.

For comment on the Interpretation Act, 1937 see note 55a Chapter 2.

Other common law presumptions which have been subsumed in this way are the presumption against confiscating property (or abolishing proprietary rights) without compensation (Article 43) and the presumption against denying a citizen access to the courts (Articles 38 and 40).

The European Communities and Sources of Law

Since the Republic's accession to the European Communities in 1972, various measures adopted by the institutions of the Communities have become part of our law. This was made possible by the Fourth Amendment to the Constitution Act, 1972, which introduced a new Article 29.4.3° which provided as follows:

> 3°. The State may become a member of the European Coal and Steel Community . . . the European Economic Community . . . and the European Atomic Energy Community . . . No provision of this Constitution invalidates laws enacted, acts done or measures adopted by the State necessitated by the obligations of membership of the Communities or prevents laws enacted, acts done or measures adopted by the Communities, or institutions thereof, from having the force of law in the State.

The sources of community law are divided into *primary* sources and *secondary* ones. It is also necessary to draw another distinction between those provisions which are *directly* applicable to member states and those which only apply after appropriate *action by the government of each member state,* i.e. those provisions which are not directly applicable. Furthermore, these distinctions overlap so that some secondary sources are directly applicable just as some primary sources are not. Each community was established by a treaty between the original members and these treaties represent the primary sources of law. Some articles in these treaties are self-executing, i.e. directly applicable, while others require further action by the member states to implement them. The secondary sources are derived from the actions of the Council of Ministers or the Commission. The power of these bodies to make law is provided for by Article 189 of the Treaty of Rome (1957) which established the European Economic Community. This article provides as follows:

> In order to carry out their task the Council and the Commission shall, in accordance with the provisions of the Treaty, make regulations, issue directives, take decisions, make recommendations or deliver opinions.
>
> A regulation shall have general application. It shall be binding in its entirety and directly applicable in all member states.
>
> A directive shall be binding, as to the result to be achieved, upon each Member State to which it is addressed, but shall leave to the national authorities the choice of form and methods.
>
> A decision shall be binding in its entirety upon those to whom it is addressed. Recommendations and opinions shall have no binding force.

The European Court of Justice is charged with the interpretation of the Treaty and must therefore, to a limited extent, be considered as a potential source of law. The court, in common with the courts of civil law countries, is not, however, bound by doctrine of stare decisis though in practice it does follow its previous decisions.

Custom as a Source of Law

We have already seen the role which custom played in the development of the common law. It has inspired developments in civil and criminal law and, to the extent that its contribution has not been modified by statute, it deserves attention as a source of law. There is no statutory definition of such important matters as murder, or consideration in the law of contract, and resort must be had to definitions drawn up by the courts and inspired by general custom.

Local customs, i.e. customs peculiar to a particular locality, may be recognised as law provided they comply with four conditions. First, the custom must be reasonable and this is a question of law upon which previous decisions on other (perhaps similar) customs are of importance. Parker J. once described the text to be applied in the following way:

> . . . [custom] must be such that, in the opinion of a trained lawyer, it is consistent, or at any rate not inconsistent, with those general principles which, quite apart from particular rules or maxims, lie at the very root of our legal system.[56]

Secondly, the custom must not be inconsistent with a statutory provision and, thirdly, it must have been exercised or observed as of right and not by force or permission. Finally, it must exist since 'time immemorial', which is fixed at 1189. The person alleging the existence of the custom does not have to establish this latter point; rather he will succeed unless his opponent can show that the custom must have come into operation since that date by establishing that it is based on practices consequent on the Statute of Labourers of the 14th century, as in *Simpson* v. *Wells.*[57] In that case the appellant claimed the customary right to erect a stall on the public highway. Blackbury J. held, however, that the practice had only been in existence since 23 Edward III (1349) and therefore did not satisfy this final condition.

Authoritative Texts

We have already indicated that the common law was developed by the courts.

On the continent, however, the development of the law took a different form. Unlike the position at common law the writings of learned scholars was an important and influential source of law in civil jurisdictions. Though 19th-century codification in most civil law jurisdictions means that such texts are no longer treated as a fundamental source of law, they continue to enjoy considerable importance. While writers in common law jurisdictions have never attained the same status as their civilian counterparts, some have long since been accepted as providing a valuable secondary source of law. The works of such eminent writers as Bracton (13th century), Coke (17th century), Blackstone (18th century) and Pollock (19th/20th century), to mention but a few, have been frequently cited in and accepted by the courts as accurate statements of legal principle. It is important to realise, however, that these writers are not the actual source of the law stated in their works but rather the recorders or 'reporters' of principles developed by the courts.

Chapter 3

LEGAL PERSONALITY

Before the substantive rules of law can be considered one must comprehend the identity of the participants. It is a fundamental premise of common law systems that all persons are equal before and subject to the law. In Ireland this is enshrined in the Constitution. It is not our purpose to examine the practical validity of such a statement in terms of a person's access to the law (that will be the subject for comment in Chapter 8). Rather, the following chapter will sketch the different capacities of persons known to the law, in order to see how and why the law may depart from the principle stated above. It will be seen that in differentiating between various social groups, the law limits personal capacity in a legal sense. The law in Ireland (and for that matter in England and many other Western states) attributes abilities and disabilities, rights and duties to particular groups in their standing before the law.

First, the three basic *legal personalities* will be identified: (i) Human beings; (ii) Incorporated associations; (iii) Unincorporated associations.

After a brief examination of the identity of each, attention will then be drawn to the differing status that the personality or subdivision of a personality may attain. For example, one may take the legal personality of a human being and the status of an Irish citizen, a child, or someone who is mentally handicapped. Finally, it is necessary to consider the rules of law as they affect and define *relationships,* i.e. combinations of personality and status. Of the many such relationships recognised by the law, the most significant of these will be illustrated. Whether the link is one of parents and child, husband and wife or student and teacher, the law provides particular rules regulating the relationship between the respective parties.

A LEGAL PERSONALITY

Human Beings

Even the most primitive of legal systems in the world recognise a *human being* as the principal personality to be subjected to the law's demand and protection. This can be termed the natural or ordinary person. However, there are, as will be shown, according to the law, different categories of human beings with varying capacities under the law. Legal rights are, generally speaking, fully afforded under the Irish legal systems to all persons of full age (i.e. of majority or, as it is known, *sui juris*) and with full mental capacity (i.e. *compos mentis*). The law will presume in any matter before the courts that such is the case unless the contrary is shown. Those not of full age, or suffering from mental incapacity or indeed as yet unborn, are recognised by the law but lack the full capacity of the human beings described above. The extent to which such an identity is limited will be discussed under the section on *status* that follows.[1] It is important at the outset to realise that the personality accorded in general terms by the law to the human being is by way of a unit of legal identity, within which there are many categories. However, it would be wrong to assume that, historically, so far as the Irish system is concerned, law has maintained such a definition. Take, for example, the situation in feudal Ireland, when the law recognised the rights of lord and, to a certain extent, vassal. It did not, for several centuries, allow the native Irish outside of the Pale to have access to the common law. Similarly prior to the feudal system when much of the 'civilised' world was empire building, legal rights were accorded to the citizens of, say, Greece and Rome. Slaves, however, were regarded as animate chattels (personal property) and were effectively denied recognition by the law. The point to stress, therefore, is that the modern legal systems of the world, with few exceptions, in theory at least, regard all human beings as being the subject of the law, i.e. with a legal capacity. The fact that each legal system may discriminate between different groups and classes of individual reflects the political, economic and cultural regimes of that particular country. In addition to the above, non-human entities have been given a legal capacity reflecting particular social structures, principally in the world of trade and commerce. By way of contrast one might note that in the Middle Ages legal personality was accorded to other groups, including the non-human animal that was apparently prosecuted for crimes.

However, of the inanimate world two forms of legal personality are known to the law in Ireland, namely, the *corporate* and the *unincorporated association.* These represent juristic or artificial persons. The growth of these personalities came with the industrial development of the 19th century although traces of the artificial person can be located earlier in history.

While most of the law relating to the personality of the human being can be more appropriately considered under 'status', it is fitting to discuss here in greater detail the concept of the artificial personality.

Incorporated Associations (Corporations)

The law distinguishes between the human being as one type of personality and the corporation as another. Although rights are given to other associations (unincorporated, e.g. clubs or trade unions) only the human beings and the company are capable of full and independent legal identity.

The corporate association is a body that is formed in ways prescribed by law and which continues until determined by law. Being such an artificial person it is not subject to the contingencies of mortality. The two main characteristics of the corporation are, first, its separate and autonomous existence as a person in its own name, and secondly, its membership is entirely human.

An example may illustrate this point. A wishes to buy a motor car from a local garage. He buys a particular car and pays £2,000 for the vehicle. He pays by cheque. His cheque is not honoured (i.e. it bounces). The car turns out to be defective. In general terms A can be sued for the amount of the cheque (i.e. in not honouring his obligation) but A could commence proceedings against the garage owners in respect of the defect in the car. If the garage is run by B and C, two individuals in partnership, then A will sue either or both as individuals. However, if the garage business is owned by a company called D Company Limited, then A will sue that company as a legal person. The fact that B and C own the shares of the company is for the present purpose irrelevant.[2]

What, therefore, is a corporation? There are two types of incorporated associations: corporations aggregate and corporation sole. Both are legal persons autonomous of their human membership.

Corporations sole are essentially offices of a public nature. They are of course filled by human beings, but the identity of such in legal terms is by virtue of the corporation and not the individual person. The fact that the office in question is held by a human being means that in his or her private capacity that person has an individual, human, legal personality. A *corporation sole* therefore is a public office which exists until legally dissolved and it may, over a number of years, have different persons occupying the office. There are many examples of this, the President of the Irish Republic for instance. The duties and powers of the corporation sole are then prescribed by law. In the case of the President of the Irish Republic the principle rights and duties are contained in the 1937 Constitution. The Ministers of a Government Department are also corporation sole, as are the bishops. In England an example of such would be the monarch.

In Ireland, as a result of the Constitutional provisions contained in Article 40, all persons are equal before the law and it is suggested that as corporation sole are legal persons they can be sued and sue in their capacity as corporations. The origins of the corporation sole are both common law, Constitutional and legislative. It is important to realise that the human beings occupying such office therefore, for practical purposes, may have two legal capacities, albeit autonomous and distinct ones. It might also be noted that in terms of litigation the corporations sole are perhaps somewhat insignificant, although in England the Crown is party to all criminal matters tried on indictment and therefore regularly 'appears' in court hearings.

Once a person leaves office, the person assuming the vacant post takes over all the former (and future) liability attaching to the corporate identity. There is of course (subject to the Constitution) nothing to prevent the Oireachtas from ending such a corporation.

Corporations aggregate are corporations involving more than the single occupation of an office, i.e. where a group of people associate to form a company for a particular purpose. It is, of course, the company so formed by the group that is the legal person, and not the individual members of the group (although each will have an individual human legal capacity).

Corporations aggregate are created in one of three ways: First, by royal charter – it must be remembered that prior to 1922 Ireland was subject, in theory at least, to the royal dictates of England and by virtue of the royal prerogative (inherent powers originating in pre-Parliamentary days, now custom and convention) corporate identity could be granted to a particular project. Examples of such still exist in Ireland, e.g. the National University of Ireland, formed by royal charter in 1908. University College, Cork, was granted such identity in 1845 (under the name of Queens College). The Incorporated Law Society of Ireland was formed in 1830. Needless to say in the Republic corporations cannot now be so formed.

Secondly, companies can be created specifically by statute – this device has for example been used to create the nationalised industries that are so important in the present economy. C.I.E., for example, was formed under the Transport Act, 1950, and the E.S.B. under the Electricity (Supply) Act, 1927. Both were then given corporate personality.

While the above two methods of creating aggregate corporate identities were and are respectively important, the third method of creating a company is the most significant in terms of modern commercial practice, that is, by compliance with the statutory requirement of the Companies Act, 1963 and 1977 (following closely the English legislation of 1948, 1967 and 1976).[3]

Before turning to the requirements of this legislation and the nature of the company so created, it is useful at this stage to outline the basic structure of the company. The usual form of a company that is created under the Companies Acts is the *company limited by shares.* The law of the company will be considered in Chapter 15 but for present purposes we can consider the form the company takes in terms of legal personality.

Once the company has complied with formal requirements contained in the legislation, it exists as a legal personality, say, in the registered name of D Company Limited. The ownership of the company is held by virtue of *shares* in the company. Supposing there are 100 shares of £1 each, the shares will be held by shareholders who in fact own their respective stake in D Company Limited. The company is a person completely autonomous from the shareholders, who simply have a say in the running of the company to the extent of their holding (by voting at the meetings of the company).

The shareholders appoint *directors* who run the company on a day-to-day basis and are in fact the company's representatives or agents. There may well be a managing director or chairman of the board appointed as overseer.

The directors can involve the company in transactions thereby acquiring assets and incurring liabilities in the company's name. It is important to understand that the profits made by the company are divisible amongst the shareholders (subject to the terms of reference of the company or, as they are known, Articles and Memorandum of Association, of which more later). Losses incurred by the company, however, are *not* incurred by anyone other than the company. All a shareholder must do is ensure that he or she has paid face value for the share, i.e. if 20 shares are owned the payment must be £20.

Such payment need only be made if the company requires it or if the creditors of the company can find insufficient assets to settle money owed. The liability of the company is therefore unlimited, the liability of the shareholders is limited in this way.

Just to confuse matters, often, especially in small companies, the total shareholding is owned by the directors (e.g. two directors with 50 shares each), but this does not detract from the principles stated above.

Given such a structure exists with the company, two relationships emerge: (i) An internal relationship between company shareholder and Director; (ii) An external relationship between company and third parties, e.g. creditors.

How therefore is such a company formed? The Companies Act, 1963, specifies three different types of company: (i) Limited by shares; (ii) Limited by guarantee; (iii) Unlimited.

The latter two are not common in practice. A company limited by guarantee exists where the shareholders undertake to pay a fixed amount in the event of the company requiring such payment, e.g. to satisfy creditors. An unlimited company exists where the shareholders' liability is unlimited. However, the most common of the companies so mentioned is the *company limited by shares.*

Before considering the method of incorporation it is relevant to note that, whatever type of company is formed, it will either be a *public* company or a *private* company. The difference between the two is essentially a matter of form and detail. The private company can only have a maximum of 50 shareholders with at least two subscribers (original members who form the company). It must also have at least one director and one secretary. It is *not* allowed to offer shares for sale to the public and the transfer of shares is restricted (must be offered back to existing members). A public company must have at least seven subscribers and has no restriction on the sale or transfer of shares. The public company, however, is subject to more detailed returns and general paperwork. Thus the public company is ostensibly made more accountable. The private company is restricted as indicated, but it is not subject to the same stringent regulations.

In either case the company is formed by sending two documents to the Registrar of Companies, namely, the *Memorandum of Association* and the *Articles of Association.* Once these are filed and the registrar is satisfied that the formalities have been complied with, the company exists. A certificate is issued confirming such identity and the personality has full capacity from that date. The memorandum is an official public statement of the company's *objects* and *powers vis-à-vis* the third parties. This, for example, will give information to persons wishing to deal with the company. It also states full particulars about the company's formation, its shares, subscribers, name and address of registered office. The articles regulate the internal administration of the company and its management (directors, meetings, division of profits).

As the law that affects companies will be examined further in Chapter 15, we now continue to examine the nature of the company, rather than the particular law applicable to it.

However, before turning away from the legal personality of the company, it may be of value to give consideration to the characteristics of the company in practice, by way of general conclusion.

As a legal 'person', the company from the date of incorporation can sue and be sued in its own name. The case of *Salomon* v. *Salomon & Co.*[4] is authority for this position. In this case S, a cobbler, formed a limited company, holding the majority of the shares. He lent money to the company by way of debentures. The company became insolvent, and S attempted to exercise his rights as a creditor of the company. The court held he could, for a company is a person from incorporation and must account for its debts in its own name. The fact that a creditor was a shareholder made no difference.

Not only is the company able to sue and be sued in its own name, but the members (shareholders) of the company are irrelevant in so far as any person dealing with the company is concerned, and the liability of the shareholders is usually limited either by shares or guarantee.

As the company has an artificial legal existence it can only be operated through agents (directors) who work in the company's name. Thus, providing the directors act within their power (*intra vires*), the company is bound by the transactions involved, and the directors are not. The artificial nature of the company, however, does limit its activities, despite the actions of the directors. A company cannot, for example, be guilty of any crime involving human commission such as rape or murder, but it can via its directors be involved in offences which as a legal person it is capable of committing, e.g. fraud.

The company's powers and those of its members and agents are regulated by the memorandum and articles of association. To act outside such powers (*ultra vires*) will render the action not binding on the parties save for certain exceptions to be considered later.

Finally, the company is legally active until wound up in accordance with the law, either *voluntarily* (with members passing appropriate resolutions and with all debts paid for and assets divided) or *involuntarily* by the court. This may take place where, for example, a company cannot meet its assets and creditors ask for the court to wind up the company. The person appointed to wind up the company's affairs is known as the *liquidator* (a receiver can also be appointed by the court to handle the company's affairs).

As will be shown later, a company is a device which offers, during its legal existence, protection for persons who hold shares in the company, for if the company cannot pay its way it can be dissolved, and if debts are not paid this is irrelevant so far as the members are concerned. It is sufficient that they have paid fully for their shares. This can be contrasted with the unincorporated association where liability is generally both joint and several on the individual members. It is to this form of associations that we can now turn our attention.

Unincorporated Associations

As mentioned, the law recognises three legal personalities: the human being, the corporation and the unincorporated associations. The latter, though, falls half-way between a group of individuals, i.e. human beings, and a separate and autonomous legal identity. The law recognises the importance in practice of groups of individuals operating towards a common aim, and gives them a special status. This, however, falls short of full autonomy.

In general terms any association that is not a corporation is for present purposes merely a group of *individuals* and as such any transaction entered into or acts done in furtherance of the common purpose are attributable to the whole group both jointly (each and every member) or severally (any particular member).

An example may illustrate this point: If A and B are farmers and amalgamate their holdings and trade under the name of A and B (farmers), any assets or liabilities attaching to this business or partnership will, short of any indication to the contrary as between the parties, be divisible equally. However, a creditor could sue either or both of them to obtain satisfaction for any money owed. If C, a creditor, sued A alone, A would have to pay the whole and would be able to recoup B's contribution, but this would be a separate matter for themselves alone to settle and would be of no concern to C. If, of course, A and B were a limited company, the company alone would be responsible and A and B as shareholders would only be liable to the extent of any unpaid shares they held.

Therefore, all groups of individuals who operate for a particular purpose and who have no corporate identity are unincorporated associations. This will include the most loosely structured society such as a youth club or the large and highly organised trade union bodies.

Before looking at the most important of these particular formations, the principal characteristics of the unincorporated associations can be set out. First, despite being merely a collection of individuals the association can act in its own name, e.g. it may trade. The only limitation here is the registration of the name if the association is trading as a business.[5] Again some of the specific regulations affecting trading associations (i.e. partnerships) will be revealed in Chapter 15.

Secondly, as pointed out above, the liability is, except in defined circumstances that will be examined below, both joint and several. The main exception to this proposition is that if a committee had been appointed with the power to control the day-to-day running of the association, the members of the committee may alone be responsible.

Finally, the property of the association, again a subject of some qualification, is either held by all of the members, or by persons appointed by the association to hold such property. If these persons are created they are known as trustees (it will be recalled that the relationship between trustee and beneficiary is an equitable one). The association itself, as it has no legal identity, may *not* own a property.

The internal regulation of the association is, subject to natural justice (a concept to be examined in Chapter 4), a matter for the club itself to decide upon. The only remedies available at law to ensure that the club does abide by its own rules are the prerogative orders of the High Court.[6]

In addition, the club must abide by the law in its external affairs and the courts reserve the right to ensure that the club acts *intra vires* to its internal rules. Consequently in this respect the court cannot be excluded from regulating the activities of the association.

In general terms such an association will cease to exist once the purpose for the association is no longer pursued or the stratum of the association has broken down.

As against these general rules, however, the law has deemed it necessary to protect certain forms of association because of their commercial, social or political importance, i.e. the law recognises the need of particular institutions; even though they do not have a separate legal personality, they do have a quasi-legal identity – a sort of half-way house.

The most important of these associations can now be considered. They fall into four categories: partnerships, charities, trade unions and friendly societies.

Partnerships: Governed by pre-1922 English legislation in the form of the Partnership Act, 1890, a partnership is defined as a 'relationship which subsists between persons carrying on a business with a common view to profit'. Therefore this is a commercial relationship of 19th century origin (as indeed were the origins of the corporate associations).

Given the scope of the partnership, that is trading, the principal characteristics of this association can be revealed. Again, as in the case of the company, it is not the intention here to set out the basic law involved but rather to highlight the capacity of such an entity under the law. Chapter 15 will deal expressly with the law appertaining to companies and partnerships.

The partnership is simply a collection of individuals whose liability, albeit under an assumed trading name, is again both joint and several. As will be seen the law recognises the importance of such a trading unit and therefore imposes regulations aimed at the protection of parties dealing with partnerships and generally controlling such business activities. Thus the number of partners, the authority of partners, the relationship of partners as between themselves, and the public liability of partners are all statutorily expressed.

Each partner is liable to the firm's creditors for all of the debts and may only set off liability as against the remaining partners so as to recoup the appropriate share.

Because of the business overlap with companies the 1963 legislation makes certain provisions, further emphasising the legal distinction between the two personalities. More accurately, it might be said that the law distinguishes between the legal personality of the corporate association and the quasi-legal personality of the partnership.

It is, however, possible for the partners themselves to regulate their internal relationship even though this cannot affect their liability in a public sense. Consequently partnership agreements are often compiled setting out the work load, share of profits and debts, and ownership of property that flow from the partnership activities. In special circumstances it is possible to have a partnership with the partners having limited public liability, but only if at least one of the partners has a general and unlimited liability.[7] Finally, it can be noted that the law goes beyond the membership of the partnership, for if a non-partner is held out to be a partner by the partnership, acts carried out by that person bind the partnership itself.

Charities: This topic is expressly included here as the law does regard the charity as having characteristics of a personality, although strictly speaking it may not be an association. However, for reasons of convenience the personality of the charity will be so explained. In terms of liability the charity will either be a collection of individuals (e.g. a club), and as such will be jointly and severally liable, or it will exist for a purpose that does not include collective activity (e.g. a fund to preserve graveyards); in the latter instance where there is no human involvement, no liability for the fund will be attracted.

More accurately, the charity of an unincorporated association has a particular legal personality in so far as the law accords certain *benefits* to that entity. The benefits are of a fiscal nature and can be listed. First, the law bends over backwards, as it were, to ensure the survival of charities for the public good. Normally a gift or bequest can only be made to a person or other legal identity. If, for example, it is left for a purpose alone, say, the maintenance of a tomb or the relief of the poor in a given area, that gift would normally *fail* and revert to the next of kin or the donor as being incapable of enforcement.

The law, however, attempts to preserve the charitable intention, and providing the gift is for a charitable purpose recognised by the law it will be applied, despite the fact that legally there is no one to administer it. In fact the gift is put into effect by the *Charity Commission.* The significance of this, of course, is to ensure the perpetuation of the cause by, *inter alia,* avoiding the normal inheritance and succession rules. Charity has a legal definition and the law is contained in the Charities Act, 1961/73. Charity is legally limited to the relief of the poor, the sick, the advancement of education or religion, or other purpose beneficial to the public. In fact if the charity being the subject of the gift has ceased to exist altogether, the law may apply the cyprès doctrine and apply the finances in similar fashion elsewhere.

There is of course nothing to stop a gift being made to a named person or association in their capacity as individuals. The essential consideration therefore, is if an entity is not a charity it must have a legal identity available to enforce and be accountable for legal transactions. In addition to the benefits outlined above the charities are also given relief from financial obligations such as taxes and rates.

Trade Unions: The law of organised labour stems from a bitter historical struggle between the work force, employers, courts and legislation. For present purposes the trade union (and indeed employers associations, e.g. the C.I.I.) is a collection of individuals in the form of an unincorporated association. This association, however, over the last two hundred years, has developed from an illegal organisation the members of which could be sued, prosecuted, and severely punished, to a highly organised national representative unit, unimpeachable by the civil law. The latter, however, requires qualification.

Further details will be considered in Chapter 16 where the liability of employers/ees is considered. It may, however, be noted here that since the Trade Union Act, 1871, the union has assumed a personality, short of full legal identity. As a result of judicial intervention[8] the extent of protection of the 1871 legislation fell into question and the Trade Dispute Act, 1906, was introduced. This is the basis of Irish law in so far as the liability of a union and its members is concerned. Generally speaking there is protection against civil action appertaining to the behaviour of the union when involved in industrial action.

A trade union cannot (since 1906) generally be sued in tort by any party claiming injury, regardless of whether the union is acting 'in contemplation or furtherance of a trade dispute'.[9] This effectively secures the funds of the union by making such tortious action unpresentable to the court. The Trade Union Act, 1941, restricts this protection to unions who are holders of negotiation licences, i.e. registered under that Act.

The only exceptions to the above are, first, where a person suffers injuries resulting from the union's activities (i.e. through its members), and where a civil action may lie, unless the member was actively involved in a trade dispute, e.g. driving negligently while on union business. Secondly, a union is liable for any breach of duty in respect of property that it controls (e.g. defective premises) unless again such breach flows from a dispute.[10]

A similar immunity extends to officials of a registered trade union in Ireland, providing the actions are carried out within the terms of their official capacity and providing the action is in contemplation or furtherance of a trade dispute. This expressly relates to picketing and similar protest.

This protection extends to the members of the union,' in so far as alleged interference with another's business (including picketing) is concerned. Their liability is individual, however, in other matters under the civil and criminal law.

In any event both the union and its members are always accountable to the criminal law, although since 1824 it has not been unlawful, at least in theory, to combine.

It is important, therefore, to stress that the trade union has a particular personality with an obvious and important practical significance.

Friendly Societies: Friendly Societies occupy a rather peculiar position under the law that reflects more their historical growth than their current social importance. The law is to be found in the Friendly Societies Act, 1896, as amended. The legislation provides a definition of a friendly society and other societies capable of registration and/or legal recognition. As the name implies, such societies are those established to provide benefits in money and kind to its members, in return for subscriptions. Thus the friendly societies are provident societies. That such organisations are permitted by law, and accorded certain advantages (mainly exemptions from taxes and representative functions for trustees of the societies), is indicative of the role that such societies perform. The State traditionally has cultivated self-help charity and assistance. The personality of such societies is more than mere individual collectivity, but is less than that of either corporate or even some of the non-corporate associations, e.g. trade unions. Its importance as a quasi-personality may perhaps become increasingly important with the current rise in co-operative enterprises, especially in agriculture and light industry. A form of friendly society known as an industrial and provident society is given corporate status. This caters in particular for initiatives run on a co-operative basis.

In conclusion, therefore, the personalities of the law are twofold: human and corporate, with a third category occupying a position short of full liability, i.e. the unincorporated association.

STATUS

While a particular entity will have a legal personality, being one or a combination of the three suggested above, that personality may be subdivided into further groupings denoting status *vis-à-vis* the law. A person may also have at any one time different stati varying with circumstance. As status is more commonly a personal characteristic, the following rule relates only to human beings but it is appreciated that associations may have varying stati depending on the activities of the group.

There are five matters to consider: nationality, age, sex, mental capacity and a miscellaneous collection of issues.

Nationality

Each human being, according to the Irish law, has a national status, be it Irish citizenship, the citizenship of another country or no citizenship. Persons in the last two categories are referred to as *aliens.*

Citizenship amounts to a relationship between individual and State involving both allegiance and protection. If one is an Irish citizen then allegiance is owed to the Republic and this concept is based in the value of national unity or loyalty. Consequently, acts carried out in prejudice of this allegiance are potentially treasonable. In return for such patriotism the State offers protection in the form of the Constitution, with specific rights and duties duly accorded. Thus an Irish citizen has the right to be treated by due process of law (with certain qualifications), the right to leave and re-enter the country, the right to take part in the democratic determination of the governing of the country, i.e. voting etc., and the right to enjoy freedom of personal liberty. The Constitution specifically enumerates, though it does not exclusively list, such rights.[11] An alien does not enjoy the same status although it is arguable that one would enjoy protection under the Constitution whilst on Irish territory.[12] The concept of nationality in so far as Irish law is concerned, therefore, relates to a particular status in terms of rights and duties under the law.

Briefly, how can nationality be acquired? Subject to the Constitutional provisions of Article 9, the law is contained in the Irish Nationality and Citizenship Act, 1956. Citizenship of Ireland is gained by birth, descent, marriage (declaration), grant of honour, naturalisation or through certain reciprocal arrangements with other countries. One might also note that according to the Constitution a person born in Northern Ireland may elect for Republican nationality.

While stressing that the above legislation formulates the *de jure* position in Ireland, the situation is further complicated by E.E.C. regulations that affect not nationality but movement of persons and, generally, the mobility of labour.

Although nationality affects the status of a person under the law, lack of the domestic nationality does not exclude a person from the auspices of the law. In other words the status of a person may be limited by lack of the appropriate nationality but that person may (in a non-beneficial sense) still be subject to the laws of the country regardless of national origin. Consequently if a German national carelessly drives into an Irish citizen in Ireland, then that person may be sued for damages caused. Likewise the criminal law would apply. In practical terms, however, enforcement of judgement could prove problematic.

Nationality therefore, allegiance apart, denotes a beneficial status in terms of legal protection. Related to the concept of nationality are *domicile* and *residence.* Domicile is residence of a person in a country coupled with the intention to remain in that country, i.e. where you have your present home. Residence is a matter of a physical presence. This is achieved by living in a country without intending to make a permanent home there. This distinction is important for it affects *access* to the law. While nationality may concern the theoretical allegiance and protection of a citizen, domicile and residence affect, in many instances, the jurisdiction of the courts to hear a dispute of concerned parties.

Perhaps the most appropriate field of law that can be used to illustrate this point is the law of the family. A person's capacity to marry, the recognition of foreign divorces, the question of legitimacy, the ability of a party to apply for the custody of and access to children, are all matters affected by the question of domicile and residence.

Just as a person has a national status, be it Irish or alien, likewise every person has a domicile. A person is deemed to have the domicile of origin, i.e. the domicile of the father if legitimate or the mother if illegitimate. according to Irish law.[13] Intention is irrelevant. Once majority is attained (in Ireland, 21) a domicile of *choice* can be made, i.e. where you reside and wish to remain. This suspends the domicile of origin. It should be noted that a woman who marries, however, automatically under Irish law acquires the domicile of her husband, called a domicile of dependency. This not only may be ideologically objectionable but has a very practical legal significance. If the husband and wife separate, the domicile of dependence continues to exist until the marriage is lawfully dissolved (by death or divorce, although the latter is strictly limited in the Republic). It has been suggested that this provision could be unconstitutional.[14] It might be added that no formal declaration is required to establish domicile; it is more a matter of conduct. Apparently if a domicile of choice or dependency is extinguished, the domicile of origin is revived until a new choice is made.

How does this therefore affect access to the courts? The courts will not normally recognise actions by courts in countries where the parties are not *domiciled* and also the Irish courts will not entertain a claim by a party unless they are either domicile in Ireland or resident for a certain period (normally 12 months). This is designed to preserve the sanctity of the domestic law and procedure preventing abuses, say, by parties flying into the country just to use the domestic courts or institutions for their own convenience. Residence therefore may, after the determination of a certain time, give access in place of domicile.

By way of contrast the United Kingdom has reviewed its domicile laws and presents a less discriminatory approach in the Domicile and Matrimonial Proceedings Act of 1973. Reform on similar lines has been mooted recently in the Republic.

The nationality, domicile and residence of a person therefore affect the *status* of the legal personality. It should be noted that the corporate association will have no nationality other than a place of origin, but will be subject to any rules of domicile and residence.

Age

The status of an individual is directly affected by *age,* i.e. the law limits the capacity, for various reasons, of both persons young and old. Historically the law has long differentiated between full responsibility and a lesser degree of accountability on the basis of youth. Consequently limits are imposed protecting children and members of the public and limiting the activities of young people in general. These restrictions are generally lifted on a sliding scale as age increases. The starting point for discussion must be the distinction between the age of majority and minority.

The Brehon Laws apparently imposed a limitation on children during the life of the parent, but the common law dictated the age of *21* as being the dividing line demarcating full responsibility. Under this age at common law the person had no civil liability but could be criminally liable from the age of 7.

While in Ireland the law still preserves a legal majority at 21, statutory intervention has meant that many of the restrictions imposed on young persons are no longer applicable. (The details of the law relating to age limitations are given under Notes and References.)[15] The age of a person may therefore determine his or her standing before the law.

Such is the anomalous situation, with *de facto* majority being attained at 18, that recommendations have recently been made to lower the age of majority in Ireland to accord with the practice in many other countries.[16]

Sex

Despite its alluring title, this section is concerned with the legal limitations on the status of persons who are treated in a particular way by the law because of gender. Thus only men can commit rape. However, this point has far-reaching and important practical consequences in Ireland, for the law treats men and women differently in many respects. The merits of such discrimination are not up for debate here but the existence of the differentiation should be noted. While, as will be illustrated, there have been a number of recent enactments to remove some of the patent discrimination suffered by women under the law, it can be seen that women still, at law and in practice, have to suffer considerable, and unjustifiable, limitation. The most significant limitations placed on women by the law are as follows.

Since 1882 women have, in theory, enjoyed the same property rights as men, i.e. the right to own, retain and dispose of personal and real property.[17] Since the Sex Qualification (Removal) Act, 1919, there have been in law no bars to prevent women from entering most professions and vocations.

However, two chief areas of inequality still remain in so far as the law actively differentiates between the sexes and their respective legal status and capacity; these concern employment and the family.

Over the past two years in Ireland there have been positive moves by the legislature to end, or at least to be seen to end, the possibility of discrimination against women. Consequently it is now both a matter of civil and criminal law if a woman is discriminated against in terms of the selection for conditions of and dismissal from employment.[18] Despite such legislation women at law are still restricted in many areas relating to the nature of the job involved and the hours of work. A more detailed discussion of the nature of such legislation will be alluded to in Chapter 16.

A woman moreover is actively discriminated against in matters relating not to the terms of the job but rather to its consequences. Thus the law generally recognises the man as the identity responsible for the compilation and return of income tax papers and, more importantly, it is the man who receives tax allowances. A tax rebate on joint income would also fall to the man. Similarly if a woman is either unemployed or normally at home looking after the house and/or the children, she is positively discriminated against through her entitlement to social welfare benefits. As a starting point the *amount* of benefit may differ. The man may receive, for example, unemployment benefit and in fact the period of entitlement to such benefit is shorter for some women than for men. By way of consolation, prior to 1979, the woman paid 7p per week less for her social insurance contribution.[19] Likewise active discrimination is felt in the other contributory and non-contributory benefits. A more comprehensive explanation of the social welfare system is given in Chapter 18.

The law apparently feels committed to regarding the woman as having at least a special status, even if that cannot be reconciled with full human activity. This is because the Constitution in Article 41.2.1 recognises the place of the woman in the home, as 'by her life within the home, the woman gives to the State a support without which the common good cannot be achieved'. Similar role-definitions are accorded to mothers.[20] The Constitution can, of course, be amended by referendum.[21]

This discriminatory recognition has so shaped legislation and policies that many laws and presumptions are geared against the woman who wishes to lead a life as an alternative (not even in addition) to the home. Women consequently are at a disadvantage in both economic, social and legal terms.

Within the family unit (some detail follows in Chapter 17) it should be noted here that women suffer different rules with regard to domicile, matrimonial actions (e.g. criminal conversation)[22] and financially (e.g. having to wait three months before claiming social welfare benefit as a deserted wife).[23]

In addition, many laws affect women in an indirect way. Areas that come to mind include the piecemeal protection against matrimonial violence, the non-availability (until mid 1980) of a State Legal Aid Service,[24] and issues of abortion and contraception. One might speculate that Ireland, in so far as the Constitution allows, will follow closely behind the slightly more liberal approach of the British.

Mental Incapacity

The chief stumbling block to full legal status yet to be examined is that of the mental state of the human being. The law presumes, *inter alia,* that a person is full *compos mentis,* i.e. accountable for his or her actions. If a person is *non compos mentis,* then a number of incapacitating consequences follow. The legal definition of the *non compos mentis,* although obviously reliant on medical assistance, is not necessarily considered in medical terms. We are therefore concerned with the legal incapacity rather than the clinical. How bizzare a person's actions are, may be indicative but not conclusive of mental incapacity as far as the law is concerned. Also a person who does not have full legal capacity owing to the mental state of mind may have intermittent capacity during lucid periods.

There are two aspects to consider: first, the person concerned will be incapacitated with regard to the benefit of and liability to the law (with certain qualifications); in addition, the law may as a result of such a state of affairs assume *control* over a person both bodily and materially. The extent of the disability will depend on the nature of the mental incapacity.

At civil law such status need not be declared (i.e. it can be discovered, for example, during litigation). A person suffering from mental incapacity may be excused civil liability except for limited circumstances, i.e. whenever lucid periods are enjoyed, as in contract.[25] Rights are accorded to such a person in a delegated way, i.e. the person will have a legal capacity but cannot implement some or all of it. For example, the right to handle money may be exercised by an appointed person known as the 'receiver'. Consequently a mentally incapacitated person may, unless subject to bodily control, come and go unaffected, except that he or she may not be able to enforce a transaction as in contract. This, however, does not mean that the transaction itself is necessarily invalid. Suppose, for example, such a person buys a watch. If no receiver has been appointed the transaction is valid. It could not be enforced by the shopkeeper (say, if the cheque bounced) as the person concerned could avoid the contract on grounds of incapacity (although some qualification is needed in this respect).[26] However, if the watch proved defective the shopkeeper could be sued. A problem, however, could arise as to who would sue. In addition, the person may suffer inabilities under the civil law, e.g. be unable to obtain a driving licence, given consent to marry, etc.

According to criminal law the mental state of mind is extremely important.[27] As will be shown in Chapter 11, a criminal act consists of doing (*Actus reus*) and the intending (*Mens rea*). The mental state of mind can negative either or both. If the person breaks a window during a fit, it is arguable that the relevant mental condition prevented the control of body movements. It is a prerequisite of the *Actus reus* that such movements be physically voluntary. More obviously, *Mens rea* can be negatived by establishing that the intention to do the act was lacking owing to the inability of the person to form it (because of the mental state of mind). The law, however, distinguishes in this context between insanity (again a legal definition) and a state of affairs short of insanity which still prevents a criminal intention being formed.[28] It is pertinent to note the significance of the finding of insanity and something less than insanity. Once a case has been concluded, if insanity is established, the verdict is guilty but insane. However, this does not mean that the person is in practice acquitted. While being not guilty the State can detain the person until it is assured that it is safe to release that person. A person not guilty by reason of a mental state falling short of legal insanity is free to go, subject to the provisions of the Mental Treatment Acts.

Control over the body and business of the mentally incapacitated can be assumed in two ways. The President of the High Court may on application by, for example, relatives of the person concerned or other lawfully entitled bodies, i.e. the court, appoint a special trustee to handle that person's affairs and the receiver is accountable to the court. The person will be given an allowance as approved by the court. Once such *wardship* is declared, then this officially deprives the person subject to the order of civil legal capacity in respect of their funds.

It remains now to consider the physical detention of a mentally incapacitated person. The law is contained in the Mental Treatment Acts of 1945, 1958 and 1961. These follow closely the provisions in England contained in the Mental Health Act, 1959. These Acts divide mental incapacity into three categories. First, long-term detention and/or treatment is specified, secondly a short-term detention is permitted under the Acts, and thirdly there are provisions relating to emergencies.

In general terms admission, detention and treatment depend either on voluntary submission by the 'patient' upon a court order, or on the intervention of an authorised person such as the police in case of emergency. The jurisdiction for such intervention depends usually on certification by doctors of the mental condition, with more stringent requirements being necessary the more drastic the proposed interference with the liberty of the person. An aggrieved person may either appeal to the Mental Health Tribunal or to the High Court for an order of Habeas Corpus[29] and/or damages for assault and false imprisonment.

The orders committing someone to such a mental institution originate either through criminal proceedings or on application to the courts outside of the criminal jurisdiction. It must be appreciated that this aspect of law involves both fundamental constitutional as well as human rights issues. The problem caused and the position of the subject must therefore be examined when considering such an incapacity.

Miscellaneous

In conclusion, there are some miscellaneous categories that have assumed a particular status under the law. These may well overlap with other categories already examined. A person, of course, may at any one time hold a number of different capacities in any given situation, e.g. a female, young person with mental incapacity.

Such additional groups can be dealt with very briefly. The law recognises a special status of foreign diplomat as provided for in the Diplomatic Relations and Immunities Acts, 1967/76. Hence come stories of parking tickets being collected and ignored by ambassadors and their staff. Much of this status stems from a *de jure* recognition of *de facto* reciprocal arrangements between international sovereign states. Consequently the diplomat is unaccountable to, but may use, Irish law. Serious breaches of law, however, may in practical terms involve the expulsion of an offender from the State.

The law also accords a special status to persons honoured by the State and persons falling into the category of corporations sole who may have a particular status, e.g. the President of the Republic.

On a more mundane level special status is given, for example, to employers and police, but these will be examined either in terms of their relationship indicated below or in more relevant subsequent chapters.

RELATIONSHIPS

So far personality and status have been identified as the two determining factors of a person or body's standing before the law. It appears logical to include in this final section of the chapter some brief notes on the relationships which the law recognises, as these too are, as it were, capacity-giving features from which both rights and duties, obligations and liabilities flow.

The most fundamental relationship which ironically will receive the least attention is that of the State and the individual. In the Republic, with its written constitution great stress is placed both in practice and in debate on the nature of this relationship, an aspect that will be elaborated upon in Chapter 9 which deals with the substance of Constitutional law. This apart, there are many special relationships imposed, upheld and generally recognised by the law, and the following categories are perhaps the most socially significant.

The Family

The nuclear family as known to the Western world consists of man, woman and, possibly, children. The law imposes complex regulations that affect the relationship between husband and wife, parents and child, and other co-habitees, i.e. unmarried couples. Of the matrimonial relationship, the law regulates the formation, duration and dissolution of the marriage. Flowing from such a relationship are matters of maintenance and ownership of property. All of these appertain to a recognised bond or *consortium.* Also as a consequence (or sometimes a prelude) of matrimony, the law has to arbitrate over the custody, guardianship and access to and of children. Each party therefore has both rights and duties that occupy much of the time of courts and legislature alike. The detail of this complex legal area is examined in Chapter 17.

Employment

Here again, owing to detailed coverage later, we merely take note of the relationship between employer and employee. This is on both a contractual (i.e. operated on terms of agreement) and tortious (i.e. civil duties outside of contract) basis. The law, subject to statutory minima (i.e. standards below which parties cannot lawfully operate), will endorse the terms of the agreement; the employer is to pay wages, honour holidays agreed and dismiss with proper notice; and the employee is to work. Statutes, however, in order to protect the tenure of the employee, have introduced additional factors that are incorporated as terms in the contract, such as the right not to be unfairly dismissed.[30]

Additional civil responsibilities are placed on this relationship. A clear example is the duty of the employer to provide a safe working environment for the employee.

Business and Commerce

This rather vague category includes the basic relationships upheld in the world of private and public commerce. The Western world has long recognised the relationship of capital to labour as indicated above,[31] and the relationship of buyer and seller. In the latter instance a mass of statute and case law exists regulating rights on buying and hiring goods. Here we will examine a few of the important relationships the law imposes, thus making large sections of commercial practice possible.

The first chapter went to some pains to highlight the growth of two very distinct aspects of the law, i.e. common law and equity. Prior to the fusion of jurisdiction in Ireland in 1877, equity had been responsible for the evolution of the *use* or *trust.* The relationship of *trustee and beneficiary* is vitally important in a legal sense. It may be recalled that a trust may be expressed or implied, i.e. by the action of the parties or by the law. In either event it is considered equitable to ensure that a person carried out the express or implied duties. The responsibilities of the trustee, i.e. the holder of the property, is to the beneficiary or the recipient. The courts using these long established equitable principles will therefore uphold the trust. It might be noted that since 1877 there has been no separate Court of Chancery.

In considering a problem a person may have recourse to *professional* advice. This occurs daily in the commercial world both public and private. While a contract may be created and thus a relationship of *buyer and seller* created, the law may regulate the parties' conduct by imposing additional requirements, e.g. on standards of competency or style of business. A convenient though by no means exclusive example is that of the solicitor and client. In addition to any claim in contract or tort (e.g. negligence) the law also requires the solicitor to operate in a particular and controlled way. This affects many items, from the handling of the client's money to advertising for business. To greater or lesser degrees, bankers, insurance brokers, estate agents and accountants may also be used to illustrate this point.

As a final example of the law and commerce in practice one can cite the relationship of company and shareholder. As previously seen, the company and the shareholder are legal personalities. The former is an artificial person, the latter a human being. The company exists as an autonomous entity and is managed by its directors (agents). The shareholders have a link with the company in the form of a financial stake which entitles them, according to the terms of reference of the company, to a share of profits or *dividend.* The shareholders, empowered by virtue of the shareholding to vote in the meeting of the company, decide the company's policy in operation. There is therefore a legally enforceable relationship between the parties peculiar to the two types of legal person.

Although different descriptions of categories of personality, status and relationship have been used, this chapter should at least have indicated the nature of legal personality and capacity. While remembering the individual categories, it is vital to stress that an entity may find a personality, status or relationship mandatorily imposed, e.g. domicile or nationality. However, at any one time and for a number of different purposes a person or body may assume the same or different capacities *vis-à-vis* that situation. In short a legal personality under Irish law may have a changing status as time and circumstances dictate. In other countries the possible combinations of such personality and status may be even wider.

As the adage has it, 'all are equal but some are more equal than others'.

Chapter 4

LEGAL METHOD

INTRODUCTION

A lawyer's supposed skills consist of three elements. First, the lawyer is familiar with the substantive rules of law and practice. Secondly, the lawyer knows how to find and utilise such material. Thirdly, the lawyer is called upon to predict the outcome of matters that are in dispute. In collating material and implementing these basic skills the lawyer works according to a definite *method.* While each individual may adopt different means of bringing about an end to a legal issue, e.g. effecting the conveyance or conducting the court hearing to its conclusion, there are defined rules that will to a large extent dictate the outcome. This chapter describes the underlying principles of such a method.

The scope of the study is, by its very nature, eclectic and often seemingly abstract. As with preceding chapters, however, an understanding of basic principle is crucial to an appreciation of the law in Ireland. The reader should therefore attempt to assimilate the information with an idea of its relevance to the law. The final chapter will attempt to criticise, one hopes constructively, some of these premises.

Qualifications apart, the chapter is divided as follows:

(i) Identification of a legal problem.
(ii) Characteristics of the common law system.
(iii) Concepts of law.
(iv) Legal technique.

The overlap between, and artificiality of, such classification is acknowledged.

WHAT IS A LEGAL PROBLEM?

It is all very well defining law by reference to its formal sources, but this approach does not, in any practical sense, define a legal problem.

A legal problem can be identified by reference to the availability of a *remedy*. The problem therefore exists for the lawyer in terms of what solution, if any, can be found within the law. There are two distinct difficulties with this approach.

First, the law is often seen as being the ultimate panacea to 'legal' problems. What should be appreciated by both reader and lawyer alike, not to mention the rest of the population, is that the law provides a remedy on its own terms. Much of what will appear in this chapter will show that the courts adjudicate a problem on the basis that two or more parties are in dispute, and that one of them must be deserving (legally) of a judgement. Law, clearly, is not such a universal remedial medium. It is submitted here that the law is but one (and perhaps not the most appropriate) of the means of settling disputes.

The second issue which should be highlighted at this stage is that in defining its boundaries the law has, with increased specialisation, conveniently pigeon-holed problems into categories with appropriate remedies. Nowhere is this more apparent than in contemporary legal education, where law is still largely taught in terms of substantive and traditional subjects. These subjects are the ones that the law is conventionally associated with, namely, constitutional law, contract, tort, property, equity, crime and jurisprudence. There is a growing realisation that legal rights and duties that can be enforced and upheld under the law exist in less traditional subjects. One may attribute the growth of this realisation to a number of sources, none the least being the recognised need of the profession to expand their market, but the end result is to 'legalise' areas that were before seen as non-legal. Family law provides a modern example of this development in the Republic. Increasingly, the law of social welfare, civil rights, and sexual equality are attracting lawyers' attention, as is administrative law.

However, there are many areas that are still not recognised as having legal relevance. Whether this is progressive or regressive is a matter for speculation. That a problem is not seen as a legal one is significant, for this is a strong determining factor on the remedies that are seen to be available in handling the particular conflict. Whatever the value of law as a catalyst in problem solving, it is important to realise both its limitations and the extent of its application.

WHAT IS A COMMON LAW SYSTEM?

Separation of Powers

The common law system grew, as we have shown, slowly and in a piecemeal fashion. A central authority existed under royal supervision and a body of adjudicators to administer the law. The law was recognised as accepted customary behaviour, supplemented by royal proclamation and later by Acts of Parliament. Judicial precedent was to be a development of the 18th and 19th centuries. The functioning of these law makers and law givers brings us to one of the fundamental characteristics of the common law system as it operates in Ireland, the United Kingdom and many other English-speaking nations: the law is administered by those lawfully entitled, but their functions are distinct. This concept is traditionally known as the *separation of powers.*

Three authorities are concerned with the function of the common law system: the *executive,* the *legislature* and the *judiciary.* Except for their joint accountability to the law and its process each supposedly operates independently of the other. As will be seen this accountability is known as the *rule of law,* i.e. no person or body is beyond the law.

The executive, or government, is responsible for the administration of the country and hence its laws. It is accountable only to the due process of law. Ministerial functions must, for example, be *intra vires* to their lawful powers. The legislature is politically related to the executive but is autonomous in terms of the mechanical creation of law. The judiciary likewise is, in constitutional terms, endowed with an independence to review and interpret the law, stemming either from the statutes or prior case-law. Its function is subject only to the law (e.g. by way of appeal) and Parliamentary intervention (in the form of new law-making).

Judicial Review[1]

In a work of this length and diversity it is not possible to examine exhaustively such undoubtedly important concepts. It is necessary, however, to stress the relationship of the three powers. This is popularly achieved under the heading 'Judicial Review'. To appreciate this concept and the application of the rule of law one must turn to the 1937 Constitution. Here the independent and distinct functions and accountabilities of the powers are considered. While not being an exhaustive authority the Constitution provides a documentary starting-point for material on the fundamental characteristics of Ireland's essentially common law system. Chapter 9 reveals the significance of these and other principles pertinent to constitutional law. In carrying out the review of the law and in compliance with it the courts have, since 1937, in Ireland dealt with three distinct aspects of judicial review:

(i) On the validity of Acts passed or drafted by the Oireachtas.[2]
(ii) On the powers of the executive, both national and regional (Local Government) and other judicial and quasi-judicial bodies.
(iii) On the extent of fundamental rights preserved by the Constitution.[3]

The rule of law, however, at this stage must be qualified by a number of exceptions to the principle. While all persons are subject to the law, the law does recognise persons and institutions that are accorded a special status. Attention has already been drawn to such exceptions, including the President of the Republic and foreign diplomats. In the United Kingdom the situation is further complicated by the presence of the monarchy and the absence of a written Constitution.[4]

Natural Justice

If the separation of powers is the first characteristic of common law systems, the principle of *natural justice* must be the second.

Despite the existence of a written Constitution the Irish courts have in their findings been able and willing to stress the relevance of this ancient principle that seems unaffected by Constitutional restriction.[5] Thus the law, certainly as expostulated by the courts, has retained the old common law principle that decision makers must not contravene certain unquestionable standards. These standards are basically twofold:

(i) The rule against bias (*nemo index in causa sua*). In the words of Hewart, Lord Chief Justice in *Regina* v. *The Sussex Justices,* 'Justice should not only be done, but be manifestly and undoubtedly seen to be done'.[6]

Thus no one can be a judge in their own cause. Any connection between the adjudicator and parties in dispute that might affect the outcome renders the adjudicator's position open to question. Even though no benefit accrues to this person as a result of a judgement, the decision given by such an interested party is null and void. A family relationship, a business connection or close friendship can rule out the adjudicator's function. The principle is clearly shown in *Dimes* v. *Grand Junction Canal Company*[7] where a decision was quashed as the judge was a shareholder in the defendant company. No advantage need be shown to accrue to the judge.

(ii) The rule of fair-hearing (*audi alteram partem*). It is also a principle of natural justice for both sides to have the opportunity of putting their case. Any authority empowered to make decisions as between two or more interested parties is bound to allow all interested persons to state their arguments fully.

The failure of a Garda Commissioner to allow a taxi-driver the opportunity to state his case as to why his tax licence should not be revoked has recently been held to be in contravention of such a principle.[8]

The two concepts therefore of natural justice and the separation of powers are common to common law systems, and Ireland is no exception. The Constitution tacitly endorses such principles.

Adversary Trial

If one were to attempt to describe a further characteristic of the system it must lie in the adversary nature of the judicial process. The way in which a dispute is judicially resolved in Ireland is known as the *accusatorial* or *adversary method.* The essence of this can be found in the old cliche 'innocent until proven guilty'. Without confusing civil and criminal liability the adversary system dictates that the person alleging a claim has the responsibility of proving it. That measure of responsibility is known as the *burden of proof.* In criminal proceedings the prosecution (State) must establish *beyond all reasonable doubt* that the person charged is guilty of the offence. In a trial before judge and jury the question of guilt is to be adduced by the jury on the evidence given and with due direction from the judge on matters of law. In the District Court the justice performs this function. The principle of accusatorial trial is an especially important characteristic of common law systems for, in theory at least, the accused need put up no defence or explanation of his or her actions until the onus has been satisfied. When the prosecution has established such an onus then the burden shifts to the defendant to disprove guilt.

In civil trials the same principle applies, i.e. the person bringing the case must prove it. One important distinction should be noted at this stage, however: the onus of proof is slightly reduced to that of the *balance of probabilities.* While 'reasonable doubt' will prevent a conviction in a criminal trial, a civil accusation that 'is more likely than not' will succeed. Again a defendant is under no duty to establish an explanation for actions or omission until the burden of proof is met by the plaintiff.

The adversary system can, by way of contrast, be compared with the trials under civil or continental legal systems. Here the process is known as *inquisitorial.* This does not, as popularly thought, mean 'guilty until proven innocent' but rather the adjudicator is allotted the task of making a preliminary examination to discover the merits of the case. Once a finding has been reached each side may then present its arguments accordingly.[9]

Law and Fact

A potential source of some confusion to readers is the distinction made by lawyers between *law* and *fact*. It is a characteristic of common law systems that the two are, though related, separate and autonomous concepts. To confuse the two is fatal to an understanding of the substance and application of law in Ireland.

An example may illustrate the point: A is charged with the murder of B. At the trial A alleges that he was never at the supposed scene of the crime. Whether this is true or not will be a question of *fact*. In the Central Criminal Court the jury will decide such a factual issue. It will, however, be a matter of law as to whether the definition of murder has been satisfied, i.e. a human being died within a year and a day because of an act or omission by A, and that A intended to bring about such result.[10]

Nowhere is the significance of this distinction more clearly illustrated, as will be seen, than in the area of social welfare law. The Department of Social Welfare and Regional Health Board have certain discretionary powers concerning the payment of benefits and the conditions imposed here for qualification for entitlement. That a particular *policy* is adopted in dealing with the exercise of discretion in defined circumstances is a matter of *fact*. Because tribunals and officials adhere to a policy lends no legal authority to that decision. The advocate may, therefore, find it useful to argue that the policy is not mandatory and should not be applied in the particular circumstances. A policy is a question of fact and not law and need not therefore be mandatorily applied.

There are further important issues arising from the law/fact distinction. The courts consider such terms when granting leave to appeal. Usually leave to appeal will only be granted on an issue of law. This is primarily due to the presumption of the appellate courts that the court of first instance is in the best position to adjudicate on the facts, being most proximate to the issues in question. In limited circumstances, as will be shown, appeals of fact may be admitted.[11]

Substantive and Adjective Law

Another characteristic of the common law system of Ireland is the difference between *substantive* and *adjective* law. We have in Ireland two complementary sets of rules of law. Those that purport to regulate specified areas, e.g. tort, contract, crime and property, are known as substantive law. The law that lays down the framework within which such specific laws can operate is known as adjective or procedural law. It has been implied in this text that the adjective law was of primary importance in the early stages of the growth of the common law. The technicalities of an action were often more of a determining factor than the merits of a case. It was the form of the law that to a large extent determined the nature of rights, especially in the private civil sense. It may be fair to say now that adjective law serves only to oil the machinery for the substantive rules to operate and while of major importance and frequently tested in the court, it is no longer fatal to a substantive action.

Codification

The final and perhaps most obvious characteristic of the common law can be found in a comparison with these civil law systems. The piecemeal development of the common law emphasises the lack of early legislative influence. There is an apparent disinclination on the part of the legislative to gather together the law on any particular point. In a word the common law system has little *codified* law. Following the French Revolution the ruling philosophy of the day was to lead to increased codification of the law on the premise that the law would then be available on one issue in one text. While a number of statutes exist in the common law framework that have this effect, most of the law in Ireland is reliant upon the variety of sources examined before.[12]

Given the limited purpose of this chapter let us now examine some of the concepts which govern the application of law in Ireland.

WHAT ARE THE CONCEPTS OF THE LAW?

Res Judicata

A starting-point can be taken with the principle of *res judicata pro veritate accipitus.* Literally translated this means that a thing adjudicated is received as the truth. The practical effect of *res judicata* is that the law presupposes that to any legal dispute there are two opposing parties, that there is a definite issue between them, that there is a court or tribunal competent to adjudicate on the issue, and that there has been a lawful determination of the case. Further, once decided subject to the appellate system, the matter cannot be raised by either party again. Precedent apart, this process is of no relevance to other parties in dispute. Consequently to challenge the presumptions of *res judicata* some primary defect in the settlement of the dispute must be shown. The means of such a rebuttal will shortly be made apparent.

Locus Standi

Incorporated with *res judicata* is the second concept, that of *locus standi. Res judicata* presumes the existence of the two parties in dispute, while *locus standi* indicates the right of a person to be a party to a dispute (a place of standing). This ancient principle has caused a number of problems for the courts, even in recent times. If A drives carelessly and damages B's property, B will undoubtedly have the *locus standi* to complain, as some interest of B's has been unlawfully interfered with. This test can be applied to the majority of legal disputes. What if the facts are changed? A, a private individual, hears of R.T.E's intention to broadcast a play on television that contains explicit sexual scenes. R.T.E's justification is that such is produced in the name of art and culture. Does A have a sufficient interest in the matter to enable an application to be made to the High Court for an injunction preventing the broadcast? There would seem to be little authority on the matter in Ireland. Perhaps, however, some guidance can be taken from the decisions of the English courts. If the case involved an application to force a statutory authority to carry out (or refrain from carrying out) a particular duty then a wide interpretation of *locus standi* may be held. This would involve an application for a *prerogative* order. In a number of judgements known collectively as the Blackburn Cases[13] *locus standi* was accorded, *inter alia,* to a private individual to call to account members of public authorities including the Metropolitan Police Commissioner (London).

In a curiously worded case in 1973 under the name of *Attorney General* v. *I.B.A.*[14] one Ross McWhirter was granted an injunction preventing an allegedly indecent film being broadcast. This was granted despite the reluctance of the Attorney General to consent to such preventative action. It would appear therefore that if a member of the public is a last resort and has any degree of interest in the matter, *locus standi* may be held to exist.[15]

Locus standi, however, does have some defined boundaries. In the area of family law, for example, grandparents are not able to challenge an access order of the courts. In contract a third party has no *locus standi* to enforce the contract to which he or she is not privy. The interest therefore must be one recognised by the law.

In Rem and In Personam

Before leaving such concepts of the law two further issues must be considered. The expressions 'actions *in rem*' and 'actions *in personam*' are often used in writings of legal and equitable interests. They require brief explanation. Quite simply these terms reflect their origins. An action based in equity recognised an equitable interest. That interest, remembering its nature, arose from a personal right created by the Court of Chancery – a right as between one person and another because of their particular relationship. Such is known as a right *in personam.* The interests preserved by the trust serve as a useful example. The trustee owes a duty to the potential recipient or beneficiary. That interest is in no way affected by the claims of the third parties, unless they too form part of the relationship. Rights *in rem* are the common law rights, e.g. to damages, possession, etc. While the principle of *res judicata* limits the decision of the court to the immediate parties, the pronouncement is good against the whole world, i.e. interests are recognised on a non-personal level, even though their application is by the individuals. The distinction is perhaps only important today in so far as it emphasises the discretionary nature of equity and the entitlement to common law remedies.

The Judicial Prerogative

Finally we must examine the operation of judicial review. It has already been mentioned that judicial review is a characteristic of common law systems and, despite certain Constitutional restrictions, is alive in Ireland. It is the purpose of the following lines to indicate the operation of such a reviewing process. How do the courts intervene in controlling power exercised by either the executive or legislature or other tribunals making judicial or quasi-judicial decisions?

The concept with which we are concerned here is that of the *inherent* power of certain courts (the High Court and Supreme Court) to interfere with decision-making at a number of levels. This authority appears to be of long historical standing and is unimpeachable on the same lines as the principles of natural justice.

For the present we will ignore the extent of the court's power to interfere in the legislative process, for this is documented later.[16]

Where a statutory or Government authority exceeds its jurisdiction (*ultra vires*) the court may grant a *prerogative order.* There are three such orders: *certiorari, mandamus* and *prohibition.* The first quashes, the second compels and the third prohibits a particular decision or action. Thus where a Minister in England refused to appoint a committee to investigate price differences in the milk industry, saying his discretion was unfettered, mandamus was granted forcing the Minister to act. To refuse was held to be *ultra vires* to his power.[17]

Where the authority is given a discretion to make a decision, an order can still lie if that discretion has not been exercised in accordance with the principles of natural justice. If the authority operates with a bias or declines to allow full representation for each side in a dispute the prerogative order is the appropriate remedy. In addition a vague duty to act fairly has been stated in the English courts as being part of natural justice although it is doubtful how far the statements of the English courts would affect decision-making bodies in Ireland through acceptance by the Irish courts.[18]

The ability of the court to make a prerogative order is also apparent where there is an error on the face of the record of a court or tribunal. Thus if the record of the adjudication is in some way defective an application for a prerogative order can be made. This can be clearly illustrated from the seemingly administrative function of the tribunal system. Over the past decade a number of tribunals have been established in Ireland to carry out decision-making in quasi-judicial areas, such as income tax, land planning and entitlement to welfare benefits. The legal implication of such must not be underestimated. It was felt in England for many years that the High Court was effectively denied jurisdiction on the grounds that such tribunals were given the task of decision-making by Act of Parliament. The argument followed that these authorities had the jurisdiction to decide an issue rightly or wrongly. The only complaint that lay under this argument was if the tribunal acted *ultra vires* to its powers. However, since 1951 in England decisions of such authority can now be questioned if an error of law appears on the record.[19] We feel it would be of highly persuasive authority if cited in an Irish court.

It can be said that the potential abuses of power by tribunal and official alike are therefore limited by the unwritten jurisdiction of the High Court and the Supreme Court to grant prerogative orders remedying the defect. The Constitution is silent on the matter, except for vesting all pre-Treaty legal powers in the superior courts.

It should, for the sake of completion, be noted that the courts can also grant declarations or injunctions regulating the exercise of the power of decision-making. The declaration is an order which pronounces the legality of a *de facto* situation. This will lie where an abuse of power has occurred and the aggrieved party wishes this to be known, without asking for a definitive cause of action. Additionally an aggrieved person may ask for a declaration where clarification of the legal position is required, even though no damage has yet been sustained. This presupposes that the person in question has sufficient *locus standi.*[20]

The injunction will lie similarly to prevent the cause of action occurring where a prerogative order would be ineffective, as the abuse has not yet occurred. An example of this would be as previously given, to prevent the broadcasting of certain allegedly obscene material.

The power of the court therefore to interfere in decision-making of courts, tribunals and officials beyond the ordinarily understood appellate procedure, and not as a court of first instance, is a concept vital to the operation and understanding of the law in common law jurisdictions. It is as such of particular relevance to Ireland.

WHAT ARE THE TECHNIQUES OF THE LAW?

It was argued in the introduction to this chapter that a lawyer not only knows the law (or some of it) and where to find it, but can use the law that is available. This final section is concerned with the use of legal material or, as we have termed it, legal technique.

Authority

The first and most essential of all techniques, for both student and practitioner alike, is to be found in the use of *authorities.* Cases are won and lost, examination questions passed and failed on degrees of understanding of this important principle. Simply put, each proposition of law must, to hold its validity, be supported by an authority. In the modern context the authority will stem either from legislation or precedent. Neither judges or examiners will be impressed by a statement of law that is unsupported by authority. One can draw an analogy here with mathematics. The answer alone is insufficient, it is the method or working out that is vital to the proof. Some judges require less of advocates than others, but the authority is the basis of legal argument.

This is not to suggest that success in a legal action depends on quoting the appropriate authorities. Indeed often the law is not in dispute and the case is decided on the *facts.* However, even in this instance, the court should hear authority to support any propositions of law that are submitted to the court.

The reader therefore should be aware, even when answering a seemingly straightforward legal problem, that statements of the law must be supported by authority. Where there are none directly on the point, principles enunciated in other cases must be argued and extended either through the use of persuasive precedent or by analogy.

Thus, to wound or cause grievous bodily harm is a criminal offence under sections 18 and 20 of the Offices Against the Person Act, 1861. The meaning of 'wound' or 'grievous bodily harm' is judicially defined.[21] It may be necessary to refer to such authority in the course of a trial to satisfy the court that the accused did nor did not commit the appropriate offence.

Presumption

The reader will recall that one of the principal characteristics of the Irish legal system is its adversary or accusatorial nature. The party bringing the action must satisfy the burden of proof. Often, however, it is unnecessary to realise evidence on particular issues; they are presumed. *Presumptions* are thus extremely important, for they do not have to be established. They arise for a number of reasons such as protecting children (presumptions against criminality under 14) or as a matter of convenience or public policy (e.g. onus on the employer to establish ground for dismissal). The presumptions are divisible into the rebuttable and the non-rebuttable. As suggested by these descriptive tags the non-rebuttable presumptions are beyond challenge. An example would be the inability of a child under 7 to commit a criminal offence (although certain legal consequences could be attracted).[22] Likewise a male under 14 is presumed incapable of committing an offence involving sexual intercourse.[23] With this category of presumption the party in whose favour they fall takes an absolute benefit.

The rebuttable presumption on the other hand is only presumed until the contrary is proven. A child aged from 7 to 14 is presumed incapable of forming a criminal intention but this could be refuted by, say, reference to the child's previous history. Likewise under the employment protection legislation a dismissal is presumed unfair and the onus then shifts from the applicant (the employee) to the respondent (the employer). The latter has the task of establishing a good reason for dismissal. It should be pointed out that unless it is admitted (it usually is) the dismissal must be proven by the applicant. This will be examined at greater length later.[24] In other areas presumptions are also important, e.g. presumption of death will be made by a court after an absence of seven years and if all due inquiries have been made. A presumption of marriage is made in favour of a man and a woman who have lived together as husband and wife and the onus of challenging the marriage will lie with the complainant party.

It must be appreciated that examples are numerous and it is sufficient for present purposes if the relevance of the presumption is seen in the shifting of the onus of proof.

Judicial Notice

On a similar tack brief mention must be made of *judicial notice.* This is an acceptance by the courts of matters which are clearly established as following particular patterns. That such matters do normally follow a particular pattern is acknowledged by the court without the need for proof. Examples of this in operation, would be the existence of a 24-hour day, or of a human gestation period of 9 months. Again it is a matter of convenience to make the proof of such unnecessary. Where appropriate, however, it is possible to refute such notice.

Convention

The next legal technique that should be commented upon is that of the *convention.* This is a misnomer in so far as it is debatable whether a convention is law (in the sense of customary practice). The convention is an accepted mode of behaviour often underlying judicial and Government activity. In countries with an unwritten Constitution, such as the United Kingdom, the convention can prove to be of some significance; in countries with written Constitutions its importance must be limited.

It is enough merely to recognise conventions for their historical and perhaps limited practical significance. By way of example, the procedure of the British Houses of Parliament is largely determined by convention, i.e. an accepted way in which matters are conducted. There would appear to be little or no authority except perhaps customary law for such behaviour to be mandatory.

Citation of Material

Finally one of the formal areas of technique can now be stated, that found in the *citation of legal materials.* If all this section does is to allow the reader to make use of the reference library, it will have been worthwhile.

Given the Irish law has its source in two countries, the citation of the pre-1922 law must be recognised in both statutory and case-law. The post-1922 British legislation may also be of interest in terms of its persuasive authority. More importantly the citations of the cases decided by Irish courts since 1922 and the Acts of the Oireachtas must be learnt. The citation of material is important for two reasons. First, it lends credibility to the particular decision or statute, and secondly, it enables the material to be located. The material is of little use without this direct or indirect access.

Statutes of the English Parliament prior to 1922 are recorded by reignal year as follows: 24 & 25 Vict. 100.

Translated, this means the 100th statute (chapter) passed in the Parliamentary session in the 24th and 25th years of Queen Victoria's reign. The statute is in fact the Offence Against the Person Act, 1861. Quoted in this form it would be known by its short title. In Ireland since 1922 statutes have been cited by their year of enactment and statute number, thus 1961 41 is the 41st statute passed in 1961, which is Civil Liability Act. The English too adopted this method of citation in 1963.

The citation of cases requires greater explanation. Two factors affect the citation of such material. Again, the English as well as the Irish form requires explanation. The determining factor in case-law citation is the name of the report. These names are simply explained by reference usually to the initials of the reporting agency. Hence the Irish Reports, the principal reports in the Republic, are cited as I.R., the All England Law Reports in England are known as All E.R. The latter report should not be confused with the English Reports, collections of old case-law reports cited as E.R. Other reports carry similar initials. A comprehensive list can be found in the current law citator or a law dictionary.

The year of the report also has some bearing on the form of the citation. If the date is recorded in conventional brackets, i.e. ( ), then the date is of secondary importance. The volume number is the key to the citation which is not necessarily related to the date. The date gives the lawyer a time-span but the citation is governed by the volume number in the particular series. An example should make this clear: (1883) 11 Q.B.D. Translated, this refers to the case of *Heaven* v. *Pender* reported in the 11th volume of the Queen's Bench Division reports. The case was decided in 1883. The pre-1922 English authorities are so reported. Sometimes the year is omitted.

The main Irish Reports since 1922 have been cited differently. The year indicates the date of the decision and the volume relates to the year. Where only one volume was compiled during a year the citation might appear (1961) I.R. If more than one volume appeared then the citation might be (1961) 2 I.R. etc. The volume number changes each year reverting back to volume one, and so on. Some of the other reports of Irish cases are, however, still cited by volume number, e.g. the Irish Law Times Reports.

The English have also adopted this more sensible mode of citation in recent years. To distinguish between the previous model and the slightly different form in England the year is now cited in square brackets, e.g. [1964] 3 All E.R.

The final addition to the citation is the page number, a figure appearing at the end of the expression, e.g. (1963) I.R. 652. This indicates the page at which the report is to be found. If a particular passage of the judgement is cited then an additional figure will be added at the end of the citation, e.g. (1963) I.R. 652 at 657.

While considering this basic material it might be useful for the reader to note here the existence of several indices:

(i) The Current Law Citator – an English compilation of case names and citations (a case may be reported in several reports).

(ii) Index of Statutes in Force – an Irish compilation with an English equivalent, listing all statutes in force and the amendments made during the index period.

(iii) Digests – various compilations both Irish and English, e.g. the English and Empire Digests, that give citations and brief facts of important cases.

CONCLUSION

In entitling this chapter 'Legal Method' our purpose was to show some of the presumptions, characteristics and techniques upon which the exercise of law is dependent.

Some of the concepts alluded to are in themselves abstract, ill-defined and inconsistently applied. This reinforces the principal features of a common law system, that it is heavily dependent on judicial review, and that the law has often been drafted (by the courts and legislature) in a piecemeal fashion in reaction to the particular problem before the lawmakers. The end result is to leave a confused picture of substantive law and its administration as well as procedural control. Each is clearly based on the principles of *res judicata* and *locus standi.* Thus, the law is still a law of, and for, individuals.

To use the law it is necessary to comprehend fully the concepts and techniques of the legal system, whether the matter be a mundane citation or a complicated review of ministerial power. For those sufficiently interested, reference is given to additional material on the points so raised.

PART II

THE ADMINISTRATION OF JUSTICE IN IRELAND

Chapter 5

THE COURTS

This chapter will examine and describe the structure and jurisdiction of the courts to be found in the Republic. The word 'courts' is used here in the strict sense, i.e. it includes all judicial bodies established by the Constitution and legislation that administer law in the country. Excepted from these are the quasi-judicial tribunals. These important decision-making units will be examined separately in the third section of the chapter.

The chapter is divisible into clear sections: first, the courts having a criminal law jurisdiction will be analysed; secondly, the civil law courts will be described. In many instances a court may have a *dual* jurisdiction, i.e. can administer both civil and criminal matters, but for reasons of convenience this jurisdiction will be treated separately. The reason for this should become clear: the procedure and nature of the proceedings are different.

The individual courts are considered in turn, starting with the District Court, leading through the Circuit Court and High Court and ending with the Supreme Court in both civil and criminal matters. The structure and jurisdiction of each court is considered and so too, briefly, is the process each court adopts leading up to trial or disposal. Finally, the appellate function of the court is noted.

The procedure attaching to each court will be considered in so far as the pre-trial process is concerned, but the detailed rules of evidence and procedure can be found in Chapter 7.

I THE CRIMINAL COURTS

A discussion of the criminal courts must be prefaced with some general comments. The criminal law makes a number of distinctions between, *inter alia,* the types of offence and this can affect the mode of trial adopted. Two such distinctions can be noted: first, the difference between the *felony* and *misdemeanour,* and secondly, *indictable* and *summary* offences.

The felony was a type of criminal offence carrying a capital sentence, i.e. death. The misdemeanour was something less serious introduced, among other reasons, to mitigate against such a severe sentence. The importance of this distinction is now primarily restricted to the powers of arrest attaching to individual offences. Generally speaking, a warrant is required for the arrest of a person suspected of committing a misdemeanour. No warrant is required to arrest a suspected felon. The emphasis on serious and less serious offences has been taken further by the terms indictable and summary offences. It is this distinction that is of particular importance to the jurisdiction of the criminal courts. Summary offences (not to be confused with misdemeanours, which may be either summary or indictable offences) are created by statute and are expressly to be tried before the district justice. As will be seen, however, to be tried before the District Court they must also be minor offences within the meaning of Article 38.2 of the 1937 Constitution. All other offences are indictable, and are, *prima facie,* to be tried in the Circuit or Central Criminal Court, i.e. before judge and jury. As will be noted, exceptions do exist to this rule under the provisions of the Constitution and Acts of the Oireachtas.[1]

The reader may well encounter some contradiction with this general principle, for some offences are indictable but triable summarily, some offences are summary but triable on indictment and some offences are triable either on indictment or summarily. The latter offences are known as hybrid offences. The confusion that might be caused by such classification will be cleared. For the time being it is sufficient to appreciate the basic distinction.

Before turning to the operation of the individual courts brief mention must be made of the instigation of proceedings. The common law position states that every person is subject to the law and can implement the law in appropriate circumstances (i.e. where a grievance exists). In criminal matters any private person could (and until 1801 had to) commence criminal proceedings as a national representative of society that had been offended by the commission of the offence. This situation has been altered by statute for, since 1924, all indictable offences are prosecuted by the State. Initially this was in the name of the Attorney General but since 1974 the Director of Public Prosecution has assumed this function.[2]

A private person may still bring summary proceedings but usually these are commenced by the Gardai. The Attorney General's consent to certain proceedings may also be required.[3]

Finally, it should be noted that in instituting criminal proceedings certain time limits must be observed. These are imposed presumably to ensure that offences are prosecuted within a reasonable time of their commission, in the interests of both the suspected offender and the public in general. At common law no time limit exists for the prosecution of indictable offences. Someone accused of murder, for example, may be prosecuted at any time regardless of how long has elapsed since the commission of the offence.

However, certain indictable offences have been subjected to limitation periods by statute. Example of such limitation can be found in the Criminal Law (Amendment) Act, 1935, where a 12-month limitation period is imposed. As previously mentioned, summary offences are all statutory in origin and a general limitation period of 6 months is imposed within which time prosecutions must be commenced. If a complaint is not made or information is not laid before the court within this time period no prosecutions can be instigated. A further limitation period is imposed for certain motoring offences. The provisions are contained in the Road Traffic Act, 1961/73, which stipulates that either a person must be warned of the possibility of prosecution at the time of apprehension or must be informed within 14 days of an intention to prosecute. If such warning or letter of intention is not dispatched within the time limit no prosecution can be brought. Failure to observe these limitation periods provides the accused with an absolute defence.

THE DISTRICT COURT

Since 1922 the District Court has held a distinct criminal jurisdiction, modelled initially on the preceding Magistrates Court, but now considerably extended by statute. The court is comprised of one justice, a full-time lawyer of 10 years' standing. The justice is assisted by the clerk of the court. The court hears offences arising within its district.

Although the court has a wide jurisdiction its powers of sentence are restricted. A maximum prison sentence of 12 months can be imposed by the court and/or a maximum fine of £100 imposed. The court does have additional powers of sentence, e.g. disqualification of a person from driving a motor vehicle or the confiscation of fishing equipment for persons contravening regulations affecting fishing rights in territorial waters.[4]

The jurisdiction of the District Court in criminal matters is sevenfold.

Minor Offences

These are offences referred to specifically in the Constitution.[5] The District Court has jurisdiction over summary offences and, as will be seen, over certain indictable offences, but in either case to be triable before the District Court the offence must be a minor one. There has been considerable legal debate over the definition of a minor offence and it now seems to be the case that the offence is within the jurisdiction of the District Court if the likely punishment is within certain boundaries. In the case of the *State (Sherrin)* v. *Kennedy and Others*[6] a possible penalty of three years' imprisonment was held to render the offence beyond the jurisdiction of the District Court. Thus the offence was not considered to be a minor offence.

Both indictable and summary offences are capable of being a minor offence and it is for the District Court initially to determine whether it has jurisdiction. The importance of this Constitutional provision cannot be over-estimated, because the classification of an offence as a minor one denies the accused the right to trial by judge and jury.

Indictable Offences Scheduled in the Criminal Justice Act 1951 (as Amended)
Providing the court considers the offence to be within the above definition, and if the accused agrees to summary trial, the District Court has jurisdiction to try an indictable offence. An example of the type of offence within the schedule to the Act is larceny, where the value of the stolen goods does not exceed £200. Such offences will, however, not be within the jurisdiction of the District Court if the accused insists on trial by judge and jury. The Director of Public Prosecution's consent is required for certain offences appearing in the schedule, e.g. larceny of goods exceeding £200 in value.

Indictable Offences Where the Accused Pleads Guilty
The District Court has the power to record a finding of guilt and sentence an accused person for the commission of an indictable offence if the accused pleads guilty and the justice is satisfied that the accused understands the charge. This facet of jurisdiction is provided by section 13 of the Criminal Procedure Act, 1967. Certain indictable offences are excluded from this jurisdiction, namely, murder, treason, piracy and war crimes. The District Court is of course limited in its sentencing powers in these matters as indicated above.

With the consent of the Attorney General, the District Court may deal with the offence summarily or it may endorse the verdict of guilty and dispatch the accused to the Circuit Court for sentence (if the court feels its powers of sentence are insufficient in the particular circumstances). In this case the accused may change his or her plea on reaching the Circuit Court.

Indictable Offices Not Triable Summarily, Not Scheduled in the Criminal Justice Act, 1951, and Not Referred for Sentence
These offences will be tried by judge and jury in a higher court, but the District Court carries out an important function in committing the accused for trial. This function is known as a *preliminary hearing.* It is the task of the District Court to decide whether or not a *prima facie* case exists against the accused and, if so, to commit the accused for trial before the Circuit Court, Central Criminal Court or Special Criminal Court. The procedure is governed by the Criminal Procedure Act, 1967. To dispense with the necessity of hearing formal evidence the process is made more efficient by requiring certain documents to be served on the accused, including statements of evidence by prosecution witnesses. Any evidence given orally is reduced to writing and known as a deposition. The parties are not later allowed to deny the truth of such statements. The whole process is intended to filter out the cases that do not contain sufficient evidence against the accused, and to collect as much evidential material as possible for cases that are committed for trial. The district justice must decide on the basis of the depositions and

submissions if the case is to be sent forward for trial. Other charges may be substituted by the District Court or, if more appropriate and within the jurisdiction of the court, summary trial can be conducted. If no case is answerable the accused is discharged. It is possible for the accused to waive the necessity of such an examination and proceed to trial on a not-guilty basis.

Offences Committed by Persons under the Age of 16

Here the District Court sits as the Children's Court to deal with charges against children under the age of 16. This Juvenile's Court differs in two respects from the ordinary Criminal District Court. First, hearings are *in camera* (in private), with only the interested parties present. Secondly, the procedure is less formal. It should be noted that certain children under 16 may be tried in the ordinary court system where serious crimes are committed, e.g. murder, or where they stand charged with defendants above the age of 16.

The Granting or Refusal of Bail

In common with all criminal courts of first instance and the appellate courts, the District Court has the power to grant bail to the accused person. The law is to be found in the Criminal Procedure Act, 1967. The concept of bail is explained in Chapter 7.

If An Accused is Tried in the District Court He or She May Be Committed to the Circuit Court for Sentence, Where the Court Feels It Has Inadequate Powers of Sentencing. This May Occur Where the Accused Is Found Guilty or Admits Guilt

Proceedings are commenced in the District Court by way of a complaint by the prosecuting party, usually the Gardai. The accused will be brought to court after having been detained in custody (arrest) or through the service of a summons specifying the accused by name, the offence concerned and the date on which the matter will be considered. The court may dispose of the case or on conviction refer for sentence.

THE CIRCUIT COURT

This is the next court of first instance to be considered.

Here, the offences tried are exclusively indictable except for those summary offences that are not minor offences within the District Court's jurisdiction. The Courts (Supplemental Provisions) Act, 1961, provides that the Circuit Court has the jurisdiction to try all indictable offences, with the exception of murder, treason, piracy and offences contained in the Offences Against the State Act, 1939. These offences, as will be seen, are reserved for the Central Criminal Court and the Special Criminal Court.[7]

All persons standing trial in the Circuit Court do so before judge and jury. If they are referred by the District Court for sentence, or plead guilty in the

Circuit Court, the sentencing is carried out by the judge sitting alone. The accused will either have been committed for trial following the preliminary examination by the District Court, or will be referred to the court for sentence only, or will have been committed having waived the right to such preliminary examination. In exceptional circumstances the D.P.P. can commit the accused for trial regardless of the outcome of the preliminary examination.[8]

As the Circuit Court is a court of first instance the accused must plead afresh regardless of previous proceedings. The trial proceeds on the basis of the indictment, which is a technical, written document specifying the name of the accused, the court of trial, the offences with which the accused is charged and particulars of the offence. The indictment may specify one or more defendants.

As will be seen in the chapter on evidence and procedure, the judge has three functions: to decide issues of the law and direct the jury accordingly, to see the rules of evidence and procedure are complied with and, where appropriate, to sentence a guilty party. The jury's sole function is to decide on the fact of the accused's guilt or innocence, and in exceptional circumstances to decide whether or not the accused is fit to stand trial.[9]

The Circuit Court has a limited appellate function under the criminal law. The Circuit Court hears appeals from the District Court that take the form of a rehearing. The right to appeal to the Circuit Court is normally confined to the accused. In these circumstances the matter is tried with a jury. The decision of the court in such appeals is final, subject to applications for prerogative writs.

The court sits on circuit and hears matters either that arise in that district or where an accused lives or is detained. The Director of Public Prosecutions can direct any trial due to be heard before the Circuit Court to be transferred to the Central Criminal Court. This might be used, for example, where it is thought that a local jury might be unduly prejudiced by pre-trial publicity.

The Circuit Court judges' powers of sentence are unlimited, except in so far as statute provides maximum penalties.

THE CENTRAL CRIMINAL COURT

The third court of first instance sits permanently in Dublin, although there are powers for it to sit on circuit. This court is a division of the High Court and as such is important for two reasons. First, as High Court judges adjudicate, their pronouncements of law are capable of forming *precedent.* The court is also important for it deals with the more serious crimes of murder, treason, etc., and the crimes referred to it by the Circuit Court.

Trial in the Central Criminal Court is by judge and jury and the procedure is by way of indictment as in the Circuit Court. Again the powers of sentence are only limited by statute.

THE SPECIAL CRIMINAL COURT

This is the fourth court of first instance to be considered. The Special Criminal Court has given rise to much controversy since its creation for it differs from the other courts of first instance in its mode and rules of trial.

The authority of the establishment of a Special Criminal Court is contained in Article 38.3 of the Constitution of 1937, which reads:

> 1° Special Courts may be established by law for the trial of offences in cases where . . . the ordinary courts are inadequate to secure the effective administration of justice, and the preservation of public peace and order.
>
> 2° The Constitution, powers, jurisdiction and procedure of such Special Courts shall be prescribed by law.

The court sits without a jury and must consist of three adjudicators. Since 1970, as a matter of practice, these have been members of the judiciary but prior to that time included non-judicial members, especially from the higher ranks of the armed services. This court has been established on two previous occasions, in 1939 and 1961, and military officers then sat.

The law governing the Special Criminal Court and its operation is to be found in Part V of the Offences Against the State Act, 1939, and the court is made effective by Government proclamation that the ordinary courts are inadequate within the meaning of the Constitution. This proclamation was last made in May 1972 and to date has not been annulled by the Government or the Dail. The Special Criminal Court is at present therefore a regular criminal court sitting in Dublin.

This court is able to try all offences that are scheduled in the 1939 Act and the Government may declare additional offences to be added to such a list. The rules of procedure are drawn up by the court in concurrence with the Minister of Justice and only a majority verdict within the court is pronounced.

The Director of Public Prosecutions can request a trial by the Special Criminal Court if he thinks fit. The decision to refer the matter to the Special Criminal Court can be made, regardless of whether these offences are scheduled offences, if the D.P.P. considers that the ordinary courts are inadequate to deal with a particular matter.

The District Court still performs the preliminary examination of matters referred to the Special Criminal Court unless the D.P.P. requests otherwise.

Trials may also be transferred to the Special Criminal Court on the D.P.Ps intervention.

The scheduled offences are offences under: (i) The Malicious Damage Act, 1861; (ii) Explosive Substances Act, 1883; (iii) Firearms Acts, 1925-71; (iv) Offences Against the State Act, 1939/72.

And the jurisdiction is extended by the Criminal Law (Jurisdiction) Act, 1970.

The subject matter of the Special Criminal Court therefore is presumed to affect the security of the State, but it has been noted elsewhere that the

Special Criminal Court is used for the trial of offences not within this general description. The merits of such must lie open to serious criticism because of the denial of due process of law accorded to the accused.[11]

THE HIGH COURT

The Central Criminal Court, being a branch of the High Court, has a criminal jurisdiction as indicated. The High Court also exercises criminal jurisdiction in an appellate sense in four specific areas. Neither of these areas involves an appeal in the strict sense of the word and both originate from the inherent function of the High Court.

First, the High Court has a power to issue prerogative orders. These have been considered elsewhere.[12] They challenge the competence of a court (*inter alia*) to hear a dispute. Thus if the court of first instance exceeds its jurisdiction or if there is an error on the face of the record of the court, a prerogative writ can be obtained.

Secondly, the power to issue a writ of Habeas Corpus lies with the High Court. This function is exercised to restrain the illegal detention of a person and, as will be seen,[13] is an order requiring the accused and his or her detainer to attend before the High Court to explain the circumstances of and justification for detention.

Thirdly, the High Court has the power to grant bail. A High Court judge may grant or refuse bail where it is denied by a lower court. Additionally, only a High Court Judge can grant bail for certain serious offences.

Fourthly, the High Court may consider an appeal by way of *case-stated.* The High Court has an inherent jurisdiction to give a ruling of law on the facts as stated by an inferior court. The District Court on its own initiative or on the application of one of the parties may submit, either before, during or after a case, the facts of a dispute in a formal document to the High Court. A request is made to the High Court for an opinion on the law as it affects the particular facts. The High Court will do so and will issue a direction to the District Court either to retry the matter, reverse the decision or simply leave the decision intact. If the matter has not yet been tried or is in the course of trial, the District Court will apply the opinion and direction accordingly. A similar process for case-stated lies from the Circuit Court to the Supreme Court.

COURT OF CRIMINAL APPEAL

This is the first of the appellate courts to be considered and was established in 1924 to hear appeals from the Circuit Court, Central Criminal Court or Special Criminal Court. The court comprises of three judges, one of the Supreme Court and two from the High Court. *Leave* to appeal must be obtained from the trial judge or from the Court of Criminal Appeal itself. Unlike the appeal from the District Court to the Circuit Court, matters referred to the Court of Criminal Appeal are not dealt with by way of rehearing. Counsel from both parties will be able to submit arguments on questions of law and, exceptionally, on fresh evidence.

Leave to appeal will only be granted where an issue of law is in dispute but in exceptional cases where fresh evidence is available and this could not have been adduced before the original court, leave to appeal may be granted.

On hearing representations the court will affirm or reverse a decision, or order a new trial, or remit, increase or otherwise vary a sentence. In essence a miscarriage of justice must have occurred, e.g. the trial judge may have misdirected the jury, or the sentence given was too severe.

The right of appeal lies with both parties, although it was thought that there was no appeal from an acquittal. Now, by virtue of Criminal Procedure Act, 1967, the Attorney General or Director of Public Prosecutions may refer a matter to the Supreme Court for a ruling, though this will not affect the acquittal of an accused. Thus this will clarify the law for the future. Although no appeal appears to have been brought it would seem that the prosecution can appeal to the Supreme Court on a verdict of not guilty by any Court of First Instance.

THE SUPREME COURT

As the final court of appeal the Supreme Court has a wide jurisdiction in criminal matters. These can be considered as follows:

(i) An accused convicted in the Central Criminal Court may choose, with leave, to appeal either to the Court of Criminal Appeal or the Supreme Court. If an accused does appeal directly to the Supreme Court there can be no appeal to the Court of Criminal Appeal.

Leave to appeal to the Supreme Court will only be granted if the Court of Criminal Appeal or the Attorney General or Director of Public Prosecutions certifies that the case involves a point of law of exceptional public importance. If the issue is not so classified the appeal can go no further than the Court of Criminal Appeal.

(ii) Under Section 29 of Courts of Justice Act, 1924, an accused may appeal from the Court of Criminal Appeal to the Supreme Court, providing the certification referred to above is granted.

(iii) An appeal lies directly from the Central Criminal Court to the Supreme Court for any interlocutory order, e.g. bail.

(iv) The Attorney General or Director of Public Prosecutions may refer a matter for determination by the Supreme Court as previously indicated, but this will not affect the acquittal of an accused.

(v) The Supreme Court may give an opinion by way of case-stated to the Circuit Court on application, with the appropriate direction. This procedure seems little used.

(vi) The Supreme Court will entertain appeals from the decision of the High Court to refuse to grant the writ of Habeas Corpus.

(vii) The refusal of the grant of a prerogative writ can also be appealed from the High Court to the Supreme Court.

(viii) The Supreme Court acts as a final court of appeal for matters decided by way of case-stated from the High Court to the District Court.

CONCLUSION

It can be seen therefore that, in accordance with the Constitution and relevant enactments, the Courts of Criminal jurisdiction are divisible into four courts of first instance, with varying jurisdictions. There are two courts dealing exclusively with appeals, although both the Circuit Court and High Court exercise a limited power of review. The D.P.P. may also intervene in this process by transferring matters between courts.

The procedure within each court and the conclusion to the proceedings (including punishments) will be examined later.[14]

The structure of the Criminal Courts can therefore be described diagramatically as follows:

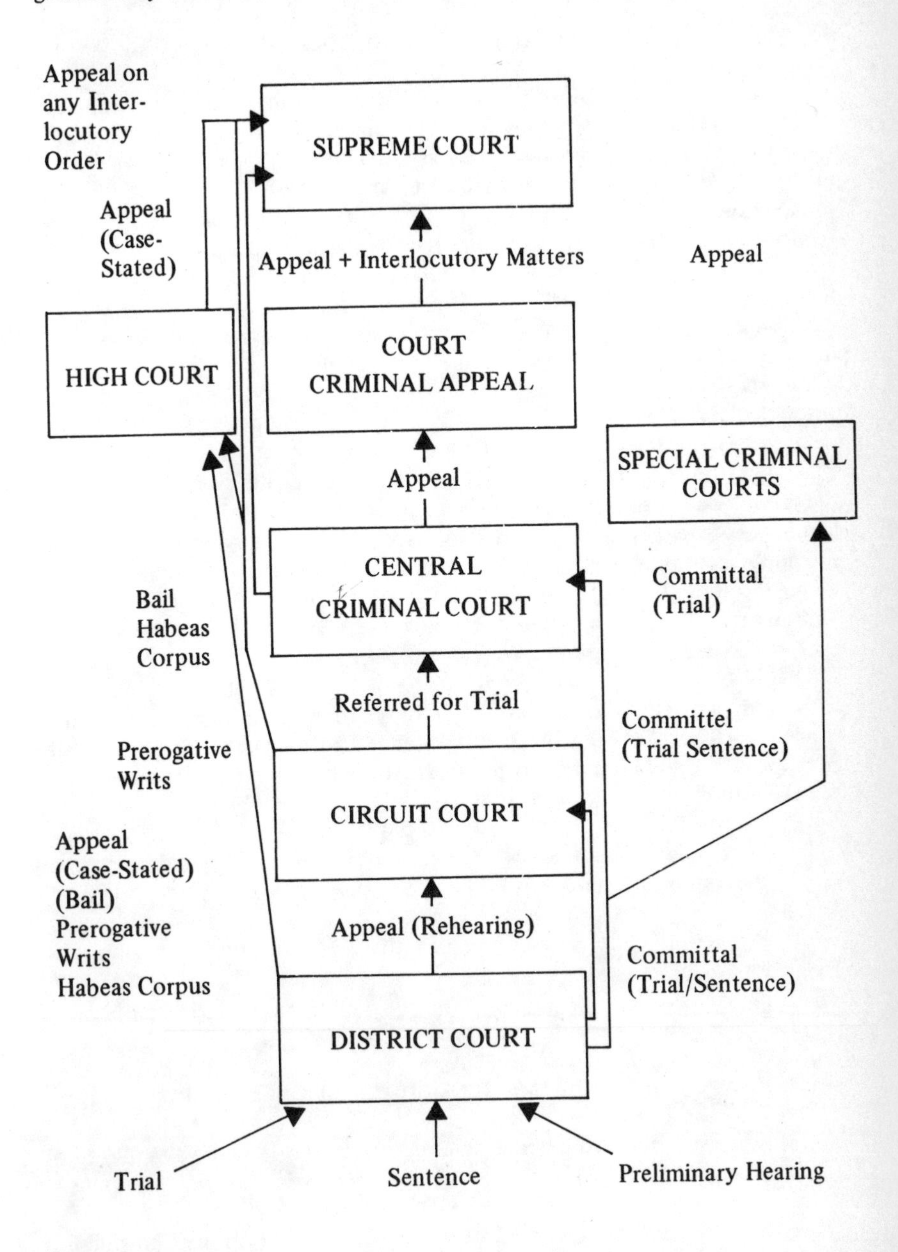

II THE CIVIL COURTS

THE DISTRICT COURT

The civil jurisdiction of the District Court, though limited by statute,[15] covers a very wide range of matters. The limitations on jurisdiction generally relate to the *quantum* of the claim and to the geographical area or *district* in which the claim arises. The District Court, as the lowest civil court in our jurisdiction, is essentially a court of first instance. The role of this court is to provide a quick and cheap forum for dealing with disputes of a local and relatively minor nature. It is, without doubt, the busiest of courts in our hierarchy and is the court (exercising its civil or criminal jurisdiction) in which most of our citizens come into contact with the administration of justice. As such it is an extremely important tribunal.

In matters of contract and tort the court has jurisdiction provided the amount claimed does not exceed £250. A similar limit is placed on claims relating to consumer credit, such as actions arising out of a hire purchase. Though without jurisdiction in relation to actions dealing with title to land, the court has jurisdiction in such related matters as ejectment for non-payment of rent and ejectment for overholding in any class of tenancy provided the annual rent does not exceed £315. In the case of proceedings under the Rent Restrictions Act, 1960 and 1967, however, in addition to the limitation on the amount of rent, the rateable value of the premises must not exceed £25 p.a. and both parties must consent to the matter being dealt with by the Court.

In addition, there are a variety of other matters in which the court is concerned. The following list is not intended to be exhaustive but merely to emphasise the wide range of matters upon which the District Justice may be called upon to adjudicate:

(i) Maintenance Proceedings on behalf of a spouse or dependent child of the family (maximum of £50 and £15 p.w. respectively).

(ii) Protection Orders (maximum of three months duration subject to renewal).

(iii) Affiliation Proceedings (maximum of £15 p.w.).

(iv) Recovery of rates by local authority (no limit to amount recoverable).

(v) Actions arising from a sale at a market or fair (where value does not exceed £5).

(vi) Enforcement of Court Orders: the District Court has jurisdiction to enforce judgement-debts irrespective of the amount involved.

Proceedings in the District Court are commenced by the issue and service of a Civil Process. Every process contains the name, description and last known place of residence or business of the parties. Corporate bodies are simply described by their corporate name. If the defendant wishes to defend the proceedings he must lodge a Notice of Intention to Defend at least four days before the date fixed for the hearing. The party who is successful before the court has the responsibility of preparing the decree or dismiss, for signature by the justice. There is also a 'default' procedure which allows a plaintiff to obtain judgement where the defendant defaults or fails to defend the action.

The District Court is comprised of a president and 34 district justices. Each justice sits alone.

THE CIRCUIT COURT

The Circuit Court has an original and an appellate jurisdiction in civil matters. Whether dealing with an appeal from the District Court or with a case at first instance, the Circuit Court judge sits alone. There is no longer any right to trial by jury in civil matters in this court.[16] The court's jurisdiction is limited in the same manner as the District Court, namely, by reference to the *quantum* of the claim and to the area or circuit in which the claim arises. For this latter purpose the country is divided into eight circuits, with a Circuit Court judge attached to each. The court is presided over by the President of the Circuit Court.

In matters of contract and tort, or proceedings brought by the State or any minister or department the court has jurisdiction provided that the amount claimed does not exceed £2,000. The Circuit Court has jurisdiction over equitable matters such as the execution of trusts, dissolution of partnerships and actions for grant (or refusal) of probate or letters of administration, provided that the property concerned, if personalty, does not exceed £5,000, and if realty, does not exceed £100 in rateable valuation. This limit of £100 r.v. is also imposed with regard to actions concerning the title to land, its partition or sale or ejectment on title. The court's jurisdiction under section 10 of the Hotel Proprietor's Act, 1963, is £2,000. A claim in excess of this limit may, however, be dealt with by the Circuit Court if the parties to the action so agree.

There are certain matters which are dealt with exclusively by the Circuit Court, irrespective of the amount claimed. Such matters include the granting of new licences under the Intoxicating Liquor Acts, claims for malicious damage and actions for a new lease under the Landlord and Tenant Acts, 1931 to 1976.

An appeal from the District Court lies to the Circuit Court, except where such appeal is by way of case-stated when it lies to the High Court. An appeal in the Circuit Court takes the form of a complete rehearing and either party may introduce new or additional evidence. The decision of the Circuit Court on appeal is final, conclusive and non-appellable. Appeals against decisions of the Circuit Court sitting at first instance lie to the High Court, except where the appeal is by way of case-stated when it lies to the Supreme Court.

Proceedings in the Circuit Court are commenced by the issue of a Civil Bill, which sets out the main points of the plaintiff's claim under the title 'enforcement of claim'. The defendant will then enter an appearance and file a defence. The action is now ready for trial. As in the case of the District Court there is a default procedure which allows the plaintiff to recover in default of appearance or defence.

The Circuit Court is comprised of a president and nine judges. Each judge sits alone.

THE HIGH COURT

The High Court has original and unlimited civil jurisdiction. Article 34.3(1) of the Constitution of 1937 provides as follows:

> The Courts of First Instance shall include a High Court invested with full original jurisdiction in and power to determine all matters and questions whether of law or fact, civil or criminal.

The High Court is also the only court of first instance in which the Constitutional validity of any law may be challenged or which may grant a Prerogative Order such as mandamus, certiorari or prohibition.

In theory the High Court may be constituted in three different ways:

(i) As a divisional court with three judges.
(ii) When a judge sits with a jury.
(iii) As a judge sitting alone.

Article 40(4) of the Constitution provides for applications for an order of Habeas Corpus. Subsection 4 of this provision is as follows:

> The High Court . . . shall, if the President of the High Court or, if he is not available, the senior judge of that Court who is available so directs in respect of any particular case, consist of three judges and shall, in every case, consist of one judge only.

As seen, the High Court sits as an appellate court for matters arising in the Circuit Court, and for appeals by way of case-stated in the District Court. The High Court has of course its inherent power to grant prerogative writs. An appeal from a decision of the High Court lies to the Supreme Court.

In practice the High Court rarely sits as a divisional court. A judge will sit alone in Chancery matters, actions for breach of contract and liquidated damages, matrimonial causes and actions relating to title to land. In most other matters the plaintiff may opt for trial by judge and jury.

THE SUPREME COURT

The Supreme Court stands at the apex of the Irish court structure. It is the final court of appeal in all matters commenced in the High Court and in all Constitutional issues. It hears appeals by way of case-stated from the Circuit Court and against the decision of the High Court on a case-stated from the District Court.

The powers of the Supreme Court on appeals vary according to whether the action at first instance was dealt with by a judge and jury, or by a judge sitting alone. In the case of the former we have already noted that the jury determine the facts and the judge instructs them on the law to apply to those facts. Either one (or both) of these matters may form the basis for an appeal. A further ground of appeal in such cases is that the damages awarded were excessive. Because the matter was dealt with by a judge and jury, the appellant can only ask for a new trial, though the Supreme Court may set aside the verdict and judgement and substitute its own therefore. A finding of fact by a jury, however, will not be set aside simply because the Supreme Court would have reached a different conclusion on the same evidence, unless the court finds that the jury's decision was not reasonably open to them on the basis of that evidence.

In the case of an appeal against the judgement of a judge sitting alone, the appellant may ask the Supreme Court to reverse the original judgement and the court may make any order which the trial judge has jurisdiction to make. Unlike the case of trial by judge and jury, on an appeal from a decision of a judge sitting alone the court may reverse with a finding of fact based on its own view of the evidence. As a matter of practice, however, the court is slow to do so.

In addition to its appellate jurisdiction the Supreme Court has original jurisdiction in a number of matters by virtue of the Constitution. These include, *inter alia,* deciding whether the provision of any bill referred to it by the President under Article 26 is contrary to the provisions of the Constitution, and power to establish the permanent incapacity of the President under Article 12.

The Supreme Court consists of the Chief Justice and six other judges as well as the President of the High Court, who is a member *ex officio.* Three judges form a quorum though the court sometimes is constituted by five judges.

The Civil Court structure can be described diagramatically as follows:

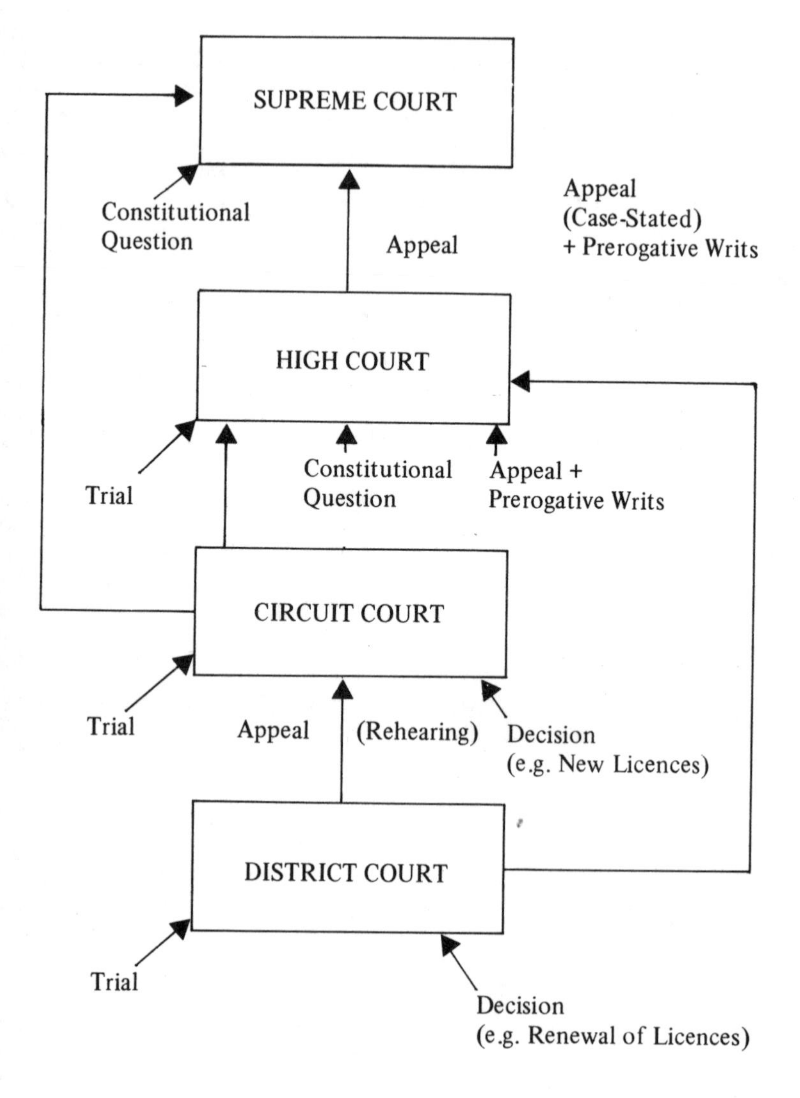

III THE QUASI-JUDICIAL TRIBUNALS

We have described the structure of the civil and criminal courts operating in the Republic. Certain bodies also exist that exercise a decision-making function apart from the formal courts. These can be broadly termed quasi-judicial tribunals. The definition of such tribunals is broad. This is to say, there are many bodies both within and beyond the Republic that have to arbitrate between the interests of respective parties. Most of the tribunals, however, are related to the traditional court structure through the process of judicial review and in limited circumstances matters of substance can be brought within the court's jurisdiction by way of appeal.[17]

Despite not being judicial in the strict sense of the word, the importance of these bodies should not be underestimated. The tribunals include both panels of adjudicators and individual officers, and they determine matters of national importance including civil rights, income tax appeals, entitlement to social welfare benefits and internal disciplinary hearings for the principal professional bodies. The distinction between the jurisdiction of the courts and the other tribunals is perhaps not so clear in practice, given the increased legalisation of many of the quasi-judicial bodies. The distinction, however, must be fully appreciated in comprehending the operation of the two distinct adjudicative processes.

The history of the tribunals in the sense presently used makes interesting reading for it was, in its origins, largely a direct response to legislation of immense social relevance. The perceived nature of the tribunal was initially administrative. This forum was seen to be a cheap, informal and efficient medium through which social legislation could be administered. That the tribunals are becoming more legalistic in style, argument and process is perhaps an indicator of the direction in which the administration of law in the Republic is heading. Whatever one's opinions about the merits of a tribunal system are, one thing is clear – this is a method of decision-making that is to be of increasing importance in Ireland.[18]

The quasi-judicial bodies can be divided into three broad categories:

(i) Extra-Territorial tribunals.
(ii) Domestic administrative tribunals.
(iii) Other domestic tribunals.

EXTRA-TERRITORIAL TRIBUNALS

Ireland is affected in a number of ways by decisions made in courts and tribunals not within the State. The basis for such can be traced to Ireland's subscription to a number of international conventions and treaties. There are three such agreements that encompass decision-making authorities potentially affecting the Republic. It should be appreciated when considering these authorities that Ireland's ability to regulate its own internal affairs is largely unaffected by affiliation to the undermentioned treaties. It is rather a matter of international diplomacy than sanctioned law that nations, including Ireland, tend to observe decisions of the authorities empowered under the relevant treaties.

The three treaties are: (a) The Treaty of Rome; (b) The European Convention on Human Rights; (c) The Charter of the United Nations.[19] Reference is given later to further material that examines the form and relevance of these treaties. For the present it is sufficient to note the existence of the decision-making organs within each agreement and their effect on the Republic.

The interpretation of the Treaty of Rome and ancillary agreements, or of the laws passed by the Council of Ministers or the European Commission of the E.E.C., and their application to member States, is the function of the Court of Justice of the European Communities. According to the treaty, Ireland, as a party to a dispute, is bound by the decision of the European Court. The relevance of this is discussed further in Chapter 10.

Ireland is also a signatory to the European Convention of Human Rights and Fundamental Freedom. This Convention established the European Court of Human Rights, that may hear applications from both individuals and Member States alleging that a Member State has violated rights contained in the Convention. Thus, inhumane treatment has fallen for discussion before the Commission on many previous occasions. Internment without trial, the birching of juvenile offenders, and interrogation methods have all been the subject of discussion.[20] The Commission issues a decision and a Member State is asked to adopt remedial action if the allegation is substantiated. An action levelled against Ireland would bring at least substantial international pressure to bear on the State. A recent and contemporary issue was discussed in the *Airey* case, when an Irish citizen complained to the European Court that she was being denied both a remedy under and access to Irish law. Her subject of complaint was in the field of matrimonial law. The case hinged, amongst other issues, on the failure of the Republic to institute a system of legal aid enabling a person to gain access to the courts despite having insufficient funds to pay. A verdict was given to the applicant.[21] The effect of this will be examined further in Chapter 8.

Finally of the extra-territorial courts, brief mention must be made of the United Nations. This organisation has a number of decision-making bodies including the *General Assembly*, the *Security Council* and the *International Court of Justice.* Decisions from either unit in the form of judicial pronouncements or resolutions are, at international law, binding on Member States. The practical relevance of such decrees again has to be judged against the political climate in which they are issued. South Africa's refusal to comply with a number of resolutions concerning the sovereignty of South West Africa (Namibia) serves as a useful example.

The extra-territorial courts have one feature in common. In the event of the subjected nation not complying with a decision the ultimate sanction of expulsion from the organisation can be applied.

DOMESTIC ADMINISTRATIVE TRIBUNALS

The courts adjudicate in a very small percentage of legal disputes. When persons initiate their claims many fall by the wayside or are settled before reaching trial. Decision-making in some important and contentious areas is carried out without reference (except for the limited process of judicial review) to the ordinary courts. Decisions as to the entitlement to benefits, allowances and consents from the State machinery has created an enormous industry that has carried with it an adjudicative process. Parliament, in drafting legislation affecting the lives of the majority of the population, has had to create quasi-judicial bodies and officials to administer the plethora of regulations. Thus domestic tribunals in Ireland have reached a position of great importance in terms of their social and legal relevance. While paying the lip-service to the law, in so far as legal arguments occur within the ambit of the tribunals, these bodies have adopted their own procedures, policies and styles. The nature of the proceedings usually reflects the issues to be solved. Although many of such entities exist, reference here will be made only to the most important. Three characteristics, however, stand out in all such institutions. First, the jurisdiction of the tribunal is frequently described as exclusive. This has been interpreted by the laws and the courts as meaning that the only judicial tool of intervention possible is by the process of judicial review. The powers of the courts to administer an appellate function on issues of law arising in such tribunals is severely limited. Secondly, the tribunals are seen by adjudicators and participants as essentially non-legal. This has significant consequences in the procedures adopted by each authority. It is arguable, though beyond the scope of this text, that far from corresponding to this description many tribunals, especially in Britain, have grown towards a more apparent legal model.

Finally, in its administrative guise the tribunal operates, within the legal framework, largely on a basis of discretion. The exercise of that discretion has, again especially in Britain, been frequently discussed by the courts.[22]

Decision-making at this level includes:

The Labour Court

This is not a court of law but rather a conciliatory body serving a number of functions in industrial relations. While serving as a liaison and arbitrative unit the Labour Court includes officers with significant powers, in the sense described above. In addition, decisions are made in relation to disputes. Equality officers are appointed by the Department of Labour and work within the auspices of the Labour Court. They investigate disputes arising through alleged discrimination under the provisions of the Anti-Discrimination

(Pay) Act, 1974, and the Employment Equality Act, 1977. The decision of the equality officer can be subjected to an appeal to the Labour Court sitting as a tribunal. Non-compliance with a Labour Court decision in these matters is a criminal offence, triable in the ordinary way. An appeal on law lies to the High Court. This is discussed further in Chapter 16.

The Rights Commissioner, Deciding Officer and Employment Appeals Tribunals

Under the provisions of the Unfair Dismissals Act, 1977, an allegation of unfair dismissal can be made to the Rights Commissioner appointed by the Minister of Labour. Likewise a claim for redundancy under the Redundancy Payments Act, 1967/71, may be referred to a deciding officer. The decisions of either of these officials is subject to an appeal to the Employment Appeals Tribunal. This tribunal may also act as a tribunal of first instance on application by either party. If the decision of the Employment Appeals Tribunal is not acted upon within six weeks of its pronouncement an appeal lies to the Circuit Court. Either the Minister of Labour or other parties may finance such an appeal.

Social Welfare Tribunals

Entitlement to social welfare benefit is calculated by officers employed by the Department of Social Welfare and the Regional Health Board. The initial decision is taken by the deciding officer appointed by the Department of Social Welfare. An appeal lies to the Appeal's Officer also appointed by the Department. The Regional Health Board has similar officers for benefits falling under their control. No formal procedure for hearing before either Officer is prescribed in detail. Benefits relating to unemployment, old age, sickness and other disabilities thus are decided upon without a formal and uniform procedure. The appropriate legislation denies access to the High Court on most issues arising out of law or fact in this decision-making process. More detailed reference can be found in Chapter 18.

The Planning Board

Certain consents are required when developing land or buildings in the Republic. A decision on the grant of planning permission lies initially with the local Planning Authority (local council). An appeal can be made against the decision of the corporation to the Planning Board. The importance of such in protecting individual interests in property is of course highly significant. In limited circumstances an appeal also lies to the Minister.

Appeals Commissioner

The calculation of income tax liability is a subject affecting a vast proportion of the population. For those in disagreement with such calculation of allowances or tax liability, an appeal lies to the *appeals commissioners* and thence on matters of law to the High Court.

Restrictive Prices / Practices Commission
This tribunal was created to review monopoly practices in industry and commerce. Criminal offences exist in the appropriate legislation and this commission adjudicates in matters of contravention of such rules directed against restrictive trade practices. A similar authority also regulates prices.

Ministerial Power
Government ministers and their departments have, in addition to the above, considerable powers of essentially a discretionary nature. Such power includes the granting of consents, exemption and regulations. The only control over this is by way of judicial review.

OTHER DOMESTIC TRIBUNALS

This miscellaneous category of quasi-judicial bodies covers two distinct areas. First, there are a number of tribunals that exercise a disciplinary function, and secondly, certain tribunals for historical reasons have maintained a limited jurisdiction in special areas.

Barristers, solicitors and doctors are all subject to overall supervision by their professional bodies. The Incorporated Law Society, the Honourable Society of Kings Inn and the Medical Association all exercise disciplinary control over their members' activities. Again, judicial review is the only control of this process but the regulations of such professional bodies usually include the right to appeal to the High Court on matters of law.

Of the second category, two examples can be given. First, *courts martial* still exist to administer military law. Usually such courts are staffed by the judiciary and appeals lie against verdicts to the High Court. Secondly, the *Ecclesiastical Courts* exercise a jurisdiction in the regulation of the internal functioning of the Church. The secular jurisdiction of the Ecclesiastical Courts based on probate and matrimonial matters was terminated by 1870.[23] Today such decision-making is in relation to the function of the Church and its own administration. It would appear that some formality, however, is still maintained and the courts sit in this capacity.

Further details concerning these quasi-judicial tribunals and officials can be located under appropriate headings in the text. Here we have merely given a brief description of their nature and jurisdictions.

Chapter 6

PERSONNEL OF THE LAW

In this chapter we are concerned with those people, apart from the individual litigants, who are responsible for carrying out the process of the law both in the courts, offices and in education. The personnel divide neatly into administrators and the profession.

Under the first heading we will consider the judiciary, the officers of the court and Government or State officials. The second heading will include barristers, solicitors, clerks and teachers of law.

The brief historical analysis of the law's evolution contained in Chapter 1 did include reference to the growth of the profession. It remains in this chapter simply to describe the function of each of the personnel of the law.

THE ADMINISTRATORS

The Judiciary

The judges are to be found in each of the courts listed in Chapter 5. Five judges including the chief justice sit in the Supreme Court. Eight judges occupy the High Court, one of whom is President of the Circuit Court. In the Circuit Court the president and ten judges are in office. In each case the judges, with the exception of the chief justice and president, are known as puisne judges (from the French 'lesser'). In the District Court thirty-five judges sit under the president.

The tenure (or legal base) of a judge's position is now founded on statute and, subject to the Constitution, lasts indefinitely, but with retirement limits and restrictions on incompetence imposed.

Historically, promotion to the Bench has been a hazardous affair, especially in Ireland, with appointment at a premium and often as a political favour. Although statutory regulations for the appointment and control of the judiciary were introduced as early as 1701[1] it was only in 1782 and 1877 that Irish judges were accorded security.[2] It is important to note the significance of these enactments for, at least in theory, they gave the judiciary independence and freedom from political manipulation.

Article 68 of the 1922 Constitution was the next regulatory provision affecting the appointment of the Irish Bench, with judges to be appointed by the governor-general on the advice of the executive. The Constitution of 1937 in Articles 9, 13.9 and 35.1 provide for the appointment of judges by the President and removal in cases of incapacity by the Oireachtas. Since 1961 resignation has been by letter to the President.[3]

District Justices, however, were not accorded security until 1946 but now enjoy the same tenure as any other member of the judiciary.[4] There are additional powers of surveillance vested in the chief justice to ensure that a district judge is discharging his or her function properly.[5]

While a judge or justice can only be removed from office for misconduct or incapacity, in accordance with the provisions of the Constitution and subsequent legislation, retirement has been compulsory since 1924. The ages of retirement in the Supreme and High Court, Circuit Court and District Court are 72, 70 and 65 respectively.

Appointment to a judicial office is the prerogative of the President (on the advice of the executive), but minimum periods of experience are a prerequisite. For appointment to the Supreme or High Court this period is 12 years as a practising barrister. The period is 10 years for appointment to the Circuit Court. In the latter case the experience may be gained by a solicitor or barrister. Subject to these limits there is of course promotion from one appointment to another to consider.

While the selection of the judiciary is largely free from the political connotations of the 19th century and before, it has been realistically noticed elsewhere that the appointment of judges is necessarily coloured by the opinions of the Government in power. Additionally, the backgrounds of the judges themselves have many common features in terms of class, culture and tradition.[6]

Before turning to other administrators of the law, it is worth examining the organisation of the judges and court sittings.

Briefly, the courts and judges sit during the four terms which comprise the legal year. This dates back to Saxon times. The original terms of Hilary, Easter, Trinity and Michaelmas were so short that it became impossible to deal with all of the pending business. The Judicature (Ireland) Act, 1877, abolished the formal terms and now the High Court sits in four sessions or sittings. While retaining the names above, the dates for the terms are now fixed by statute, namely, 11th January – March 22nd, 4th April – May 26th, 6th June – July 31st and 1st October – December 21st. The lower courts sit as often as circumstance demands. The Supreme Court also responds to demand. The District and Circuit Courts in the main urban areas are permanent features throughout the year. The sittings, however, are of practical importance as an action in the High Court (except for emergencies) can only be brought during the period in which the court is sitting. In addition to its sittings in Dublin the High Court travels on circuit throughout the country to hear appeals from the Circuit Court.

Overall there are eight regions or circuits in Ireland which the courts operate; these, with the areas covered by the District Court, handle the administration of justice in the country. These administrative divisions are also important for, as will be seen, other court officials are responsible for oiling the machinery without being accorded judicial rank as such. It is these persons to whom we now turn.

The Officers of the Court

A number of court officials warrant mention at this stage for their important administrative and sometimes quasi-judicial functions. The history of these posts is well documented elsewhere.[7] It is sufficient here to identify the main officers and their duties.

The *master* is the chief administrator of the High Court. This is a very important post in practice for many procedural issues prior to trial are adjudicated over by the master, as are post-trial issues such as questions of costs. Since the restructuring of the courts in Ireland in 1924, and by virtue of the Court Officers Act, 1926 (as amended), a central office under the master of the High Court has been created.

On circuit, the county registrar fulfils the administrative function, handling pre- and post-trial matters for and on behalf of the Circuit Court. Both the master and registrar therefore work, as it were, behind the scenes, but their importance in the day-to-day life of litigation should be appreciated.

Also of importance is the role of the *sheriff.* Again this officer has a long history and today the sheriff is mainly occupied with the enforcement of judgements, the serving of court documents and generally ensuring obedience to dictates of the courts.[8] In some areas the sheriff is also given the task of acting as registrar.

Finally, there are various *clerks* responsible for administration. Prior to the Constitutional changes of 1922, the clerk in the Magistrates Court was (and in Britain still is) very important. The magistrates were usually lay-persons and were advised by a clerk who was a qualified lawyer. This person therefore advised the justices on the law. Today district justices are lawyers themselves and the court clerks are now purely administrative in nature. They assist the court in its function, take a record of proceedings, conduct the procedural matters and draw up the court orders.

Government and State Officials

Prior to independence there were many officials appointed to act on behalf of and to advise the Crown. The posts of Prime Sergeant, Attorney General, Solicitor General and King's Advocate were all abolished in the 1922 legislation. In 1924 the post of Attorney General was created; under Article 30 of the 1937 Constitution the post is preserved. In general terms the Attorney General is the legal advisor to the Government, instituting and defending proceedings to which the State is a party. It is not now customary for the Attorney General to appear personally in these cases. The Attorney General is appointed by the President on nomination of the Taoiseach and at the Premier's discretion. The Attorney General may be requested to resign and will do so on change of Taoiseach. It has been noted elsewhere that since 1974 the Attorney General is no longer responsible for instituting prosecutions in the criminal courts, but the consent of the Attorney General may be required to bring proceedings.[9] In addition, the Attorney General may still be heard in issues where the interpretation of the Constitution arises, and he may intervene on matters of national security.

The other official worth noting at this juncture is the Minister for Justice.

This important Government post carries with it the governmental responsibility for the administration of justice in the State, and the minister is therefore accountable to both the Government and Oireachtas.

THE LEGAL PROFESSION

Academic Lawyers

Before turning to the practising legal profession, a brief account should be given of the role of the academics or teachers of law.[10]

This group is included for two reasons. First, by way of practice and tradition there has been (and largely still is) a strong link between law teachers and the practising profession. This link is manifested, for example, in the subjects that the educational institutions make available for study. In other words the content of courses essentially complements the requirements of practice. Secondly, many academics provide a positive input to the law by way of commentaries, articles, books and advice and opinions on commissions of enquiry.

In Ireland there are three types of institution at which law is studied and where academics make their contribution. Each of the four universities in Dublin, Cork and Galway offer courses which lead to a degree in law. While each is independent of the legal profession the content of such courses reflects the tacit demands of legal practice. It is perhaps fair to note that this is increasingly less so with the gradual introduction of non-core subjects, e.g. social welfare law. In order to qualify as a practising lawyer not only will a person usually take a law degree, but a prescribed set of courses must be undertaken and a series of examinations passed. These are controlled by the Incorporated Law Society and the Honourable Society of King's Inns for solicitors and barristers respectively. Each therefore acts as an important educational source, albeit directly serving the profession's interests. The details for qualification are again noted elsewhere.[11]

Law is also taught in a number of regional technical colleges in the country and, importantly, law is taught often as part of other subjects (e.g. business studies). This multi-disciplinary approach is significant for law here is necessarily seen as one aspect of a particular study rather than independent of other forces. To date, however, these courses mainly serve business interests.

It is important therefore to note the role of academics as teachers, researchers, and commentators of, and on, the law.

Barristers

It has been seen[12] that for many centuries the barristers, through the King's Inn, controlled the training, conduct and operation of practising lawyers. Today the Bar, as it is collectively known, is one autonomous aspect of the legal profession. It is sufficient to note here the principal functions of the barrister or counsel. After passing a set of academic obstacles both in law and in Irish, a person may be called to the Bar. If the newly admitted barrister wishes to practise, he or she must undergo an informal apprenticeship for 12 months, known as pupilage.

Barristers are, by law, self-employed, but practise in chambers. There are two types of practising barrister, senior and junior counsel. This division indicates expertise and seniority. To become senior counsel (on application to and approval by the Chief Justice, with the sanction of the Government) a person must 'take silk', an old expression relating to a different style of gown that the senior counsel wears. The senior barristers and judges who achieved appointment from the ranks of counsel also sit as a disciplinary body known as benches, or the inner bar.

The work of a practising barrister is twofold: first and foremost the barrister is an advocate, which means he or she will address the court on behalf of the client. However, in this respect rules of tradition or etiquette control the barrister's activities. The barrister is not permitted to work directly for the client but is engaged by the solicitor. This is known as a 'brief', being a formal document requesting the barrister's assistance. Also a barrister is expected, unless there is a good reason, to act on a brief; this has been described as the 'cab rank' rule. The role of tradition is still important with, for example, a barrister being unaccountable to any person (e.g. a client) except the court. Thus no proceedings for negligence lie if the court of proceedings is not satisfactorily completed.[13] In addition, a barrister may not sue a solicitor for fees owed. A barrister has right of audience in all courts and must only address the court in accordance with instructions. A senior counsel will usually appear backed by a junior.

The second and largely forgotten function of the barrister is known as paperwork. This covers the drafting of pleadings and the giving of opinions. Again a solicitor must brief counsel and counsel will reply by sending to the solicitor the requested documentation.

Thus the barrister is used as an expert on matters of legal opinion and as an advocate, especially in the higher courts.

The Solicitor

With separate training and disciplinary powers, the Incorporated Law Society has, since the 19th century, controlled solicitors.

The reader will recall that solicitors and barristers arose from the same origin but the work-load of the two soon gave rise to a division in the profession. If the barrister is principally the advocate, the solicitor is the administrator. This description is, however, over-simplified. While much of the solicitor's work is preparatory and conducted in an office rather than a court, a little more detail is required to appreciate a solicitor's function. There is now considerable overlap between, but differences in, the two sides of the profession. A solicitor's work can be divided into three: non-contentious office work, contentious office work and advocacy.

The non-contentious work is perhaps the best known of a solicitor's skills and includes all matters where there is no patent dispute in hand. Thus the purchase and sale of houses (conveyancing), the formation of companies and partnership, and the drawing up of wills and administering deceased person's estates (probate) comprise much of a solicitor's work. These matters are mainly concerned with drafting appropriate documents. The contentious work in the office is concerned with the preparation and/or settlement of issues in dispute. Thus, civil law disputes in contract, tort, land law and family law are important. If the dispute goes to trial the solicitor will interview witnesses, brief counsel if necessary, conduct correspondence and attend preliminary hearings prior to trial. Many issues, especially where insurance companies are concerned (e.g. personal injury cases), may well be settled out of court and the solicitor will (with or without counsel's opinion) conduct the correspondence.

Since 1971[14] the solicitor has had a right of audience before all courts in Ireland but as a matter of practice tends to restrict appearance to lower courts (especially the District Court). A solicitor may well therefore appear as an advocate, without counsel's assistance. This appearance may be before courts and quasi-judicial tribunals (e.g. employment appeals tribunal). Where the solicitor does appear on behalf of the client in either criminal or civil cases the solicitor is not required to wear the traditional wig and gown of the barrister, but in all other respects the rules and procedures must be obeyed.

To qualify as a solicitor sets of examinations must be passed and approximately two years' apprenticeship must be served. Historically the solicitor is an officer of the court but today is accountable in practice to the Incorporated Law Society.[15]

It can be seen therefore that there is considerable overlap between the two sides of the profession and many ancient rules of etiquette that are perhaps inappropriate to modern society. This is noted elsewhere.[16] But all attempts to introduce significant change have failed. Indeed, by way of comparison, in Britain the Royal Commission on Legal Services reviewed the possibilities of fusion and change but recommended no significant alteration in the style and form of the legal profession.[17] The training and operation of lawyers will, it is submitted, be a constant topic for discussion.

Clerks

Again it is worth noting the function of clerks who operate in the legal profession. Many unqualified persons work in lawyers' practices under supposed supervision, dealing with the administrative work, e.g. conveyancing, probate. In Britain internal regulations have been introduced to afford certain clerks status and qualification; these are introduced through the Institute of Legal Executives.

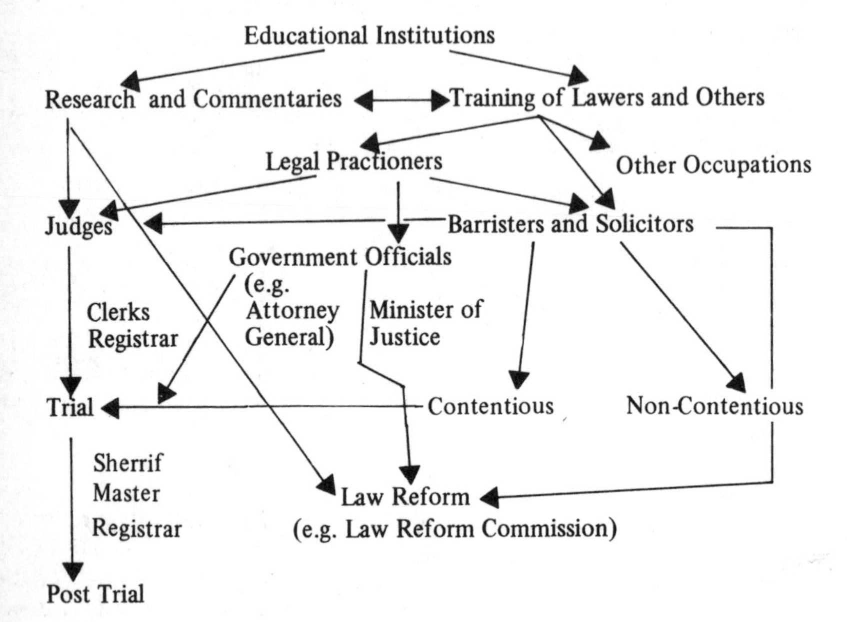
Educational Institutions
Research and Commentaries
Training of Lawers and Others
Legal Practioners
Other Occupations
Judges
Barristers and Solicitors
Government Officials
(e.g.
Attorney
General)
Minister of
Justice
Clerks
Registrar
Trial
Contentious
Non-Contentious
Sherrif
Master
Registrar
Law Reform
(e.g. Law Reform Commission)
Post Trial

Chapter 7

PROCEDURE AND EVIDENCE

This chapter examines, against the background of the structure of the administration of justice, the principal rules of evidence and procedure operating within the Irish legal system.

The procedure attached to the criminal law is described. The civil law process is analysed. The most important of the rules of evidence are set out, as they affect, in general terms, all litigation. Where rules specifically apply to either civil or criminal cases, references are made.

PROCEDURE AND THE CRIMINAL LAW

In examining the process of the criminal law many pertinent issues are raised before a case is ever referred to the courts. Consequently one must have regard to the regulations affecting the law-enforcement agencies as well as the proceedings before the courts. This section is structured by three situations: pre-arrest, arrest and in court. The implementation of the criminal law is therefore examined in context, involving both the police and the judicial process.

Pre-Arrest

The first contact people may have with the criminal law is when apprehended by a law-enforcement agency. This will usually be the Gardai, but could include security guards and defence forces. It is a fundamental characteristic of the common law system that the police have no more power to interfere with personal liberty than the ordinary citizen. This must be qualified by reference to certain statutory powers which permit the Gardai to act over and above the common law. Thus both the police and citizens have the power, right and, in some cases, duty to prevent crime. When police powers are considered in this light, subject to the statutory exceptions, the Gardai have in theory a strictly limited right of law enforcement. Consequently a person is not generally speaking obliged to give information, disclose identity or address, or in any other way assist the police. Furthermore if a person is detained against their will or otherwise affected by police interference, that person may take reasonable steps to avoid the interference. While it may be advisable to co-operate with the Gardai, there is no general obligation to do so. Likewise in common law there is no general power of search or seizure. The nature of such powers relates to the type of activity concerned. The Gardai, for example, under the provisions of the Offences Against the State Act, 1939, stop, search and interrogate the persons suspected of being involved in the commission of offences against the State. Also the name and address of a person suspected of committing offences specified in Section 18 of the Criminal Law (Jurisdiction) Act, 1976, must be given on demand. These offences include burglary, possession of firearms, damage to property and fatal offences. Such a person may be searched and their property is also liable to be seized.[1]

Short of these powers the Gardai are not legally empowered to search, seize or question in a pre-arrest situation.[2]

The powers, however, are increased in additional circumstances where a warrant is granted by a peace commissioner or a district justice or senior police officer, or where an arrest is made. Although the warrants can be issued without an arrest (e.g. to search premises) their use can best be examined in the following section.

Arrest

The state of affairs known as arrest is of legal importance, for a number of consequences may flow from this situation. An arrest takes place where a person is taken into (police) custody and held, regardless of the wishes of the accused. This may occur verbally (i.e. 'I am arresting you') or physically (forcible retention).

Two issues must be mentioned here. First, when can an arrest be made? Secondly, what are the consequences of the arrest?

A person can be arrested in a number of instances:

(i) Where a felony has been committed. The arrest can be made by the police or a private citizen.

(ii) Where any offence is committed and a warrant is issued for that person's arrest. The person named in the warrant can be arrested by a police officer.

(ii) Where a breach of the peace has occurred the police can arrest without warrant, despite the offence being a misdemeanour.

(iv) Certain statutory powers entitle the police to arrest, e.g., drunken driving.

To arrest without a warrant the citizen needs to show reasonable cause to suspect the person to be in the act of committing a felony or having committed a felony. The Gardai need to show either reasonable cause to suspect a person to be in the act of committing a felony (or an offence for which statutory powers of arrest exist) or that a person has committed, or is about to commit, a felony. In all other instances a warrant is required.

In any of the above cases the arrest is unlawful if either adequate reason is not given for the arrest, as soon as is practically possible, or the warrant is defective, e.g. a person is incorrectly named. If too much force is used in the arrest the arrest itself will become unlawful. A person subject to an unlawful arrest for any of the above reasons will have the right to use reasonable force to resist.[3]

Once a person is lawfully arrested a number of consequences arise. First, the person can be lawfully detained. The period of detention depends upon the relevant common law or statutory authority. At common law a person can be detained for such period as is necessary for investigations to be conducted but should be brought before a court within a reasonable time depending on the facts. However, longer periods of detention are provided for by statute. Under the Offences Against the State Act, 1939, a person can be detained for up to 48 hours if suspected of committing or being involved with the commission of offences against the State. The Emergency Powers Act, 1976, circumvented this provision in so far as detention for up to 7 days could be effected. The Act was only in force for 12 months from October 1976.[4] While in custody and once arrested the accused may be asked his or her name, personal details, may be searched, photographed, finger-printed and tested (e.g. in the use of firearms) and articles in his or her possession may be detained. Various offences exist if the accused does not comply with these requirements. The accused's property not in personal possession, e.g. house or car, may be searched and goods seized if relevant to the crime of which the accused is suspected, or any other crime. Theoretically a warrant is required for the searching of such premises. Some exceptions do exist, however, e.g. where stolen property is involved, where firearms are suspected or where drugs are concerned. Where a warrant, however, is not required any evidence collected by the police unlawfully may still be admitted in court. The relevance of this will be explained. The Criminal Law (Jurisdiction) Act, 1976, in fact goes beyond this common law position and extends the power of search and seizure. Premises may, short of search, be entered to effect a lawful arrest.

Therefore much depends on legal authority of the arresting/searching party. Wrongful arrest or search lays the interfering party liable to both criminal and civil proceedings. However, evidence of a crime unlawfully obtained is admissible at future court hearings, subject to the approval of the court.[5]

Once in custody a number of 'rights' exist, at least in theory. First, the accused may demand release, subject to the time periods relating to the detention. If a charge is levied within the time period, the person can be detained against his or her will, but must be brought before the court within a reasonable time, again subject to statute.

Secondly, stemming from the implicit rights of the Constitution, a person has entitlement to legal advice and representation. A person should also be given the opportunity to contact a lawyer and immediate family.[6] A young person (under 17) should only be interviewed in the presence of parents or guardian. Writing equipment should be provided on request. A caution that anything said by the suspect may be used against him or her at trial should also be given. Further, no question should be asked of the accused once charges have been laid.

What is the significance of such 'rights'? Regrettably, subject to Constitutional protections, the rights listed above have no force of law. They are, rather, recommended procedures which should be adopted. Collectively they are known as the *Judge's Rules.* First formulated in 1912, the Judge's Rules are guide-lines for police pre-trial behaviour aimed at preserving fair play. Breach of such rules may, in the discretion of the trial judge, mean that any evidence obtained could be rendered inadmissible. Beyond that, however, the apparent 'rights' are more a matter of practice than law. This can be contrasted with the more vigorously applied protections of the United States' criminal procedure.[7] The courts in Ireland have on a number of occasions, however, stipulated that a flagrant breach of Constitutional rights will render evidence inadmissible.

Finally, the pre-trial situation may give rise to the question of bail. Before a person is brought before the court, the police have the power to release that person on bail. Bail is examined in further detail elsewhere.

Court Proceedings

A person will come before the criminal courts in one of three ways. If a person is arrested a court appearance will follow either with the person released on police bail and surrendering to the court, or being detained in custody and being taken to the court. If a person is not arrested attendance at court will be commanded by the issue of a summons.

Two matters determine the procedure of the court:

(i) Whether the offence is triable summarily or on indictment.
(ii) Whether the accused pleads guilty or not guilty.

As has been seen before, trial on indictment is heard before judge and jury. Summary trial is before the District Justice.

The jurisdiction of the court and, if relevant, the wishes of the accused (possibly the intervention of the D.P.P.) will determine where the offence is tried. Although trial on indictment is more formal than summary trial the same principles of procedure and evidence apply to not guilty and guilty pleas in both courts. This procedure can now be examined.

Guilty Plea: Where a person pleads guilty either before the district justice or judge and jury, two options face the court. Either the court can accept the plea and sentence the accused on hearing an outline of the evidence, or the court can refuse to accept the plea. In the latter case reason for refusal will normally relate to the dissatisfaction of the court that the accused understands the proceedings. Where the accused is unable or unwilling to plead, the court will, if it is satisfied that the accused is fit to plead, enter a plea of not guilty on the accused's behalf. Trial will then proceed. Where the court is of the opinion that the accused is unfit to plead no verdict is entered.

The accused will be detained at an appropriate institution until deemed fit to plead. This matter can be raised by either the prosecution, defence or the court. The question of fitness to plead is left to the district justice or jury, as appropriate. If a person regains fitness trial can proceed at a future date.

Once a guilty plea has been entered the prosecution must outline the circumstances of the offence to the satisfaction of the court. However, usually no formal evidence is given. The court will then hear an account of the accused's antecedents (if any); this is the criminal record of the accused. Such previous convictions must be accepted by the accused or strictly proven by the prosecution. The purpose of this is to assist the court in determining sentence. In giving such information the prosecution may inform the court of the accused's domestic circumstances. This is usually left, however, for the defence.

The defence then has the right to address the court. This will be carried out by the accused or the legal representative. The purpose of this address is twofold. First, other offences can be admitted by the accused. These are known as offences to be taken into consideration. The accused may reveal details of such for a number of reasons; the most important is that if the court accepts such admission the accused can never be prosecuted for those offences. However, the court has a discretion to punish the accused at this instance in time. The accused, therefore, is given the chance of clearing his or her name. The police often ask the accused if he or she will accept responsibility for such crimes, as it clears police records too. In addition, an unprompted admission must stand to the accused's credit. The court can, however, refuse to accept such and, for example, order trial on issues arising.

The second function of the defence is to address the court in mitigation. This is an attempt to persuade the court with regard to sentence. Extenuating circumstances, family background, repentance, etc. may all be raised. In addition, either the defence or the court may request reports from specialist agencies, e.g. a social worker or medical expert. When hearing all the appropriate submissions the court will then sentence the accused. The range of punishment will be considered shortly.

Not-Guilty Plea: Where the accused pleads not guilty the procedure is as follows. The plea will be entered if the accused denies guilt, or stands mute or otherwise fails to indicate a plea and the court is satisfied that the accused is fit to plead. This procedure is known as arraignment, if the trial is on indictment. On this basis the trial will commence. The prosecution will address the court outlining the evidence against the accused. The evidence in chief is then given, i.e. the prosecution calls witnesses to substantiate the allegations made. There are a number of important procedural rules affecting the conduct of such examination. The most important can be noted. The prosecutor must not ask leading questions or put hearsay forward as evidence to the court.[8] Any previous conviction of a witness must be revealed to the prosecution if demanded. The defence may cross-examine the prosecution witness and the prosecution may re-examine the witness on issues arising out of the cross-examination. The judge or justice may also intervene in clarification of points raised. When all the witnesses have been called the case is thereby concluded for the prosecution.

At this stage of the proceeding an application can be made by the defence for a direction from the judge or justice. The basis of the application will be that the prosecution has failed to make out a case against the accused and the case should be dismissed. In the absence of this application or if the application is refused by the court the defence may then call its own evidence in the same way as indicated above. If the accused wishes, he or she may give unsworn evidence which precludes the right of cross-examination. This, however, will necessarily carry less weight with the court.

The prosecution may with leave of the court call further evidence to refute issues raised in the defence which the prosecution could not reasonably foresee, e.g. a surprise alibi. The defence then addresses the court on submissions of law and matters arising in the evidence. The prosecution may also address the court.

The question of guilt must then be settled. In trials on indictment this issue is for the jury to decide. The role of the jury is considered below. The judge will, for the jury's benefit, make a summing up. This involves an explanation of the jury's function, a summary of the evidence, an emphasis of contradictory material, and an explanation of the law. If appropriate the judge may direct the jury as to its verdict, e.g. if there is no case to answer. The facts, however, are for the jury alone to decide. Any attempt to influence their decision will amount to a misdirection, the verdict liable to be quashed on appeal. The judge, therefore, may highlight the relevant material and indicate how the law is to apply once the facts are determined. In the District Court the justice must decide these issues.

In a trial on indictment the jury must attempt to decide on guilt. A unanimous verdict must be given, otherwise a retrial is ordered. If the accused if found not guilty he or she must be acquitted. If guilty the procedure is one leading to sentence as described before. The only appreciable difference is that an address in mitigation is inappropriate for obvious reasons.

It should be noted that when asked to make a plea the accused may submit that there is a defect in the proceedings. This is known as a *motion to quash* proceedings. Although rarely used it could be raised where, for example, the offence tried on indictment is not indictable. The accused may also plead *autrefois acquit* or *autrefois convict* where he or she has been acquitted or convicted of the particular offences previously.

Although the principal rules of evidence remain to be examined it is appropriate to note in outline here the court's powers concerning illegally obtained evidence. As seen before, the court has a discretion to admit evidence unless it has been obtained in direct violation of constitutional rights. Thus material seized unlawfully, e.g. without a warrant, or confessions extracted involuntarily may be inadmissible.

Punishment

Once a person has been convicted the court must pass sentence. There are four categories of punishment. In the District Court sentencing is limited to a maximum of 12 months' imprisonment and/or a £100 fine.

First the accused may be *deprived of his or her liberty.* This can be achieved by imprisonment that will either be with hard labour (for less than two years), penal servitude (three to five years) or simple imprisonment. The ultimate deprivation is of course death, but since the Criminal Justice Act, 1964, the death penalty has been removed from all offences except treason, capital murder and certain military law crimes. It is not possible to execute or imprison a person aged under 17.

A prison sentence may also be suspended, i.e. not implemented unless further offences are committed within a certain time period.

The second category of punishment involves *supervision.* This can be direct in the form of probation, where the subject must liaise with a probation officer on specified terms. The supervision may be indirect, where a discharge is given and conditions attached. Here a person will be told not to commit further offences within a specified period, failing which the court will have the power to sentence the person for the offences committed and this offence in question. A discharge may also be absolute, i.e. unconditional where a guilty plea or finding of guilt is entered but the court in the circumstances do not wish to punish. As in the case of the suspended prison sentence the ideal of the conditional discharge is to warn the person of punishment, allowing that person to make amends by avoiding trouble in the future.

The court also has the power to bind the person over to keep the peace, regardless of conviction.

The third category of punishment is *pecuniary,* i.e. a financial penalty. This can be either a fine (with or without time to pay), compensation, (e.g. for a victim suffering as a result of crime) and/or costs of the court (an order to pay a percentage of the court's cost).

The final category of punishment involves some form of *confiscation.* Here the court deprives the guilty party of a benefit, e.g. banning a person from driving for a limited period, confiscating fishing equipment, offensive weapons, etc.

Additional punishment also exists for particular types of offenders, such as young persons (including Borstal for 16 to 19 year olds, reformatory schools for 12 to 17 year olds, and industrial schools for those under 12). Detention in mental institutions may also be ordered.[10]

In this context it is appropriate to note the existence of the Criminal Injuries Compensation Tribunal, which since 1974 has had the power to grant an *ex gratia* payment to compensate victims of violent crimes. The compensation is only payable for personal injuries. This is unrelated to punishments inflicted on a person convicted of crime. Malicious damage to property may also lead to a claim for civil compensation from the local authority.[11]

Two further issues relating to criminal procedure, bail and juries, should be taken into account.

Bail

As previously mentioned all criminal courts (with some limitation) have a power to grant bail. The question of bail will only arise where a person is detained in custody. The grant of bail involves the release of a person subject to three conditions:

(i) That the person will appear at court on a specified day.

(ii) That if the person does not, a fixed sum of money will be forfeited. A forfeit can be applied in relation to the accused and/or sureties; the latter are persons who promise to pay a certain sum to the court in the event of the accused not appearing. This potential forfeit is known as a recognisance.

(iii) That any other conditions are observed, e.g. reporting to the police each day, orders not to leave the country, etc.

The law is contained in the Criminal Procedure Act, 1967. Sections 21 – 33 lay down the requirements. Section 31 gives the police the power to grant bail prior to any court appearance. This power can be exercised by the officer in command of the station above the rank of sergeant. Again the conditions enumerated above can be imposed.

Section 28 of the Act specifies that the court or a police commissioner shall admit an accused person to bail if it appears to that person that this is a case in which bail ought to be allowed. Section 29, however, specifies that where a person is charged with treason, murder or other serious offences only the High Court has the power to grant bail. If bail is refused by the court the accused may appeal to the High Court and against an order of the High Court to the Supreme Court.

In 1966 in the case of *O'Callaghan* the Supreme Court reviewed the law concerning bail. It was held that the refusal of bail should depend on the probability of the accused evading justice and not any other reason. Thus the seriousness of the crime charged, the possibility of interference of witnesses or the likelihood of the accused not appearing at court might be good reasons for refusing bail. Further, subsequent decisions have indicated that bail ought to be allowed unless such an evasion of justice is likely. Reasons that are not sufficient to deny bail would be the lack of a fixed address or the likelihood of commission of further offences.[12]

It should be noted that bail is the process by which a person can be released from lawful custody. This can be contrasted with an application for a writ of Habeas Corpus which lies for the release of a person from unlawful custody.[13]

Juries

As seen above, the jury has a distinct function in adjudicating questions of fact. The law governing the selection, function and capacity of juries is contained in the Juries Act, 1976. All persons on the electoral register are liable for jury service unless exempted or disqualified from service. The former category includes lawyers, priests, those under 18 and those with a reasonable excuse (e.g. a doctor). Those disqualified include persons convicted of crimes and sentenced to certain terms of imprisonment. The jury consists of 12 members. Before each is sworn or empanelled the defence and prosecution may have up to 7 pre-emptory challenges. Further challenges can be made providing good reason is given. The effect of such challenges is to exclude the juror. This process may be used if, for example, a juror is known to have a prejudicial attitude, say, where the accused is of an ethnic, minority group. The first 7 objections, however, need not be justified.

The jury is selected by the county registrar and a ballot is held in court to determine membership of each jury panel.

PROCEDURE AND THE CIVIL LAW

Proceedings in the civil courts originate either in the District Court or High Court. As the nature of the Irish system is accusatorial, proceedings must be commenced by the party making the allegations. A civil action is commenced by the use of a writ or summons. The details of the District Court have already been noted.[14]

Pleadings

Once an action has been commenced, the trial is not an immediate consequence as in the case of procedure in the criminal courts. Each court to a greater or lesser extent relies on standard documentation, which sets out the facts, demands and allegations. These are known as pleadings. As the procedure is at its most formal in the High Court this can be described, as in principle the same rules apply to the rest of the courts of first instance. In the District and Circuit Courts, however, there is less formality and adherence to the documentation. It is important to realise, however, that the pleadings described below are generally applicable in outline if not in detail.[15]

A High Court action is commenced by the issue and service of an originating summons. There are three kinds of originating summons. (i) A plenary summons. (ii) A summary summons. (iii) A special summons.

Generally speaking, a summary summons is appropriate in actions where the plaintiff seeks only to recover a debt or liquidated demand in money payable by the defendant under a contract or trust, or where a landlord seeks to recover possession of land against a tenant whose term has expired or been terminated by notice to quit or for non-payment of rent. It is also provided that procedure by summary summons may be adopted by consent of the parties in any other cause of action. Summary proceedings do not invoke any further pleadings and may be with or without oral evidence.

Procedure by special summons is adopted in a number of special cases outlined in Order 3 of the R.S.C. These actions include, *inter alia,* many equitable matters such as the administration of the estates of deceased persons, the execution of trusts, the construction of deeds, wills and other written instruments, and disputes of a matrimonial nature such as judicial separation on the custody of children.

Cases involving pleadings and oral evidence, e.g. case of trial by judge, are commenced by the service of a plenary summons, which contains a very brief statement of the plaintiff's cause of action and the remedy (usually general damages) which he seeks. After the defendant has entered an appearance and served a Memorandum of Appearance, the plaintiff files his Statement of Claim. This is a more thorough account of the plaintiff's case, where appropriate setting out details of the alleged special damage (hospital expenses, loss of earnings, etc.) sustained by the plaintiff. It is common, however, for the defendant to seek even further information and this he may do by means of a Letter for (Further) Particulars. After he receives the plaintiff's reply the defendant will lodge his defence. It is usual for the defence to comprise of a simple but total denial of all of the allegations made by the plaintiff. Such a total denial is usually more a question of strategy than anything else in that it places the onus on the plaintiff to *prove* all of his allegations.

At this stage of the pre-trial process two further matters may arise. The defendant may, in spite of the terms of his defence, recognise that the plaintiff will win on the issue of liability (i.e. will be awarded *some* compensation) and may decide to offer a sum of money in settlement. These negotiations between the parties will take place in confidence or 'without prejudice', which means that the parties cannot give evidence of such negotiations at the trial. If these negotiations fail, the defendant may nonetheless lodge a sum of money in court which he asserts is sufficient to meet the plaintiff's claim. This is known as a lodgement and it is frequently, though not necessarily, made at the time of filing the defence. The significance of a formal lodgement of this kind is that if a plaintiff refused it and in the subsequent trial fails to obtain a greater sum, he will be liable to pay the defendant's costs (as well as his own) from the date the lodgement was made. It should be noted that in a subsequent trial before judge and jury the former will be aware that a lodgement has been made but not of its amount, while the latter will know nothing about it.

Another matter which may arise for consideration at this stage is the question of a counter-claim by the defendant. The incident or event which gave rise to the proceedings may have been one in which the defendant, as well as the plaintiff, sustained loss and injury. In such circumstances the defence, in addition to a denial of liability by the defendant for the damage sustained by the plaintiff, may also contain a claim by the defendant for compensation for his loss. Such a claim is known as a counter-claim and permits both claims to be dealt with at the one trial.

The pleadings are followed by a Reply and Rejoinder from the plaintiff in which he joins issue with the defendant upon his defence (except in so far as the latter may contain admissions), and the Notice of Trial in which the plaintiff informs the defendant of the day appointed for the trial of the action between them.

The Trial

While the pleadings play an important role in the outcome of a case, there is no doubt that in common law jurisdictions the most important aspect is the trial itself. The first preliminary step involves the empanelling of a jury of 12 persons where the action is to be tried before judge and jury. The plaintiff (usually through his solicitor or counsel) opens the case by giving a brief résumé of his cause of action and the manner in which he intends proving his allegations made in the pleadings. He then calls his first witness. Examination by the plaintiff of his own witness is known as the 'examination-in-chief' and the plaintiff may not put leading questions to such a witness.[16] At the conclusion of the examination-in-chief the defendant may, if he wishes, then examine the witness. This is known as the 'cross-examination' and there is no prohibition on leading questions. When the defendant has concluded his cross-examination the plaintiff may re-examine the witness, but only to clarify matters which have been raised in the cross-examination. After all the plaintiff's witnesses have been heard the defendant may apply to the judge for a 'direction', i.e. the defendant requests the judge to withdraw the case from the jury and/or dismiss it because the plaintiff has failed to make out a *prima facie* case. If the judge is of opinion that there is no case to answer then he will grant the request, otherwise the defendant proceeds to call his witnesses who are subjected to the examination-in-chief and possibly cross-examination and re-examination. When the final defence witness has been heard the defendant may once again apply for a direction. If refused, the defendant will then usually close his case with a final address to the jury. This is followed by the plaintiff's closing address. Finally, and this part of the trial should not be underrated, the judge will direct the jury. In the course of his direction the judge will summarise the evidence, often indicating the areas of conflict of discrepancy, and will inform the jury of the appropriate legal principles. The jury's function is to determine the facts and apply them to the law as outlined by the judge. The task of the jury is usually facilitated by the judge providing them with a number of specific questions. In a case involving a motor accident (without a counter-claim) these questions might be formed as follows:

(i) Was the defendant negligent?

If the jury answer to this is in the negative, this concludes the issue; only if they find the defendant negligent will they then proceed to the next question.

(ii) Was the plaintiff negligent?

If the plaintiff has contributed to his own loss (i.e. contributory negligence) then the jury will proceed to question (iii). If the answer is in the negative then they will skip question (iii) and move directly to question (iv).

(iii) Apportion negligence between plaintiff and defendant.

E.g. Defendant 75% negligent; plaintiff 25% negligent.

(iv) Assess the damage to the defendant.

This requires the jury to arrive at a lump sum which, in their view, will (as far as money can possibly do) put the defendant in the position he would have been in had the accident not occurred (e.g. £12,000).

The jury will return to the jury box and these answers will be handed to the judge, signed by the foreman of the jury (the foreman is the first person empanelled). In our example the plaintiff would be awarded 75% of £12,000, the deduction of 25% being made because he had contributed to this degree to his own loss. The plaintiff will then recover £9,000. Unless he has failed to beat a lodgement he will normally also be awarded his costs. Either party may bring an appeal against the decision but notice of such an appeal must normally be lodged within 10 days.

Enforcing a Judgement

The enforcement of court orders is a crucial feature of any legal system since there would be little point in obtaining a court decree if a defendant could ignore it with impunity. The methods available for enforcing court orders are basically related to the nature of the order and are essentially of four kinds:

(i) Contempt Proceedings: A person who is directed to take or refrain from a particular course of action in civil proceedings and who fails to comply with such direction may be committed to prison for contempt of court. Thus a person who ignores an injunction, a decree of specific performance or an order of Habeas Corpus, may be committed to prison until he is willing to comply with the decree.

(ii) Execution Orders, Stop and Charge Orders, etc.: The word 'execution' in its widest sense signifies the enforcement of, or giving effect to, the judgements or orders of the courts. In a narrower sense it means the enforcement of such orders by a public officer under orders of sequestration, *fieri-facias,* charging orders, stop orders and orders for possession or delivery, etc.[17] Under these orders a defendant's property may be seized and, where appropriate, sold in order to satisfy the judgement debt.

(iii) Proceedings under the Enforcement of Court Orders Act, 1926 and 1940: These Acts provide for the situation where the sheriff certifies that the defendant does not have any property which can be seized in order to satisfy the judgement debt. The general scheme of the Acts is to permit the District Court to enforce such judgements (irrespective of the amount) by way of an instalment order. The court will assess the means of the debtor and then order him to pay a certain amount on a periodical basis until the judgement debt has been paid in full.

(iv) Attachment of Earnings Orders: This is an order directed to a debtor's employer, which directs the employer to deduct a certain amount from the debtor's weekly or monthly earnings and to transmit such amount to the District Court. Attachment of earnings orders are confined to maintenance-type cases in family law and are used to enforce maintenance orders, affiliation orders and certain other analogous orders.

Chapter 8

ACCESS TO THE LAW

In order to take part in legal proceedings a person must have the requisite *locus standi.* Given that a person does have sufficient legal interest and a cause of action, how may that person put the law into operation and what consequences may attach to the decision to implement the law? The determining factors in gaining access to the law are both numerous and complex. This chapter highlights the most important of these and indicates the nature of significant proposals that are currently being debated in this country.

Three such determinants are suggested as influencing the decision and ability to mobilise the law. The extent to which access is, or is not, achieved, may depend on one or more of these factors. There are three principal considerations: (i) non-recognition of a legal problem; (ii) non-accessibility of lawyers; (iii) cost. The causative reason for each will require explanation.

As a starting-point, however, one must inevitably turn to the Constitution. The right of access to the law for citizens of the Republic is not specifically mentioned in the Constitution. The extent to which the fundamental rights found in Article 40 are exclusive is discussed in Chapter 9. The Constitution declares that:

> All citizens shall, as human persons, be held equal before the law . . . . [and further] The State guarantees in its laws to respect, and, so far as is practicable, by its laws to defend and vindicate the personal rights of the citizen.[1]

Moreover in criminal matters, with certain exceptions, a person cannot be deprived of personal liberty without trial by jury and due process of law.[2]

However, these provisions do not provide a comprehensive declaration of equality of access to the law and more significantly neither the Constitution nor subsequent enactments yet provides for the means of such access. This will be discussed in greater detail shortly.

The inherent, albeit latent, presumption of viable access to the law has in fact been taken a stage further by the issues of Constitutional interpretation. Such is the international recognition of the right of access to the law, coupled with the machinery, financial and otherwise, to implement it, that Ireland has been pressured into a position of introducing a legal-aid scheme as outlined herein.[3]

To return, however, to the determinants of access, the definition of *legal dispute* is worthy of note.

NON-RECOGNITION OF A LEGAL PROBLEM

Access to the law may be effectively denied owing to the failure of potential litigants and other agencies (including lawyers) to acknowledge that a particular problem is one suited for solution by the law. This has been examined in some depth elsewhere.[4] It is sufficient for present purposes to note that the law has traditionally been concerned with interests in land, rights of inheritance, commercial practice and criminal behaviour. Problems arising, for example, in the areas of housing, employment and social welfare have largely been ignored as having little or no relevance to the law or lawyers. This is clearly reflected by both the orientation of lawyers in their practice and education and in the plethora of legislation, especially in recent years, introducing regulations that are largely seen as administrative in nature. It is not suggested here that the law is necessarily the most appropriate course of action to solve disputes.[5] However, where rights or entitlements do exist, so do legal remedies. The law is therefore one way of adjudicating between the interests of two or more parties.

To digress further one might speculate as to the reasons for the increased legislation of hitherto-neglected areas. 'Rights' are now receiving greater publicity. Lawyers too are becoming more aware of the relevance of law. One might also add that these newly discovered areas are pools of untapped work for lawyers, though without a system of legal aid there is often little or no remuneration involved. It is argued elsewhere[6] that the identification of legal problems is one of the principal barriers to access to the law and that the much-needed injection of funds via a legal aid scheme in fact does not address this obstacle of gaining access.

NON-ACCESSIBILITY OF LAWYERS

If a problem is recognised as having a legal solution the person who seems most likely to assist is a lawyer. It is suggested here, however, that, with certain qualifications, lawyers are effectively inaccessible to a vast majority of the population except in cases that are closely identified with a lawyer's work, e.g. house purchasing, matrimonial disputes and crime. Three reasons seem to underlie this. First, many people are concerned about the cost of using the law and the lawyer. This topic will be pursued in the following section. Secondly, for a variety of political, social and cultural reasons people may not approach a lawyer. Many people have little or no contact with the law and are therefore apprehensive and unsure as to its application. Thirdly, the geography of the law would seem extremely relevant. The austere and formal city-centre office is enough to ensure that many people do not cross its threshold. These issues have been comprehensively examined in a variety of empirical and theoretical studies.[7]

The combinations of these reasons again can result in a lack of exercise of the 'right' of access.

COST

The most obvious and perhaps widest held view of the difficulties in using the law relates to its proceed cost. The cost of using the law for the client is twofold: the expense involved in consulting a lawyer, and the cost of court action if pursued. One thing is certain: as in many other specialised trades or professions, the law is expensive. It is not the purpose of this examination to condone or criticize the value given or the reasons for such expense. It is sufficient to recognise for the present, that a person using the law may be responsible for expenses arising from a variety of sources. The cumulative effect is to deny access to many people on financial grounds. To argue, however, that this is the primary or exclusive obstacle to access would be artificial. The following pages will analyse this cost. The finances of the law can be divided into three areas: (i) State provision for the administration of justice; (ii) Personal cost of bringing proceedings; (iii) State provision of legal services.

State Finance

In discussing the cost of the law one should note that the State assumes responsibility for providing a system for administering justice. The Royal Courts of medieval times were expected to be self-financing with the courts, officials and judges paid for through fees levied on litigants. Today public funds support the courts and judiciary. This of course is paid from revenue raised by taxation.

Access to the courts is, at least on one level, assured therefore by establishing the cogs of the machinery. The State, however, does not provide finance for the use of the courts. At civil law, litigants pay fees to commence proceedings and may be ordered to pay a contribution towards the cost of the other party's action. In the criminal courts there is a greater degree of public financial charge with the cost of prosecuting largely falling on the State. The nature of the proceedings (ostensibly preserving public order) is such as not to work on a self-supporting basis. The cost therefore of providing the structure of the administration of justice falls on the State and is paid for by the population through taxation. This, however, is not the real 'cost' of the law so far as the individual client is concerned.

Personal Cost

The personal cost of the law is the expense of employing a lawyer. As will be seen it is not a legal requirement to use a lawyer, i.e. one may represent oneself in proceedings. However, for obvious reasons of skill, familiarity and competence, much of the work will be handled by a lawyer on behalf of the client. Simply put, each person using a lawyer is responsible for the cost of the lawyer and expenses incurred. An example should make this clear: A employs B, a solicitor, in defending a criminal charge. B advises A, obtains medical evidence in A's defence and instructs a barrister to appear at A's hearing. At the conclusion of the hearing A receives an invoice as follows: For services rendered, advice and assistance *re:* assault charge before the Cork Circuit Court,

My fees			100
V.A.T. @ 10%			10
			£110
Disbursements			
Counsel's fee	22		
Dr's medical fee	12		
	£34	=	£ 34
TOTAL			£144

The charges comprise first, profit costs (the lawyer's fee) with the appropriate level of taxation. Secondly, any expenses are added, and these are known as disbursements. The total is known as the *solicitor/client charge.*

Whatever the outcome of the proceedings the person employing the lawyer will be responsible for the solicitor/client charge. There is an implied authority (which can be limited expressly) given by the client to the lawyer to incur expenses in acting in the client's best interests. The amount the lawyer charges is not limited in law unless either a fixed fee has been agreed upon (i.e. a contractual term) or a financial limit is imposed prior to expenses being incurred so that if the person feels that the charge is excessive a complaint may be made to the Incorporated Law Society, who may examine the charge and certify as to its reasonableness. If the lawyer was at fault in performing his or her task then proceedings for negligence or breach of contract may arise.

This, however, is not the end of the matter. If a case reaches court, or indeed if a case is settled prior to court, either of the parties may have to pay a contribution to the costs of the other side. This will either arise by agreement (e.g. where a case is settled) or by court order. The court has a discretion at common law to order a party to proceedings to pay costs in addition to any judgement made. Generally speaking costs follow the event, i.e. the successful party is awarded costs against the unsuccessful. On what basis are the court costs calculated? The reader might be forgiven for imagining that the losing side would pay all the expenses of the winner. After all the losing side is implicitly responsible for causing the successful party to incur expenses in having to commence or defend proceedings. Regrettably this is not the situation. A party awarded costs will receive what is known as *party and party costs.* Two factors determine the relevant calculation. First, costs are allowed that were reasonably incurred in the conduct of the case. These will include the cost of preparing court proceedings, the filing of documents and attendance at court. They will not include any steps taken that were not strictly necessary. When preparing a case all possible ends should be examined and tied up. No costs will be awarded for the energies put in outside of the immediate issues at stake. Likewise interviews and correspondence with the client will not be awarded if made in preparation that was not absolutely necessary. Secondly, rules exist relating to different types of dispute and values at stake. Costs claimed in each case may not usually exceed the scale in question. Thus for each item a maximum figure can be claimed. For example, in an action where total damages was less than £100 attendance at court may be allowed at a maximum of £20, correspondence between the solicitors may be allowed at £2 per letter, etc. Party and party costs therefore can fall short of the actual solicitor/client cost charged.

The party and party costs may be agreed as ordered or in settlement without trial, but in cases where the costs ordered by a court are in dispute the aggrieved party may apply to a court officer to have the costs taxed. Taxation involves an examination by a taxing master (or Circuit Court registrar) who examines the claim and adjudicates on it. Each item of the claim will be scrutinised. Taxation itself is a complicated procedure involving its own costs. It should be pointed out that the liability to pay the solicitor/client charge is incurred regardless of the order for costs. In the absence of the order of costs being obeyed the outstanding amount ranks as a civil debt and the person against whom the order was made may be pursued in the normal way as a debtor. The non-payment of costs may also amount to contempt of court. It may be appreciated therefore that the costs, in addition to being a considerable barrier to access, also act as a strong determinant to the outcome of proceedings, and an agreement in settlement may well be influenced by the costs at stake. An example should make this clear. A is injured in a road accident and B admits liability. A's solicitors contact B's insurance company.[8] B's insurance company offer £2,000 damages and £200 as a contribution towards A's cost. If A's solicitor thinks (with counsel's opinion) that the claim is to be worth, say, more than £2,000, the offer could be refused. However, if the court were to award less than £2,000 at the hearing A would lose any claim for costs that would otherwise lay.[9] The reason for this is that B may be seen by the court to have made all effort to settle outside of court. Where substantial costs are involved a settlement will often be achieved to avoid the risk of gaining no more in damages and losing the issue of costs. Costs therefore dictate both degree of access and the chance of pre-court settlement.

Legal Aid

In mentioning the cost of going to law one must have regard of the relevance of legal aid. In Ireland legal aid is as yet underdeveloped. The concept of legal aid can be explained first, and its relevance to the Republic will follow.

Legal aid is a system of financial subsidy towards legal expenses. It can be broadly described as a welfare benefit, in so far as those satisfying certain meritorious and financial criteria may receive legal services either free or at a reduced rate. However, the operation of such a scheme will be discussed shortly. Civil legal aid has recently been made available in the Republic following the outline of a scheme recently laid before the Oireachtas.[10] A limited criminal aid scheme is also in operation.[11]

Bearing in mind the contemporary relevance of legal aid, how will this affect access to the law? Based on the British experience, upon which the Republic's scheme draws heavily, the operation of a legal aid scheme can be described as follows. A legally aided person in either civil or criminal cases is a person who applies for legal aid from the relevant authority and who is granted a certificate on satisfaction of specified criteria. The usual grounds operating include a means test and an appraisal of the merits of the case. A means test simply examines income, capital and expenditure; a person's disposable income and capital (i.e. after allowable deductions) is related to a contributory scale. Below a set figure a person is entitled to legal aid without making any payment, and above a set figure a person is disqualified from legal aid. Between these extremes a person may be granted legal aid subject to the payment of a specified amount by instalments or in a lump sum. Legal aid will cover all the eligible legal expenses on payment of the requisite contribution, if any. The merit criteria, at least as operated in Britain, is not supposed to be concerned with the likely success of the action, but rather whether if the person concerned had the funds, they would still pursue a claim.[12] This is broadly known as the reasonableness test.

Civil legal aid, as can be seen in reference to the Republic's present scheme, may be refused additionally if the dispute is not within the terms of reference of the scheme, for example appearances before tribunals, and the certificate may be limited, for example to allow investigation up to but not including trial, thus saving expense.

In criminal cases, the certificate will name a lawyer of the applicant's choice (on a legal aid panel who is willing to undertake such work) who will conduct the case on behalf of the legally aided person. The case is supposed to be conducted on the same basis as if the client were paying in the normal way for such services. At conclusion of the hearing (which again should take no account of legal aid) the lawyer submits a report to the authority concerned and claims payment. The costs claimed are subject to taxation. In civil cases if the legally aided person recovers any property or money in a judgement this is subject to a charge. This means that the legal aid authority can deduct any expenses paid from the legal aid fund out of the monies recovered by the litigant. It should be noted that if a person is legally aided then, subject to the contribution, no payment can be demanded towards legal expenses outside of this charge. Thus the lawyer cannot charge the client for legally aided work direct. The lawyer must recover fees as indicated above. The issue of legal aid only extends to the solicitor/client costs of the aided person. Consequently if the legally aided person loses a case, costs can be awarded against that party in favour of the other. This works on the principle outlined above that costs follow the event. As a matter of practice, however, the British experience would indicate that the discretion towards costs is seldom exercised against a legally aided person.

The Republic's system of civil legal aid is still in its early stages and it is too early to determine whether it meets the needs identified by the Pringle Report. Altready, however, there are indications that the law centres are understaffed and overloaded with cases. In Britain since 1949, legal aid is available for legal advice sought before or without court action (this is known as 'the green form scheme'). In addition, the scheme covers the legally aided person's costs and expenses arising from civil and criminal litigation. Appeals against the refusal of legal aid can also be made.

To conclude, therefore, access to law may be affected by a variety of factors, including a combination of political and social barriers and the undoubtedly high cost of going to law.

Against this background how may a person physically exercise access?

Pursuing a Claim under the Law

The simple answer to the question above is for the person concerned to employ a lawyer and pay for the requisite services. It may be argued that a lawyer's time should be purchased in exactly the same way as any other commodity. It is not our intention to enter into this debate although we submit in passing that fundamental services such as law, health and education should not be sold in the open market to the highest bidder. It is an essential tenet of modern welfare societies that a minimum standard of living should be assured to all.

If a person is unable or unwilling to pay for legal services through the private profession, how can advice and representation be obtained in the Republic? The following options, which may overlap, are available.

Legal Aid: In certain criminal cases a defendant may be granted legal aid to provide for representation. The law is to be found in the Criminal Justice (Legal Aid) Act, 1962, and is available for all criminal offences where the court deems the charge or charges appropriate for legal representation to be provided at the State's expense. A means test is also applied. There would appear to be little material available on the practical scope of this scheme but the matter has received judicial attention in so far as a denial of legal aid might amount to a breach of constitutional rights.[13]

The civil legal aid structure envisaged in the recent proposals laid before the Oireachtas will be examined shortly.

Do-It-Yourself: Providing a person has the locus standi, he or she can appear in court without legal representation. All courts are without exception open to hear the original parties to a dispute. There are of course many reasons why a person will not represent him or her self. Lack of legal knowledge, self-confidence, articulacy and ignorance of procedure are but a few of the reasons which mitigate against self-representation.

Charity: Many lawyers to a greater or lesser extent provide advice and representation on a charitable basis by making a reduced charge for their services or waiving their fees altogether. Similarly many voluntary agencies may provide assistance, and these will be noted more fully below. While this level of servicing may be commendable on an individual basis it is, we submit, highly unsatisfactory to rely upon an *ex gratia* and charitable system to provide such a vital service.

To Obtain Assistance from a Friend: Nothing prevents a person obtaining advice from a friend or colleague, though one may question their legal skills. The courts will not, however, as a rule allow representation by persons without locus standi or legal qualification. Thus a friend may help but may not speak on behalf of a litigant, except as a witness.

To Obtain Assistance Directly from the Court: Officers of the court, for example the clerk, may not give legal advice but are generally prepared to assist an unrepresented person, for example in explanations of procedure. In non-contentious matters, upon payment of a small fee the court may conduct a person's business on his or her behalf, for example in the extraction of probate. This latter point is particularly relevant where a court official is by name involved in proceedings, e.g. in the enforcement of maintenance orders.[14]

Insurance: Principally in road traffic cases a person may rely on insurance cover to meet legal expenses.

Societies and Associations: Members of benefit societies, trade unions and clubs may have access to funds and/or lawyers by virtue of their subscription.

Payment Out of 'Winnings': In areas not open to legal aid representation may be gained by entering into an agreement with the lawyer that a person will be represented and a charge will only be made if the action is successful and damages recovered. In this way both sides take a qualified gamble. It is submitted that this informal device would be unenforceable at law on grounds of public policy.

Habeas Corpus Applications: In 1967 an undertaking was given on behalf of the Attorney General that an applicant's legal expenses will be defrayed by the State where the court thinks it appropriate to do so in the interests of justice and of the applicant's financial circumstances. This has since been extended to all State-side applications.[15]

Intervention by State Officials: A litigant may benefit by the discretionary intervention of certain Government officials, e.g. the Minister for Labour may bring a case of unfair dismissal before the Circuit Court on behalf of an applicant, and if so the State will bear expenses incurred.

Advice Agencies: A person in need of legal advice may use one of the centres in the Republic without charge. There are two main types of centre: those run by the Free Legal Advice Centres (F.L.A.C.) and those established by The Citizens' Advice Bureaux. A number of other voluntary agencies also exist. The principal limitation here is that most such agencies, being voluntary and part-time, do not offer representative services. Thus advice and/or assistance only is offered. Indeed some agencies expressly decline to give legal advice. If legal services are required the agencies will usually refer a person into the profession. It would seem therefore that the function of each centre varies considerably from area to area and depends upon overall policy and local energies.[16]

Law Centres: As will be seen shortly the concept of law centres features strongly in the Pringle Report and the recent proposals for civil legal aid in Ireland. In addition, the role and function of law centres has occupied much debate in Britain (where the centres originated). It has been argued above that to ensure equality of access to legal services both financial assistance (legal aid) and other devices are necessary in promoting legal services. The law centre is one approach in tackling the problem of provision of legal services. As will be stressed later the term 'law centre' is not consistently used to mean the same thing. The model as presently operated in Britain and as is found in Ireland's only law centre (at Coolock, Dublin) specialises in welfare law and offers a full service, albeit one that concentrates on a particular locality. The term 'community law centre' is a more accurate description of the role of the law centre in this capacity. The management and hence the policy of the law centres in this guise is shaped by representatives from the local community which the centre serves.

The law centre therefore is an important agency in terms of developing access to law. Individual cases within the scope of each centre are pursued but in addition educational material is produced to emphasise 'rights' of which the local population may not be aware. It should be appreciated that this approach is some way removed from the traditional concept of providing legal services.

RECENT CHANGES IN THE LAW

We have now examined some of the difficulties relating to access to the law and the ways in which access can be gained or implemented. A true appraisal of this topic would be incomplete without mentioning recent developments relating to the provision of legal services. In June 1974, under Pringle J., the Minister for Justice appointed a committee to 'advise on the introduction at an early date of a comprehensive scheme of legal aid and advice in civil matters and to recommend on the form, nature and administration of the scheme'.[17]

The committee took over three years to consider evidence and opinion from a variety of sources, finally producing a comprehensive volume in December 1977. Some two years later the Minister laid before the Oireachtas Regulations introducing a non-statutory civil legal aid and advice scheme.

Both the Pringle Report and the Minister's White Paper contain the bones of a legal aid scheme. As the two documents contain several common strands brief comment can be made of the relevant details.

First, it is worthwhile to remind ourselves of the principal recommendations of the Pringle Report, for the regulations take much of their framework from the report itself. Secondly, the Regulations can be considered.

Three main provisions are to be found in the report. A Legal Aid Board was envisaged by the committee, independent of, but with representatives from, the profession. This body should be responsible for the administration of legal aid, including the granting of aid, the handling of a legal aid fund, regular research into and review of legal services, and publicity of legal services generally.[18] The Regulations in part two deal expressly with such a board appointed by the Minister for up to five years and consisting of 12 persons and chairperson, of which two will be practising barristers and two solicitors. Membership is to be part-time unless the Minister otherwise provides. The functions of the board are enumerated in section 2.2 although the research function contained in the Pringle Report is not listed.

The report's second and most far-reaching set of recommendations concern the introduction of a comprehensive legal aid scheme which had the following characteristics: it was to apply to all Irish civil law; it was to apply to both advice and representation; it was to include hearings before court and tribunals; eligibility should depend on satisfaction of a test based on an examination of means, coupled with 'a reasonableness test' (balancing individual interest with public interest); and the advice and representation was to be provided by lawyers in private practice, law centres and legal advice agencies.[19]

The report realistically recognised that the political and economic climate may not favour such a wide-flung legal aid net and so as an alternative suggested an interim scheme shaped by the comprehensive structure outlined above. This was to be limited to issues of family law, landlord-and-tenant dispute and consumer protection, with priorities reviewed at regular intervals. It was not to be made available to tribunals, was to be limited to the 'lower income groups' and need not include legal advice (providing the State made sure advice agencies contributed ground-cover).[20]

Interestingly the Regulations fall some way between the comprehensive scheme and the compromise version. One might argue that on one front this is to be welcomed, i.e. the scheme goes beyond the caution inherent in the interim scheme contained in the Pringle Report. However, conversely, the scheme now proposed will operate on a potentially wide, but practically limited, basis and will perhaps be a stumbling-block to achieving the comprehensive scheme set out above. In any event, as the second half of this section argues, the concept of legal aid, important as it is, must be seen in context. The removal of the financial obstacle is but one of the inroads into problems of access to law.

What of the Regulations themselves? A distinction is made between legal advice and legal aid. The former amounts to advice or assistance, with the exception of court proceedings. The latter covers representation in the four courts of civil jurisdiction.[21] The Regulations are extremely vague on the practical administration of legal advice but more comprehensive *vis-à-vis* legal aid. However, excluded from the scope of either aspect of the scheme are criminal law matters, defamation, debt collecting, conveyancing, disputes concerning interest in land (property covered by the Rent Restriction Acts and Landlord and Tenant Act excepted), civil bills for less than £150 and certain less important matters.[22] The financial criteria for eligibility are clearly set out[23] and the board is to be given a wide discretion in the granting or refusal of legal aid based on the merits of the applicant in his or her case. The system, as recommended in the Pringle Report, is to be contributory.

Perhaps, in light of the following submissions on the lessons to be learnt from the British system's failings, it is appropriate to mention the inclusion of law centres in both the report and the Regulations. The third aspect of the Pringle Report is enshrined in the Regulations and deals with the function of the board in the creation and maintenance of legal service centres. These centres, either presently existing or to be created, are seen as supplemental but complementary to services available in private practice. However, in the Regulations services under the scheme are to be *entirely* the domain of centres created or sponsored by the board. Section 6 of the Regulations set out, somewhat scantily, the conditions under which these services will be made available. The staff of such centres will be engaged by the board and services will be open to all eligible persons regardless of place of residence. This has the potential of removing community control or influence from the type and emphasis of service offered. It is significant that the term 'community' law centre, stressed by the Pringle Report, is entirely absent from the details of the Regulations. The criteria upon which such centres are to be located are set out. Uniformity, legal need and efficient use of resources are the principal guide-lines. The board, almost by way of postscript, is to take account of 'local and other interests' but the final decision is vested in the board. It is not clear from the Regulations how far the engagement of lawyers will be on a full or part-time basis and what rules will apply in the selection of lawyers to staff the centres.

In conclusion, therefore, it is suggested that it is unrealistic to think of the law as an objective yardstick accessible to all. Certainly this is the type of presumption that underlies such juristic concepts as the rule of law. We have seen that law serves particular needs and effectively ignores others. It should therefore come as no surprise for the reader to learn that people use the law in terms of the issues they see the law dealing with. It is a matter of perception of relevance of the law that dictates access. Financial difficulties are of course relevant too, and the introduction of a long-overdue legal aid scheme will provide much assistance for those who would otherwise suffer. Consequently access to the law will only be made available to those who are involved in traditional areas of legal dispute, e.g. criminal and family matters.

If access to law is to be made open to all, the powers that be must consider how legal services should be delivered or otherwise vast areas (e.g. social welfare) will go untouched.

PART III

SUBSTANCE OF THE LAW

Chapter 9 *

CONSTITUTIONAL LAW

INTRODUCTION

In recent years there has been an increasing number of Constitutional issues litigated before Irish courts. In addition, there has also been a noticeable and welcome growth in the public awareness of 'Constitutional rights'. The reader who turns to this chapter in search of these elusive 'Constitutional rights' will not be entirely disappointed but will also quickly realise that they are but a part, if an important part, of Irish Constitutional law. For the Irish Constitution goes beyond constitutionally guaranteed liberties and establishes a legal framework for Irish law and society as a whole. Two further points are worth noting. First, leaving aside the five Articles dealing with fundamental rights, the remaining 45 Articles have remained, for the greater part, unlitigated. Much of this chapter, in consequence, is descriptive. Secondly, the interest of the public in general in Constitutional matters may not run very deep; the recent referenda on the Sixth and Seventh Amendments to the Constitution attracted a national poll of less than 20%.

The Constitution of 1937 is the successor of the Constitution of Dail Eireann (1919) and the Constitution of the Irish Free State (1922). The 1937 model, however, represented a considerable change in the nature of the State, as expressed in various Articles. It created the Constitutional framework which subsequently permitted the transition from the Irish Free State to the Republic of Ireland to be (easily) accomplished by an Act of the Oireachtas.

THE NATION AND THE STATE

Article 1 of the Constitution asserts Ireland's claim to nationhood and self-determination. The national territory is the whole island of Ireland[1] but, pending reintegration, Irish law applies only to that area to which the laws of the Irish Free State applied, i.e. the 26 counties.[2] This qualification was

**See also 1988 Supplement pp. 327-332.*

necessary to avoid the immense juridical (as well as political) difficulties which could otherwise have arisen. But for the interim provision of Article 3 all matters, criminal as well as civil, and disputes arising in Northern Ireland would have been justifiable before the courts in the Republic.

Article 5 provides that Ireland is a sovereign, independent and democratic state. Sovereignty is a concept used by international lawyers to refer to the right to govern and legislate. Independence is not a term with a defined legal meaning but is generally understood to include the right to act without interference or intimidation from others. Democracy entails essentially the right of the people to select the government, though whether the people can democratically decide to substitute another political theory (e.g. dictatorship) for democracy is a difficult question. In any event it is clear that the Oireachtas cannot do so without the appropriate Constitutional amendment.

THE PEOPLE

All powers of government, legislative, executive and judicial, are vested in the people.[3] But the people themselves are not the source of these powers, which are said to derive under God. Moreover while the people are the ultimate decision makers, these rights must be exercised 'according to the requirements of the common good'. These qualifications highlight a significant difference between the ideas of European liberal thought and those which motivated the framers of the Constitution. The power of the people is not absolute but must be exercised having regard both to its source and the common good. These restrictions are reflected later in the recognition of certain rights as rights which cannot be abrogated even by the people. But they also represent a Christian (and, later, a Roman Catholic) influence. The result has been an attempt 'to reconcile the notion of an alienable popular sovereignty with the older medieval conception of a theocratic state'.[4]

THE PRESIDENT

The President is the formal head of State who represents Ireland at ceremonial functions. He also performs a number of ceremonial duties such as the appointment of the Taoiseach on the advice of the Dail, the appointment and removal of ministers upon the advice of the Taoiseach and the appointment of the judiciary and officers of the defence forces, upon the advice of the Government. Besides these formal and ceremonial duties there are other particular ways in which the President plays an important role under the Constitution. All of these latter duties or powers treat the President as a kind of protector or guarantor, not only of fundamental rights, but also of the Constitutional framework as a whole. It is these powers which elevate the office of President above that of mere ceremony or symbolism. At the same time, however, it is important to emphasise that the President is not

Head of the Government (that position is reserved to the Taoiseach), nor does he (unlike the President of the United States) exercise any executive role in Government. These powers, namely, those exercisable solely upon the discretion of the President, must be distinguished from those already mentioned, which are exercisable only upon the advice of the Government or according to law. The main Presidential discretionary powers are as follows:

(i) Article 26: This provides that, with the exception of a money bill, (see p. 170 *infra*) the President may[5] refer any bill to the Supreme Court for a decision on the question as to whether such bill, or any provision thereof, is repugnant to the Constitution. Five bills[6] have been referred to the Supreme Court under this provision and only in one of those cases has the court held that the provision in question was repugnant to the Constitution.

Once the Supreme Court reaches a decision the President must then act in accordance with that decision by signing or not signing the bill, as the case might be. If a bill referred by the President is found to be constitutionally valid, the validity of that bill cannot be challenged again *at any time.*[7]

(ii) Article 27: The provisions of this article are not as commonly known as those of Article 26 and have never been exercised. A majority of the members of Seanad Eireann and not less than one-third of the members of the Dail may address a joint petition to the President requesting him to decline to sign or promulgate any bill, on the grounds that the bill contains a proposal of such national importance that the will of the people thereon ought to be ascertained. The President, after consultation with the Council of State, may decline to sign the bill on these grounds unless a referendum approves the bill or the bill is approved by a resolution of the Dail, *after* a general election.

(iii) Article 13(2)(ii): This provision is brief and may be stated in full. 'The President may in his absolute discretion refuse to dissolve Dail Eireann on the advice of a Taoiseach who has ceased to retain the support of a majority in Dail Eireann.'

This power must be contrasted with the duty of the President, under the first paragraph of the same section, to summon and dissolve the Dail upon the advice of the Taoiseach. It would appear, therefore, that in this regard the President need follow the advice only of a Taoiseach *with* a majority. If the Taoiseach has ceased to hold súch a majority, the President has an absolute discretion in the matter. One writer, Professor Chubb, has expressed surprise at such an outcome and has made the following observation:

> Under Article 28(10), a Taoiseach is required to resign from office 'on his ceasing to retain support of a majority in Dail Eireann' unless on his advice the President dissolves [the Dail] . . . . [but] the President may in his absolute discretion refuse a dissolution in such circumstances. If he does so refuse, the Taoiseach must resign, thus giving the opportunity to the Dail to nominate a successor. But this is to prevent the people from making what is surely one of the most important decisions it can make, that of who is to be the Government of the State, and at a juncture when it would seem particularly appropriate for them to do so.[8]

There are a number of difficulties with this objection. First, although if the Taoiseach resigns, the Government is also deemed to have resigned,[9] the people did not choose either the Government or the Taoiseach in the first place. It is common knowledge that the Taoiseach will be chosen by the party with a majority in Dail Eireann and that, in practice as well as in Constitutional theory, the Government is selected by the Taoiseach. It does not follow that because a Taoiseach lost *his* majority in the Dail, that the *party* has also lost its majority. If the Taoiseach resigns in these circumstances, a general election is not necessarily a welcome consequence or side-effect. Professor Chubb's view would result in a Government or party being unable to remove and replace a Taoiseach without a general election. Fortunately, however, such a problem has never arisen in practice.

(iv) Article 13(2)(iii): The President may, at any time, after consultation with the Council of State, convene a meeting of either or both Houses of the Oireachtas. Moreover the President may also, again after consultation with the Council of State, communicate with the Houses of the Oireachtas by message or address on any matter of national or public importance.[10] The only condition to the exercise of either of these powers, is *consultation* with the Council of State. While this is also the only condition to addressing the nation,[11] the content of any such message or address must have the approval of the Government.[12] It would seem, therefore, that the President may address the Houses of the Oireachtas when he pleases and, when doing so, he may say as he pleases. While free to address the nation, what he says in these circumstances is subject to Government approval. Since all proceedings in both Houses of the Oireachtas are usually recorded and regularly reported, one wonders whether this is a practical or necessary distinction. It would seem more consistent with his role as protector of the Constitutional framework to permit the President to freely address the nation.

Other Presidential Powers

Article 13(6) provides that the right of pardon and the power to commute or remit punishment imposed by any court exercising criminal jurisdiction are vested in the President, but such powers may, except in capital cases, also be conferred by law on other authorities. Such a power is exercisable only upon the advice of the Government.

Other powers may arise under the Constitution itself or be conferred upon the President by law.[13] Except where otherwise provided (i.e. the discretionary powers discussed above), the Constitutional powers are exercisable only upon the advice of the Government.[14] Where a power has been conferred by law such power is expressly stated to be exercisable or performable only on the advice of the Government.[15]

Absence or Incapacity of the President

In such circumstances, or in the event of the President's death, resignation, removal from office or failure to exercise the Presidential powers and functions, these powers may be exercised by a Presidential Commission.[16] The Commission consists of the Chief Justice (or President of the High Court), the Chairman or Ceann Chomhairle of the Dail (or his deputy) and the Chairman of the Senate (or his deputy).[17] Should a contingency arise (perhaps, for example, the kidnapping of the President) which has not been provided for under these provisions, the Council of State may make such provision as seems appropriate.[18] The President is not permitted to leave the State without the consent of the Government.[19]

Impeachment of the President

Subject to the powers of impeachment provided by Article 12, the President is immune from any liability for the exercise of his powers or any act done or purporting to be done in the exercise of those powers.[20] The President can only be impeached for *stated misbehaviour.*[21] The *proposal* to prefer such a charge against the President in either House must be supported by at least 30 members of that House.[22] The charge is then investigated by the other House[23] and the President has the right to appear and to be represented at such investigation.[24] If at least two-thirds of that House support a resolution that the charge has been sustained and that the misbehaviour was such as to render him unfit to continue in office, such resolution operates to remove the President from office.

THE NATIONAL PARLIAMENT AND THE GOVERNMENT

The national Parliament is known as the Oireachtas and consists of the President, Dail Eireann and Seanad Eireann.[25] As the role of the President has already been discussed, we shall concentrate here on the Dail and the Seanad.

All legislative[26] and executive[27] powers are vested in the Oireachtas and the Government respectively, and the issue here is how the former powers are distributed between the Dail and the Seanad. The general position is that the balance is struck heavily in favour of the Dail. The initiation of Money Bills (e.g. the bill to implement the 'budget') is reserved to the Dail.[28] Bills other than Money Bills may be initiated by Seanad Eireann but, if subsequently amended by Dail Eireann, are deemed to have been initiated by the Dail.[29] While all bills passed by the Dail must be submitted to the Seanad, the power of the latter house to amend a bill referred from the Dail is limited in a number of ways:

(i) If, within 90 days of receiving the Bill, the Senate does not pass it, the Dail may resolve (at any time within a further one hundred and eighty days) that the Bill shall be deemed to have been passed by both Houses.[30]

(ii) Any rejection of the Bill by the Seanad, or any amendment by the Seanad which the Dail does not agree with, is subject to the same provision.[31]

(iii) The period of ninety days is reduced to twenty one days in the case of a Money Bill, at the expiration of which the Bill is deemed to have been passed.[32]

(iv) These periods of ninety days and twenty one days may be abridged if the Government considers (and so certifies to the Chairman of each House and the President) that the Bill is urgent and immediately necessary for the preservation of the public peace and security, or by reason of the existence of the public emergency, whether domestic or international. The President must concur in such opinion. Such bills, however, can only remain in force for ninety days unless both Houses agree that such a Bill should continue for a stated period.[33]

A further indication of the relatively subordinate position of the Seanad is that elections and appointments to the Seanad are dependent upon elections to the Dail.[34] Elections to the latter must take place at least every seven years[35] according to the Constitution.

The Government must consist of not less than 7 and not more than 15 members. They are appointed by the President on the advice of the Taoiseach,[36] who is head of the Government.[37] The Taoiseach nominates a member of the Government to be the Tanaiste, and the latter acts on behalf of the Taoiseach whenever the Taoiseach is incapacitated or absent from office.[38] The Taoiseach, the Tanaiste and the Minister for Finance (the latter two offices have frequently been held by the same minister) must be members of the Dail.[39] All other members of the Government must be members of the Oireachtas,[40] with a maximum of two from the Seanad.[41]

These Constitutional provisions do not of course tell us the whole, or the real, story of Government in Ireland. In reality practically all legislation is first proposed by the Government, and the Parliamentary role of members of the Oireachtas who are not members of the Government is usually confined to debate and, depending on the party to which they belong, voting in favour or against the measure proposed.

THE COURTS AND JUDICIAL REVIEW

The structure and jurisdiction, as well as the Constitutional basis, of the criminal and civil courts has been set out in Chapter 5. In the next section of this chapter we will focus on the natural, fundamental and personal rights as enshrined in the Constitution and as developed and interpreted by the courts. Here we will simply highlight some of the features of, and basis for, the process of judicial review.

We have already referred to the jurisdiction of the Supreme Court to determine the Constitutional validity of a bill referred to it by the President. But the Supreme Court[42] and the High Court[43] have jurisdiction to review the Constitutionality of any *laws.* This jurisdiction involves the use of one of two devices.

First, it is necessary to remember that all laws in force prior to the enactment of the Constitution were carried forward by Article 50, *provided they were not repugnant to the Constitution.* But no provision was made for any comprehensive review of such laws. Instead, some of them have been the subject of litigation from time to time. If such a law is found to be repugnant to the Constitution it is held never to have been carried forward by Article 50.

Secondly, laws passed since the enactment of the Constitution are declared 'invalid' if found to be repugnant to the Constitution. While this means that such laws cease to have any effect, it does not mean that they are automatically repealed. This is important because, due to the element of flexibility introduced into the doctrine of stare decisis by the Supreme Court (see Chapter 2), it is theoretically possible that such laws might be revived by a later court. It is of course equally possible that a decision based on Article 50 might also be reversed by a later court.

It is worth noting that Mr. de Valera, the principal draftsman of the Constitution, did not intend the Supreme Court to enjoy such powers, certainly not with regard to post-1937 legislation. Professor Kelly has shown in some detail that Mr. de Valera did not intend 'to shackle the legislature in the future in a way in which it is not shackled today'.[44] The latter's intention was rather to set 'headlines' for the legislature to aim at. But all Mr. de Valera could do was to say what he *thought* he was doing. It was for the courts to determine what he did. As we shall see in the next section, the courts have adopted a different view to that of Mr. de Valera.

Only in one limited respect has the de Valera view prevailed. Article

28(3)(iii) expressly excludes from judicial review all acts passed in time of war or armed rebellion or armed conflict.

On 1st September, 1976 the Oireachtas (repealing a resolution which had existed since September 1939) adopted the following resolution:

> Dail Eireann hereby resolves [pursuant to Article 28(3)(iii)] that, arising out of the armed conflict now taking place in Northern Ireland, a National Emergency exists affecting the vital interests of the State.[46]

Later that month the Emergency Powers Bill, 1976, was passed by both Houses but, on 24th September the President referred the bill to the Supreme Court under Article 26. The bill was upheld but what is of significance here is the approach of the court to the restriction of Article 28(3)(iii). Though recognising that there was a presumption that the facts were as stated in such a resolution, the Court reserved the question whether it had power to review such resolution. Moreover the Court held that Article 28(3)(iii) only applied to invoking the Constitution in order to invalidate an Act of the Oireachtas. For other purposes, e.g. determining the validity of detention, the Constitution may be relied upon.

Finally, the *one judgement rule* has been considerably restricted by the court. Article 34(4)(v) provided that, in cases in which the validity of a law is challenged, the decision of the Supreme Court is to be delivered by one judge 'and no other opinion on such question, whether assenting or dissenting, shall be pronounced, nor shall the existence of any such opinion be disclosed'. The Supreme Court has construed the term *law* in this paragraph as being applicable only to laws passed under the 1937 Constitution and not to laws carried forward by Article 50. The reader will find nothing in the section on statutory interpretation in Chapter 2 which would support such a construction.

FUNDAMENTAL RIGHTS

Articles 40 - 44 of the Constitution appear under the general title of 'Fundamental Rights', and it is this section of the document which has attracted the greatest share of popular and judicial attention. Indeed, with regard to the latter, Professor Heuston has recently remarked that the cases 'seem to go to the furthest limit of judicial law-making'.[47]

The extensive development of personal rights by the Irish Supreme Court has been the result of two developments of its own. First, in what may yet become the most important Irish decision of this century, the Supreme Court in *A.G.* v. *Ryan*[48] (see also the discussion in Chapter 2), upholding the decision of Kenny J. in the High Court, held that the personal rights guaranteed by the Constitution were not confined to those rights specifically enumerated under Article 40, but also included a number of unspecified or unenumerated rights. This decision has been buttressed by the development of the view that the rights guaranteed by the Constitution are of a dynamic rather than static quality. The Chief Justice has expressed this view in the following manner:

> In my view the preamble makes it clear that the rights given by the Constitution must be considered in accordance with concepts of prudence, justice and charity which may gradually change or develop as society changes or develops, and which fail to be interpreted from time to time in accordance with prevailing ideas. The Preamble envisages a Constitution which can absorb or be adapted to such changes. In other words, the Constitution did not seek to impose for all time the ideas prevalent or accepted with regard to these virtues at the time of its enactment.[49]

Even more revolutionary, however, (and equally difficult to justify) has been the fact that the High Court[50] has employed the Directive Principles of Social Policy expressed in Article 45 (said to be for the guidance of the Oireachtas only and 'not to be cognisable by any Court under *any* of the provisions of this Constitution') in testing the constitutionality of pre-1937 legislation. Once again this was achieved by restricting the word 'laws' to those laws enacted since 1937.

In addition to the distinction between specified and unspecified rights, a further distinction must be drawn because certain rights are described as 'natural rights'. The Constitution expressly recognises at least three natural rights or, in other words, three rights which do not derive their validity from the Constitution. First, under Article 41, 'the State *recognises* the Family as the *natural* primary and fundamental unit group of society', possessing rights 'antecedent and superior to all positive law'. Secondly, under Article 42, the State *acknowledges* the role of the family as 'the primary and *natural* educator of the child'.[51] Thirdly, under Article 43, the State '*acknowledges* that man . . . has the *natural* right . . . to the private ownership of external goods'.[52] It is submitted that the use of the word 'natural' in each of these Articles, linked as it is in each case with words such as 'recognises' and 'acknowledges', can only be construed as indicating that these rights are derived not from the Constitution but from the higher authority of *natural law.* If this is a proper construction these particular rights are, in theory, incapable of amendment or abrogation. But their very recognition in the Constitution is at least their source of effective legal authority and persuasion, if not their organic or legal source. Without a Constitutional foundation they become, in reality, little more than platitudes or philosophical aspirations. To this extent, such rights are as dependent upon the Constitution as those 'Constitutionally created' rights. And, in this context, the warning of Professor Kelly is appropriate:

> . . . the ultimate protection of human rights in a democracy lies with the people themselves. If they allow villains into Government, a piece of paper will not protect them from the consequences, nor must they expect a few learned men in wigs and gowns to save the fools from the knaves they have elected.[53]

Nonetheless, if such rights are derived from natural law, the implication is that they cannot be amended or abrogated as long as the present Constitutional framework prevails. This in itself is of significance even though they may ultimately stand or fall with the Constitution. It is also interesting to speculate whether, in view of our discussion above on the development of personal rights, the courts will recognise any other (personal) rights *of this nature.*

The rights of the family are expressed as 'inalienable and imprescriptable' under Article 41. The right (and duty) of parents to provide for the religious and moral, intellectual, physical and social education of their children under Article 42 is expressed as 'inalienable' only. Inalienable means incapable of surrender or transfer, while imprescriptable means incapable of being lost through not being used or exercised. The familial rights under Article 41 are not qualified or limited as are those under Article 42 (and others). Whether the terms 'inalienable' and/or 'imprescriptable' distinguish Articles 41 and 42 from the others in the area of fundamental rights is an issue to which an Irish court has yet to address itself. One practical implication, however, is that legitimate children are generally considered to be ineligible for adoption as a result of Article 41.

We can now briefly examine those substantive fundamental rights found in the Constitution, as developed by the courts.

Personal Rights: Article 40

(a) Equality: All citizens, as human persons, are to be held equal before the law. Legislation may have due regard, however, to differences in physical and moral capacity, and of social function between citizens. Accordingly, special voting procedure for blind persons does not violate this provision,[54] while the guarantee was deemed to have been violated by the exclusion of women (except upon application) from jury service.[55]

(b) Expressed or Enumerated Rights: The State guarantees in its laws to respect and, as far as practicable, by its laws to defend and vindicate the personal rights of the citizen. The right to one's life, person, good name and property are specifically mentioned.

(c) Unenumerated Rights:[56] These cannot be exhaustively listed since, as the product of litigation, they are 'discovered' by the courts from time to time. The following rights have been recognised as falling within this category:-

(i) employment rights including the right to work, to earn a living, and to join (and to refuse to join) a trade union.

(ii) right to due process of law including the right to be heard, to consult and be represented by a lawyer, the right to litigate and to have access to the courts.

(iii) the right to free movement within the State.

(iv) the right to marry and to marital privacy.

(d) Personal Liberty: It is provided that no citizen is to be deprived of his liberty save in accordance with law. At one time this guarantee was restricted by a very positivist interpretation of the phrase 'in accordance with law'. According to this view 'law' meant ordinary legislation and any deprivation of liberty which was in accordance with ordinary legislation was 'in accordance with law'. Gradually, however, this view has been replaced by the view that such 'law' must accord with ordinary principles of constitutional law. In order to protect the right to personal liberty, Article 40.4 contains detailed provisions for challenging the legality of any deprecation of liberty. This procedure is referred to as *habeas corpus.*

(e) Inviolability of the Dwelling: The dwelling of every citizen is inviolable and must not be forcibly entered save in accordance with law.

(f) Rights subject to Public Order and Morality: Article 40.6(1) guarantees liberty to exercise certain rights subject to public order and morality. In addition to this general restriction, there are specific limitations in each clause also. The following areas are provided for:–

(i) *freedom of expression:* citizens are guaranteed the right to express freely their convictions and opinions. It is provided also, however, that 'the State shall endeavour to ensure that organs of public opinion, such as the radio, the press, the cinema, while preserving their rightful liberty of expression, including criticism of Government policy, shall not be used to undermine public order or morality or the authority of the State'. Examples of restrictions upon freedom of expression are the Offences Against the State Act 1939, the Official Secrets Act 1963 and the Censorship of Films Act 1923 to 1970. The Constitution itself provides that the publication or utterance of blasphemous, seditious, or indecent matter is an offence.

(ii) *freedom to assemble peaceably and without arms:* the State may enact legislation, however, designed to prevent or control meetings which are determined in accordance with law to be calculated to cause a breach of the peace or to be a danger or nuisance to the general public and to prevent or control meetings in the vicinity of either House of the Oireachtas.

(iii) *freedom of association:* the citizens have the right to form associations and unions, but laws may be enacted for the regulation and control in the public interest of the exercise of this right. The right has been held to include the right to disassociate i.e. the right to obtain from or refuse membership of an association or union. The Offences Against the State Act 1939 (as amended in 1972) contains detailed provisions prohibiting the formation or membership of subversive or illegal organisations. Laws which regulate or limit the freedom to associate must be free from political, religious or class discrimination.

While it is clear that the overall restrictions on the rights guaranteed are substantial, the expression of such 'freedoms' in a written constitution is a valuable instrument against, at the very least, severe or extreme forms of oppression. Professor Chubb has pointed out[57] that the presence of such solemn declarations as those contained in Article 40 has an important political (if not legal) influence upon government.

Familial Rights: Article 41

These rights are dealt with in Chapter 17 on family law, and will not be repeated here.

Education: Article 42

Under this Article the State acknowledges that the primary and natural educator of the child is the family, and guarantees to respect the inalienable right and duty of parents to provide, according to their means, for the religious and moral, intellectual, physical and social education of their children. Children must, however, receive a certain minimum standard of education, whether at home or in private or State schools. The State cannot oblige parents to send their children to State schools or any particular type of school, contrary to the parents' conscience and lawful preference. The Supreme Court has defined 'education' in the following terms: 'Education essentially is the teaching and training of a child to make the best possible use of his inherent and potential capacities, physical, mental and moral.'

Religion: Article 44

This Article has been amended by the Fifth Amendment of the Constitution Act, 1972, which deleted provisions conferring a special status on the Roman Catholic Church and which specifically mentioned other (but not all) religions found in the State in 1937. The Article, however, continues to contain elaborate provisions for the protection of freedom of religion. There is also an important limitation. Section 2(1) provides as follows: 'Freedom of conscience and the free profession and practice of religion are, *subject to public order and morality,* guaranteed to every citizen.[58]

In addition to guarantees of religious freedom, the Article prohibits religious discrimination, whether through the imposition of disabilities or the granting of endowments to a particular religion, or the confiscation of property. The latter, however, may be diverted 'for necessary works of public utility and on payment of compensation'.

Private Property[59]

While Article 43 deals specifically with the right to private property, the issue is also dealt with by Article 40(3) and Article 44(2)(v) and (vi). Here we shall confine our attention to Article 43. It is provided by section (1) that the State acknowledges that man, in virtue of his rational being, has the natural right, antecedent to positive law, to the private ownership of external goods. Accordingly under section (2) the State guarantees to pass no law attempting to abolish the right of private ownership or the general right to transfer, bequeath and inherit property. Whenever social justice requires, however, the State may delimit these rights in the interests of the common good.

It has been noted earlier that the right to private property is a *natural* right which is acknowledged, but not created, by the Constitution. One other point should be noted: the State may not freely interfere with the right merely in the interests of the common good. The criterion for intervention is social justice,[60] a vague list but one which the courts will not shrink from applying where necessary.[61]

CONCLUSION

The Constitution of 1937 is therefore the *de jure* foundation upon which, *inter alia,* the legal system and law is based. That most of the Constitution has not been the subject of litigation is indicative of its largely descriptive nature and also of the traditional perception of law, untouched by a documentary yardstick. We suggest that at least in this latter respect the Constitution will play an increasingly important role in shaping society in Ireland.[62]

Chapter 10*

THE LAW AND INSTITUTIONS OF THE EUROPEAN COMMUNITIES

THE INSTITUTIONS

By the end of the Second World War the economies of most European nations lay in ruins. Six years of war had left its mark not only in human casualties but in economic terms as well. The concept of nationalism, which in its extreme form had led to two world wars, had lost considerable popularity among political scientists and politicians and the concept of internationalism or supra-nationalism was beginning to take its place. The allies had combined successfully in time of war and now there was a growing belief that they could also do so in times of peace. The Treaty of Versailles which concluded the First World War and which led to the economic castration of Germany was a warning against exacting excessive economic retribution from the vanquished by the victors. And yet there remained the need to ensure that Germany would not yet again equip herself secretly for further warmongering. The solution, first proposed by the French Minister Schuman and finally adopted, was the pooling of French and German coal and steel resources (the most crucial of war's raw materials) under joint control. This was achieved through the establishment of the European Coal and Steel Community. In April 1951 France, Germany, Italy, Belgium, Holland and Luxembourg signed a treaty in Paris which brought the community into existence. The Treaty established the following five institutions:

(i) A Special Council of Ministers.
(ii) An Assembly.
(iii) An executive, known as the High Authority.
(iv) A Consultative committee attached to the High Authority.
(v) A Court of Justice.

In the following years various other efforts at broadening the scope of European integration were undertaken. A notable failure in 1954 was the rejection by France of the idea of a European army. This failure led to increased efforts on the economic front and the Treaty of Rome, which established the European Economic Community, was finally signed on 25th March, 1957. The second Rome Treaty, setting up the European Atomic Energy Community, was also signed on that day. Both treaties, which were subsequently ratified by the domestic Parliaments of the original members of the E.C.S.C., became operative on 1st January, 1958. Ireland, Britain and Denmark joined all three communities on 1st January, 1973. Irish accession

**See also 1988 Supplement pp. 327-332.*

was preceded by a national referendum which adopted the necessary Constitutional amendment by an overwhelming majority.

With the exception of the Court of Justice, the Rome treaties provided for similar but separate institutions to govern the E.E.C. and Euratom. Merger of these institutions was finally completed on 1st July, 1967. The following are now the institutions through which each of the communities operates:

(i) The Commission.
(ii) The Council of Ministers.
(iii) The Committee of Permanent Representatives.
(iv) The Parliament.
(v) The Court of Justice.

Though we will examine each organ separately it is important to stress that each organ or institution interacts with the others. The legislative function is divided between the Commission, the Council and, frequently, the Parliament. Disputes between the institutions and Member States (or individuals), or even among the institutions themselves, may be brought before the Court. Thus, there is frequently considerable interaction between all of the institutions. That is not to say of course that the decision-making power is in any way divided equally between them. For example, the role of Parliament is essentially that of a consultative rather than that of a decision-making body. In fact in most instances it is the Council of Ministers (within which national interests are foremost) which has the decision-making power, though this view must be slightly modified in view of the role of the Commission.

The Commission

Formerly known as the High Authority under the E.C.S.C. Treaty, the Commission represents the supra-national dimension of the communities. In a sense it is the civil service of the Community and, like any such service in any state, possesses considerable influence, if not power, with regard to the development of the communities. The Commission consists of a President and 12 commissioners, each of whom is assigned a particular department or section such as agriculture, energy or taxation. But the Commission is a collegiate body with collective responsibility. It is provided by the Treaty that each Member State must have a national on the Commission. In practice the larger members, e.g. Italy, France, Germany and Britain, have two.

A commissioner does not represent his state but rather is he present as an individual representing the European idea. He is not permitted to engage in any other employment during his term of office and must be careful on leaving office not to take up any position inconsistent with his former position as a commissioner.

The powers and functions of the Commission are diverse and various, but some of the more important ones deserve mention. As guardian of the treaties the Commission performs a watch-dog or policing role to ensure that Community law is observed. Acting as an executive body it frames proposals for the Council of Ministers. This is a crucial feature of the Commission since, in most instances, a proposal from the Commission is a prerequisite for Council action. It also plays a representative role representing the communities in legal proceedings and maintaining relations with non-member states and other international organisations.

The Council of Ministers

The Council represents the national aspects of the communities. It is here that national interests are protected and considered. Each State is represented by one minister, usually its foreign minister, though the composition may vary according to the subject matter under examination. Thus in matters of agriculture it will be the ministers of agriculture from the nine Member States who will usually be in attendance. The Council is presided over by a President elected from among the foreign ministers each six months. The office rotates in alphabetical order. At the time of writing Ireland has assumed the Presidency for the second time since accession. We were preceded by France and will be succeeded by Italy.

In order to appreciate fully the powers and functions of the Council it is necessary to understand the relationship between the Council and Commission. The Treaty contemplates a very close relationship between these two organs. A proposal from the Commission is a prerequisite for the Council's action in most cases. The Council may request the Commission to submit a proposal and, in the event of the latter failing to comply, may bring the matter before the Court. Generally speaking the Commission frames proposals concerning Community policy and development which, if acceptable to the member states, are adopted by the Council.

Council decisions are reached by either a simple majority, a qualified majority or a unanimous vote. A simple majority is sufficient only in a handful of relatively less important matters. The greater part of the Council's decision-making powers is exercised by a qualified majority. For this purpose each Member State has been assigned the following number of votes:

France, Germany, Italy and the U.K.:	10 votes each
Belgium and the Netherlands:	5 votes each
Ireland and Denmark:	3 votes each
Luxembourg:	2 votes each
Greece:	5 votes

A vote by qualified majority requires 45 votes from the total of 63 votes available. Accordingly no such majority can be recorded by the 'Big 4' acting alone without the support of at least one of the smaller members. If a measure does not receive the support of at least three of the Big 4, a qualified majority cannot be achieved. In certain cases where the Council is permitted to act on its own initiative (i.e. without a proposal of the Commission) the qualified majority must, to be effective, include six Member States.

In order to relieve a Member State of its obligations under the Treaties, a unanimous vote is necessary.

The Assembly of the European Communities (the European Parliament)
The European Parliament is the only Community organ to which members are directly elected by the peoples of the communities. It consists of 434 members elected from each Member State in the following numbers:

France, Germany, Italy and the U.K.:	81 members each
The Netherlands:	25 members
Belgium and Greece:	24 members each
Denmark:	16 members
Ireland:	15 members
Luxembourg:	6 members

It is important to appreciate that the elected members do not sit at national delegations but organise themselves into groups based on political philosophy and ideologies. The representatives of Ireland are members of such groups as the Socialist Group, the Christian Democrats and the European Progressive Democrats.

Another distinctive feature of the Parliament is that it operates by way of standing committees. There are 14 such committees, each specialising in a particular aspect of Community activity, e.g. Monetary Affairs, Agriculture, Legal Affairs, etc. Accordingly most of a European Parliamentarian's time will be devoted to committee work. Apart from this there are eight plenary sessions involving the entire assembly each year. These sessions are of one week's duration.

Parliament is essentially a deliberative rather than a decision-making forum. For the greater part its functions are confined to consultation where, in certain limited circumstances, Parliament *must* be consulted before action is taken by the Council or the Commission. Members of Parliament may ask questions of the Commission and Parliament may vote the entire Commission (though not an individual commissioner) out of office. Parliament also plays an increasingly important role in the field of budgetary control.

The Court of Justice
Article 164 of the E.E.C. Treaty provides that the role of the Court is to 'ensure that in the interpretation and implementation of [the] Treaty the law is observed'. Advocate-General Lagrange has described the principal functions of the Court as the protection of the rights of individuals against illegal acts of the administrative authorities and the maintenance of the institutional balance and the limits imposed by the Treaty on the powers delegated by it.

The Court is composed of nine judges and four advocates-general. This means that each Member State has a national on the Bench, who holds office for six-year renewable terms. The treaties provide the judges and advocates-general are to be be selected from persons qualified to hold the highest judicial office in their respective Member States. In practice the Irish appointees have been the Chief-Justice and the President of the High Court. The Court is presided over by a President, elected from their number by the judges for renewable terms of three years. In order to facilitate the dispatch of business the Court usually sits in two chambers, each with its own President.

There is no office in our jurisdiction which corresponds precisely with that of advocate-general. Based essentially on the function of the *Commissionaire du Gouvernement* in the French *Conseil d'Etat,* his function is to assist the Court in reaching its decision. To this end he will make reasoned submissions to the Court which will include proposing an appropriate solution to the issue before the Court, having regard to the existing law and its possible implications for future development within the communities. He is an independent officer representing neither individual nor institutional interests.

The jurisdiction of the Court may be divided as follows:

Administrative Jurisdiction: In this capacity the Court deals with actions brought by individual or enterprises against the actions (or inaction) of the Community institutions. In fact the greatest number of actions heard by the Court have been brought by individuals and enterprises regarding the acts or omissions of the former High Authority or the Commission. There are four grounds for such an action:

(i) Legal incompetence (i.e. *ultra vires*): a complaint that the Community organ has acted beyond the limits of its powers.

(ii) Major violation of procedure: a complaint that the organ has failed to adopt an administrative act by the requisite number of votes or has failed to give sufficient reasons for its actions, where required to do so by the treaties.

(iii) An infringement of a Treaty provision: a complaint that a community organ is in breach of a Treaty provision or a secondary source of law, such as a regulation.

(iv) Abuse of power: a complaint that an organ has exercised a power to achieve an end for which the power was not intended or granted.

Constitutional Jurisdiction: In this respect the Court can be seen as the supreme arbiter between the central organs of the communities and the governments of Member States, the guardian of common interests and the guarantor of national prerogatives. It is the function of the court to maintain on the one hand the balance of power between organs of the Community *inter se,* and on the other the balance of power between the Community and Member States. Thus the Court may be viewed as a constitutional court which enforces the separation of powers envisaged by the treaties. A Member

State or the Council may bring an action against the Commission on any one of the grounds mentioned in relation to the administrative jurisdiction. Similarly an action may be brought by a Member State or by the Commission against the Council.

International Jurisdiction: The E.C.S.C. Treaty provides that any dispute between Member States may be brought before the Court. The position under the Rome Treaties is more restrictive. Under the latter a Member State can bring such a dispute before the Court only when it alleges that the other Member State is in breach of a Treaty provision. In addition, such a dispute must first be referred to the Commission for its reasoned opinion. Only after this has been done may proceedings be instituted before the Court.

Civil Jurisdiction: The civil jurisdiction of the Court includes the following matters:

(i) Disputes between the communities' civil servants and the institutions that employ them.

(ii) Actions for damages in tort brought against the communities or individual civil servants.

(iii) The Court's jurisdiction might be provided for in a contract, under private or public law, to which the communities are a party or which is concluded on their behalf.

There are certain other areas which do not fall conveniently into any of these categories but are areas in which the Court exercises jurisdiction. On occasions, for example, the Court acts as a disciplinary tribunal. In this capacity the Court could remove a commissioner or even one of its own judges from office.

Some points concerning procedure before the Court are worthy of attention. Drawing heavily on the civil law tradition, there is far greater attention to the written procedure than one usually finds in a common law jurisdiction. Generally speaking the written stage is usually accusatorial, while the oral proceedings tend to be inquisitorial. Only one judgement is delivered and no dissenting opinions are made public.

ASPECTS OF SUBSTANTIVE LAW OF THE E.E.C.[1]

In order that the reader may gain some impression of how E.E.C. law impinges on Irish life and the economy, we will deal with two of the areas which have been dealt with by Community law, but no attempt is being made to provide an exhaustive study of that ever-growing body of rules. At the outset it is appropriate to note Article 2 of the Treaty, which provides as follows:

> The Community shall have as its task, by establishing a common market and progressively approximating the economic policies of Member States, to promote throughout the Community a harmonious development of economic activities, a continuous and balanced expansion, an increase in stability, an accelerated raising of the standard of living and closer relations between the States belonging to it.

The general terms of this Article make it difficult to conceive of it as having any direct operative effect, but it has been used by the Court (*Walrave & Koch* v. *Assoc. Union Cycliste Internationale,* Case No. 36/74, [1974] E.C.R. 1405) to indicate the matters which may not be subject to Community law.

Article 3 sets out the activities which the Community may engage in for the purposes of Article 2 and, in doing so, it summarises in convenient form the principal areas of Community law. For the sake of completeness the Article is quoted here in full:

> Article 3
>
> For the purposes set out in Article 2, the activities of the Community shall include, as provided in this Treaty and in accordance with the timetable set out therein.
>
> (a) the elimination, as between Member States, of customs duties and of quantitative restrictions on the import and export of goods, and of all other measures having equivalent effect.
>
> (b) the establishment of a common customs tariff and of a common commercial policy towards third countries.
>
> (c) the abolition, as between Member States, of obstacles to freedom of movement of persons, service and capital.
>
> (d) the adoption of a common policy in the sphere of agriculture.
>
> (e) the adoption of a common policy in the sphere of transport.
>
> (f) the institution of a system ensuring that competition in the common market is not distorted.
>
> (g) the application of procedures by which the economic policies of Member States can be coordinated and disequilibria in their balances of payments remedied.
>
> (h) the approximation of the laws of Member States to the extent required for the proper functioning of the common market.

(i) the creation of a European Social Fund in order to improve employment opportunities for workers and to contribute to the raising of their standards of living.

(j) the establishment of a European Investment Bank to facilitate the economic expansion of the Community by opening up fresh resources.

(k) the association of the overseas countries and territories in order to increase trade and to promote jointly economic and social development.

We shall now examine briefly the legal developments in two of these areas, namely, agriculture and the free movement of persons.

Agriculture[2]

The Treaty recognises the importance of agriculture to the Community as a whole and, in a sense, has provided a separate regime for agriculture. This regime is founded on two basic principles. First, it is envisaged by the Treaty that the rules governing agriculture will derogate from the rules which establish the common market (Article 38(2)). Thus Article 42 exempts agriculture from the competition provisions of Articles 85 and 86, while Article 92 which prohibits state aids does not apply to agriculture. Secondly, Article 38(4) provides that the operation and development of the common market for agricultural products must be accompanied by a common agricultural policy. As Professor Lasok so aptly puts it, 'It follows that there is no question of the co-ordination at the Community level of the various national policies but of the one policy for the whole Community'.[3]

The purposes of the common agricultural policy are set out in Article 39(1) as follows:

(a) to increase agricultural productivity by promoting technical progress and by ensuring the national development of agricultural production and the optimum utilization of all factors of production, in particular, labour.

(b) thus to ensure a fair standard of living for the agricultural community, in particular by increasing the individual earnings of persons engaged in agriculture.

(c) to stabilise markets.

(d) to provide certainty of supplies.

(e) to ensure supplies to consumers at reasonable prices.

In order to achieve the aims of the common agricultural policy Member States are obliged under Article 40(2) to adopt a common organisation of agricultural markets. Such markets have now been organised with regard to many products such as cereals, eggs poultry, fruit and vegetables, milk and wine. The first market to be organised was the cereal market and while each market differs from sector to sector, it provides a useful illustration of the manner in which markets in general are organised. The basis of this organisation is *the price system,* which comprises a *target* price, an *intervention* price and a *threshold* price.

The Council of Ministers, acting on a proposal from the Commission, sets the *target price* annually. It is not a fixed price but one which is intended to enable producers to plan their production for the coming year. Real market prices may subsequently exceed, or fail to reach, this target price.

The *intervention price,* which is determined in the same way, is the minimum price which a national government will pay producers who are unable to sell their produce on the market. It is, in essence, a guaranteed price. The intervention price, unlike the case of the target price, is not uniform throughout the Community but will vary from area to area. The *basic* intervention price, however, has been fixed in relation to the market conditions in Duisburg (West Germany), because that area is regarded as having the lowest production of cereals.

Finally, there is a *threshold price* fixed for cereals imported into the Community. In the case of cereals it is determined by deducting from the target price the cost of importing goods into Duisburg through Rotterdam in Holland. Levies are imposed to prevent the influx of foreign products at a price below the desired market price.

Besides the creation of markets, the work of the Community institutions also involves measures for structural improvement and the establishment of the mechanism for the financing of the common agricultural policy and the establishment of rules governing the expenditures borne by it. It has been estimated that more than 90% of all acts of the Community institutions have been concerned with the various aspects of the common agricultural policy.

Free Movement of Persons

Under Article 3(c) *supra,* Member States are bound to abolish obstacles to the free movement of persons, services and capital. Here we will briefly examine the developments with regard to free movement of persons. The position is governed by Articles 48-58.

A distinction is drawn by the Treaty between 'workers' and others. The term 'workers' is not confined to manual or physical labour but comprises all wage-earners and persons employed. Article 48 provides that the freedom to be enjoyed by such workers shall include the following matters:

(a) the abolition of any discrimination based on nationality between workers of Member States as regards employment, remuneration, and other conditions of work and employment.

(b) the right to accept employment in any Member State.

(c) the right to move freely between Member States for the purposes of employment.

(d) the right to remain in a Member State after cessation of employment there.

There are, however, two important qualifications: first, the Article does not apply to employment in the public service; secondly, the freedom of movement is subject to limitations justified on the grounds of public policy, public security or public health. Directive 64/221 provides that measures taken on grounds of public policy or public security cannot serve economic ends and must be based exclusively on the personal conduct of the individual concerned. Moreover previous criminal convictions do not, *in themselves,* constitute grounds for expelling, or refusing to admit a foreign worker.

Finally, Article 51 authorises measures in the area of social security as are necessary to provide freedom of movement for workers. Thus an Italian living in Belgium is entitled to his old age pension in Belgium like any Belgian citizen,[5] and the daughter of a foreign worker in France is entitled to be admitted to an educational course under the same conditions as a French girl.[6]

The importance of these provisions may be judged from the fact that in 1970 it was estimated that there were almost one million E.E.C. nationals who were 'foreign workers' in the Community.[7]

Under the title 'right of establishment', the free movement of persons other than wage-earners is provided for by Articles 52-58. Freedom of establishment includes the right of foreign nationals to take up and pursue activities as self-employed persons and to set up and manage undertakings, in particular, companies and firms, under the conditions laid down for its own nationals by the law of the Member State where such establishment is effected.

Chapter 11*

CRIMINAL LAW

In our introduction the substance of the law was divided into two categories, public and private law. Private law, it will be recalled, is the body of rules affecting individuals *vis-à-vis* each other. Public law, on the other hand, is concerned either with inter-State relations or State and individual interests. In the latter category Constitutional law and criminal law stand to the fore. This chapter is concerned with the prohibitions and restrictions imposed by the State against individuals. Breach of such regulations renders the offender liable to prosecution in the Criminal Courts, as previously described.[1]

The essence of the proceedings is society (in the guise of the State machinery, e.g. the D.P.P. gardai or private individuals) prosecuting a suspected offender and punishing that offender on conviction. This can be directly contrasted with civil proceedings that attempt to preserve the *status quo* and/or compensate individuals for loss suffered. With this concept in mind the law can be considered.

First, a number of elementary points must be appreciated. These principles apply generally to all criminal offences and indicate the extent of criminal responsibility. After this introduction to liability the principal offences will be outlined. They fall into the following categories:

(i) Offences against the person (fatal and non-fatal).
(ii) Offences against property.
(iii) Offences against the State.
(v) Miscellaneous offences.
(vi) Inchoate offences.

PRINCIPLES OF CRIMINAL LIABILITY

Actus reus and Mens rea

As a starting-point the maxim *Actus non facit reum nisi mens sit rea* can be taken. This indicates the nature of liability and, roughly translated, means that the commission of an act will not constitute a criminal offence unless there is criminal intention. Two expressions from the maxim stand out as fundamental to liability, *actus reus* and *mens rea.* The prosecution must show beyond all reasonable doubt that the accused both committed the act or omission in a physical sense and had the intention to commit the same. The former is known as the *actus reus* and the latter the *mens rea.* Unless the law clearly indicates to the contrary, both must exist and coexist. The English case of *Fagan* v. *The Metropolitan Police Commissioner* illustrates the point well.[2]

F drove his car accidentally onto a policeman's foot. By doing so F had

**See also 1988 Supplement pp. 327-332.*

(as will be seen) committed the *actus reus* of battery, i.e. the application of unlawful force. However, at the time of the commission of the act F did not intend to drive onto the policeman's foot. He was asked to drive off but refused. At that moment he was held to have formed the *mens rea* for the offence. The *actus reus* and *mens rea* coincided and F was guilty of the offence charged. Thus when considering whether an offence has been committed (i.e. guilt) one must have regard to the *actus reus* of the offence and the *mens rea* required.

The duty of the prosectuion is to establish both aspects of liability and is, subject to limited exceptions, unequivocable. The burden of proof must be satisfied before an accused need establish a defence or explanation.

The *actus reus* can be briefly dealt with as follows: each criminal offence requires either an act, e.g. hitting, or an omission, e.g. failure to feed a child;[3] certain circumstances must exist at the time of and/or certain consequences must flow from the act or omission. The proof of all these prerequisites must be established to show the existence of the *actus reus.* The example of murder will illustrate the point. Disregarding for the time being the *mens rea* required, the *actus reus* is the unlawful killing, by act or omission, of a human being with death resulting within a year and a day of that act or omission. It can be seen that certain circumstances must exist, that there must be an act or omission that is unlawful and a human being must be subject to the act or omission. Certain consequences must flow, i.e. death of the victim within a year and a day. The total is the *actus reus.* An *actus reus* is required for every offence, including inchoate or incomplete offences.[4] The particular problems with regard to the *actus reus* in individual offences will be examined shortly.

What is meant by *mens rea*? This is known as the criminal intention, but what must be intended for liability to exist? It has been stated helpfully elsewhere that criminal intention can be categorised in three ways.[5] First, there is direct intention. This is where an accused commits the actus reus (or attempts to do so) intending to bring about defined consequences, e.g. the *mens rea* of murder will be satisfied by a person intending to kill. This is the most obvious form of intention. Secondly, there is an oblique intention. This will occur where a person knows that defined consequences are substantially certain to follow, even though they were not necessarily wished by that person. Thus foresight of certainty can amount to intention to satisfy the requirements of *mens rea,* e.g. if A sells B a gun, knowing it is to be used for a murder, A may be guilty of participating in crime even though no harm is wished on the intended victim.[6]

The *mens rea* can also be satisfied where a person commits, or attempts to commit the *actus reus* and is *reckless* as to the consequences. Simply put, this is where a person takes an unjustified risk knowing the nature of the risk, or where that person ought to have known the risk. This is perhaps a watered-down version of oblique intention in so far as foreseeability of harm is concerned. An example should illustrate these distinctions.

A wishes to kill B. A picks up a gun knowing it to contain three bullets in a chamber with a capacity of six. A fires the gun at B and B dies. A can be said to have had direct intention.

A wishes to frighten B. A picks up a gun knowing it to contain three bullets as above. A fires the gun at B and B dies. A can be said to have had oblique intention.

A wishes to frighten B. A picks up a gun not knowing whether it is loaded. A fires the gun at B and B dies. A can be said to have been reckless.

The overlap is considerable and the boundaries difficult to define but on using the above tests of foreseeability, intention can be gauged.

Mention should also be made at this stage of the existence of ulterior intention. This where the *mens rea* comprises of two or more degrees of intention, e.g. burglary. In this offence the *actus reus* is entering premises as a trespasser and carrying out an unlawful act,[7] and the *mens rea* is intending to enter as a trespasser and either at the time of entering or after entering forming an additional intention to carry out an unlawful act.

One addition to the above must be made: according to section 4 of the Criminal Justice Act, 1964, a person is assumed to intend the natural consequences of his or her actions if these actions result in an unlawful killing.

Finally on this point it should be noted that *mens rea,* although generally presumed to be required, need not be present in certain offences. As will be seen these are offences for which either mere negligence or no intention at all can give rise to criminal liability. The latter are known as strict liability offences.[8]

Defences

In understanding the nature of criminal liability the reader must consider the ways in which the law tolerates certain behaviour. These can be broadly described as defences, although some are total and others partial exemptions from liability. The defences fall into four main categories, namely, defences relating to the offender, defences relating to the circumstances and consequences of the offence, defences specifically provided by statute, and special defences relating to particular crimes. The latter category will be discussed when considering the substantive offences. The first two categories are common law in origin.

It is sufficient for the present purpose to list such general defences, with further explanation provided.

Of the defences relating to the offender, the principal ones are as follows:

(i) *The age of the offender:* At common law no liability exists for crimes committed by persons under the age of 7. There is a presumption against a person having mensrea if that person is aged under 14. This is rebuttable. There is an irrebuttable presumption against a male under 14 having the capability of committing an offence involving sexual intercourse.[9]

(ii) *Sex:* Certain offences can only be committed by men, e.g. rape.[10] Likewise, only women can commit particular offences.[11]

(iii) *Automatism:* It is a prerequisite of the actusreas that an act or an omission is voluntary. Where an action is a result of a person's lack of control over physical movements there can be no conviction. It is thought that there are two types of automatism, sane and insane. In the former the person will be acquitted,[12] in the latter the rules appearing below will apply. The defence hinges on the physical voluntariness of the accused's behaviour.

(iv) *Insanity:* This may result in automatism but may also involve negative liability as the person did not realise the nature and quality of the act involved (as opposed to physical incapacity to control movements owing to insanity). Insanity is given a legal definition and is popularly referred to as the rule in the *M'Naghten* case.[13] This case involved an assassination attempt on the life of the English Prime Minister Peel. The accused attempted to assassinate the person he thought was Peel, but in fact levelled a shot at Peel's private secretary. It was held that as the accused did not appreciate the nature and quality of the act owing to a disease of the mind, the accused was insane. The verdict in such cases in the Republic is guilty but insane, and the consequence is that a person is not sentenced but detained in a suitable institution until fit for release.[14] As the detention can be for a greater period than the maximum sentence for the offence in question, it is seldom pleaded. In addition, it is a defence which must be established beyond all reasonable doubt by the accused and therefore there are considerable difficulties of proof.

(v) *Drunkenness:* In days when the criminal law was applied with unmitigated rigour drunkenness, far from being a defence, was often an aggravating feature. Sentences were often increased in severity to reflect this factor. Today, however, drunkenness has a limited effect on criminal liability. If a person is intoxicated by drink or drugs this will only provide a defence if either insanity is caused or if a specific intention is required by the offence and drunkenness prevents this intention being formed. The first instance falls within the common law rules. The second can only be pleaded where the law clearly requires a particular form of intention. For example, the offence of murder requires malice aforethought on the part of the accused and if such a state of mind is not present owing to drunkenness there can be no conviction for this offence. However, there may well be conviction for other offences.[15] Drunkenness, though, will never be an excuse where intoxication was self-induced to provide the accused with the courage to commit the act in question.[16]

However, when considering a person's state of mind drunkenness must be taken into account to see what the person actually intended (subjective).

(vi) *Mistake:* This may negative the mensrea in limited circumstances. The defence is only available for mistake of fact and not law, and will only be tolerated if reasonable.[17] Consequently a mistake by A to practice self-defence, even though no threat was ever in fact involved, may if reasonable, provide a defence. A mistake of law, however, will not affect liability although it may mitigate against sentence.

(vii) *No coincidence of the actus reus or mens rea:* This has been examined before.[18]

(viii) *Lack of intention* for any other reason than is mentioned above. This is a question for the jury and must be examined subjectively, i.e. what did A intend?

The defences relating to the circumstances or consequences of the offence can similarly be listed.

(i) *No satisfaction of the actus reus,* e.g. a person does not die within a year and a day.

(ii) *The accused is forced to commit an offence* by threats of the third party. This is known as *duress* and can only be pleaded where an accused is placed under unlawful pressure by the application of force to that person or to his/her immediate family. The actus reus and mens rea exist, but the behaviour is nevertheless excused. The nature of these threats must place the accused in an unavoidable dilemma. In deciding whether or not duress exists the court must balance the harm threatened with the gravity of the offence committed by the accused. Using such criteria it would appear that no threat of any kind will excuse the commission of a fatal offence.[19]

(iii) *Necessity:* This defence will be available when an accused is placed in an unavoidable dilemma that does not consist of an unlawful threat compelling the commission of a criminal offence. Again the offence and risk must be balanced. Examples of the application of such a defence can be found where the accused pleads self-defence, the accused acts under superior military orders, or the accused acts in prevention of crime. A somewhat gory example shows the limits of such a defence. In *R.* v. *Dudley and Stephens* three people were shipwrecked and were adrift in a small boat. Two of the occupants killed and ate the weaker third. Both were, on rescue, convicted of murder, as necessity was held to be no defence to a fatal charge.[20]

(iv) *Consent of the victim:* It is possible for an accused to plead that the victim of an alleged crime consented to the commission of the actus reus. The law, however, does restrict the ability of a victim to consent where either the victim is under 17 or of unsound mind, or where the harm caused to the victim substantially interferes with that person's health or comfort.[21] However, where appropriate, the defence is an absolute one.

Finally, statute provides a number of specific defences, which can be noted in outline only. The Larceny Act, 1916, the Road Traffic Act, 1961, the Consumer Information Act, 1977, all contain defences to specific offences. Where appropriate these will be noted.

In addition, it should be recalled that the prosecution must establish the actus reus and mens rea *beyond all reasonable* doubt and negative any defences raised similarly. The defendant, where insanity is pleaded, however, must carry the burden and proof.[22]

Statutory Time Limitations of the Prosecution of Offences

In addition to the offences disclosed above the prosecution may, in order to secure conviction, have to commence proceedings within certain statutory time periods. At common law no period of limitation existed during which prosecution had to be brought. Consequently a person could be prosecuted for the commission of an offence at any time after the event. This is still the position with regard to the majority of indictable offences, e.g. murder. The Criminal Law (Amendment) Act, 1935, now provides, however, that offences coming within the scope of the Act must be made subject to prosecution within a 12-month period, commencing on the date of the commission of the offence. Similarly time limits are imposed for certain other offences, e.g. an offence under the Sale of Food and Drugs Act where a prosecution must be brought within 28 days. Summary offences, however, are subject to a time-limitation period, being six months from the date of the commission of the offence. Unless there are exceptional circumstances a prosecution cannot be brought after the lapse of such a period. Finally, under the road traffic legislation a person must be warned at the time of the commission of the offence or within 14 days thereafter of an intention to prosecute. Failure to observe this technicality renders any subsequent prosecution void.

Participation in Crime

As a general principle the criminal law treats as equally responsible all parties related to the commission of the offence, its procurement or its concealment. The person present at the commission of the offence and who causes the actus reus to be committed (either directly or through an innocent agent) is known as the principal in the first degree. Those present who merely assist in the commission of the offence rather than cause the offence to be committed are known as the principals in the second degree. If not present but gave assistance prior to the offence the person is known as an accessory before the fact. Those assisting after the commission of the offence are known as the accessories after the fact. Where felony is committed the principals in the first and second degree and accessory before the fact carry equal responsibility. There is no such distinction in misdemeanours, where all collected parties are treated as principals. There is, however, no accessory after the fact where a misdemeanour is committed. It may also be an offence to otherwise lend assistance to persons committing a criminal offence.[23]

With a basic understanding of such principles of liability the categories of crime previously listed can now be examined in detail.

SUBSTANTIVE OFFENCES

Fatal Offences against the Person

There are two types of fatal offences against the person. First, there is the offence of killing another person. Within this category there are the offences of murder, manslaughter, abortion, infanticide and genocide. Secondly, there is the offence of self-murder or suicide.

Each offence can be considered in turn, listing the requirements of the actus reus and mens rea (if any). Any special defences attaching to the individual crime will be mentioned.

Both murder and manslaughter involve the unlawful killing of a human being, that death occurring within a year and a day of the accused's act or omission. If the commission was accompanied by malice aforethought (intention), then it is murder, if without, the offence is manslaughter. Several problems have been encountered in the criminal courts in relation to this definition. Ignoring for the present the constant difficulty of establishing the requisite intention sufficient for culpability, the courts have had to decide what is an unlawful killing and to what extent an act or omission causes death. Taking the first problem: if A punches B and B dies, A will either be guilty of murder or manslaughter, depending on intention. If A collides with B during a game of football and B dies, then no liability will attach as, *prima facie,* the action was lawful.[24] The second problem, that of causation, requires more detailed explanation. The law says that if the injury inflicted was a substantial cause of death so as to accelerate death, it is sufficient for the actus reus of murder.[25]

If an act occurs to intervene and break this causative chain, liability may be avoided. Cases of this nature have occurred where, for example, medical treatment has been administered and the accused was intolerant to that treatment. Even though such treatment would have been unnecessary except for the injury, there will be no liability on the accused if it was the treatment rather than the injury that killed. However, the cases indicate that the treatment must be palpably wrong before the chain can be broken.

While considering the mens rea it is worth noting that an intention to kill (direct, oblique or reckless) or to inflict grievous bodily harm will suffice for murder. The definition of grievous bodily harm can be found elsewhere.[26]

In addition to the definitions of murder or manslaughter given above, an aggravated form of murder also exists. This is known as *capital* murder.[27] The aggravating circumstances here reflect the identity of the victim. The murder of a member of the Gardai, a prison officer, or Head of State or Government for political motives makes the offence capital and punishable by death. The common law offence of murder carries a mandatory statutory sentence of life imprisonment. The court has a discretion in sentencing a person convicted of manslaughter. The sentence will reflect any mitigating circumstances that exist.

Attempted murder is a statutory offence contained in the Offences Against the Person Act, 1861, and reference to such inchoate crimes will shortly be made.

One special defence exists in this context: if an accused successfully pleads provocation, a charge of murder is reduced to that of manslaughter. Provocation occurs where a person is in some way goaded to take a course of action, e.g. because of taunts, discovery of infidelity, etc. It would now appear that if a person behaved reasonably, i.e. if a person in his or her position (with his or her sensitivities) would have so reacted, then the charge is reduced.[28] Provocation, however, does *not* appear as a defence to any other charge, though it might be a mitigating factor when sentence is considered.

It has been stated that if the act is unlawful in itself but no mens rea exists, the offence of manslaughter will have been committed. Manslaughter may be voluntary or involuntary. The former will occur where the accused intended to kill but has a legal excuse, e.g. provocation. The latter will apply when no mens rea exists. This may occur for a number of reasons. Accidental death from unlawful action provides one instance. Intoxication may provide another where the drunkenness for example prevents the specific intention required for murder being formed.

The other fatal offences can now be mentioned.

Infanticide is the murder of a young child. It is separated from murder in the strict sense in that the law recognises that certain after-effects may exist following the birth of a child that can result in a mental imbalance on the part of the mother. No exact boundaries appear to be set in this context but apparently a killing up to 12 months after the birth has been held to amount to infanticide. The offence is akin to manslaughter and the law is contained in the Infanticide Act, 1949. This offence avoids the necessity of proof and application of the M'Naghten rules.

Abortion is prohibited by section 58 of the Offences Against the Person Act, 1861. The Act deals, as will be seen, with many aspects of Offences Against the Person and is current law despite its age. The offence is procuring a miscarriage. It can be committed by a man and/or a woman. It is an offence to administer any noxious substance or otherwise interfere with the foetus. It is not necessary to secure a conviction against a man, for the woman in fact to be pregnant, but the woman must be pregnant for conviction of herself. In neither case is a miscarriage required. It is also an offence to conceal a dead body, e.g. where the child is stillborn.[29]

The last offence under this category is that of *genocide*. This originated in the United Nations Declaration of 1946 adopted by Convention in 1948. Ireland's law is to be found in the Genocide Act, 1973, which makes it an offence to intend to destroy a national, ethnic, racial or religious group by, for example, killing its members or preventing births. Irish law ratifies the International Convention to which the country is a party.

Finally comes the consideration of self-murder or *suicide*. Two aspects of this must be mentioned. First, killing oneself, and secondly, suicide pacts. If a person commits suicide a felony is committed. Persons privy to a suicide pact or agreement may, if they survive and others die, be guilty of murder. Attempted suicide, however, is only a misdemeanour.

Throughout this section nothing has been said about the identity of the victim. Providing that the actus reus is satisfied in respect of fatal (and non-fatal) offences and the mens rea (if any) exists, an offence will be committed. The identity of the victim is irrelevant providing the actusreas is in every way complete. Thus if A wishing to kill B fired a gun and hit C, who died, A is guilty of murder or manslaughter depending on the mental state of mind. This doctrine is known as *transferred malice* and is equally applicable to the non-fatal offences.[30] These offences can now be examined.

Non-fatal Offences against the Person

There are four categories of non-fatal offence against the person, namely, assaults, sexual offences, offences against children, and a miscellaneous category.

Assault is used here in a generic sense and covers assaults at common law and aggravated versions created by statute. Technically an assault is putting a person in fear of the immediate application of unlawful force to the person.[31] The application may be direct or indirect. The extent of force applied is irrelevant except that if injury results a more serious statutory charge may lay.[32] The actual application of the force is known as a battery, and the threats of the force as an assault. The statutory assaults include both assault and batteries as defined at common law. The principal aggravated batteries are contained in the Offences Against the Person Act, 1861. Section 47 makes it an offence to commit an assault causing actual bodily harm. Section 20 prohibits unlawful wounding or the infliction of grievous bodily harm. The former involves the severing of the skin and the latter amounts to serious harm or injury.[33] Section 18 provides for the most serious of the statutory assaults and consists of a wounding or infliction of grievous bodily harm, coupled with intention to cause grievous bodily harm. The Act also contains a number of other assaults including obstruction of peace officers (e.g. Gardai), administration of noxious substances, and use of traps, firearms and explosives.[34] Thus non-fatal offences against the person consist of a number of offences on a sliding-scale of seriousness.

Two specific defences should be mentioned at this stage, although their application is not exclusively in this domain. All of the above rest on the unlawful nature of the threat or force. If lawful excuse exists no offence will have taken place. For example, a parent, guardian or teacher has the right to exercise a reasonable chastisement of children in their care. A person also has the right to use reasonable force to prevent crime taking place.[35] The latter power is particularly relevant where law-enforcement agencies are concerned.

The relevance of the victim's consent must also be noted. This was referred to in the section concerning general defences. The accused may allege that the victim consented to force applied or threats levied. As previously mentioned, the validity of such a contention is hedged by two limitations. First, a person cannot legally consent to force that substantially interferes with health and comfort, and secondly, a person under 17 or mentally unstable cannot consent.[36]

The law also prohibits certain sexual behaviour that may or may not amount to assault. There is a wide category of such offences to consider. The most significant will be mentioned here.

Rape is unlawful (i.e. extra-marital) sexual intercourse without the consent of the woman. It can by definition only be committed by a man. This offence is particularly problematic in terms of evidence required for a conviction. The circumstances of such behaviour tends to reduce the relevant evidence to a series of contradictory allegations by the man and the woman. The difficulties that this places the victim and the accused in has been noted both judicially and otherwise. One example will indicate such difficulty: in the case of *R.* v. *Morgan* an English court had to deal with the problem of the accused's belief that the woman involved was in fact consenting even though she resisted advances. The court decided that if the accused believed that consent existed (subjective), no offence would be committed. This was later reversed to an objective test by legislation. The Irish courts have yet to decide this point but it is suggested that an objective test should be applied.

A separate but potentially overlapping offence involves unlawful sexual intercourse. This is where intercourse takes place and the victim is under 17 or suffers from mental disability. If the victim is aged 15 to 17 then the offence is one of unlawful sexual intercourse, but cannot be rape if the woman consents. A person under 15 cannot consent and the matter is an aggravated offence known as statutory rape.[37]

The law prohibits the abduction of girls and women for sexual intercourse, marriage or property. Also it is an offence to abduct a person under sixteen from the custody of their parents or guardians.[38]

Any action carried out in circumstances of indecency will amount to an indecent assault (e.g. touching) and applies to both men and women. Likewise it is an offence to indecently expose oneself in public view or to behave obscenely. Gross indecency between males is also prohibited. The majority of these offences are contained in the Criminal Law Amendment Act, 1935.

It must be appreciated that of all of the substantive offences at criminal law the sexual offences perhaps come closest to the relationship between law and morality. The remainder of the sexual offences certainly fall within this category.

Buggery is an offence consisting of sexual intercourse *per anum* between a man and a woman, or a man and a man, or *per anum* or *per vaginum* between a man, a woman and an animal. Thus consenting homosexual males will be guilty of buggery. This might be contrasted with the more tolerant legislation of the United Kingdom. The prohibition is found in section 61 of the 1861 Act.

Contraceptives: The Health (Family Planning) Act, 1979, now governs the importation and sale of contraceptives,[39] prohibited until then.

Bigamy is the attempt by a married person to enter into a second or further marriage while the first marriage validly exists. It is therefore an offence to 'marry' twice. Complicated provisions exist to regulate the recognition of foreign divorces, etc., in order to facilitate further lawful marriage. This is mentioned elsewhere.[40]

The law also prohibits sexual intercourse between persons within certain degrees of consanguinity (that is blood relations). It is an offence for sexual intercourse to take place between father and daughter, mother and son, etc. The offence is known as *incest.*

The last of the sexual offences to be discussed here relates to the activities of prostitutes. It is an offence to solicit in public, to keep a brothel or for a man to live off immoral earnings. It is no offence, however, to practice as a prostitute providing that the above regulations are not breached.

In addition, offences also exist to *protect children.* Again there is considerable overlap with matters above mentioned. In addition to assaults and sexual offences it is an offence at common law to wilfully neglect a child where a person is entrusted with a care of that child. It is also an offence under the Children's Act, 1908 (as amended), to practice cruelty in respect of children.

Of the miscellaneous *non-fatal offences against the person* mention can be made in pssing only of the common law offence of kidnapping (stealing and carrying away), false imprisonment, and child stealing, which may or may not involve the commission of previously mentioned offences.

Offences against Property

This third category of criminal offence can be divided into three. First, offences of dishonesty can be mentioned. These will be generally referred to as offences of larceny. Secondly, malicious damage to property can be examined, and thirdly, the offence of forgery will be mentioned.

Larceny in its simple form involves the taking of peoperty belonging to another without the consent of the owner and with the intention of permanently depriving that person of the property. The law is to be found in the Larceny Act, 1916, and subsequent cases. By comparison much of the law in the United Kingdom on larceny has been codified by the 1968 Theft Act.

Taking involves a change of possession and can be obtained directly or indirectly. The former would occur where, for example, A removes a book from B's possession, and the latter where A practises a trick, false pretence, intimidation or induces a mistake so as B parts with possession 'voluntarily'.

The goods must be capable of being stolen and, simply put, this includes all property with the exception of land and things attached to the land.[41]

The goods must in addition be carried away, i.e. physically moved by the accused. The extent of the removal is irrelevant.

The goods also must be owned at the time of the larceny. Consequently, abandoned goods cannot be stolen.[42]

The intention to permanently deprive the owner must also coexist with the actus reus. This can occur at the time of the gaining of possession or later. For example, larceny will be committed if A is given change for a £5 note when in fact a £1 note was tendered. Although no offence is committed at the time of possession changing hands, larceny occurs at the time of the failure to disclose the mistake when the taking and mens rea will coincide.

Some very difficult points exist in the law, however, where a person is given a *prima facie* lawful title. If, for example, A goes into a restaurant, eats a meal and leaves without paying, a conviction would not follow unless some trick of false pretence was practised, or the effect of the action is to obtain credit by fraud.[43]

In addition to this concept of 'simple' larceny certain forms of aggravated larceny also exist. The significance of this distinction lies, as might be expected, in severity of sentence. The aggravation can be because of the nature of the property (e.g. cattle, State secrets), or the manner in which the property is stolen (e.g. by force), or the place where the goods are stolen (e.g. residential premises), or the nature of the person stealing the property (e.g. a tenant). The most important of these aggravating features are in robbery, burglary and blackmail. Robbery is provided for in section 23 of the Larceny Act as amended by the Criminal law (Jurisdiction) Act, 1976. The essence of the offence is larceny coupled with an assault or battery. Further aggravations can occur where the robbery is carried out with firearms or explosives. Section 23a of the Larceny Act (as amended) creates the offence of burglary. This is committed where a person enters a building as a trespasser either with the intention to steal, cause grievous bodily harm, rape, or cause criminal damage, or after entering as a trespasser forms the intention to steal or inflict grievous bodily harm or attempt such. The offence is again further aggravated where the accused possesses a weapon. It should be noted that this offence includes two aspects of the mensrea, an intention to enter as a trespasser, with the ulterior intention of stealing, etc.

Embezzlement, false accounting and fraudulent conversion are all also included within the broad definition of larceny.[44]

Section 29 of the Larceny Act applies to the extortion of property by menaces, or as it is more popularly known, blackmail. This involves the demanding of property coupled with menaces, i.e. the unlawful application of a threat or other pressure.[45]

The final offence to be considered under the heading of larceny involves an association with property subject to larceny. This is known as receiving or handling stolen property. Section 33 of the Larceny Act prohibits such activity. A number of elements must exist, namely, the accused must have taken goods into possession, the goods must have been stolen and the accused must know of such (subjective). The last element can be satisfied by reference, however, to the accused's prior history of receiving stolen property.

Malicious Damage: The second aspect of offences relating to property, covers damage or destruction. The law is to be found in the Malicious Damage Act, 1861. The offences under this Act involve the damage of any property, both real and personal. Any deliberate act will be sufficient for conviction providing that it can be established that the accused intended to cause such damage or was reckless as to whether the damage occurred.[46] For example, if A throws a punch at B, B avoids the blow and A breaks a window, A will not be guilty of malicious damage unless intention can be shown in relation to the property. There may, however, be an assault. At common law one type of damage was considered to be more serious than any other, that of arson. This involves the burning of a dwelling house. The common law offence has now been supplemented by the Malicious Damage Act, 1861. This extends arson to non-residential property. It is apparently no offence to burn one's own property unless there is an additional intention to injure or defraud. Today arson is one type of criminal damage.

It is convenient at this stage to mention the offences created by the Prohibition of Forcible Entry and Occupation Act, 1971, that, *inter alia,* creates an offence to forcibly enter property (or a vehicle) or remain on property once told to leave.

The last offence against property to be looked at in this section is that of *forgery.* The law has been consolidated in the Forgery Act, 1913, and covers the creation of a false document for use as the genuine article. Document here includes both seals and dies, as well as written manuscript. To amount to a forgery the document must not only tell a lie but must also tell a lie about itself.[47] The fact that a document discloses false material will not make it a forgery unless it purports to be an original document. The intention for this offence is satisfied if an intention to deceive exists, should the document be of a public nature. Where the document is of a private nature fraud must be shown. Fraud involves deceit coupled with deprivation. Additional offences may also exist with regard to the forging of public and other documents.[48]

Offences Against the State

This broad category includes what might be described as 'political' offences, public order offences and offences against the administration of justice. The first category of offences involves direct violations of State interests. Treason, historically, has occupied a peculiar position at common law. It is viewed as the most serious crime one can commit against the State, and as it is ostensibly an offence against the people as well as the State machine. It has been treated as a special offence. The present law is contained in the Constitution of 1937, Article 39, as expanded by the Treason Act, 1939. It is an offence for a person to levy war against the State or assist in the levying of such war. The offence applies to all persons within the State or Irish citizens and persons normally resident in the State who commit treasonable acts beyond the State boundaries. The penalty is death.

Offences against the State are also created under the Offences Against the State Act, 1939 and the Official Secrets Act, 1963. The latter deals with betrayal of State secrets and applies to the publishing or possession of information prejudicial to the State.

The 1939 legislation, as amended, extends to prohibit:

(i) Usurption of functions of Government, e.g. setting up a non-constitutional Government body. This offence may also amount to treason.[49]

(ii) The obstruction of the Government, i.e. the prevention of the Government from carrying out their lawful function.[50]

(iii) Obstruction of the President – this includes any interference with the President's powers and duties.[51]

(iv) Unlawful interference with the military, police or State employees.[52]

(v) The promotion of secret societies in the military or police.[53]

(vi) Carrying out any unauthorised military exercise, including drilling, training, etc.[54]

(vii) Administering or taking unlawful oaths.[55]

(viii) Membership of any unlawful organisation, including organisations that are treasonable, anti-constitutional, criminal or otherwise illegal.[56]

The second aspect of offences against the State consists of offences against public order. The following offences can be briefly noted:

(i) *Sedition:* This is concerned with publication or uttering of material or words intended and likely to cause public disorder. This is an indictable offence at common law and is also contained in sections 10 – 12 of the Offences Against the State Act, 1939, and Article 6.1(1) of the Constitution.

(ii) *The unlawful seizure of vehicles:* This is prohibited by the Criminal Law (Jurisdiction) Act, 1976. It is an offence to seize with force a vehicle including motor vehicles, boats, trains and aircraft. The force may be directed against either the vehicle, the owner or occupier. The offence is popularly termed 'hijacking'.

(iii) *Unlawful assembly:* An offence will only be committed if three or more persons meet together with the intention of carrying out a purpose likely to involve violence or cause a reasonable person to fear the application of violence. Once the meeting to carry out such plans takes place this is known as a rout and once the violence is applied the situation is called a riot. The offence can be found in the collective activities of the persons concerned. Individual liability may often exist for the previously described offences against property and people. An associated offence of an affray may also exist in this context, and consists of the fighting of two or more persons in public where such is potentially frightening to reasonable people.

(iv) *Unlawful public meetings:* Meetings which are held in support of unlawful organisation will in themselves be unlawful. In addition, any meeting may be rendered unlawful by an officer of the Garda Siochana not below the rank of Chief Superintendent serving the appropriate notice. The law is contained in section 27 of the Offence Against the State Act (as amended). In addition, meetings likely to influence a person in authority may be unlawful, e.g. a protest meeting levelled at a Government minister. In all of these cases one must bear in mind Article 40 and the fundamental rights preserved by the Constitution and the validity of legislation that restricts such rights. This is enlarged upon in Chapter 9.

At common law offences against public order can also be found under the antiquated names of forcible entry and detainer, challenge to fight and creation of a public nuisance. Such are generally termed breaches of the peace and as such are offences which attract arrest without a warrant.

The third category of offences against the State consists of behaviour that is aimed at interfering with or disrupting the administration of justice. Any court in Ireland has the inherent power to deal with persons who stand in contempt of that court. Failure to obey a court order, or disrespect in face of the court, are two instances where contempt can occur. Theoretically a person can be jailed until repentant. Contempt can be viewed in two ways. If the action is intended to interfere with the administration of justice, it will itself be an offence (misdemeanour at common law). Also, however, the court may imprison for contempt if the person concerned is otherwise disrespectful, e.g. failure to comply with court order. This does not in itself involve an offence but rather brings the inherent powers of the court to bear upon that person in a quasi-criminal way.

In addition, a number of statutory and common law offences also exist in relation to the administration of justice and these can be enumerated.

(i) *Perjury:* This is a false statement made on oath, either orally or in writing, made deliberately by a person who does not believe the statement to be true or who is ignorant as to its truth. This prohibition affects, for example, witnesses at a court hearing, and parties who swear document on oath.

(ii) *Escape from lawful custody:* This is a common law offence. If force is used during such attempt the offence becomes an aggravated offence of prison breaking. If a person is rescued from lawful custody the rescuer commits an offence akin to prison breaking. In addition, any person aiding or abetting an escape from lawful custody commits an indictable offence.

(iii) *Perverting the course of justice:* This involves any behaviour aimed at interfering with the judicial process, e.g. destroying evidence, and is akin to creating public mischief, which is also a common law offence.

(iv) *Miscellaneous categories* of offences relating to the administration of justice exist. It is sufficient to note these offences by name only. These include frivolous arrest, public corruption, taking or offering a bribe, embracey (undue influence of juries), and champery and maintenance (interference with third parties in court actions, e.g. providing funds for action, or a person agreeing to share judgement damages by way of contract).

Offences of Strict Liability and Negligence

It is a general proposition of law that mens rea is required in addition to the actus reus for conviction in any criminal matter. Two categories of offences do not require mens rea, namely, offences of negligence and strict liability. Strict liability offences are absolute offences in so far as the intention is irrelevant. However, certain defences may exist in relation to the actus reus. Negligence in certain instances can be enough, coupled with the actus reus, to convict, where the law imposes a duty on a person to behave reasonably (objective). Some examples, provided by the motorist, should make this clear. To drive without due care and attention is an offence and amounts to negligence, i.e. not behaving as a reasonable driver would.[57] To park in a prohibited place (e.g. on double yellow lines) would be an offence of strict liability where intention is irrelevant. A defence, however, might be raised in relation to the actus reus, e.g. an emergency (necessity). These offences are either offences of a trivial nature, or behaviour that it is in the public interest to prohibit regardless of intention. Another example of prohibition of this nature includes the regulations regarding the sale of food and drink. The intention of the person dispensing drink in circumstances of contamination is irrelevant. The law in fact goes one stage further here and holds employers liable for criminal acts of employees in such circumstances. This is akin to the principle of vicarious liability as encountered in tort. Thus if a barman dispenses drinks outside of licensing hours the proprietor of the premises can be held guilty as well as the barman for breaches of the licensing regulations.

Miscellaneous Offences

Many offences that exist under the Irish criminal law do not conveniently fit into the above categories. The following are the most important:

(i) *Firearms and explosives:* A number of serious offences exist, mainly statutory, regulating the possession and use of firearms, explosives and other dangerous weapons or equipment. The Firearms Acts, 1925/64, as amended by the Criminal Law (Jurisdiction) Act, 1976, provide the bulk of the law. It is an offence to possess a firearm and if such is possessed with the intention to endanger life or cause damage to property the offence appears in an aggravated form. Certain firearms, however, can be lawfully possessed with the requisite licence. The use of a firearm or possession in certain circumstances may create additional offences, e.g. burglary or robbery.

The control and possession of explosives is similarly prohibited by the Malicious Damage Act, 1861, the Explosive Substances Act, 1883, and the Criminal Law (Jurisdiction) Act, 1976. Again the use of explosives may render the accused liable to prosecution for additional and aggravated offences.

(ii) *Misuse of drugs:* The apparent seriousness of the offences contained in the misuse of drugs legislation cannot be overemphasised. The fact that the relevant legislation creates maximum penalties often far in excess of penalties for offences against persons and property renders the topic of great importance, even though the number of prosecutions are limited. The law is now to be found in the Misuse of Drugs Act, 1977. This Act creates classes of controlled drugs. The possession, manufacture or sale of such drugs is an offence. Sentence varies with the degree of involvement and class of drug concerned.

(iii) *Offences against the environment:* This is an area of increasing importance covering not only the seemingly minor offence of littering but the pollution of rivers, seas and the air by both industry and transport. The offences are mainly statutory and many are offences of strict liability.

(iv) *Economic offences:* Again this is an area of growing importance in our developing and credit-conscious country. Offences here relate to international money dealings, consumer protection and customs and excise control. Also, counterfeiting currency is an offence.[58]

(v) *Offences against the motorist:* It has been mentioned elsewhere that the motorist is liable to prosectuion for a number of offences, many of which do not require proof of mens rea. Negligence and strict liability can inculpate the accused.

(vi) *Offences and the working environment:* The Factories Act, 1955, and its amendments have introduced a number of criminal and civil prohibitions in relation to the working environment. One example that can be given here is the legal obligation under the criminal law for employers to provide safeguards when employees have to handle dangerous machinery. A factory inspectorate is charged with the duty of enforcing such important provisions, although prosecutions seem few.

(vii) *Criminal libel and blasphemous material:* It is an offence at criminal law to defame a person occupying an official office, e.g. the clergy or Government ministers, or to defame an institution, e.g. the Church. The rules here are similar to the tortious requirement, that there must be a publication. In addition it is also an offence to produce material that is offensive concerning God or religion generally.

(viii) *Licensing regulations:* The sale of alcohol, tobacco and other restricted substances is subject to a number of regulations, again mainly strict liability in nature concerning the place, hours and method of sale.

Inchoate Offences

Where an offence is in some way incomplete it is said to be inchoate. Commission of an inchoate offence generally renders the accused guilty of a crime for which the penalty is the same as if the crime envisaged had been committed. It is of course a crime in itself to commit the inchoate offence. There are three types of such offence: first, attempts, secondly, conspiracy and thirdly, incitement.

To *attempt* a crime renders a person liable to the same punishment as if the crime had been completed.[59] Attempts must be as sufficiently proximate to the act as to render the accused guilty. Otherwise the same requirements in terms of the actus reus and mens rea must exist. Attempts, however, may be made where it is not possible to commit the envisaged offence. If an attempt is absolutely impossible there can be no conviction, e.g. if A puts powder in B's drink in an attempt to kill B and the powder is not poisonous, A will not be guilty of attempted murder. However, if A puts an insufficient amount of poison in drink intended for B he may be guilty of attempted murder as this was only relatively 'impossible'. If the offence is legally impossible, e.g. attempting to handle stolen property and goods, and the goods are not stolen, no offence will apply.[60] This has created some difficulty in relation to attempted larceny committed by the popularly termed 'pickpocket'.[61]

A *conspiracy* is an agreement between two or more persons to commit an unlawful act. That act may be a crime or a breach of civil law, e.g. tort, or in some other way outrageous to public decency. The offence is in the agreement itself, but the agreement must involve an unlawful act.[62] Certain protection exists here, however, for members and officials of trade unions holding negotiating licence under the Trade Union Act, 1941, and who are acting in contemplation or furtherance of a trade dispute.[63]

Incitement is the encouragement of others to commit a crime and, regardless of the commission of the offence, is an offence in itself.

CONCLUSION

In this chapter we have described first, the basis of criminal liability, and secondly, the main characteristics of the principal substantive offences. Any commentary upon the criminal law in Ireland would be incomplete without emphasising the nature of the criminal law. It is an area of public law in the sense that the State prohibits, throughout the country, certain behaviour. In addition, delegated powers may be granted to bodies to introduce supplementary regulations establishing criminal liability, e.g. local authority by-laws. The aim of the criminal law in this public sense is to preserve life and liberty, private property and State machinery. This can be contrasted with the civil law that traditionally preserves individual rights *vis-à-vis* other individuals. There is, however, an increasing volume of law that is concerned with State interests. The point is well illustrated by the recent legislation affecting the commission of offences in extra-territorial jurisdictions.[64]

The structure of the criminal law courts, the process and jurisdiction of these courts, and the principal rules of evidence and procedure can be found in chapters 5 and 7.

Chapter 12*

THE LAW OF CONTRACT

INTRODUCTION

Nowhere in the Irish law are the principles of legal study more clearly applied than in the law of contract. As such, therefore, the law of contract provides ideal material for the reader to test his or her knowledge of the law as it works. In addition, contract law is concerned with particular rules appertaining to *legally enforceable* agreements, and the law therefore involves substantive rules. The following chapter illustrates the operation of Irish contract law, as well as explaining the details of that body of regulations.

Contract law is found in a variety of sources, both *common law* and *statutory*, and the reader must rely on knowledge of legal method to comprehend the principles involved.

Furthermore, the law of contract clearly underpins basic social values. In Ireland this is particularly pertinent, for the Constitution in Article 43 declares that:

> The State acknowledges that man . . . has the natural right, antecedent to positive law, to the private ownership of external goods . . . . [and further] The State accordingly guarantees to pass no law attempting to abolish the right of private ownership, or the general right to transfer, bequeath and inherit property.[1]

The law of contract relies entirely on the presumption of the 'right' to own and dispose of private property, otherwise it would be meaningless. The use of the term 'property' is here used in a generic sense, i.e. in reference to goods and services.

The history of contract has been briefly alluded to. Initially the law only enabled agreements that were made under *seal* to be enforced but through writs that related to debt and wrongful detention of property, and with the use of writs on the *case* (assumpsit), the law recognised by the 16th century a general law of *agreement*. Under this, broken promises could be enforced. Despite increased legislative interference it is this law that is still enforced today. As will be seen, a distinction is still made between contracts made under seal and otherwise.

Given the contract's base in the preservation of private property, on what principles does the contract work? Three words adequately summarise the answer to this question: *sanctity, privity* and *objectivity*.

The law will (all other matters satisfactorily existing) enforce the contract in accordance with the agreed terms. That such terms might be unfair, unreasonable or inadvisable is theoretically irrelevant. One can point to the maxim *caveat emptor*. This means 'let the buyer beware', or more generally put, the parties to an agreement must, as it were, look before they leap.

See also 1988 Supplement pp. 327-332.*

Interrelated with this concept is the vital principle of privity. The law will only enforce the agreed terms as between the agreeing parties. Thus if a third party attempts to enforce a contract, the courts will not entertain such a claim, on the basis that the party concerned was not *privy* to the agreement. Confusion has been caused in the past when subjects of a contract have tried to sue for breaches of an agreement. The courts have only been willing to entertain such an application if the plaintiff was involved in the agreement (rather than merely in its terms). An example can best illustrate the point:

A agrees with B that for £5 A will mend C's car. If B pays A the £5 and A does not mend C's car, C is not privy to the contract and cannot legally complain. B would be the only party with the *locus standi* to sue A.

The concept of privity has been litigated on many occasions, with widespread practical as well as academic debate. Certain exceptions also exist to this rule including the relationship of trustee and beneficiary, the assignment of contractual rights and obligations, and the principle of agency.[2]

Although the courts will only enforce agreements as between the contracting parties and in accordance with the terms of that agreement, it is often the task of the court to decide what those terms are. In the absence of more explicit evidence the courts have adopted an objective standpoint and will hold agreed that which would reasonably appear to have been agreed. This is not to be confused with reasonable terms. The courts try to understand, using this test, what the parties agreed between themselves. An example of this approach occurred in the case of *Sullivan* v. *Constable*[3] where the last act in the chain of events was deemed to reasonably indicate the intention of the parties.

Thus a contract is enforced in terms of the actual agreement (as perceived by the court) and only between the agreeing parties.

The following pages deal with the law by considering, firstly, the elements of an enforceable contract, i.e. whether there is sufficient information about the agreement for the courts to enforce. Here one needs to know the identity of the parties, whether they actually reached agreement, whether they gave consideration for the agreement and whether they intended to be bound by it.

Secondly, the interpretation of the content or terms of the contract will be considered, and thirdly, factors that occur after a *prima facie* contract has been agreed that invalidate the contract will be examined.

Next, the termination of the contract must be regarded, i.e. how does contractual liability end? Finally, the remedies available if a breach of contract occurs will be noted.

From the above it will be seen that the passage of the contract from formation to determination will be followed.

In a word, the parties to a potential contract must *negotiate.* This can take the simple and mundane form of buying a loaf of bread or a pint of beer, or can be a highly complex transaction. The essence of both in terms of a contract is the agreement. In order to make such an agreement there must be an offer and an acceptance. The former can be made subject to a number of conditions and qualifications but the latter must be unequivocable.

The law has been called upon to draw sometimes highly technical distinctions between the two terms, and a host of other pre-contractual negotiations. Simply put, an offer is a proposition capable of unconditional acceptance. The acceptance is a complete concurrence with the terms of the offer. As the definitions are self-reliant, an example might render this more apparent:

A wishes to sell his car for £200. He places an advertisement in the local paper. B reads the advert and writes to A offering to pay £150. A telephones B and agrees to sell for £150. The transaction is then completed.

These facts give rise to a number of developments of legal significance in terms of the technicalities of agreement. It is of vital importance to define each stage of the process as only an offer is *capable* of being accepted, and only an acceptance will complete the agreement, i.e. form the basis of the contract. The offer, therefore, regardless of any conditions contained within it, must be capable of being accepted and must be something more than a mere statement during the negotiation. Consequently an offer can only be made in a form that can be legally accepted.

One must here distinguish between offers and gifts, offers and mere negotiations and, more particularly, offers and *invitations to treat.* The latter term has been subject to much litigation and is an example of the process of pre-contractual negotiation. The point can be clearly illustrated by the case of *Pharmaceutical Society* v. *Boots.*[4] This dispute involved the sale of drugs. Under the law qualified supervision was required in the sale of certain products. The legal argument hinged on whether at the time of selection of the goods by the customer there was a sale (i.e. a contract). If so the retailers were in breach of their supervisory requirements. It was held that the display of goods was only an invitation to treat and as such could not be accepted (by picking the goods off the shelf). The selection by the customer was the offer and this could be accepted by the retailer at the cash desk. Similarly advertisements are normally held to be invitations to treat.

It is also important to consider to whom the offer is made (i.e. defining who can accept), how the offer is made and when the offer ends. As general propositions, it can be said that the offer must be communicated to the relevant party, it can be made to one or more individuals or to the whole world, depending on the context,[5] and it will end either when withdrawn by the offeror or when accepted. It can be made either orally or in writing or by conduct. It may also contain certain conditions which if accepted may form part of the contract.

Once a valid offer has been made it is capable of being accepted, and the acceptance, too, is covered by technical legal rules and definitions. Three propositions of law govern the style of, and effect of, this other aspect of the agreement. First, the acceptance must be unconditional, i.e. being in total agreement with the offer. Secondly, the acceptance can be in any form, except for imposed silence,[6] unless a specific form of acceptance is mentioned in the offer. Finally, the acceptance is only generally valid when communicated to the offeror. This is subject to one important practical exception known as the postal rule, which says the acceptance is valid once a letter containing the affirmation is posted rather than received.[7]

Any attempt to renegotiate an offer will not amount to an acceptance but will, probably, be a counter-offer, itself being capable of acceptance.

In addition to the mechanics of agreement, however, it is also necessary to satisfy other requirements before a valid contract will exist. As part of the agreement the terms of the contract must be sufficiently clear.[8] The court is not concerned at this stage with the actual construction of the terms, but rather that the parties have in fact agreed terms sufficiently obvious to be enforced. Until this takes place there can be no contract. Thus the subject-matter of the contract, the quantity and quality of the subject, the price and details of delivery, etc., might be required to be specified. Once the courts hold such are sufficiently stated, then the contract (other things existing) is viable. The ascertaining of such terms can be gleaned from the express agreement (written or oral) or from the parties' conduct both past and present, as, for example, in the case of previous dealings between them.[9]

A further essential element required before a contract can legally exist is that the parties must have intended to create a legally binding transaction. This point may seem to the reader to be stressing the obvious, but the courts have clearly indicated a distinction between purported contracts negotiated by parties in a commercial sense and other situations where, say, a more domestic relationship has been involved. The courts have tended to operate a presumption that the parties do intend to be bound by their dealings (re-inforcing the doctrine of sanctity and privity of contract) unless there is a special relationship between them such as family ties, or a position of trust and reliance. This would appear to be a matter of public policy, not to wish to enforce a contract in such relationships. Consequently the courts have often refused to enforce contracts between husband and wife, even though each has the capacity to contract, unless they are in some way estranged, e.g. separated or divorced.[10] The connection between the supposed contracting parties is therefore of importance. The decision of the courts in fact goes far beyond this domestic definition. In this area of labour law there is a common law presumption that there is no intention to be bound by negotiations appertaining to a contract of employment.[11]

In enforcing these legal provisions, however, the courts have been able to resort to other devices in order to attach a civil liability to the parties, especially in the domain of equity, i.e. the use of the trust.[12]

Two other essential elements remain to be examined. First, to create an enforceable contract *consideration* must be given, and secondly, the law may require the contract to be in a particular form.

Consideration is required for all enforceable contracts, except those under seal. The topic of consideration is both complex and abstract, and has given the judiciary as well as students many problems. Simply put, consideration is the *value* given by the parties in respect of the contract. Difficulties arise, however, in defining both the nature of such value and who must give it.

The questions here are perhaps best answered with reference to the *types* of consideration that can exist. There are three types of consideration, all of which are subject to two rules. The consideration may be *executory, executed* or *past.* These terms will be examined shortly. In any event, to amount to a valid (that is legally effective) consideration it must firstly 'move' from the person wishing to enforce the contract, and secondly must be of *sufficient* value. The first rule means that if a plaintiff is attempting to enforce a contract he or she must show, *inter alia,* that a value was given. The most common example would be either money or goods/services changing hands, but the essence of the requirement is that the person either gives a benefit or suffers a detriment. Usually the advantage of this will pass to the other contracting party, but this is not legally required. The second stipulation is that the benefit given, or detriment suffered, must have a value known to the law. Providing it does have such a value the law is not concerned, in the absence of fraud etc., that the value is a reasonable or market one. This endorses the law's preservation of sanctity of contract. Thus, for example, a payment of £10 for a Rolls-Royce motor car will be good consideration.

If the consideration is given in the form of a promise to do something in the future, it is known as executory. If it is in the form of an act actually carried out, it is executed. In either case it must relate to the terms already agreed between the parties. If the act is done before such agreement it is not good consideration. It will be known as *past,* or invalid consideration. The only exception to this proposition is that past consideration may be acceptable in contractual terms if carried out on the tacit understanding that an agreement existed, e.g. if previous dealings had been so handled.[13]

It must be remembered that consideration is required if a contract is to be enforced by the courts, but a lack of such will not render in any sense unlawful the purported agreement. Many 'contracts' are adhered to that would not be capable of enforcement if issue was taken.

In either of the instances discussed above the concept of the giving of consideration involves the imparting of benefit, for example money, or the suffering of a detriment, for example declining to sue some person, where the other contracting party had no right to demand such. Problems have arisen in the past on this very point. Take, for example, the following facts:

A and B enter into a contract to sell and buy respectively a motor bike.

It is beyond dispute that all the formalities of an initial contract exist, that is to say A offered to sell, B accepted, both intend to be bound by the transaction, the terms are clear and good consideration has been given. The consideration may have been the transfer of the vehicle and the promise of £100 (A and B's consideration respectively). Notwithstanding that B has not yet paid the money, the consideration is legally sufficient (executory). If B falls on hard times and is only able to pay £60 on the agreed date, then legally B is indebted to A for the balance. Supposing A says that he will accept £60 if paid the next day and B manages to raise this sum, can A then go back on this secondary agreement and sue B for the balance?

The simple answer to this question would be 'yes', although some qualification is required. On the facts A was entitled to £100, this sum being the amount agreed between them. By paying a lesser sum B has given consideration to any additional agreement over and above the contract, i.e. to buy and sell the bike for £100. B was already indebted on making the contract to A to the extent of £100. Consequently any contract whether, as in this case, in its original form, or whether altered or added, must be backed by fresh consideration to be enforceable. This common law principle has been long established by the case of *Foakes* v. *Beer.*[14] In these cases the party in A's position can effectively go back on this promise to accept less because of the lack of consideration on B's part for this new agreement.

When therefore a contract has already been formed (with valid consideration etc.) and an additional agreement is entered into, when can this additional agreement be enforced? Clearly this secondary 'contract' can be enforced, even if it gives less than the first, if extra consideration is given. For example, if B had given A £60 and a bottle of champagne, then the agreement would stand, because A *had* received something not originating in the first contract, i.e. the champagne. One other exception to the common law rule also exists. This is known as *promissory estoppel.*

The reader will recall from the historical introduction to this text that a body of the law has arisen to mitigate against the inadequacies of the common law, that of equity. Estoppel is an equitable principle that effectively bars a person from denying the truth of a promise or statement previously made.

In this context it can be applied to the example of A's promise to accept less than contractually entitled. Under limited circumstances equity will provide a defence to B if B is later sued for the balance of the monies. This will be allowed if a promise is made that it was, on the facts, intended to be binding and it was acted upon by the other party (the one to whom the promise was made). Thus if the courts consider it, for these reasons, inequitable for A to sue B for the balance, a defence in the form of estoppel will prevent A's claim. The law here has been substantially litigated in England in the famous case of *High Trees* v. *Central Property.*[15] Needless to say in preservation of the sanctity of contract and its common law origins, estoppel is of very limited though significant application.

Finally it falls to consider the *form* of the contract. Generally speaking a contract can be made orally, in writing or by conduct or in any combination of the three. As a matter of practice the more substantial pecuniary transactions tend to be recorded in the written form. The law does, however, prescribe a required form in limited circumstances. These rules are principally to be found in the Statute of Frauds (Ireland), 1695.

This ancient piece of legislation was, as the name suggests, introduced to eliminate the potential for defrauding persons in commercial transactions. The requirements of the Act are to render *unenforceable* contracts of particular kinds unless they are evidenced by writing.[16] The contract itself need not be, but often is, in writing, but to be enforceable a memorandum of evidence of the contract must exist. This could be in the form of, for example, a letter. The contracts affected are as follows:

(i) Contracts by personal representatives to pay a deceased's debts.
(ii) Contracts of Guarantee.
(iii) Contracts and Consideration of Marriage.
(iv) Contracts to be performed more than 12 months after the agreement.
(v) Contracts for the sale of interests in land.
(vi) Contracts for the sale of goods worth more than £10.

In addition, the contract may be affected by the specific legislation covering that particular transaction, e.g. hire purchase agreement.

Therefore in order to have a legally enforceable contract five elements must coexist: an agreement (offer/acceptance), certainty of terms, consideration, intention and form.

TERMS OF THE CONTRACT

Once it has been established that the prerequisites of a binding contract have coincided, then and only then will the contents of the contract fall for examination. Here one is concerned with the legal significance of the actual terms agreed, either expressly or implied, from words, documents or conduct. The law is concerned with the extent and meaning of such terms. Consequently one can view this aspect of contract law from the point of collation of the terms as well as the classification of certain types of terms.

As a starting-point one might ask how the terms can be defined, for it is only when a term of the contract has been broken that a remedy is called for. As will be seen the type of term can determine the type of remedy applicable.

There is some necessary overlap in this notion with the previously stated idea of certainty of terms referred to. A contract will not exist if its terms are not certain, or capable of being ascertained. If the terms are expressed, either orally, in documentary form, or by conduct, then the problem is simply one of interpretation. If the terms alleged are not expressed the court may infer them from the previous dealings of the parties[17] or otherwise from the parties' conduct.[18] In holding such implied terms the courts have in the past used a number of fictions and devices to which reference can be made, attempting to apply some commercial efficacy to the transaction.[19]

The courts therefore have attempted to preserve contractual significance by upholding agreements notwithstanding a seemingly vague or unspecified content. This does not detract from the general requirement of the law but rather indicates the innovatory way in which the courts will attempt to encourage contractual validity where the intention of the parties is clear. The English courts in particular have, especially in commercial matters, taken this course of emphasis but have indicated that from the conduct of the parties some agreement must be clear.[20] It is therefore the details rather than the principles of liability that may be inferred. In addition, as will be seen, terms may be implied by statute. Reference here can be made to sections 12 to 15 of the Sale of Goods Act, 1893.[21]

Given that the courts have accepted what terms were agreed it remains to consider the relevance and meaning of such terms. The important issue to stress here is the relative weight of each term. If a contract is broken, say for example by one party not paying for goods, then the term that is broken (non-payment) may, depending on its legal relevance, entitle a party to claim damages. This remedy amounts to the difference between what was given and what ought to have been received under the contract. In the alternative the breach may be such as to enable the injured party to refuse to honour the relevant obligations, under the contract or, in other words, *rescind* the agreement.

Thus the terms fall broadly into two categories: major terms and minor terms. Generally speaking the former give a right to rescind and the latter a right to compensation or damages. To further complicate the issue one must also distinguish between *conditions* and *warranties.*

These are technical terms referring to the major and minor terms respectively of a contract, or more particularly, a contract for the *Sale of Goods.*

The English decision of *Hong Hong Fir Shipping Co.* v. *Kawasaki*[22] of course is of no binding precedence in Ireland, but indicates its disapproval of artificially classifying matters as conditions or warranties, and emphasises that a term of a contract will be considered in its context as to whether or not in itself it is vital to the existence of the contract. If a term is of such importance and is broken, the plaintiff is entitled to rescind.

The technical terms, however, cannot be ignored, as they are enshrined in the Sale of Goods Act.[23] Thus the reader must be aware that a condition is an important term of the contract and a warranty is something less, the significance being that only damages can be claimed for breaches of the latter. Here the aggrieved party would still be liable under the contract. In a contract not relating to goods the terms, conditions and warranty are perhaps inappropriate and the concept of major and minor breaches more understandable. The end result in terms of a remedy is the same.

It is therefore very important to decide whether a term is a major or a minor one in considering the appropriate remedy that may be available to an aggrieved party. The details of the remedies themselves are included later. How, then, does the court decide? Briefly, there are four ways:

(i) That legislation, for example the Sale of Goods Act, implies such in the contract, e.g. section 14 of the Act says it is an implied condition that goods will be of merchantable quality and fit for the purpose for which they are sold, *or*

(ii) The parties have agreed in words or conduct that some terms are vital and others are not, e.g. delivery time, or particular quality of goods.[24] *or*

(iii) That because of the special relationship of the parties it is inferred that such be a condition, i.e. where one party has specialised skill or knowledge.[25] *or*

(iv) That the courts imply the relevant weight to the term because of its meaning to the contract. If the contract is pointless without such a term it must be of major significance to the contract.

There may be considerable overlap between each category. An example should make this clear:

A hires B to sing at a concert. B fails to turn up for rehearsals in accordance with agreed terms. A prevents B from performing at the concert saying that the rehearsals were essential. B sues A for wrongfully rescinding (ending) the contract. If B's breach was a major one (condition) A had the right to end the contract. If this was a minor breach (warranty) A had no such right, and could only sue for damage if the performance was consequently impaired through such a breach.

In the case of *Bettini* v. *Gye*[26] on similar facts the court held A's action to be wrongful repudiation. Failure to attend for rehearsals was not therefore seen to be a major term of the contract. As wrongful repudiation is a major breach (preventing a party from performing a contract) this reversed the tables and allowed B to repudiate. A's remedy was only one of damages.

By way of completeness it should be noted that under the Sale of Goods Act, however, once goods are accepted, regardless of the nature of the breach, an aggrieved party is only entitled to damages. Likewise, if a right to rescission exists and the aggrieved party delays in some way, damages only can be awarded. It is therefore vital to understand the nature of the individual terms.

What of the meaning of specific terms, notwithstanding they might be major or minor? A number of types of terms need explaining. First, contracts may contain clauses that are meaningless. Secondly, the contract may contain a clause that is ambiguous. As a general rule these two categories can be dealt with by saying that the meaningless term is ignored by the courts and the ambiguous clause will be interpreted against the drafter, in other words giving the other party the benefit of any doubt. Consequently if A buys from B a lucky horse he has not legal grounds for complaint if the horse proves to be singularly unlucky and falls in its first race. It should be noted, however, that if a technical word is used this should be given its technical meaning, e.g. a legal term.

One of the most litigated points in the law of contract so far as interpretation is concerned must however be examined in greater detail here, that of the exemption clause. These are clauses that purport to limit or exclude a party's liability that would otherwise have been incurred as a result of the contract. It has already been seen that the courts will uphold the sanctity of an agreement and this includes the right to limit liability as part of the contractual agreement. Indeed section 55 of the Sale of Goods Act specifically allows such. The problems litigated in this area, however, reflect the often one-sided nature of such clauses, and both the courts and now more recently the legislature have limited this doctrine principally for the protection of the consumer.[27] When, therefore, will such a clause be upheld?

In the absence of legislative prohibition the courts in Ireland have followed closely the English experience by ensuring that such limitation or exemption clauses only apply where it has been agreed in a positive sense that obligations under the contract can be avoided. The reader might assume that the cases involved have created devices to avoid the full rigours of the general sanctity of contract, i.e. in this context not to be bound by the exemption clause.

Early cases clearly show the legality of the exemption clause, emphasising the importance of reading the small print. In *L'Estrange* v. *Graucob*[28] the parties entered into a contract involving the sale of a fruit machine (the gambling variety) that later proved to be defective. The contract signed by the plaintiff was upheld even though it contained an exemption clause absolving the supplier from total liability. The parties had agreed such terms. Consequently the rules establish that if a person does not read the small print and accepts the term, e.g. by signing the contract, then all of the terms of the contract including such an exemption will be valid.

This result can, however, be avoided in specific instances. An exemption clause will not apply, i.e. it will be disregarded, if it cannot be said to have been incorporated in the agreement. Examples of this include clauses that are drawn to a person's attention after agreement has been reached,[29] or where sufficient attention is not drawn to the existence of such a clause at the time when the contract is made.[30] Thus one is concerned here with ensuring that the clause is agreed and not unilaterally imposed by the party in whose favour the clause is drafted. If, however, a person signs a contract containing such a clause the party will be bound by this provision as positive agreement has been evidenced. The courts have now decided that the sufficiency of attention necessary to point out the existence of an exemption clause depends on the circumstances. Clauses are common knowledge, e.g. on the reverse of a bus ticket or railway timetable, then it is siffucient that some reference be made to them either specifically by the contracting parties or impliedly, by reference on the ticket for example, of the existence of such a clause. If exemption clauses are not normally found in these transactions then greater attention must be used.

If the exemption clause does not fall down at this level, then it is *prima facie* valid. The courts have at this stage recognised the existence of the clause as a term of the contract. The effect of the clause may still be avoided. First, the courts may consider the interpretation of the clause. If on its construction it is ambiguous, or when literally interpreted does not cover the facts in question, it will be avoided. In *Curtis* v. *Chemical Cleaning Co.*[31] a clause limiting damage to buttons and sequins, was not held to include the staining or shrinkage of a particular item. Thus the drafter of the clause has to ensure its application. If the clause is wide enough it may still be avoided if, for example, A has a claim against B arising, say, in tort and is not privy to any contract with B. Here any clause contained in a contract, say, between B and C would be of no concern to A. Mention of privity is important here, for in the *A.M. Satertwaite* case[32] the courts implied, in the reverse to the above proposition, privity of contract, to allow reliance on a commercial contract and the inherent exemption clauses – a clear policy decision encouraging business efficacy.

Again, in the absence of legislative intervention, if the clause survives these obstacles it may fall at the final hurdle. This is known as the doctrine of *fundamental breach.* Simply put, if a clause is otherwise valid it may still be avoided if the matter which the clause purports to exclude is vital to the contract. The test applied is whether a breach of contract makes the performance of the contract radically different from that which was intended. If so, any clause excluding liability for such a breach is to be disregarded. An example may serve to illustrate this point:

A contracts with B for the supply of a new car. Between ordering and delivering B replaces certain parts of the car with second-hand equipment; this could amount to a major breach of contract. An exemption clause purporting to exclude B's liability if the car is defective might be avoided if the breach was so fundamental to the contract that it could not be relied upon, i.e. the clause only applied to matters within the contemplation of the contract. This apparent safeguard, however, can still be ineffective if, in construction, the exemption clause appears to specifically cater for this particular breach. It can be seen therefore that the nature of the breach, albeit fundamental to the contract, might in the circumstances be included in a limitation clause. This was established by the influential English decision known as the *Suisse Atlantique,*[33] a complicated commercial case where a clause imposing compensation was inserted in the contract, i.e. a limitation of liability. The court held that despite a fundamental breach of the contract such a clause could validly exist, as it was specifically designed for that breach. It is suggested that this doctrine has very limited application.

So long as a contract validly exists and the exemption clause does not fall foul of any of the obstacles cited above the clause will be upheld. In this respect it is no different from any other term of the contract.

On the important subject of the significance of the terms of the contract, it is useful to note the possible legislative controls on total or partial exemption clauses. Since 1973 the English have had legislation making any attempt to exclude liability under the Sale of Goods Act, 1893, void. Consequently attempts to limit liability for defective goods are generally ineffective. In Ireland the Sale of Goods and Supply of Services Act, 1980 has been enacted by the Oireachtas and now it has legislative effect. Similar protection to that operating in England is now available in the Republic. The private consumer is now largely protected from the operation of exemption clauses. This clearly is a reflection of the balance of power between the retailer and the consumer.

Before turning to the next section on factors affecting a seemingly valid contract, it is convenient here to mention briefly the *collateral contract.* In practice contracts are often agreed and later terms are added, altered or substituted for the original. The collateral contract is a device used to incorporate either third parties or additional subject matter, after the original contract has been agreed. This is not to be confused with the variation of contractual terms by the parties where simply the contract itself is altered. The collateral concept involves additional subject matter or persons being included by reference to, but independent of, an original contract. Again, an example might illustrate the point:

A wishes to buy a motor bike on hire purchase. B is willing to sell on such terms. C company agrees to finance the transaction. In legal terms B contracts with C company for the sale of the machine. A contracts with C company for the hire purchase paying for the machine by instalments. Legally A has no contract with B. If the machine is, say, defective A would have to bring action against C company. To avoid this (given that the company may be many miles away from the place of sale and may offer no expertise such as after sales service) the courts appear to have inferred a collateral contract between A and B, thus bringing A and B into contractual obligation collateral to the main transaction.[35] Similarly additional subject matter may be included.[36] The collateral contract therefore is concerned with an avoidance of the practical limitations of sanctity and privity.

As can be seen it is vitally important to understand what the contractual terms are, where they come from and the effect they have in respect to the contracting parties' liability.

CONTRACTS THAT ARE, OR BECOME, UNENFORCEABLE

Presuming that the essential elements of the contract exist it must be recognised that events may occur either at the time of contracting or afterwards that render the contract unenforceable. These 'contracts' fall into two categories: the *void* and the *voidable*.

In other books the capacity of the parties is seen as being a prerequisite to the concept of the binding contract. We choose to approach the issue from the viewpoint that the elements repeated earlier are essential to the contract and do not include capacity, as this is not necessarily such a prerequisite. For example, a child has not, as will be seen, full contractual capacity but can in fact enforce the contract. We prefer to deal more with the vitiating factors on the presumption that a contract is *prima facie* in existence.

Returning to the distinction between the *void* and the *voidable* contract, a void contract, despite complying with the formative prerequisites, has never legally existed because of an aggravating factor, e.g. if the purpose of the contract is to perform some illegal act; a voidable contract contains a defect which allows a person to avoid or ratify the agreement, e.g. a contract made by a child which can, once the child attains a majority, be either rescinded or ratified.

The following pages will attempt to examine the most important of such factors. The elements to consider are as follows:

(i) Where either or both of the parties are *mistaken* as to the terms of the contract.

(ii) Where a *misrepresentation* concerning the contract and/or its terms is made.

(iii) Where unlawful force *(duress)* or *undue influence* is used to bring about agreement.

(iv) Where the contract or its performance is *illegal.*

(v) Where the parties lack the *capacity* to contract owing to age or mental capacity.

These can be considered in turn for the effect each has on the contract and the parties' rights.

Mistake

As a general rule the law is not concerned with whether or not the parties are mistaken in entering into the contract. Hence if A thinks that the sale includes certain land but in fact it does not, in the absence of any misrepresentation (as will be seen), A will have no remedy.[37] Mistake is therefore irrelevant. A reader may find that other texts on the subject preface this debate with reference to unilateral and bilateral mistake. Without demeaning such an approach we find it more relevant to explain the exceptions to the above proposition by reference to factual situations in which the courts have allowed relief either by considering the contract *void* or *voidable*. In other words certain situations may occur where a mistake is made by either or both parties that may vitiate a contract. There are, it is suggested, six such instances.

First, there may be a mutual mistake as to the terms of the contract. If A believes the contract refers to X and B believes it applies to Y, then the contract is void as the terms are uncertain. This overlaps with our previous examination of the contractual prerequisites.[38]

The second instance involves a mutual mistake as to the *existence of the subject matter*. Similar to the above, if the parties are in agreement but the subject does not exist, e.g. it has been destroyed (prior to the contract), there can be no contract. It is void.[39] It may be noted on a similar tack that a contract is also void if by mistake a party purports to buy his or her own property.[40]

The law does, however, allow in a number of instances a mistake by one of the parties to affect contractual validity. The first of these, and the third in our list, is where there is a mistake as to the *quality of the subject matter*, and this is known by the other contracting party. Differing and difficult legal argument surrounds this exception,[41] but for present purposes it is sufficient to note that mistake as to quality alone is not thought to be sufficient, but if the mistake was realised by the other party it renders the contract voidable.[42] Consequently if A knows that a mistake has been made but does not inform B, when B later discovers the existence of the mistake he or she may be able to avoid the terms of the contract. For one party alone to be mistaken as to the quality of subject matter will be to no avail.[43]

The fourth exception relates to the *identity of the parties*. It is clear that this can render a contract void or voidable. If A intends to deal with B, and C pretends to be B, then the contract between A and C is void.[44] If, however, A contracts with C who calls himself B then the contract is valid so long as A intended to deal with C (regardless of C's purported identity).[45] A distinction exists here between contracts where identity is essential to the contract and where it is not, e.g. where a fictitious name is used, however deceitful such might be, A will be bound by the contract as it was intended to deal with that person regardless of fraud perpetrated. The law, however, has proved more strict where the parties are face to face.[46] Here there is a presumption that the parties do intend to deal with each other and aggravating circumstances may exist to rebut such. For example, if a seller makes exhaustive enquiries as to the creditworthiness of a buyer and then relies on assurances of the buyer and accepts a cheque which is later dishonoured, the contract may be avoided. In the important English decision of *Lewis* v. *Avery*[47] it was held that mistaken identity in a face-to-face encounter in such circumstances will render the contract voidable, and therefore the aggrieved party must avoid the contract at the earliest opportunity.

The relevance of this seemingly pedantic distinction is more real than apparent, for if a contract is void the buyer, for example, gains no title to the goods concerned and cannot pass such on to a third party, however honest that person may have been. If the contract is voidable a good title does pass and can be transferred, until such time as the contract is avoided. The only remedy a plaintiff would then have would be for breach of contract (if any) where, for example, a cheque is not honoured, or an action in tort for any fraud that may exist and/or a criminal prosecution.

The fifth situation where mistake can be pleaded in contract relates to the mistaken identity of documents, or *non est factum* (not his deed). If a person signs a document and is mistaken as to the nature of it, under limited circumstances any contract so concluded will be void. This was established in the case of *Foster* v. *McKinnon.*[48] It is now accepted that this defence is only available if due care is exercised by the person concerned. Certainly the English authorities indicate that only the aged or illiterate might avail themselves of it.[49] In any event the document signed must be radically different from that which was originally intended. Again we see the stress on a qualitative rather than quantitative mistake, a point that seems to underline all of these exceptions.

The final exceptions to the general proposition that mistake is irrelevant arises where one of the parties seeks an equitable remedy, e.g. specific performance. Equity may, given its theoretically discretionary nature, refuse a remedy if to grant such would be inequitable.[50]

Such therefore is the relevance of mistake. As will be seen in the conclusion of this chapter, in the example given, mistake may in itself overlap with other areas of the law of contract, including breach and misrepresentation. It is to the latter that we can now turn as the second of the vitiating factors, following contractual formation.

Misrepresentation

A misrepresentation is a false statement of fact made or omitted, prior to a contract, that induces a party to enter into a contract with the person making the representation. As such it is quasi-contractual in nature, for to sue for misrepresentation involves suing on events appertaining to the contract rather than on the contract itself, but the effect can be to render the contract voidable. Thus it is a vitiating factor in the present context. Misrepresentation is essentially tortious in nature.

A further complication arises in that if the statement has become a term of the contract (as previously explained) then the plaintiff can opt to sue in contract. It will later be shown that this dual possibility of legal action is important, for the measure of calculation of damages in contractual and tortious actions is different.[51]

To turn to the contents of the definition given above, any statement of fact that is made in contemplation of a contract is known as a representation. Such may or may not become a term of the contract. If it is false it will be a misrepresentation.

For example, A induces B into buying A's car by saying it is very economical, it can be driven at over 100 m.p.h. and it will seat five people. These statements may or may not be terms of the contract (depending on what was actually agreed, expressly or impliedly) but they will be representations. If false an action could lie.

The statement must be one of fact and not opinion[52] and the plaintiff must acually rely on the representation if an action is to succeed, i.e. the person would not have formed the contract if it were not for such a statement; but the person to whom the representation is made is under no obligation to check upon its truth or relevance, even if given the opportunity.[53]

It is usually necessary for the statement to be expressed, though an omission can amount to a misrepresentation if it arises by a failure to impart certain information. These cases involve contracts that are *uberrimae fidei* (a special relationship of confidence or good faith), such as where a person owes a duty to another because of the relationship between them, e.g. father and son, insurance company and insurer, trustee and beneficiary. Also, if a statement is made and then circumstances alter, the representator is under a duty to inform the other party of this circumstantial change. An omission to do so will be a misrepresentation by implication. In the case of *With* v. *O'Flanagan* the court held that a person must reveal changes in the income of a business after having disclosed its turnover to a prospective purchaser. A failure to disclose an adverse change in this matter was held to be a misrepresentation by way of omission.[54] There is, though, no general duty to disclose information outside of such special relationship.

It is important to differentiate between different kinds of misrepresentations that can arise, again because of the remedies flowing from the statement. There are three principal types of false representation. If the statement is made by a person who knows it is not true, or is reckless as to its truth, the representation is known as *fraudulent.* The remedy for such is based in tort and entitles the aggrieved party to damages for the fraud, i.e. putting the aggrieved party in the position he or she would have been in had the representation not been made. The subtle distinction must be noted here. Had the representation been a term of the *contract* then the damages would be different, putting the person in the position they would have been in had the representation been true, e.g. suing in contract. However, if the representation is fraudulent the contract is *void.* No title can therefore pass and as the contract does not exist the only damages to be claimed will be in tort.[55]

Secondly, the misrepresentation might be made *negligently.* Here A may make up a false representation, believing it to be true, but if this is not what a reasonable person would have said the matter becomes actionable. Such will render the contract voidable, that is on discovering the error B may rescind the contract and/or sue for damages, either in tort or in the contract, depending on whether the representation has in fact become incorporated as a term of the contract. The negligent misrepresentation seems to stem from the English decision of *Hedley Byrne* v. *Heller,*[56] where the court decided that an action only lay for negligent misrepresentation where a statement was made and this was relied upon by the relevant party. An example of such a relationship can be found where there is a special fiduciary relationship between the parties, such as banker and client.

Finally, a misrepresentation may be entirely innocent, i.e. neither fraud nor negligence exists. Here the common law provides no remedy, but equity renders any contract that flows from the representation *voidable.* There is no right to damages for such a statement although equity does allow an indemnity for any expenses incurred as a result of reliance on the representation.[57] As the equitable remedy of rescission (i.e. ending a voidable contract) is discretionary, a remedy may be refused if the plaintiff is not deserving in the eyes of the court, e.g. there has been undue delay. This issue was closely mooted in the case of the *Bank of Ireland* v. *Smith,*[58] where an entirely innocent misrepresentation was held to render the contract unenforceable. In addition damages were allowed as the representation had become a term of the contract, in the manner indicated above.

The importance of the above is in relation to the termination of the contract and/or claiming financial compensation. It is a difficult area of law, being closely related to both tort and contract, principally affecting the measure of damages. None of this will, of course, preclude an action for breach of contract if the representation has become a term of the contract itself. This can only be gleaned from the facts.

By way of completeness it can be noted that this area of law in the United Kingdom has since 1967 been clarified by legislation in the form of the Misrepresentation Act, but Ireland has not as yet opted to follow this development.

The topics of mistake and misrepresentation are perhaps, at least in practical terms, the two most important of the so-called vitiating features. Account can now briefly be made of the remaining factors that may render a contract unenforceable. The first category of these remaining features affects the capacity of the parties concerned and the second relates to acts of illegality inherent in the contract.

Duress and Undue Influence

In attributing contractual liability it is presumed that the agreement between the parties is *voluntary.* Consequently if there is a *de facto* agreement which has been brought about by unlawful force or pressure, then this will undermine the agreement, rendering the contract voidable.

Duress here means the unlawful application of force in order to extract an agreement. This would occur, for example, if A were to hold a gun to B's head forcing B to agree to sell his car to A. Undue influence is a less direct form of persuasion in the nature of pressure arising from a relationship that incorporates a dominated and a dominant party. Where one party, such as a parent, teacher or professional advisor uses a position of dominance to achieve an agreement, then a contract so formed may be avoided.

In either case the pressurised party can avoid the contract but must do so as soon as the pressure ends. In other words the contract has a latent defect owing to the duress or undue influence exerted. In the case of duress the pressure must give the person no real option, in the latter instance any undue influence will, while it subsists, render the contract voidable. As soon as the dominance ends the aggrieved party must avoid the contractual provisions and not ratify the situation. A number of simple examples have been litigated. In *Mutual Finance* v. *Whetton* a threat of prosecution was held to be duress as it was levied by an unauthorised party[59] and in *Allcard* v. *Skinner* the dominance of the leader in a religious order was held to amount to undue influence, although the action failed owing to the delay on the plaintiff's part to avoid the contract once the dominant relationship had been terminated.[60]

Children and the Mentally Incapacitated

Two further presumptions are made by the law in ascertaining the capacity of the parties to contract; that the parties are both *sui juris* (of full age) and that the parties are *compos mentis* (not suffering from any mental disability). Generally speaking a contract made with a person lacking capacity by virtue of age or mental state of mind is voidable, i.e. it cannot be enforced against the person during the currency of the incapacity, but must be avoided if and when such incapacity ends. Consequently when attaining the age of majority a person who has purported to enter into a contract during minority must avoid the contract if it is not to be binding on that person. To clarify this general rule a child (legally) is in Ireland a person under 21 years of age. A person *non compos mentis* can be so as a result of a mental disorder or any other factor rendering the actions of a person unintentional, e.g. drunkenness. The only qualification to the last sentence is that the other contracting party must know or should have known of the incapacity.

A major exception to both instances of seeming incapacity, however, is to be found in the Sale of Goods Act, 1893, section 2 of which says contracts for goods, although in such instances voidable, give the seller the right to receive a reasonable price for the goods providing such are *necessary* to that person. A reasonable price does not necessarily accord with contract. The cases here seem to reflect the economic and social climate, for in an old English case, a gold watch was held to be such a necessity.[61] Perhaps today this would have a more contemporary relevance.

While necessities are only specifically mentioned in the Sale of Goods

Act in this context the courts have held that contracts of employment of children are to be presumed beneficial for the child and on a similar tack therefore enforceable, thus being a further exception to the general proposition stated above. This is clearly illustrated by the case of *Doyle* v. *White City Stadium* involving the famous County Cork boxer.[62] The presumption of contractual benefit can be refuted, e.g. if the employment contract contains an unduly onerous provision.

Finally, on this point, it can be noted that although a child cannot be sued on a contract, unless within the above exceptions, until attaining the majority, the child can sue on the contract if, for example, defective goods are supplied.[63] The law here is to be found in the Infants Relief Act, 1874.

If the reader is, however, under 21 and sees this incapacity as potentially beneficial a word of warning might be attached to the above. Several remedies exist for an aggrieved party who is prevented from suing on the contract. If, for example, a 17 year old hires a bicycle and then refuses to pay, a remedy may lie in equity for restitution of property, in tort for conversion and at common law for a total failure of consideration.[64] In addition, the goods may be necessary and therefore a reasonable price can be charged.

Illegality

The final issue capable of nullifying a contract can now be considered. This occurs when either the consent or performance of the contract is in some way against the criminal or civil law, i.e. illegal or unlawful. We will mention the most important of the numerous examples available, with particular reference to contracts totally or partially in *restraint of trade.*

Five varieties of illegality in contracts can be found. Certain contracts are void by statute, i.e. they are not criminally illegal but are not recognised as existing, or in other words are unenforceable. Gambling contracts are an example by virtue of the Gambling Act, 1845. Some contracts attract a *fine* by virtue of illegal performance, as in where an appropriate licence is not obtained for the sale of tobacco or alcohol.[65] In this case, however, the contract itself will be recognised. The third variety of this generic illegality are contracts that are *criminally illegal* by *statute* and void. Not only is the contract void but criminal prosecution may also follow. An example of this can be found in the case of *Anderson* v. *Daniel.*[66] In this particular example the law differentiates between the statutory illegality inherent in the substance of the contract, i.e. its purpose, and the performance of the contract. In either case the contract is void, however, if performance is illegal and one party is entirely innocent, that person can recover any value given. Otherwise the loss will lie where it falls.

The *common law* can also render a contract *criminally illegal* and void. A colourful example of this can be found in the old case of *Everitt* v. *Williams.*[67] Here the parties were partners as highwaymen. They fell out over their 'business' relationship and asked the court to adjudicate. They were both hanged for their trouble!

Finally, contracts can be *void at common law* without being illegal, similar to the first example given. It is within this example that the practical importance of illegality becomes more obvious. On the grounds of public policy certain contracts or parts of them are rendered unenforceable. Most texts give three examples here, the contracts which oust the jurisdiction of the court, contracts which prejudice marriage and, most importantly, contracts that are in *restraint of trade.*

The general rule is that such contracts are void in so far as they are in whole or part against the public interest. Thus either all of the contract is void, or the part which offends. This can be contrasted with the other examples that render the whole contract void.

What therefore is restraint of trade? Over the last three centuries the law has readily reacted against activities that impinged upon the perceived 'right' to conduct business without interference from any source. This has been most obvious in the rise of the trade unions. In the present context any contract or term of such contract that restricts the freedom of trade may be struck down by the court. Following the English case of *Esso Petroleum* v. *Harper*[68] a two-tiered test seems to apply in these situations. A contract may be in restraint of trade if it creates an unfair balance between the contracting parties *and* it is against the public interest to allow such a restriction.

Some examples will make the application of this doctrine more clear. A contract may be in restraint of trade if it restricts the right of a person to work in a particular employment if the present job is vacated, or if one contracting party is forced under the contract to obtain all products from the same source.[69] It has in such cases been held to be against one of the party's interests and public policy to allow such restriction. Much depends, however, on the nature of the contract and the relative imbalances involved. Thus in one exceptional case restrictions against competition in trade world-wide and for life were not deemed to be in restraint of trade.[70]

It can be seen therefore that progress has now been made from the formation of the contract through its terms and intervening events. What remains to examine now is the termination of the contract. How does a contract end, and what are the consequences?

TERMINATION OF THE CONTRACT

Contracts which are *void* are not contracts at all and therefore these will be disregarded, except in so far as certain remedies contained herein may be applicable (e.g. damages for misrepresentation). What we are rather concerned with are the ways in which an otherwise valid contract, one that is duly formed and is not void, can be terminated.

Basically it can be terminated by either its *performance* (thus ending the parties' obligations), its *breach* (where the aggrieved party rescinds the contract), by *frustration* (where the contract cannot, due to the fault of neither party, be performed) or where the parties naturally *agree* to terminate the contract before completion.

Little need be said of performance, except that it must be *'precise and exact'*.[71] Anything short of precise performance will disentitle the defaulting party from claiming the consideration under the contract. Here the aggrieved party is faced with two options: either the contract may be rescinded, thus ending both parties' future obligations, or the aggrieved party could sue for damages. If the latter course of action is decided upon the effect is that the aggrieved party is enforcing the contract and therefore the obligations falling on the aggrieved party are still current. Therefore if the aggrieved party insists on the performance of the contract the contract will end by performance or if the aggrieved party is to be put in the position in financial terms he or she would have been in had the contract been performed, then the remedy is one of damages. In other words, although performance must be precise and exact, something short of performance may give rise to damages, in which case both parties' obligations will be valid; but if there is a major breach of contract this may entitle the aggrieved party to rescind, in which case the party at fault is entitled to nothing. If a person is prevented by the other party from performing the contract, then short of insisting on performance (i.e. suing on the contract) that party can rescind and claim expenses known as suing on the *quantum meruit* basis).[72]

The parties can mutually decide to accept something different than contractually entitled. If they are in an agreement, such will end the contract, but two qualifications should be noted. First, if no consideration is given this cannot be *enforced.* Where only one party agrees to end the contract after having performed his or her obligations extra consideration or estoppel is necessary if that party is to be prevented from going back on the agreement. Secondly, some of the *terms* of the contract may be altered by agreement or waived that may not (unless the contract is thereby substituted by another) end a particular contract, e.g. allowing extra time for delivery.

A contract may end because of a breach of one of the terms. This has to a certain extent been examined previously, as a major breach *entitles* a party to rescind. Rescission is an equitable remedy that ends the contract, i.e. putting the parties back to the position they were in (if possible) before the contract was made. It is a negation of all obligations. The only question to ask therefore is whether or not the breach entitles the party to rescind. If it does, then, subject to the discretion of equity, rescission will be upheld back to the time the aggrieved party took steps to end the contractual obligations. The case of *Bettini* v. *Gye* again provides a clear example.[73] This therefore is a remedy that confirms the *de facto* position.

A claim for damages does not end, in itself, the contract, but rather relies upon it. The acceptance of the damages and fulfilment of the other obligations will end the contract, otherwise rescission or agreement must be relied upon.

There is, however, one further issue to be considered in this light, that of frustration. A contract may end if an event, unforeseen by the parties, occurs rendering the contract either impossible to perform, or, if it can be performed, radically different from what was intended. Here the event must arise independently of, and be the fault of, neither party.[74] This point can be well illustrated by the case of *Taylor* v. *Caldwell*,[75] where a concert hall burnt down and a concert could not be given. Here the contract to perform ended automatically because of the frustrating event. Whether this does end the contract is therefore a matter of construction.[76] If the parties choose to carry on, then a new contract may be formed.

If any value has changed hands the loss lies where it falls, unless there is a total failure of consideration[77]

It should be pointed out that a frustrating event, if foreseen by the parties, may be incorporated in the contract, and the contract will not end on such a contingency. Here it cannot be said that the contract is radically different.

If the contract ends, or has been breached, and either or both of the parties are aggrieved, then a *remedy* may be sought. What are the principal remedies in contract? Before answering this question one needs to know when a remedy will be awarded. As the rest of this chapter indicates, remedies can follow where one or both of the parties threaten to be, or are in breach of, tneir obligations. It will be seen below that the type of remedy awarded depends on both the nature of the breach and the circumstances of the parties. The principal remedies are as follows:

Rescission

This is aimed at putting the parties back in the position that existed prior to the contract. It is only granted if in accordance with equitable principals and is only awarded for serious breaches, for example a breach of condition where defective goods are sold.

Damages

Here, the parties are put in the position they would have been in had the contract been performed. This is the purpose of damages in contract. It will be seen that in tort, for example misrepresentation, the purpose is somewhat different.

Thus if goods are worth £1, cost £5 and are said to be worth £10 the measure of damages in contract is £9 (the difference between the price paid and the purported value). The measure of damage in tort is £4 (difference between the cost and the value of the goods).

The objective behind damages is therefore clear. How are such calculated? Simply put, the law will allow damages to cover any matter that was seen to be in the contemplation of the parties and, further, that naturally arise from the contract. Thus as in *Hadley* v. *Baxendale*[78] damages were allowed for breach of contract (the late delivery of a repaired millshaft) but not for the loss of profit, as the court held such was in the minds of the parties, as a likely loss. This strict interpretation has, to a certain extent, in the United

Kingdom been watered down. Damages have in the last four or five years been allowed, for example, for the loss of enjoyment of a holiday as well as its *prima facie* value.[79]

In any event the injured party must do as much as is reasonably possible to mitigate loss. The injured party must, therefore, not allow matters to get any worse.[80] It will be remembered, however, that as damages are claimed at common law, this is a remedy as of right contrasted with the equitable remedies previously mentioned.

In addition mention must here be made to attempts by the parties to predict the possibility of loss being suffered. If there is a provision in a contract that purports to allow for such a contingency this will be enforced by the court, providing it is in the nature of compensation rather than a penalty. If the compensation is liquidated, i.e. a specified amount is contained in the contract, this may be endorsed by the court; however, if an unliquidated sum is mentioned, i.e. it is not specified in terms of quantity, this may be interpreted as a penalty. Much therefore will depend on the terms of the particular contract and whether or not the parties have tried to reasonably estimate losses involved.

As previously seen a remedy similar to damages known as *quantum meruit* may also lie in the form of expenses incurred in contemplation of the contract. This will occur where, for example, A does not fulfil obligations under the contract and is thus in breach, and neither does B, but B prevents A from performing such obligations. As A cannot perform the contract it is not possible for A to sue on it but expenses can be claimed for labour and materials, etc. Any consideration already given may also be claimed back if there has been a total failure of consideration on the part of B, i.e. no consideration has been received at all.

The calculation of damages in contract can be contrasted with the tortious measure, for in the latter case, it is not the test cited above, but a wider one of reasonable foreseeability.[81] Contractual damages are concerned with what the parties agreed and not what the reasonable person contemplated.

Rectification

In limited circumstances equity will allow a contract or subsequent document to be altered to accord with the 'real' intention of the parties. It appears to be little used.

Specific Performance

This famous equitable remedy is, as the name suggests, in the form of an order from the court commanding a certain task contained in a contract to be performed. As equity supposedly puts only a gloss on the common law it will not be awarded unless the common law remedy of damages is inadequate. Consequently specific performance will only be ordered if, for example, goods are of a particular value. Land is usually included in such orders as it is recognised as having an unique identity. Perhaps the growth of the symmetrical housing estate will alter this concept.[82] Also, as a matter of policy and practicality, specific performance will not be granted if it amounts to enforcing an employer/employee relationship,[83] although some limited exceptions do exist. The usual equitable bars to relief apply, e.g. delay or unwarranted behaviour.

Injunction

Similar to specific performance this equitable remedy orders or forbids a particular behaviour and is subject to the same limitations. It will not, however, be granted if tantamount to specific performance and where specific performance would not be granted, e.g. in the contract of employment. The injunction is granted to prevent, for example, a breach of contract. The injunction, if mandatory, will order a contracting party to do a particular act, e.g. deliver goods in a particular way. If prohibitory it will stop a particular activity, e.g. stopping a student from printing his lecture notes.[84]

Statutory Provisions

In addition to the common law and equitable remedies mentioned above, certain remedies also exist under statute. These are mainly to be found in the Sale of Goods Act, 1893, and include, for example, the right to a reasonable price if the price is omitted from the contract (providing the contract is not otherwise void for uncertainty).[85] The Act also covers other matters, e.g. if goods are not delivered or if the price is not paid.[86]

Finally, although loss can only be recovered once, i.e. damages or specific performance in respect of the same matter, several remedies may be claimed that, together, compensate for the loss. An example here would be rescission and damages: if A refuses to deliver goods to B this may be a major breach of contract. B may choose to rescind the contract in consequence. If B then has to pay more for similar goods from another source B may claim the difference between the contract price between A and B and the price he has now paid, i.e. the damage suffered.

This chapter deals briefly with a complex and major area of Irish law, while taking into account the influence of decisions of the British courts. The law of contract is clearly an example of the common law regulating and shaping the law to conform with modern commercial demands.

Chapter 13*

THE LAW OF TORT

It has been said that the law is generally divisible into criminal and civil matters and that the latter can be subdivided into categories that concern particular interests found, for example, in agreements, land, personal property and personal liberty. The law of tort or torts is perhaps the widest-reaching of all of the divisions of civil law, growing as will be seen in a piece-meal fashion to provide remedies for particular civil wrongs.[1]

Whereas contract deals with voluntary agreements between identified parties, tort caters for numerous situations where injury or damage results from the unwarranted action of one or more persons. While the law prescribes for the general protection of society, a tortious remedy compensates rather than punishes, thus it can be distinguished from the criminal law. This chapter is therefore concerned with the general civil duty on persons not to cause wrongful loss or damage.

The chapter is divided into the following headings that together cover the principal rules of tort as well as some of the substantive rights and duties: (i) *Introduction and basic principles.* (ii) *The protection of interests in land:* Trespass; Nuisance; Rule in *Ryland* v. *Fletcher.* (iii) *The protection of interests in chattels:* Trespass; Conversion; Detinue. (iv) *The protection of personal interests:* Trespass to the person; Negligence; Liability for dangerous premises; Defamation. (v) *Conclusion.*

INTRODUCTION AND BASIC PRINCIPLES

Historical

As noted in Chapter 1, during the early days of the common law no one could bring an action in the king's court without a writ. We also noted that where there was no writ there was no cause of action. The main source of the law of torts lies in two of these writs, namely, the writ of trespass and the writ of trespass on the case. Trespass was available for all forcible and direct injuries to a person, his land or his chattels. If the injury was not direct or forcible then the remedy might lie in 'case', so-called because the particular circumstances of the case were set out in the writ. The early distinction between these two forms of action lay in the fact that the plaintiff did not have to establish damage in order to recover in trespass. The essence of the defendant's wrong was that by his conduct he had increased the tendency of retaliation or an affray. Direct and immediate aggression to the person, chattels or land of the plaintiff rendered the defendant liable. Redress was less readily forthcoming when the defendant's conduct was indirectly (rather

**See also 1988 Supplement pp. 327-332.*

than directly) the cause of the plaintiff's injury. As one writer has pointed out, the prevailing philosophy of early tort law was that 'responsibility was based on causation rather than fault and the headway made by the latter was made in the context of action on the case'.[2] In an action on the case a plaintiff has always been obliged to establish damage.

The impact of the Industrial Revolution on the development of the law of tort was not insignificant. In particular it led to the development of the action on the case and to its extension to various forms of loss, until, in 1932, it was finally and formally established as the action for negligence. Prior to the Industrial Revolution the action only lay against persons such as solicitors, doctors and others who pursued public callings and who were considered to have placed themselves in a special relationship with the public. As we shall see in greater detail later, the action on the case has now been extended beyond these narrow confines to cover negligent conduct by any person which causes damage to another. It must also be noted, however, that while most of the law of tort has its basis in fault (no liability without fault) there are still some occasions upon which a defendant is strictly liable for his actions without any proof of fault.

The Nature of a Tort

A tort is a civil, as opposed to a criminal, wrong and as a civil wrong, it must be distinguished from a breach of contract. In the case of contract, generally speaking, the parties determine the nature of their respective liabilities. In the case of tort, however, the liability is imposed by the State though, as will be seen, often either party may release the other from that liability. Contractual liability is derived from the agreement between the parties, while liability in tort arises independently of any agreement, though it may be modified or excluded by such agreement or by consent.

The function of the law of torts is essentially to compensate a plaintiff for the civil wrong committed against him by the defendant. As a general rule its purpose is to compensate the plaintiff rather than punish the defendant, though in exceptional circumstances punitive damages may be awarded. Subject to this latter qualification, if the defendant is found liable, usually his duty will be to restore the plaintiff (as far as money can achieve this) to the position he would have been in had the wrong not been committed. In some exceptional situations the plaintiff may obtain an injunction to protect him from further damage by the defendant. Injunctions may be the sole remedy sought by the plaintiff though usually an application for an injunction be coupled with a claim for damage already sustained.

The terms 'damage' and 'damages' must be distinguished. In tort (as well as in contract) the term damage is used to signify that loss or injury, of a personal or financial kind, for which a remedy is available. The amount of compensation awarded by the court is referred to as damages (sometimes general damages). A man does not have a right of action for every injury he might suffer during his life. The Latin phrase *damnum sina injuria* is sometimes used to refer to those injuries which do not amount to damage and for which no action will lie. An example will help to illustrate the point. If, while attending a football match, a man becomes so excited that he suffers a heart attack, he will have sustained loss and injury but he will not have suffered any *damage.* On the other hand if the same person was injured as a result of the defective and dangerous state of the football ground, he would have suffered damage and might recover damages (i.e. compensation) in a subsequent action. It should also be noted that damage must be proven by a plaintiff to succeed in most, though not all, torts.

Concurrent Wrongdoers and Vicarious Liability

As a general rule a person is liable in tort for his own actions only. In some exceptional cases, however, he may also be answerable for the acts of others. One Australian judge has described the rule in the following terms:

> . . . If a number of persons jointly participate in the commission of a tort, each is responsible, jointly with each and all of the others, and also severally, for the whole amount of damage caused by the tort, irrespective of the extent of his participation.[3]

This means that a plaintiff may sue only one defendant, any combination of defendants or, of course, all defendants, to recover his loss. The Civil Liability Act, 1961, refers to such persons as 'concurrent wrongdoers' and provides, *inter alia,* that persons may become concurrent wrongdoers 'as a result of vicarious liability of one for another, breach of joint duty, conspiracy, concerted action to a common end or independent acts causing the same damage'. It is also provided that it is immaterial whether the acts constituting concurrent wrongs are contemporaneous or successive.

It will be seen that concurrent wrongdoers fall into two general categories: First, the defendants may be jointly and severally liable because they all actually participated in the commission of the tort. Thus where the plaintiff is injured by the negligence of A and the negligence of B in driving their respective cars, A and B are concurrent wrongdoers. Secondly, persons may be concurrent wrongdoers because one person is held liable for the tort committed by an employee while the latter is acting in the course of the employment – a factory worker on a production line, a builder's labourer employed by a construction company, a postman or a bus driver for C.I.E. are all classed as employees or, as the law more traditionally calls them, *servants* in this sense. An employee must be distinguished from an independent contractor. The latter, though employed, is not subject to the same control and supervision as a servant, and the employer as a general rule is not liable for the torts of an independent contractor. A person who retains a building contractor to build a house, a hospital which retains a consultant surgeon or a dance-hall owner who books a band to perform in his hall, are all engaging independent contractors rather than servants. Finally, it should be noted that an employer is not liable for *all* torts committed by his or her employees but only those committed in the course of employment. There has been much litigation on the meaning of this phrase and the cases draw some very fine distinctions. It suffices here to say that an act is committed in the course of employment if it is of a class of act which the employee is expressly or impliedly authorised to do. Usually it consists either of a wrongful act authorised by the master or of an unauthorised mode or method of doing an act authorised by the employer. The C.I.E. bus-driver referred to earlier who injures a pedestrian while performing his duties, will render his employer liable. On the other hand if the injury was caused while the bus was being driven by the bus conductor (without the express or implied authority of C.I.E.) then the employer would not be liable. The liability of the employer is incurred on the principle of vicarious liability. In case of liability either the employer or the employee could be sued (but damage only recovered the once).[4] For financial reasons, however, it is usually the employer who will face the claim.

General Defences

There are a number of general defences in tort. Inevitable accident and voluntary assumption of risk are probably the most important, though others such as self-defence, consent and statutory authority should also be kept in mind.

(i) *Inevitable accident:* As a general rule liability in tort is based on fault. As a result injury, which is the result of an incident or event which could not be avoided by taking ordinary and reasonable precautions, is not actionable. It is not necessary for the defendant to show that the accident was 'inevitable', in the literal sense of the word, but merely that no 'reasonable' precaution would have prevented its occurrence. What is reasonable will depend on the circumstances of the case.

(ii) *Volenti non fit injuria* is the Latin phrase frequently used to express the rule that a person who undertakes to run the risk created by the defendant cannot subsequently complain if, while doing so, he is injured. It is essentially a particular application of the general rule that the consent of the plaintiff to the actions of the defendant provides the latter with a good defence. In order to amount to *volenti* the consent must be an informed consent. Mere knowledge of the risk is not sufficient. The defendant must show that the plaintiff understood the physical risk and acquiesced in it to the extent of surrendering his legal rights.

Survival of Actions

At common law the death of either party could affect rights of action in tort under two separate rules. First, under the common law maxim *actio personalis moritur cum persona* any personal action (i.e. an action based on the personal acts or conduct of the defendant or causing personal injury to the plaintiff) was barred by the death of either party. Secondly, under the rule in *Baker* v. *Bolton*[5] the death of a human being could not be complained of in a civil action. The outrageous result of this latter rule was that while a defendant who severely injured a pedestrian was civilly liable, one who killed such a pedestrian was not. Both of these rules have now been altered by statute and the matter is now governed by the Civil Liability Act, 1961. Under the Act all causes of action survive the death of the parties except an action for defamation, seduction, criminal conversation or a claim for compensation under the Workman's Compensation Act, 1934. The action may be brought by or against the estate of the deceased. Where the death of a person arises from the circumstances which give rise to the cause of action, the damages recoverable must not include exemplary damages, or damages for any pain or suffering or personal injury, or for loss or diminution of expectation of life or happiness. In such a case the maximum which may be awarded for mental distress to dependants is £1,000.

PROTECTION OF INTERESTS IN LAND

There is here considerable overlap with rules of land law or real property, but the following have evolved as the most important torts protecting interests in land, and can be described separately.

Trespass to Land

There are essentially three ways in which this tort may be committed: (i) By unlawfully entering upon land in the possession of the plaintiff. (ii) By remaining upon land after the authority to be there has expired or has been withdrawn or abused. (iii) By placing or projecting any material object upon land without lawful justification.

(i) The first is often said to be the commonest form of trespass to land. It involves the personal entry of the defendant upon the land of the plaintiff. It should be noted that even the slightest intrusion can constitute a trespass, such as putting a hand through a window or a fence. Trespass to land is, like other forms of trespass, actionable *per se* (i.e. without proof of damage) and it is no defence to show that the trespass was the result of mistake of law or fact.

(ii) Trespass by remaining upon land arises where a person remains on land after his right of entry has ceased. The latter right may be withdrawn expressly, as in the case of the express revocation of a licence[6] or may be lost through abuse, as where the plaintiff, from a highway crossing the defendant's land, deliberately interfered with a shoot by scaring the grouse. After refusing to desist he was held down by the defendant's servants. The plaintiff sued in assault but the action was dismissed. By his unreasonable use of the highway he had constituted himself a trespasser and therefore the defendant was entitled to use reasonable force to restrain him.[7]

(iii) It is a trespass to place any chattel upon the plaintiff's land or to cause any physical object or noxious substance to cross the boundary of the plaintiff's land, or even simply to come into physical contact with the land, though there may be no crossing of the boundary.[8] Thus the plaintiff has recovered in trespass where he caused a Virginia creeper to grow upon the defendant's land. This aspect of trespass also covers such conduct as the throwing of stones upon the plaintiff's land or turning cattle upon land.

The Parties: Only the person actually in possession is entitled to sue in trespass. A reversioner can only sue for damage arising from the trespass which affects his proprietary interest. A person in *de facto* possession can maintain an action against anyone except the person with the right of entry or of immediate possession.

Defences: There are a number of general defences to an action for trespass:

(i) Entry by legal authority: As seen in greater detail in Chapter 11, the criminal law authorises the entry of premises in a number of situations such as to prevent the commission of a felony or to prevent a breach of the peace or under the authority of a warrant issued by the court. The civil law also has similar provisions with regard to a landlord's right to distrain (i.e. to take the tenant's goods) for rent or the sheriff's right to seize a judgement debtor's goods under an execution order.

(ii) Entry made to abate a nuisance (see p. 240 *infra*).

(iii) A person may enter the land of another to retake goods wrongfully placed there by that other or by the felonious act of a third party.

(iv) That the trespass complained of was accidental and without negligence, e.g. where the defendant's car, through the negligence of a third party, is forced onto the plaintiff's land.

(v) Entry made in pursuance of permission or licence.

Remedies: A person may use reasonable force to prevent a trespass to his land and may also do so to remove a trespasser. In modern times this latter right has been replaced by an action for ejectment or overholding in landlord and tenant situations.

The injured party may seize any chattels (e.g. cattle) which are upon his land and are causing or have caused damage there and detain them until he has been paid compensation for the damage caused. This right is known as the right of *distress damage feasant.* As long as the injured party is exercising this right, his action for damages is suspended.

The injured party may, subject to this, bring an action for damages and/or an injunction.

Nuisance: The Nature of the Tort

It is important to distinguish nuisance from trespass to land. Trespass arises from direct and forcible interference with the plaintiff's land, while in nuisance the interference is indirect. More importantly, however, in order to recover in nuisance the plaintiff must prove damage, while trespass is generally actionable *per se.* Accordingly, while planting weeds on the plaintiff's land would amount to trespass, merely permitting such weeds to spread from the defendant's land to the plaintiff's would amount to nuisance, provided, of course, that in the latter case the plaintiff can establish damage.

There are two forms of nuisance, public and private. A public nuisance is one which affects a cross-section of the community and amounts to a criminal offence. It is only actionable as a civil wrong in tort when it causes some special or peculiar damage to the plaintiff. Examples of public nuisances are obstructing the highway or keeping a common gaming house.

Private nuisance is a civil wrong only. It can take one of the following two forms:

(a) Any wrongful disturbance of an easement or other servitude appurtenant to land.[9]

(b) Wrongfully causing, or allowing the escape of, deleterious substances into another's land, e.g. smoke, fumes, noise and vibrations, or any unlawful interference with the enjoyment of land generally.

Easements and servitudes generally are beyond the scope of this work, but it will suffice to give some examples of the way in which the tort of nuisance may arise from their invasion.

(i) Obstruction of a private right of way.

(ii) Interference with the support of land.

(iii) Interruption of light. This is actionable when the obstruction renders the plaintiff's building unfit for any ordinary purpose for which it was fit before the obstruction occurred.

With regard to the second category the occupier of land is entitled to be protected from certain interferences with his right to enjoy that land. It must be borne in mind, however, that modern living conditions make it almost inevitable that unrestricted enjoyment of land cannot be achieved. The law recognises this in distinguishing between conduct which merely causes a person discomfort and conduct which causes material damage to land. This distinction was drawn in the following way by Lord Westbury:

> It appears to me that is very describable to mark the difference between an action brought for a nuisance . . . that . . . produces material injury to property, and an action brought for a nuisance on the ground that the thing alleged to be a nuisance is productive of sensible personal discomfort. With regard to the latter, namely, the personal inconvenience and interference with one's enjoyment, one's quiet, one's personal freedom, anything that discomposes or injuriously affects the senses or the nerves, whether that may or may not be denominated a nuisance, must undoubtedly depend greatly upon the circumstances of the place where the thing complained of actually occurs. . . . But when an occupation is carried on by one person in the neighbourhood of another, and the result of that trade or occupation, or business, is a material injury to property, then there unquestionably arises a very different consideration.[10]

Any material injury to property is a nuisance without regard to surrounding circumstances. In the case of personal discomfort, however, the discomfort must be substantial and regard must be had to the locality. With regard to the level of discomfort one judge has described the appropriate test in the following way:

> Ought this inconvenience to be considered in fact as more than fanciful, more than one of mere delicacy or fastidiousness, as an inconvenience materially interfering with the ordinary comfort physically of human existence, not merely according to elegant or dainty modes and habitats of living but according to plain and sober notions among . . . people.[11]

Even if this test is satisfied the surrounding circumstances must be taken into account. One writer has put the matter in the following terms:

> The standard of comfortable living which is to be taken as the test of a nuisance is not a single universal standard for all times and places, but a variable standard differing in different localities. The question in every case is not, whether the individual plaintiff suffers what he regards as substantial discomfort or inconvenience, but whether the average man who resides in that locality would take the same view of the matter. He who dislikes the noise of traffic must not set up his abode in the heart of a great city. He who loves peace and quiet must not live in a locality devoted to the business of making boilers or steamships.[12]

Finally, if the damage to the plaintiff or his property is due to the unusual sensitivity of either, no action will lie.

The Parties: Only the person actually in possession is entitled to sue in nuisance, though a reversioner is so entitled if he can prove damage of a permanent nature to his proprietary right. As a general rule the person who creates a nuisance is always liable for it and for any continuance of it, whether he is the owner or occupier or even if he no longer has power to bring the nuisance to an end. Thus a person who builds a house which obstructs a private right of way continues to be liable even after he has let or sold the offending building.

Defences: There are essentially three general defences to an action in nuisance, namely, consent, prescriptive right and statutory authority. At one time it was thought that a consent could be implied from the fact that the plaintiff came to premises knowing of the nuisance, but that no longer represents the law. It may nonetheless be relevant with regard to personal discomfort which, as we have seen, is judged according to the locality. A defendant who claims the prescriptive right to continue a nuisance must prove that he has been doing the acts complained of openly and with the knowledge of the plaintiff (or his predecessor in title) for at least 20 years. It is essential that the defendant can show that the *nuisance itself* has existed *with regard to the plaintiff's property* for the entire period. In the case of a public nuisance this defence is not available. The defence of statutory authority needs no explanation but examples in Irish law are the Railway Causes Acts, 1845.

Finally, as a general rule, the fact that the defendant has exercised all reasonable skill and judgement is no defence to an action in nuisance.

Remedies: The injured party may resort to a form of self-help known as abatement. If the nuisance can be abated from his own land, for example, by cutting overhanging branches, the injured party is not obliged to give any notice of his act to the defendant. Where, however, it is necessary to enter the land of the defendant in order to abate, the injured party must, except in the case of an emergency such as fire, give the defendant notice and a reasonable time to terminate the nuisance. Abatement is an *alternative* remedy to damages.

An action for damages needs no further comment here, nor does the equitable remedy of injunction which is appropriate in the case of a continuing nuisance.

Liability under the Rule in *Rylands* v. *Fletcher*[13]

The rule itself may be briefly stated as follows:

> any person, who for his own purposes brings on his lands and collects and keeps there anything likely to do mischief if it escapes, must keep it in at his peril, and if he does not do so is *prima facie* answerable for all the damage which is the natural consequence of its escape.[14]

In *Rylands* v. *Fletcher* the defendants had constructed a reservoir on their own land in order to supply water to a mill. Unknown to the defendants a disused coal mine shaft ran between their land and the plaintiff's mine. When the reservoir was filled, the water escaped through the shaft and flooded the plaintiff's mine. The defendants were held liable on the above-mentioned principle which was enunciated by Blackburn J. in the Court of Exchequer Chamber.

The distinction between liability under this rule and liability in negligence is important. In negligence it is necessary to establish fault or, in other words, to prove that the defendant failed to exercise reasonable care. Liability under the rule in *Rylands* v. *Fletcher* is strict, i.e. once the plaintiff can bring his case within the rule, the fact that the defendant took reasonable care is immaterial. He is liable because his actions caused damage to the plaintiff. Strict liability is based on *causation,* while negligence is based on *fault.*

There are a number of important features of the rule to note. First, there must be an escape from the land of the defendant. In *Read* v. *Lyons*[15] the appellant, an amunitions inspector, was injured by an explosion which took place in the respondent's factory while she (appellant) was on the premises. One of the grounds upon which her appeal was dismissed was that there had not been an escape from the land. Secondly, a person is not strictly liable for damage caused by everything which escapes from his land but only for those things which are classed as dangerous things. This part of the rule is sometimes expressed by saying that a person is only strictly liable for damage caused by the non-natural (rather than natural) user of his land. It has been pointed out by one learned writer, however, that the latter distinction is difficult to draw in practice and has little to recommend it in principle. Things may be dangerous because of their inherent qualities, e.g. dynamite, or because of the quantity or amount of the thing brought onto the land, e.g., gallons of water. Furthermore, ideas change from one time to another about the natural use of anything, including land. Professor Heuston puts the point as follows:

> 'Extraordinary', 'exceptional', 'abnormal', are words that are sometimes used in substitution for 'non-natural' and they suggest the true principle underlying the doctrine. It is a question of fact, subject to a ruling of the judge, whether the particular object can be dangerous or the particular use can be non-natural, and in deciding this question all the circumstances of the time and place and practice of mankind must be taken into consideration so that what might be regarded as dangerous or non-natural may vary according to those circumstances.[16]

There are a number of possible defences available to the defendant:

(i) If the plaintiff has consented to the defendant bringing onto or keeping the dangerous things he cannot subsequently sue in *Rylands* v. *Fletcher* though he may, of course, be able to recover in negligence, depending on the terms of the contract.

(ii) Where the escape has been caused by the plaintiff's own default, the defendant has a good defence.

(iii) Where the escape is due to the act of a stranger there is no liability under *Rylands* v. *Fletcher* though, here again, the defendant may be liable for negligence.

(iv) Act of God: As Salmond points out, there has been only one reported decision in which this defence succeeded. The term 'act of God' signifies an event over which human control cannot be exercised, such as an extraordinary flood or storm. Such an event will provide a good defence unless reasonable care would have avoided the consequential damage.

(v) Statutory authority: A statute may, by its provisions, exclude liability under *Rylands* v. *Fletcher.*

PROTECTION OF INTERESTS IN CHATTELS

We are here concerned with the manner in which the law of torts protects a person's interest in goods or chattels. Such protection is not of course exclusively confined to the law of torts. Other branches of the law, e.g. the remedy of tracing in equity, may also be relevant in determining the full extent of the law's protection but here we are only concerned with the contribution of the law of tort. There are three different actions which may lie against a person who unlawfully interferes with the interest of another in certain chattels.

Trespass to Chattels

Any direct (in the sense in which the word was used at p. 232 *supra*) physical interference with chattels in the possession of another amounts to a trespass. The tort may be committed against animate (e.g. cattle or sheep) or inanimate (e.g. a book or a ring) objects. Moreover as long as there is some physical *interference,* actual physical *contact* is not necessary, so that wrongfully driving cattle out of a field or, *ex hypothesi,* summoning a dog or moving a book by levitation, would amount to a trespass.

While trespass is actionable without proof of damage it now seems that, in Ireland at least, in order to succeed the plaintiff must prove intention or negligence.[16a]

It has also been held in England[16b] that inevitable accident is a good defence to an action in trespass to goods. Like trespass to land trespass to goods provides protection for possession rather than ownership. Accordingly the plaintiff must establish that he was in actual possession of the goods and it is no defence to show, except in the case mentioned below, that his possession was wrongful. It also follows that the owner of goods who is not in possession is not entitled to sue in trespass but could himself be liable in this regard if he wrongfully interferes with the lawful possession of another, e.g. a bailee or the 'purchaser' under a contingency sale.

A recent judicial development in Ireland has enlarged the immunity of Gardai with regard to the seizure of goods under a search warrant. In *Jennings* v. *Quinn* the law was summarised as follows:

> "In my opinion the public interest requires that the police, when effecting a lawful arrest, may seize, without a search warrant, property in the possession or custody of the person arrested when they believe it necessary to do so to avoid the abstraction or destruction of that property and when that property is:
>
> (a) Evidence in support of the criminal charge upon which the arrest is made; or
>
> (b) Evidence in support of any other criminal charge against that person then in contemplation; or
>
> (c) Reasonably believed to be stolen property or to be property unlawfully in the possession of that person."[17]

Thus it would appear that a Garda can seize any goods which he reasonably believes are connected with any crime, and not just the crime he is then investigating.

Conversion

Conversion is any wilful and unlawful interference with a chattel of another which is inconsistent with the right of possession of the other or which results in the other being deprived of the use and possession of it. Conversion is based on the *fact* of an interference which is inconsistent with the plaintiff's right *and* on the *intention* of the defendant to deny the plaintiff's right or assert a right which is inconsistent with the plaintiff's. Both of these are essential features of this tort. Thus in *Fouldes* v. *Willoughby,*[18] where the defendant refused to carry the plaintiff's horses on his ferry and put them ashore, the court held that his conduct did not amount to a conversion as the act was not inconsistent with the plaintiff's title. The defendant was, of course, liable in trespass. In *Ashby* v. *Tolhurst,*[19] however, a car park attendant who *negligently* permitted the plaintiff's car to be stolen was not held liable in trover since he lacked the necessary intention. The following are some of the ways in which conversion may occur:

(i) *Conversion by taking:* A person who commits the crime of larceny is also liable in conversion. Conduct falling short of larceny, however, may nonetheless amount to conversion as where an escaped prisoner takes a car merely to make his escape without the intention of permanently depriving the owner thereof. The intention merely to temporarily deprive a person of possession is sufficient to constitute conversion.

(ii) *Conversion by detention:* A person who, after receiving a demand note for the return of a chattel, ignores or refuses to comply with such demand, thus showing an intention to retain the goods in defiance of the plaintiff is liable in conversion.

(iii) *Conversion by wrongful delivery:* A person who deprives another of his goods by delivering them to a third party is liable in conversion. It is no defence for the defendant to show that he acted in good faith.

Finally, a person who destroys an object, or fundamentally changes its identity is liable in conversion (e.g. by turning grapes into wine).

Detinue
Detinue consists of wrongfully denying possession of goods to the person entitled to immediate possession. It is the appropriate form of action in two particular cases. First, where the plaintiff seeks the actual recovery of the goods, as distinct from mere damages, he will sue in detinue. The court always has a discretion as to which remedy is appropriate and an order for specific restitution is normally only granted where the goods are of some special value or interest and damages would not be an adequate remedy. Secondly, detinue is the appropriate form of action where there has been no denial of title and thus an action in conversion will not lie. This may occur where, for example, a bailee has negligently lost the goods.

PROTECTION OF THE PERSON AND PERSONAL INTERESTS

Trespass to the Person
Trespass to the person has traditionally been divided into three categories, namely, assault, battery and false imprisonment.

Assault: An assault may be defined as any unlawful act which puts another in reasonable fear for his personal safety. It should be emphasised that the actual application of force is not necessary to constitute the tort of assault. Thus shaking a fist in a person's face is sufficient, even though no actual physical contact is made. It is essential, however, for the plaintiff to show that the conduct complained of would, in the circumstances, have placed a reasonable person in fear for his safety. Thus to shake one's fist at another from a distance would not usually be sufficient, though pointing an unloaded gun (when the plaintiff was unaware of this latter fact) would amount to assault.

Battery: A battery consists in the unlawful application of force to the person of another. Any unlawful touching, however trivial, may amount to a battery.

Thus placing a hand on a person's shoulder, an unwanted kiss and the unlawful taking of fingerprints, amount to batteries. As a form of trespass they are, of course, actionable *per se* but there is some controversy as to whether it is necessary to prove that the act complained of was intentional or wilful.[20]

False Imprisonment: The tort of false imprisonment may be defined as any unlawful act which prevents a person from exercising his right to leave the place where he is. Imprisonment does not just refer to unlawful detention in a prison or jail but to any place in which a person might be confined e.g. a room, a car or even a street. It is crucial, however, for the plaintiff to show that he had no means of leaving that place and it is not sufficient if he is merely deprived of one means of departure while others are available. Such alternative means must not be dangerous or illegal.

Negligence[21]

It has only been in this century that negligence, hitherto an important ingredient in other torts, has emerged as an independent tort. While it has long since passed through its embryonic stage, receiving its formal baptism in 1932, its scope has yet to be fully developed.

It is important to appreciate at the outset that, while 'careless' may be a useful adverb to describe the act or omission of a negligent defendant, not everyone who is careless will be liable in negligence. A defendant who drives at 100 m.p.h. may undoubtedly be careless or indifferent to his own safety or that of others, but if he completes his journey safely and without causing damage there can be no question of him being negligent as far as the law of torts is concerned. Moreover even where the carelessness or indifference of the defendant causes injury to the plaintiff, the latter will not be able to recover in negligence unless he can show that the law imposes a duty upon the defendant to take care to avoid injury to the plaintiff and that the defendant was in breach of that duty. Two crucial concepts which immediately arise, therefore, are duty of care and breach of a duty of care. A plaintiff will only succeed in a claim in negligence provided he can establish that the defendant owed him a duty of care and that as a result of a breach of that duty the plaintiff has suffered damage.

While a *moral* code may prohibit any act which is likely to harm another, the law is much more selective in this regard. It is only in certain limited circumstances that the law imposes a duty of care. Lord Atkin, in the leading case of *Donoghue* v. *Stevenson,* put the matter as follows:

> The liability for negligence . . . is no doubt based upon a general public sentiment of moral wrongdoing for which the offender must pay. But acts or omissions which any moral code would censure cannot in a practical world be treated so as to give a right to every person injured by them to demand relief. In this way, rules of law arise which limit the range of complaints and the extent of their remedy. The rule that you are to love your neighbour becomes in law, you must not injure your neighbour; and

> the lawyer's question, who is my neighbour? receives a restricted reply. You must take reasonable care to avoid acts or omissions which you can reasonably foresee would be likely to injure your neighbour. Who, then, in law is my neighbour? The answer seems to be – persons who are so closely and directly affected by my act that I ought reasonably to have them in contemplation as being so affected when I am directing my mind to the acts or omissions which are called in question.[22]

The duty of care, therefore, is based on 'reasonable foreseeability'. The crucial question is whether the defendant, as a reasonable man, ought to have foreseen that his acts or omissions were likely to injure the plaintiff. If the answer is in the affirmative, then a duty of care existed. A reasonably-minded motorist ought to foresee the likelihood of injury to other road users if he drives in a reckless or hazardous fashion. Such a motorist owes a duty of care to other road users. It will be noted that the test is an objective rather than a subjective one. It is not a question of whether this particular defendant recognised or ought to have recognised the danger, but rather a question of whether a reasonable man, in the position of the defendant, ought to have recognised it. In the final analysis this is, of course, a question of policy to be determined by the court. Lord Denning put the point as follows: 'It is, I think, at bottom a matter of public policy which we, as judges must resolve. This talk of 'duty' or 'no duty' is simply a way of limiting the range of liability for negligence.'[23]

In *Donoghue* v. *Stevenson* a manufacturer of a bottle of ginger-beer was held liable to the ultimate consumer. The manufacturer had prepared the goods in such a way as to show that he intended them to reach the ultimate consumer in the form in which they left him and with no reasonable opportunity or expectation of any intermediate examination of the goods before consumption. The House of Lords held the manufacturer liable to a plaintiff who had consumed a bottle of beer which contained the remains of a snail and which had caused injury to the plaintiff. It will be remembered that it was in this case that Lord Atkin made his now famous (obiter) remarks about the 'neighbour' principle. Since then, the term 'manufacturer' has been extended to cover erectors, assemblers and repairers, while 'products' has been held to cover hair dyes, tombstones and underwear.[24] But there have been limits imposed also. In the case of careless statements resulting in financial or economic loss, the courts have imposed a duty of care only when some special relationship exists between the parties, and even here there are a number of exceptions. In *Hedley Byrne & Co. Ltd.* v. *Heller & Partners Ltd.*,[25] the House of Lords finally rejected the old common law rule that the duty to take care was restricted to injuries to the person or property of another and held a defendant could be liable in *negligence* for a careless statement which the plaintiff relied upon and which caused him financial loss. While this area of negligence is still far from clear it can be stated that there is no liability without some form of special relationship and that a disclaimer of liability at the outset, as was the case in Hedley Byrne, will render the defendant immune.

Yet another area in which the courts have been reluctant to permit recovery in negligence has been in the field of mental suffering.

Thus, while the possible list of situations in which a duty may be said to exist is never closed but remains open-ended, 'it is not easy to predict when the courts will use the neighbour principle to extend the law and when they will refuse to do so'.[26]

Given the existence of a duty of care in any particular case, the next issue is whether the defendant complied with the proper standard of care in the circumstances. It is not necessary for the defendant to take all *possible* care but only such care as is reasonable in the circumstances of the case. Conversely the fact that the defendant has done his personal best to avoid causing injury to the plaintiff will be no defence if that standard falls below the standard of reasonable care:

> The standard of foresight of the reasonable man eliminates the personal equation and is independent of the idiosyncrasies of the particular person whose conduct is in question. Some persons are by nature unduly timorous and imagine every path beset by lions. Others, of more robust temperament, fail to foresee or nonchalantly disregard even the most obvious dangers. The reasonable man is presumed to be free both from over-apprehension and from over-confidence.[27]

In assessing whether the defendant conformed to the proper standard of care, a number of factors must be taken into account. Most forms of activity are fraught with some risk and the issue in a negligence action could be said to be whether a reasonable man would have taken the risk which the defendant took and which manifested itself in harm to the plaintiff. It is necessary to balance the social value of the activity and the expense or difficulty of rendering it harmless against the probability and extent of the possible harm.

While the defendant must guard against reasonable probabilities, he is not bound to guard against fantastic possibilities. In *Bolton* v. *Stone,*[28] the plaintiff was struck by a cricket ball while standing outside the cricket ground. It was established that the cricket ball had travelled 100 yards and crossed a 17-foot fence near the end of this distance. Such feats had only been achieved about six times in the preceding 30 years. The plaintiff's action was dismissed. Even where the risk of injury is small, however, a defendant may be negligent in failing to take adequate precaution if the resulting injury would be great. Thus a person would be expected to take greater care when dealing with nuclear waste than that required of the defendant in *Bolton* v. *Stone,* even if the likelihood of 'escape' is mathematically the same in both cases. Another important consideration is the cost or difficulty involved in taking the necessary precaution. A very high cost or degree of difficulty in taking adequate precautions, particularly where the likelihood of injury is very small, would sometimes justify a reasonable man failing to take such precaution.

It should be noted that while a plaintiff may recover for negligently caused damage to his person, his chattels or his land, under the general tort of negligence some interests have their own appropriate form of protection to which negligence does not apply. Such interests as those as personal reputation and marital privacy have not been brought under the umbrella of negligence. In addition, there are areas of law, such as the liability of occupiers, where the relationship of other rules to negligence is far from clear.

Finally, we must briefly explain the role of *contributory negligence* in modern Irish law. Until the enactment of the Civil Liability Act, 1961, if the plaintiff had contributed, however slightly, to his own damage this afforded the defendant complete defence. The Civil Liability Act abolished the *defence* of contributory negligence but introduced a system of comparative negligence. Under this latter system the 'fault' or 'negligence' may be apportioned between the parties, and, the plaintiff's recovery will be reduced in proportion to his share of the fault, i.e. his contributory negligence.

Liability for Dangerous Premises

The liability of an occupier of premises for injuries caused to persons while on those premises is generally referred to as 'occupier's liability'.

Occupier's Liability: The law traditionally has divided persons who come upon property occupied by the defendant into three categories: invitees, licensees, and trespassers. The duty of care owed by an occupier to a person coming onto the property has, at least until recently, depended upon the category to which the visitor belonged. If he was on the premises because of some material or pecuniary interest mutual to himself and the occupier, then the visitor was classed as an invitee. To such a person, the occupier was liable for injuries caused by dangers of which the occupier actually knew, or ought to have known. The following have been classed as invitees by Irish courts: a paying patron at a dance; a delivery man while on the premises for delivery; persons on premises for refreshments, while using the toilet facilities; a stevedore on the deck of a ship superintending the unloading of a cargo; a boy delivering milk to a creamery while in the boilerhouse sheltering from the rain; and a person who paid a fee for a conducted tour of a castle.[29]

Persons permitted onto another's land, but whose visit does not materially benefit the occupier, are known as licensees. The crucial distinction between a licensee and a trespasser is that the former enters with the permission, express or implied, of the occupier while the latter has no permission at all. The following persons have been held to be licensees by the Irish courts: the owner of a car admitted, by a mechanic after hours, to the garage where his car was kept; a worshipper visiting a church, the doors of which were open to the public; persons resorting to public parks and playgrounds and a schoolchild in school.[30] A licensee, it has been said, must take premises as he finds them. To such a person an occupier is liable only for concealed dangers of which he was actually aware. The licensee must take care of himself and cannot complain of obvious dangers or those which could reasonably be expected.

Persons who enter the premises of another without his consent, express or implied, are classed as trespassers. The law on the question of what duty is owed by an occupier to a trespasser has been recently the subject of judicial examination by the courts of ultimate jurisdiction in Ireland and England. The old common law rule was that the occupier owed no duty of care to a trespasser. This was sometimes expressed by saying that the only duty of the occupier was a duty not to set a trap for the trespasser. Though this harsh approach to trespassers had been slightly mitigated by judicial developments in recent years, it was not until the decision of the House of Lords in *Herrington* v. *British Rly. Board*[31] and that of the Irish Supreme Court in *McNamara* v. *E.S.B.*[32] that any clear and deliberate change becomes evident. In the Herrington case all of the five law lords were agreed that an occupier owed a duty of care to a child-trespasser. While the matter is far from clear it would seem that this duty arises only when the occupier knew or ought reasonably to have known of the presence of the trespasser *and* that there was a serious risk to the trespasser. In addition, there is no question of the standard of care being the same for a trespasser as for an invitee or licensee. The occupier is merely expected to act in a humane manner towards the trespasser. The approach of the Supreme Court was considerably different in that the Irish court went much closer to adopting a straight negligence approach. Walsh J. appraised the problem in the following manner: 'Was it reasonably foreseeable to the defendants that the children (trespassers) might enter their premises unless reasonable steps were taken to keep them out?[33]

Commenting that the jury, on the evidence before them, were entitled to answer the question in the affirmative, he continued: 'The question must then arise of whether the steps taken by the defendants to keep out children were, in all the circumstances, reasonable.'[34]

Both Griffin J. (with whom Fitzgerald C. J. concurred) and Henchy J. also accepted the reasonable foreseeability test. It would seem, therefore, that the duty owed by an occupier to a trespasser is to be determined according to the ordinary principles of negligence discussed earlier. What effect, if any, this may have upon the position of an invitee or licensee awaits further judicial decision.

Liability of Builders, Vendors and Lessors:[35] It would be misleading to think that all damage sustained by persons as a result of defective premises are dealt with as questions of occupier's liability. A contract or lease between a landlord and tenant may contain an express or implied term governing the question of liability. A vendor of premises may be liable in contract, as may a builder. Consequently the law of contract and the law of property may have to be also considered by a person who suffers damage as a result of defective premises.

Defamation

We have so far concentrated on torts which are designed to guard against the invasion of a person's property and his personal interests of freedom from physical injury or restraint. Defamation is designed to guard a person's good name, more specifically, his interest in his reputation.

A defendant is liable in defamation when he unlawfully communicates any false information to a third party which would tend to lower the plaintiff in the esteem of right-thinking people in society. The tort is divided into two categories, libel and slander. The basis of the distinction is essentially the form which the communication or publication takes. Matter published in permanent form such as writing, tape, effigy or film is classed as libellous, while matter which is published in transient form such as words or gestures is classed as slander. We will first examine the common features of libel and slander and then indicate the consequences of the distinction.

The essence of a defamatory statement is that it is false; the publication of matter which is true, no matter how cruel, tasteless or embarrassing can never amount to the tort of defamation though, as will be seen later, it may constitute a crime.

Besides being false the statement must tend to deprive the plaintiff of his reputation among ordinary, reasonable, right-thinking people in society. The tendency to produce such an effect is sufficient, so that a statement will be actionable even though no-one actually believes it. Furthermore it is the likely effect upon the minds of right-thinking members of society which is important. Therefore to say of a man that he is a police informer or to falsely state of an Irish civil servant that he 'helped jail Republicans in England'[36] does not amount to defamation since co-operation in the administration of justice is an act which, the courts have held, would tend to raise rather than lower a person in the esteem of right-thinking people. Defamatory statements generally take the form of an attack upon the moral character of the plaintiff, but this is not necessarily the case. Statements which are defamatory include those which reflect upon the capacity or fitness of the plaintiff in his profession or trade or upon his solvency in business or his physical or mental health.

Since the plaintiff alleges that the statement is defamatory of him, he must prove that it refers to him, expressly or by implication, in such a way as to be understood by others as referring to the plaintiff. Until recently this rule was rigidly applied to the extent that even if the statement was true of someone else to whom it referred, the plaintiff could nonetheless recover if he showed that it also referred to him. Thus in *Newstead* v. *London Express Newspapers Ltd.*[37] the defendants reported in their paper that 'Harold Newstead, a thirty-year-old Camberwell man' had been convicted of bigamy. The story was true with regard to a certain Harold Newstead, but not of the plaintiff who not only had the same name but also lived in the same area and was about the same age. The plaintiff succeeded in his action because the words clearly, though innocently, referred to him. The position has now been modified by the Defamation Act, 1961, which provides that where defamatory matter is innocently published the defendant may make an offer of amends (which usually involves the publication of an apology and correction). If the offer is accepted by the plaintiff it is a complete bar to any further proceedings. If the plaintiff rejects the offer, then, provided it was made within a reasonable time, it affords the defendant a good defence in subsequent proceedings.

Publication of the defamatory matter is another important feature of defamation. Since the essence of the wrong is the loss of the plaintiff's reputation *among others,* there can be no defamation by publishing to the plaintiff himself without publication to at least one other person. Publication simply means communication and neither publicity nor publication in the narrow sense is required. Sending defamatory matter to the plaintiff through the mail may amount to publication depending on the circumstances. Thus sending an open postcard or even a letter which the defendant knows will be opened by the plaintiff's secretary would amount to publication, while sending a registered letter to the home address of a plaintiff living alone would not. The fact that the defamatory matter has been originally published by one defendant will not excuse a second who publishes (repeats) it again.

Defences:

There are three main defences: justification, privilege and fair comment; we shall examine each separately:

Justification: As already noted, a statement which is true cannot be defamatory. It is not necessary, however, to show that every detail of the statement is true provided that the statement as a whole is substantially true. The point is now governed by the Defamation Act, 1961, s.22, which provides as follows:

> In an action for libel or slander in respect of words containing two or more distinct charges against the plaintiff, a defence of justification shall not fail by reason only that the truth of every charge is not proved, if the words not proved to be true do not materially injure the plaintiff's reputation having regard to the truth of the remaining charges.

Thus a defendant would succeed in a defence of justification if, having alleged that the plaintiff was 'a murderer and a thief who failed to pay a parking ticket', he established the truth of the first two, but not the last, allegation.

Privilege: Our law recognises certain occasions when a person is free to make a defamatory statement about another with either total or partial immunity. Such occasions are classed as being either occasions of absolute or qualified privilege. Absolute privilege attaches to statements made by judges, jurors, lawyers, parties or witnesses, with reference to judicial proceedings. The occasion is not confined to the trial itself but includes statements made in connection therewith, e.g. statement made to a solicitor before the trial. It also covers fair and accurate reports of statements so made. It also applies to statements made in either House of the Oireachtas and to reports thereof. Qualified privilege, which only applies to statements honestly made without malice, arises when a person is under a duty, legal or moral, to make a statement regarding another. A helpful example is that of a former employer who is called upon to provide an intending employer with a reference in respect of an employee. Statements made in the course of a reference of this kind cannot give rise to an action in defamation unless they are made maliciously, i.e. with some improper motive.

Fair Comment: A statement of opinion which is a fair comment on a matter of public interest is not actionable. There are a number of important points to note. First, the statement must be one expressing an opinion or comment, rather than a statement of fact. The facts upon which it is based, however, must be substantially true. No comment can be fair if it is based on false or invented facts. Secondly, the person making the comment must honestly believe it to be true. Malice destroys a defence of fair comment. Thirdly, the matter commented upon must be of public interest or concern. Examples of such matters are the administration of justice, the activities of the Oireachtas and works of literature.

Apology and Mitigation: A defendant cannot escape liability for the publication of matter defamatory of the plaintiff by simply apologising. Evidence of such an offer of apology, however, if made before the commencement of the action, or as soon afterwards as the defendant had an opportunity of doing so, may be given in mitigation of damages at the trial.

The Importance of Distinguishing between Libel and Slander: It was noted earlier that the law classifies defamation as slander or libel, depending upon the form in which the defamatory material is published. The importance of the distinction lies in the fact that slander, though not libel, is actionable only upon proof of special damage, i.e. actual material loss. To this general rule there are a number of exceptions. Slander, like libel, is actionable *per se* in the following circumstances:

(i) An imputation that the plaintiff has committed a criminal offence punishable with imprisonment.

(ii) An imputation that the plaintiff is suffering from an existing contagious disease.

(iii) An imputation of unchastity in a woman.

(iv) An imputation which is calculated to disparage the plaintiff in any office, profession, trade or business.

In each of these situations the plaintiff need not establish any special damage in order to recover for slander.

Defamation and the Criminal Law: A libel which tends to cause a breach of the peace is a criminal offence as well as a tort. Originating in an effort by the Court of Star Chamber to reduce what to the Court appeared to be the serious threat to public order arising from the (then) new art of printing, the crime of libel differs from its civil counterpart in two important respects. First, the truth of the statement made provides no defence unless publication is also in the public interest. Section 6 of the Defamation Act, 1961, provides as follows:

> On a trial of any indictment for a defamatory libel . . . the truth of the matters charged may be enquired into but shall not amount to a defence . . . unless it was for the public benefit that the said matters charged should be published . . .

Moreover if the accused, having raised this defence, is nonetheless convicted, it is provided that 'the court may, in pronouncing sentence, consider whether his guilt is aggravated or mitigated by the said plea and by the evidence given to prove or disprove same'.

The second difference between criminal and civil libel relates to the question of publication. As already noted, in the case of civil libel, communicating the defamatory matter to the person defamed does not amount to publication. There must be publication to a third party. In the case of criminal libel, however, communication or publication to the defamed party is sufficient since such publication may tend to cause a breach of the peace.

CONCLUSION

Such therefore is the diverse scope of the law of tort. It is easy to see why some debate has arisen as to whether this study should be called tort (indicating a general duty not to cause loss) or torts (to represent the range of interests protected). In describing the most important rules we have omitted reference to a number of other areas of tort, or torts, themselves, but we have attempted to concentrate upon the more important issues in a practical sense. Civil wrongs also occur in a family or domestic context, and torts of criminal conversation, enticement and harbouring should be noted too.[38]

Finally, it would appear that tortious liability can be incurred if business or economic loss is caused. This was particularly relevant in the early days of trade union organisation where loss resulted from industrial action. Its importance, however, despite some judicial intervention, is diminished today because of the protection offered to registered trade unions. This will be pursued in Chapter 16.[39]

Chapter 14*

LAW OF PROPERTY

Property is generally considered a most difficult and technical body of law. There is some justification for this view. For the beginner it frequently appears as a highly abstract and complicated field, full of ancient terminology and related to fact situations which are difficult to understand. Compared with other core subjects such as contract or tort there is much less familiarity with 'property' and property disputes. Concepts such as negligence and defamation can call upon familiar knowledge of car accidents and name-calling, while contractual doctrines such as consideration and implied terms can call upon the equally familiar practices of buying records and travelling in buses. But in the case of property there are fewer examples available to which the beginner can relate. The average reader may not have encountered the distinction between the house in which he or she lives and the title to the land upon which it rests, nor can either be expected to have felt the effects of distinctions between different kinds of title. For these reasons this chapter begins with a general introduction to the kinds of functions or roles that property rules perform before considering the main rules themselves.

A useful way to introduce the study of the law of property is, strangely enough, by reference to another behavioural discipline, economics. A basic assumption of economics is that all physical resources are scarce. This is merely to state the obvious. Resources such as land, oil, metals and water (economists would include labour) are finite or exhaustible. Accordingly there is a need to organise the distribution or sharing of resources. Each share may be considered as a claim or a right to particular resources. These rights are of course property rights and this term 'property rights' tells us what the law of property is about. When I say 'This book is mine', I am telling the world of my claim to a share of the limited resources of books in the world, of which the book I refer to is a part.

In the above example, however, I have merely indicated the object (i.e. the book) to which I have a claim. I have not said anything about the nature of my claim or how it will be protected or supported by the legal system. Can I do anything I like with my book? May I alter its form, e.g. by burning it? May I give it away in whole or in part to whoever I please and, if so, may I effect a transfer by simply handing the book to my friend or must I draw up (execute) a formal document of transfer such as a deed? Finally, is the book mine for a month, a year or perhaps forever so that upon my death I can bequeath it to someone who will continue to enjoy the rights that were once vested in me? The answers to these and other such questions are found in the law of property.

**See also 1988 Supplement pp. 327-332.*

It should now be clear that the principal function of the law of property is just as much to determine the *nature* of a person's claim to a particular resource as to identify the *object* of the claim. The astute reader will now be troubled by an alarming possibility suggested in this analysis. Though accepting that resources are limited he will also know that the number and variety of objects in Ireland must run into billions upon billions. If each object can be the subject of a number of claims, and if each object has its own unique set of claims, the study of property rights, he will say, is an impossible task. Fortunately the study is facilitated by a number of basic principles of property law.

First, while each object may be different from the next in a real sense, generally speaking the law has grouped all objects into classes, which are known as 'real property' and 'personal property' respectively. Subject to a minor exception mentioned later, any object such as a book, a cow or a house can be fitted into one or other of these classes. The law has achieved this organisation by identifying those objects which belong to the class known as real property and simply classifying everything else as personal property. Real property consists of land and anything which is permanently affixed to the land, such as a house. At common law if a man was wrongfully dispossessed of his farm he could bring an action to recover the property. This form of action was known as a 'real' action because the successful plaintiff recovered the farm itself. Common law, however, was less accommodating in restoring objects other than land to a successful plaintiff, who usually could only expect to recover damages. This latter (and perhaps less satisfactory) form of action was known as a 'personal' action. It was from the type of action available to recover an object belonging to each class that the classes derived their respective labels, real and personal property.

Only one object has managed to avoid being classed as either real or personal property and that is because it is really a hybrid of both. A lease, which gives the leaseholder certain limited rights to possess and use land, was subject to a personal action only. For this reason it might have been classed as personal property. But because of its very close connection with land the label would be slightly misleading. In a type of compromise it is known as a 'chattel real'. The term 'realty' is commonly used as a synonym for real property, while 'personalty' is similarly substituted for personal property. These terms will be used interchangeably throughout the remainder of this chapter.

Secondly, tangible objects of real property, e.g. a house, a river, or a coal mine, are known as *corporeal hereditaments,* while tangible objects of personal property, e.g. a book, a horse, or a lamp, are known as chattels. Accordingly all physical objects are either corporeal hereditaments or chattels.

Thirdly, the claims or rights which exist with regard to realty or personalty are limited and, for the greater part, clearly defined. A more detailed set of claims has always existed with regard to realty because, as will be seen, land is indestructible. But even here it is possible to identify all the possible claims or rights which can exist.

Finally, while all tangible objects are subject to rights (or claims), property rights may, in a special sense, exist without any corresponding tangible object. Personal property provides the easiest example. Suppose I lend a neighbour £10 and the time for repayment has now arrived, I have a right to £10 from my neighbour. I have a right, but not to any particular tangible object such as the £10 note in his coat pocket. (Indeed, if I take that note without his consent, or the authority of the court, I will be prosecuted for larceny.) At best my right is to an *intangible* object, a *debt.* In the case of personalty such rights are known as *choses in action.* Similar though not identical rights, such as the right to use a right of way or not to have the light to my house diverted by my neighbour's house, also exists as realty and are known as *incorporeal hereditaments.*

To summarise, there are three forms of property known to law, namely, realty, personalty and chattels real. The objects which are subject to claims are either corporeal hereditaments or chattels. Rights (or claims) may also exist in intangible matters and are known either as incorporeal hereditaments or choses in action. In the remainder of this chapter we will examine land law and succession separately, but three final comments may be made. First, the common law has developed a far more sophisticated and detailed body of rules with respect to realty than personalty.[1] This reflects both the historical importance of land as a source of wealth and the nature of land itself, the rights over which are generally more difficult to ascertain and thus more likely to be the subject of fraud. Second, the superiority of land as a source of wealth is more relevant to the past than the present. Changes in Western society over the past century or so indicate that personal property, rather than realty, may now be more relevant to more people. This chapter makes no attempt to discuss what has been termed the 'new property', which includes, for example, a person's right to his job or to social welfare, a form of property which, according to one view at least, may prove to be more important than realty and personalty combined.

LAND LAW

Let us suppose that I am the owner of *all* rights over a plot of land which we will call Happyacre. The term 'land' also includes everything which is permanently affixed to the land, so that if I have built a house on the land, my claims also extend to that. As owner of all the rights over Happyacre I can be said to be the *absolute* owner of the land. Now this is precisely the type of theory that prevailed under common law, with the king as the absolute owner of all land in the kingdom. Of course the king did not need or require all the land; but he did need the support of his subjects in various ways. Having retained certain lands to provide for his personal wealth he then granted various tracts of land to his subjects in exchange for various kinds of services. These services varied from a subject's duty to provide a number of days work on his lord's property to the duty to provide a certain number of armed soldiers for the lord's army in times of need. As mentioned in Chapter 1, those people who received their land direct from the king were known as *tenants-in-chief.* The latter would frequently make sub-grants, also in return for services, to persons who were known as *mesne tenants.* This process, called *subinfeudation,* might continue until at the end of the pyramid we have persons referred to as *tenants in demesne.*

Tenure

The crucial point about the relationship between the king, the tenants-in-chief, the mesne tenants and the tenants in demesne was that it was based on the provision of services in exchange for land. This system is known as the system of *tenures.* As indicated earlier the type of service required might vary so that we find a number of different tenures.

There were essentially two general categories of tenure, free tenure and unfree tenure. We shall briefly discuss each.

Free Tenures: The following diagram sets out the main forms of free tenures:

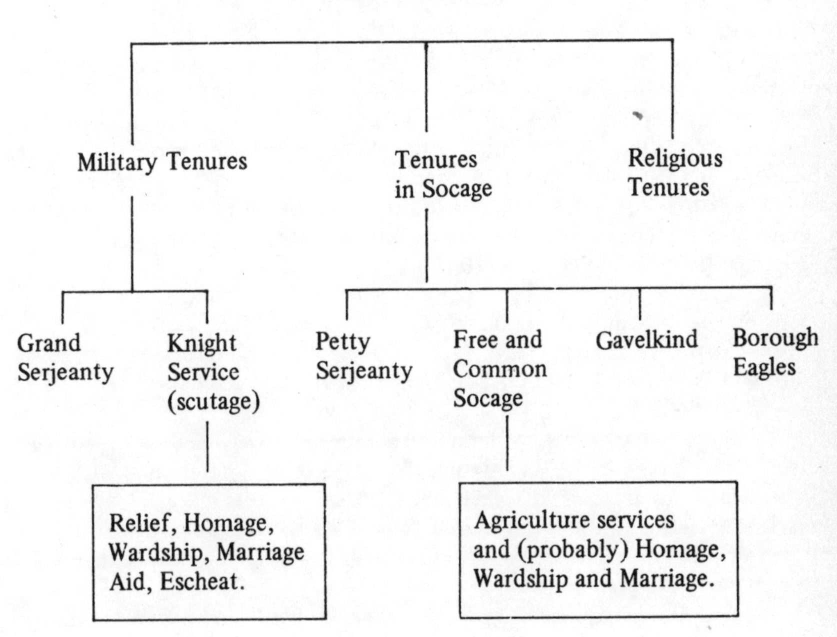

The main division was between military tenures and tenures in socage. Grand serjeanty was a very special form of military tenure confined to tenants-in-chief and under which certain personal services were due to the king. At the outset knight service, which was much more common than grand serjeanty, involved the provision by the tenant (who might be a mesne tenant or tenant-in-chief) of a number of armed horsemen for the lord's army for a specified period of each year. It would appear, however, that from the 13th century in Ireland (and even earlier in England) this obligation was commuted to a money payment known as *scutage.* For the remainder of the feudal period the importance of tenure by knight service lay in the various incidental rights it conferred on the lord or, from the tenant's perspective, the various incidental duties to which it gave rise. The tenant was obliged to pay *homage* to his lord by swearing to abide by his feudal obligations and by attending his lord's court. The lord had the right to *wardship* of his deceased tenant's heir. This meant that he not only exercised control over the person of the heir but also, until the heir reached majority, the lord enjoyed valuable rights of management over the land to be inherited. In such circumstances the lord also had the right to *choose a spouse* for his ward, and if the lord's wishes were not complied with he could fine the ward. The lord was also entitled to payment of a sum of money (usually equivalent to one year's profit from the land) whenever the land was succeeded to by an heir of full age. This right was known as *relief.* Other payments (known as *aid*) might also be demanded at specified times, e.g. to ransom the lord or upon marriage of the lord's eldest daughter or when his eldest son received a knighthood. Finally, the lord enjoyed a most valuable right known as *escheat.* Because of the system of tenures the early common law did not permit a man to dispose of his land by will. Instead it passed to his heir under a system known as *primogeniture* (see p. 260 *infra*). If a tenant died without an heir the property reverted back to the lord who might dispose of it as he thought fit. This right was known as the right of *escheat.* In addition, the property would also revert to the lord if the tenant was convicted and sentenced to death for the commission of a felony. This latter aspect of escheat should not be confused with *forfeiture* under which a tenant's land reverted, not to his immediate lord, but to the king, if the tenant was convicted of high treason. It is worth noting at this stage that land may, to the present day, revert to the State as ultimate successor when a deceased dies without any surviving next-of-kin (see p. 273 *infra*).

The most popular form of tenure in socage was *Free and Common Socage.* Indeed in Ireland it is likely that Petty Serjeanty never applied,[2] while *Gavelkind* and *Borough English* are just two of the more widely known variations which arose in certain English localities. Similar Irish variations were derived from the Brehon Laws but were rejected by the common law courts[3] (see Chapter 1 *supra*).

Free and Common Socage essentially required the provision of agricultural rather than (as was the case in knight service) military services. There was some controversy as to the extent of the incidents of common socage but, in Ireland at any rate, the practice seems to have been to claim rights of homage, marriage and wardship.

Before leaving the subject of free tenures, brief mention must be made of a third form, namely, religious tenures, of which the most common was known as *frankalmoign.* A tenant holding by *frankalmoign* was obliged to provide services of a spiritual (e.g. praying for the lord) rather than a temporal nature. Such tenures were confined to persons occupying religious offices.

Unfree Tenures: We know very little about the extent of various forms of unfree tenure in Ireland. Our knowledge can be summarised in two statements. First, unfree tenure meant that the status of the tenant was little better than that of a slave. As an unfree tenant he could be bought and sold and was frequently regarded as part of the land itself. Secondly, for technical reasons, (see below *infra*) he did not have access to the king's court. While the quantity of his agricultural services might be fixed the quality was freely determined by the lord. The common form of unfree tenure known as *copyhold* had little application in Ireland.

This was the system of landholding introduced by the Normans into Ireland over eight hundred years ago. It was, as it frequently pointed out, as much a system of government as a system of holding land. A 20th-century purchaser of an acre of land or a semi-detached suburban home would be unlikely to tolerate subjection to such obligations to the vendor of the property and, of course, little, if anything, of the feudal system of tenure remains in Ireland today. Tenures, in the feudal sense, were almost completely abolished by the Tenures Abolition (Ireland) Act, 1662, which transformed all tenures into free and common socage, which subsequently became known as *freehold.* But a form of tenure unknown to feudalism also emerged. This was known as *leasehold* and will be dealt with later in this chapter.

Estates

Tenure was but one of two crucial concepts developed by feudalism. It indicated the terms upon which the land was to be held. The other concept developed by feudalism, one which permeates modern land law, is that of *estates.* Whereas tenure determined the terms upon which the land was held, the *estate* determined the duration of the holding.

A major distinguishing feature between land and other forms of property is the relative indestructability of land. Whatever the complications generated by the ability of modern science to transform matter into energy, land is likely to outlast, not only man, but all other forms of property. This was even more certain and obvious during the feudal period than today. This durability of land and, by definition, anything permanently affixed to the land, gave an element of security to long-term dealings in land which was impossible with other forms of property. Men have always been willing to pay more for the enjoyment of land for, say, 500 years rather than 20 years because they could depend on land to exist for the longer period. Thus a 500-year lease is a valuable asset. A 500-year loaf of bread or automobile, however, is close to absolute nonsense. It was as a result of this permanent quality of land that the common law was able to develop a system of estates. Moreover the development of the concept of estates was not the work of common law alone, for equity also made important contributions, combining with common law to produce a tapestry of intricate detail.

Estates in land generally fall into two main categories, freehold and leasehold, and we will deal with each separately, noting the influence and contribution of equity where appropriate.

Freehold Estates: There are four main types of freehold estate, Fee Simple, Fee Farm Grants, Fee Tail (or Estate Tail) and Life Estates. The size of an estate may be measured in terms of time, i.e. the duration for which the property is likely to remain with the person holding the estate or his successors. On this basis the four types of estate mentioned above are listed according to size, with size representing the possible duration of a person's rights or claims, rather than the physical dimensions of the object of these rights.

(i) *Estates in Fee Simple:* A fee simple is the largest estate because, on the death of the present holder, it may pass to any next-of-kin surviving him. In the early days of common law when disposing of property by will was prohibited, the fact that there was no limitation other than that of a blood relationship between the deceased and the claimant meant that the land was unlikely to ever escheat to the lord. In contrast with the fee tail, where heirs could only be selected from among descendants (e.g. children, grandchildren) and not ancestors (father, grandmother), it was far closer to absolute ownership. Today with the availability of testamentary succession (i.e. people may dispose of any property by will) the likelihood of a fee simple escheating is even more remote. But the real advantage to the holder of a fee simple estate is that, subject to his contract and conveyance as well as other branches of law, he is free to deal with his property as he wishes. During his life he may deal with it as he pleases and upon his death may dispose of it to whoever he wishes. Such an estate is known as a *fee simple absolute.* But a fee simple estate may also exist as a *modified fee.* The two main forms which such an estate may take are known as a *determinable fee* (e.g. a grant to A and his heirs while A remains a solicitor) and a *conditional fee* (to A and his heirs provided that if A ceases to be a solicitor) respectively. The distinction between these two forms of modified fee is a highly technical one with which the beginner need not concern himself. It is important to realise, however, that the attachment of a condition to a fee simple does not affect the estate which is taken. Certainly upon the event specified occurring, the estate may automatically revert to the grantor, but the event may never occur.

(ii) *Fee Farm Grants:* A fee farm grant may be defined as a conveyance of a fee simple subject to payment of a perpetual rent by the grantee, and his successor in title. Such estates are common in Ireland and they have some very special features.

(iii) *Fee Tail:* A fee tail is a smaller estate than the fee simple because, as indicated earlier, succession to a fee tail is confined to descendants of the deceased. Entailing property was a popular device before the Industrial Revolution because it kept the property in the family for several generations. Common law developed various rules which either sought to limit the power of a grantor to tie up an estate indefinitely or forever (e.g. a rule known as the Rule against Perpetuities) or which provided a means for disentailing entailed land. This latter process is known as *barring the entail* but it can only be effected *inter vivos* and not by will. While a fee tail restricts succession to descendants, stricter forms such as *tail male* or *tail female* restrict succession even further, in this case, to male and female descendants respectively.

(iv) *Life Estate:* A life estate is essentially what its name suggests. It is an estate which will last for a life only, and the life chosen may be that of the grantee of someone else (e.g. to A for as long as B should live). In the latter case it is known as an *estate pur autre vie.* The important distinction between a life estate and the other two forms of freehold estate should be obvious. The latter estates will survive the current holder of them – they are *estates of inheritance* – while the life estate is not available for succession.[4]

So far we have confined our attention to those estates developed and recognised by common law. These estates are known as *legal estates.* But the Court of Chancery also made substantial contributions to the development of estates generally through its concept of *equitable estates.* The point is best explained by considering two examples, one relating to *trusts* and the other to the sale of land. In a more general way, however, equitable estates developed because of a defect in common law previously noted in Chapter 1, namely, that the form rather than the intent was everything at common law.

First, let us consider the case of trusts or *uses,* as they were formerly known. In certain cases while a grantor may wish X to have the enjoyment or *use* of the land, he may wish to vest the legal title or estate in someone else, Y. There are a variety of reasons why a grantor may wish to resort to such a device. He may be providing for his son, a spendthrift, whom the grantor fears will dissipate the property very quickly. To avoid this he places legal control of the land in the hands of someone he knows to be responsible and prudent, e.g. his solicitor or banker. Alternatively, he may wish to avoid certain taxes, though this possibility is becoming very remote as a result of modern legislation. Thus a grantor might convey the land to Y for the use of, or in trust for, X. Now at common law only the legal conveyance was recognised. To the common law courts the legal title was vested in Y and (this is the crucial step) X had no claim to the land. The Court of Chancery, however, was prepared to recognise and enforce X's claim. Because it was originally enforceable in the Court of Chancery only, X's right became known as an *equitable estate,* as distinct from the *legal estate* recognised by common law. In a sense the equitable estate was a shadow of the legal one and equity accordingly adopted similar nomenclature to that developed by common law. Thus if the grantor had conveyed a legal fee simple to Y in trust for X, equity treated X as the holder of an *equitable fee simple estate.* If the estate conveyed was a fee tail or life estate, then X held an equitable fee tail or equitable life estate, as the case might be.

For our second example let us consider the sale of land. The process of transferring an estate in property from A to B is known as *conveyancing.* Among the many steps in the process two are of interest here, namely, the contract for sale and the conveyance itself. The actual transfer or conveyance of land is usually preceded by a written contract in which the parties set out the terms of their agreement. Because of the usual time-lag between signing the contracts and effecting or executing the conveyance, the question may arise as to whom the title to the land belongs during this period. Common law, where the form was crucial, held that since the land had not been conveyed title remained in the vendor (seller). Equity, however, recognising that the position was not as clear-cut as that, divided the estate into legal and equitable parts. At equity, while the legal estate remains vested in the grantor, the contract has the effect of transferring the equitable estate to the purchaser. So, after signing or exchanging contracts, and until completion, legal title will vest in the vendor while equitable title will vest in the purchaser. Once again the 'size' of the equitable estate will be a shadow of the legal one, so that if the vendor is selling a legal fee simple the purchaser will hold an equitable fee simple between contract and completion. When completion takes place the two estates will merge in the purchaser but he may, of course, split them again at any time in the future.

It is important to realise that the equitable estates in property may be dealt with in any of the ways in which legal estates are dealt with. Hence it can be sold, mortgaged or disposed of by will. It may be held by more than one person at the same time (see p. 267 *infra,* dealing with joint ownership) and, as we shall shortly see, be the subject of future interests as well as immediate possession.

Before leaving the question of freehold estates two further matters must be mentioned briefly. Frequently lawyers will say that the crucial difference between freehold and leasehold estates is that the holder of the former has *seisin* while the holder of the latter does not. The concept of *seisin* is difficult to explain and while it is related to the concept of possession, it signifies something more. Common law developed two important rules about seisin: first, only the person holding a freehold estate under freehold tenure could have seisin, second, there must always be some person seised at any particular time. The importance of the first rule is not only in what is expressly stated, but also in what it implies – while a leaseholder might have possession, he could not have seisin.[5] The second rule prohibits the creation of a gap in seisin. I cannot convey my fee simple interest in Happyacre 'to X next year', because between now and next year no one would be seised.

The second matter which must be briefly explained is known as *words of limitation.* We have already mentioned the importance of formality at common law. One of the consequences of this was that in order to grant or convey a particular legal estate certain precise words had to be employed. The term *words of limitation,* therefore, refers to the words which identify the nature of the estate granted. Thus, for example, in order to transfer my fee simple estate to A I would convey it either 'to A and his heirs' or to 'A in fee simple'. If I used the term 'to A and the heirs of his body' he would get a free tail, while conveying simply 'to A' would merely create a life estate. These rules are relaxed in the case of wills, as opposed to an *inter vivos* transaction, and as one would expect are much less rigidly adhered to in the creation of equitable estates.[6]

For the beginner it may appear strange that in the above examples the words 'heirs' and 'heirs of his body' merely indicate the nature of the estate to be taken by A and confer nothing on the heirs themselves. Where the words 'heirs' or 'heirs of his body' are construed as conferring an interest in the heirs (as is frequently the case in equitable estates) the words are then known as *words of purchase* rather than *words of limitation.*

So far we have assumed that all rights in land imply a right to immediate possession. It is now necessary to dispel this notion and to explain how future interests (rights) may coexist with immediate or present rights of possession.

The rules relating to future interests are perhaps the most difficult rules of land law. Yet, provided the reader clearly understands our discussion on estates, the basic principles are not difficult to grasp.

Our starting-point is the distinction drawn earlier between different estates and the reason why we can say that a fee simple estate is *larger* than either a fee tail or a life estate. Let us employ some simple figures for a moment. It is elementary mathematics that the subtraction of a smaller quantity from a larger one will leave something remaining; in other words, '4–1 = 3'. Now this mathematical principle is equally true of estates in land. If I hold the fee simple in Happyacre and convey a life estate to X, clearly (as a life estate is *smaller* than a fee simple) I have not disposed or parted with all of my estate. That part which remains is known as a *reversion* or *reversionary interest.*

In the example given it includes my right to resume possession after the termination of A's life estate. It is a proprietary interest and, as such, may be transferred to others. Its value, of course, will vary inversely with the value of the estate I have granted to A and will depend on how long the estate is likely to last. Though a right to the *future* enjoyment of land, it may be quite valuable if A is 80 years old.

Let us take this example a stage further. Again, as the holder of the fee simple estate in Happyacre I grant a life estate to A and a fee tail interest to B, the latter to take effect after A's death. The words of limitation would probably be 'to A for life and on his death to B and the heirs of his body . . .' I have, as in the earlier example, given A an immediate estate in possession. From this moment until his death he is entitled to enjoy the property. Unlike the previous example, however, the property will not revert to me upon A's death, but rather will B then have a fee tail in possession. Until A's death B's interest is merely a *future interest* which we refer to as *a remainder.* But it should not be overlooked that I, too, still retain an interest in Happyacre. I have given away less than I started with. My future interest is my *reversion.*

Accordingly, rights in land may be classed either as rights (or interests) in possession, or future interests. A future interest is either a reversionary interest (the term used when the grantor retains an interest in the estate) or a remainder (the term used when the grantor disposes of part or all of what remains after creating the immediate estate in possession). It is not unusual to find a reversion, an estate in possession and one or more remainder, all co-existing with respect to the same land.

A few general points can now be made. First, the remainders in our example were all *legal* remainders and as such are subject to strict legal rules. These rules are designed to prevent a landowner from tying up his land perhaps forever. Secondly, equity also developed future interests, two of the most common being called *springing* and *shifting* uses. Finally, as a side-effect of the Statute of Uses (Ireland), 1634, we have a type of legal/equitable hybrid which is known as a legal executory interest.

Leasehold Estates: While freeholds were an integral part of the feudal system, leaseholds were not recognised during the feudal period and are a much later development. Indeed early in the history of the common law[7] a lease for a term of years was considered purely as a personal contract between the parties, with the doctrine of privity of contract (see Chapter 12) operating to exclude anyone but the parties (e.g. their successor's in title) from relying on the 'lease'. It should be noted that because of its (later) historical development, a leasehold has always been regarded as less than a freehold estate.

In modern land law, leasehold interests are generally divided into the following four categories:

(i) *Leasehold Estate for a Term Certain:* These types of leasehold, particularly for long terms (e.g. 999 years), are very common in Ireland.

The term is *certain* only with regard to the maximum period of duration and it is usual for the parties to provide for its termination after a short period, e.g. forfeiture for non-payment of rent.

(ii) *Periodic Tenancy:* These are leases without any maximum (or minimum) duration but which may continue indefinitely. Common examples are weekly or monthly tenancies which continue from month to month, or week to week, until determined by either party in the appropriate fashion.

(iii) *Tenancy at Will:* This tenancy may also continue indefinitely but may be terminated at any time by the will of either party. It offers little security to a tenant and nothing that he can dispose of.

(iv) *Tenancy at Sufferance:* This form of tenancy is very similar to a tenancy at will with regard to the tenant's security. The essential difference is that in the case of a tenancy at sufferance the tenant is 'holding-over' after his earlier tenancy which has been terminated. There is also a form of statutory tenancy which will be discussed later.

The modern doctrines of landlord and tenant (not to be confused with the feudal model) are, to an ever-increasing extent, governed by statute. In Irish history the plight of the tenant was an unenviable one, subject as he was to sudden increases in rent and even eviction at the whim of his landlord. Since the lease was originally regarded as little more than a special kind of contract, the doctrine of freedom of contract ensured that in practical terms a landlord was free to impose almost any terms on his tenant. Indeed Deasy's Act of 1869, which in many ways still underlies much of Irish landlord and tenant law, gave statutory expression to the idea that the basis of the relationship between the parties was one of contract.

Agrarian troubles in the 19th century saw the organisation of rural tenants to demand reform. Their demands are expressed by the 'three F's' – fair rent, fixity of tenure and freedom of alienation. It was a long and bitter struggle but by the early part of the 20th century these objectives had been achieved. In addition to the 'three F's' a system of land purchase was introduced and developed during this period. The system provided loans from State funds to tenant farmers to assist them in buying out their landlords.

The position of the urban tenant has only been improved in more recent times. Legislation such as the Landlord and Tenant Act, 1980, provides security of tenure for tenants who (after establishing a 'long family equity') find that their leases have expired. They are now entitled to new tenancies and, if the parties cannot agree, the matter may be referred to the court. The Landlord and Tenant (Ground Rents) Act, 1967, provides a means whereby certain urban tenants can now buy out the freehold title to their land and the

Rent Restrictions Acts, 1960 and 1966, restrict the right of a landlord to increase the rent of dwellings to which the Acts apply. Moreover, further restrictions or controls on the use of property, and this applies equally to freeholds, have been introduced by such legislation as the Local Government (Planning and Development) Act, 1963, which imposes statutory duties on planning authorities to generally control and supervise the development of land in their locality.

There is little else, conceptually, which can be said in an introductory work about leaseholds in Irish law. It comprises a wealth of detail in which, over a period of about one century, the legal balance has been shifted from being heavily biased in favour of the landlord to, some might argue, being heavily biased in favour of the tenant.

Incorporeal Hereditaments

We must now examine those property rights which are known as incorporeal hereditaments. The nature of such rights was suggested at the outset of this chapter by drawing a distinction between rights which were linked to tangible objects and those which were not. The essential feature of an incorporeal hereditament is that it gives the holder rights, not over land of his own, but over the land of another. In a sense it is a right of enjoyment of land in the possession of someone else. These rights take many forms but we will confine ourselves here to the two most common types, *easements* and *profits.*

An *easement* is a right enjoyed by the owner of land to use the land of his neighbour in a particular way. It is important to realise that easements exist to benefit or improve the enjoyment (and hence the value) of *the land.* The land over which an easement is exercised is known as the *servient tenement,* the land which has the benefit of the easement is known as the *dominant tenement.* Thus if the holder of the fee simple in Happyacre has an easement (e.g. a right of way) over his neighbour's land, Happyacre is the dominant tenement and the land of the neighbour, the servient tenement. Of course it may also happen that the neighbour has an easement (e.g. right to support) over Happyacre and so, for the purposes of this latter easement, the positions are reversed.

While the same land can be the dominant and servient tenement for the purposes of different easements, it cannot be both with regard to the same easement. Provided two adjoining plots are not owned *and* occupied by the same person, one plot may enjoy an easement over the other. No easement can exist, however, in favour of one plot over the other, if both plots are owned and occupied by the same person. Moreover if unity of possession and ownership occurs after easements have been created, such easements are *extinguished* and are not *revived* by a subsequent separation of possession and ownership. Examples of easements are rights of way, light, support and water.

A *profit* or, to give it the proper title, a *profit à prendre* is the right to go on the land of another and take from it something regarded as belonging to it naturally, e.g. turf, fish, minerals, etc. These rights are similar to easements but there is one vital distinction. As already indicated, an easement requires a dominant tenement. A profit, however, may exist without any such dominant tenement (though frequently there is such a tenement). A profit of this kind is known as a *profit in gross.*

Joint Ownership: Earlier in this chapter, when dealing with estates, it was observed that concurrent estates could exist in the same land, e.g. a grant by a fee simple owner 'to A for life and on his death to B in tail male'. While the holders of such interests clearly have concurrent interests, it is equally clear that *they will enjoy possession successively,* and not concurrently. In this section we are concerned with the situation where two or more persons are entitled to concurrent ownership or possession. Such cases are referred to as *joint ownership* or *co-ownership.*

There are four main categories of co-ownership: *joint tenancy, tenancy in common, coparcenary,* and *tenancy by the entireties.* We will deal only with the first two of these, which are the most popular in Ireland.

Joint tenants and tenants in common share many characteristics. In both cases third parties must treat them as a single unit for the purpose of certain transactions relating to the land. In both cases each tenant is entitled to possession of any part of, or all, the land, and no co-owner can exclude another from such possession. As well as the similarities between these two forms of co-ownership, however, there are also important distinctions. First, in the case of a joint tenancy, the common law rule is that no co-owner can dispose of his interest by will and that the last surviving co-owner takes all. The rule is known as the *jus accrescendi* or *right of survivorship.* Equity, however, leans against joint tenancies and in certain cases will mitigate the harshness of the common law rule by treating the survivor as a trustee of the land for himself and the successors of his deceased co-owners, in proportion to their respective contributions to the purchase price. This will occur, for example, where there has been a disparity in the original contributions. In such a case equity will presume (and it is only a presumption) that the parties *intended* to take as tenants in common (to which the *jus accrescendi* does not apply) in spite of their taking in the *form* of a joint tenancy. Secondly, while both forms of co-ownership require unity of possession, a joint tenancy must comply with three *unities.* These are *unity of interest* (they must all hold the same *estate,* whether freehold or leasehold, fee simple or a fee tail), *unity of title* (they must hold their estates by virtue of the same document or transaction) and *unity of time* (each interest or estate must vest at the same time). A joint tenancy may be converted into a tenancy in common by what is known as *severance.* There are two main ways of affecting a severance: by the acquisition of a further interest in the land by one of the joint tenants, or by the *inter vivos* disposition of his interest by one of the tenants. The result is that the parties are then treated as tenants in common.

Either form of co-ownership may be determined by *partition* or *union* in a sole tenant. Partition may mean the division of the land by agreement or court order, or, and this is more common in the cases of land not easily divisible, the sale of the land and the division of the proceeds of sale. Union may occur, in the case of a joint tenancy, as a result of the *jus accrescendi*, and in the case of both, by the transfer of all interests, e.g. by sale to one co-owner.

SUCCESSION

Succession may be described as the process through which the owner of property disposes of that property after his death. Rules of succession are as old as the rules of land law, and this is not surprising. Land would always survive the deceased, and a system of property rights which did not define succession rights would fall into chaos in one generation.

As we shall see, the rules themselves have varied considerably over the centuries, but they can nonetheless be seen as representing three different ideas. First, in the early period land could not be disposed of by will. Secondly, there was a period during which total freedom of disposition prevailed. Finally, comes the modern stage where this freedom is restricted in the interests of the deceased's immediate family.

When a person disposes of all his property by will he is said to have died *testate*. When he dies without disposing of any property by will he is said to have died *intestate*. Frequently a person may dispose of some, but not all, of his property by will. In such cases he may be said to have died *partially* testate or intestate.

Upon death the property of the deceased passes, in the first instance, to his *personal representatives*. These are the people who will pay the deceased's debts and funeral expenses and then distribute the remainder according to the appropriate rules. They are known as executors when applying the terms of a will and administrators when dealing with an intestacy. There is a detailed body of rules dealing with the powers and duties of personal representatives but we shall not discuss further their role here.

The remainder of this section is divided between testamentary and intestate succession, with a brief comment on the consequences of a partial intestacy.

Testamentary Succession

Testamentary succession is now governed by the Succession Act, 1965.[8] There are a number of separate issues which deserve attention.

(i) *Capacity:* Section 77 of the Act provides that a person must have reached 18 years or be, or have been, married (note that persons may marry under 18 years, see Chapter 17) and be of sound disposing mind. There is a presumption in favour of a testator's 'sound disposing mind' and the onus lies on the person asserting the contrary to prove it. 'Sound disposing mind' essentially means that the testator understood what he was doing and the consequences of his dispositions.

(ii) *Form:* Section 78 provides that all wills must be in writing. Any form of writing, such as ink, pencil, type or print, will suffice and it may be presented on any kind of surface, e.g. paper, timber, metal or stone. The prudent testator, however, will select a form of writing and a surface which will endure at least until after his death.

The will must be signed by the testator. The signature may take any form such as initials, a mark or a stamp. Formerly the rule that such signature had to appear at the foot or end of the will was rigidly applied. The matter is now governed by the Act which provides such a wide interpretation of 'at the foot or end thereof' that it is to be questioned whether anything is to be gained by saying the rule still exists.

(iii) *Attestation:* The signature (not the *will* itself) of the testator must be witnessed or attested by two witnesses. The easiest method of complying with this provision is by all three persons signing, together in each others' presence, though this is not strictly necessary.

(iv) *Content:* Each will is designed to meet the needs of a particular individual and, in attempting to interpret wills (as opposed to documents executed *inter vivos*), the courts are quite liberal in their interpretation of language. The goal is to find the intention of the testator. Most wills will begin with the testator declaring that this is his 'last will and testament', and revoking all previous wills or dispositions made by him. Next will follow the various *specific* devices (of realty) and *bequests or legacies* (of personalty), e.g. Happyacre to John Murphy, my collection of legal texts to Mary Murphy, etc. These clauses may be highly technical or utterly simple. Usually they are followed by a *residuary clause* which disposes of everything not specifically devised or bequeathed, though there may be separate residue clauses for realty (residuary devise) and personalty (residuary bequest or legacy). Such a residuary clause may be inserted even though the testator believes he has disposed of all his property in the specific clauses. A testator may acquire further property between the time of executing the will and the time of his death and he may find it inconvenient to constantly return to his solicitor and alter his will. Alternatively, a testator may have overlooked some property belonging to him or believed that property belonging to him belonged to someone else. But there is a third and more important reason. Some of the specific clauses may not be able to take effect. If the testator attempts to give property to one of the persons (or the spouse of such person) who attests his signature, such a gift will fail. When a beneficiary predeceases the testator, the beneficiary's interest is said to *lapse* (i.e. it cannot take effect). In both of these cases the property concerned will pass on intestacy unless a residue clause is inserted.

(v) *Execution:* A will is said to be executed as soon as the testator and attesting witness have completed the proper formalities described in (ii) and (iii). The will does not become operative or effective, however, until the testator dies. In the meantime no interests are created and the testator may alter his will at any time.

(vi) *Alteration and Revocation:* A will may be altered or revoked in one of three ways. First, if the desired alteration is only slight the testator will usually execute what is termed a *codicil.* Codicils are subject to the formalities of execution (signature and attestation) discussed previously. If the desired alteration is substantial it may be more expedient to execute an entire new will, including a phrase such as 'I hereby revoke all previous wills or testamentary dispositions made by me'. In the absence of such a clause the general rule is that *later* dispositions prevail over earlier ones to the extent that there exist contradictions or inconsistencies between them. Secondly, a will may be revoked by *destruction* provided there is also an intention to revoke. Destruction may take the form of burning or tearing or any other effective means. Finally, an earlier will is revoked by a later marriage unless the will was made in contemplation of *that* marriage.

(vii) *Limits of Freedom of Testation:* This was perhaps the most controversial part of the Succession Act, 1965, and gave rise to much discussion. The limitations of freedom of testation are of two kinds: first, those designed to protect the interests of a surviving spouse, and secondly, those designed to protect the interests of children.

Section 3 provides that if a deceased is survived by a spouse only, then, irrespective of the provisions of the deceased's will, the surviving spouse is entitled, as of *legal right,* to one half of *all* the deceased's property (the term *estate* is commonly substituted for *property* in this context) at the time of death. If the deceased is survived by a spouse and children, the spouse is entitled to one third of the deceased's estate. This *legal right* takes priority over all bequests and devises. The right may, however, be surrendered by agreement and such a clause is regularly found in separation agreements. Unless a contrary intention is expressed, a provision for a spouse in the deceased's will is treated as being in satisfaction, in whole or in part (depending on the proportion it bears to the entire estate), of the legal right of such spouse. The surviving spouse must elect to exercise his legal right otherwise he will take under the will.

Another valuable right is conferred by section 56. This provides that if the estate of the deceased spouse includes a dwelling in which, at the time of the deceased's death, the surviving spouse was ordinarily resident, such spouse may require the personal representatives to appropriate the dwelling and any household chattels towards satisfaction of the spouse's share in the estate.

Section 117 permits the court, on application by, or on behalf of, a child of the testator, where the testator has failed in his moral duty to make proper provision for the child as it thinks just. The court is to view the question from the point of view of a just and prudent parent, taking all the circumstances into account.

Intestacy

Since the Succession Act only applies to intestacy arising after 1st January, 1967, brief mention must be made of the rules applicable before that date, since title to property may still depend on them for its validity.

There were different rules applicable, depending on whether the property was realty or personalty. If realty, this is where the property went to the heir, who was chosen from among the blood relations of the deceased. Descent was traced from the land *purchaser,* a technical term to describe the last person who gave value for the property. The heir who succeeded to the property on intestacy was the heir of the last purchaser (or the purchaser himself, if alive), who might or might not be the heir of the deceased. Land descended lineally so that persons such as children and grandchildren took before other blood relations. Among children males were preferred to females, while among males, the elder was preferred to the younger. Among females there was no preference and they took as co-owners (coparceners). The lineal descendants (e.g. children) of a *deceased* heir stood in his place. This is known as the doctrine of representation. Thus, if the deceased has no surviving issue, his grandson would take before his sister or brother. If there were no lineal issue, the *paternal* ancestral lineal line was preferred to the maternal.

At one time all the deceased's personalty went to the bishop of the diocese in which the deceased lived. Later it seems that a deceased's wife and children could claim two-thirds of the personalty and the deceased might dispose of the remainder as he wished. Finally, the Statute of Distributions (Ireland), 1695, gave full freedom of testation over personalty. It also provided, however, for the distribution of personalty on intestacy. Since all of a married woman's personalty vested absolutely in her husband, these rules were only of real importance to men. If the deceased was survived by a widow and children (or other issue), the widow took one-third and the remainder was divided among the children. If the deceased was survived by children only, the children took all. If his widow but no children survived, the widow took one-half and the other half was divided among the deceased's nearest blood relations.

These provisions were modified, first by the Intestates Estates Act, 1890, and in 1954 by an Act with a similar title. The result of the latter Act was that, prior to 1st January, 1967, a widow was entitled to the whole estate (realty and personalty) if she was the sole survivor (i.e. no issue) and the value of the estate was less than £4,000. If the value exceeded this amount, the widow's claim was limited to £4,000. All of these provisions have now been replaced by the Succession Act, 1965.

The first point to note about intestacy rules under the Act is that the long-standing distinction between realty and personalty is abolished. The new intestacy rules determine the distribution of all the deceased's estate, whether realty or personalty. The following are the main rules:

(i) *Surviving spouse and children:* Spouse takes two-thirds, remainder divided among the children.

(ii) *Surviving spouse – no children:* Spouse takes all.

(iii) *Surviving children -- no spouse:* Divided equally between children.

(iv) *No spouse, no children:* Deceased's parents take in equal shares. If only one parent, that parent takes all.

(v) *No spouse, children or parent:* Deceased's brothers and sisters take equally. As long as one brother or sister survives, the children of a deceased brother or sister will share their deceased parent's share. If no brother or sister survive, their children take in equal shares.

(vi) *Next-of-Kin:* Where no one qualified under rules (i) – (v) above, the estate is distributed to the next-of-kin in equal shares. Next-of-kin is the person (or persons) who, at the deceased's death, stood nearest in blood relationship to him.

Let us suppose that the deceased is survived by a grand-nephew (i.e. his deceased brother's grandson) and by a second cousin, sometimes called a first cousin once removed (i.e. his deceased father's-brother's-grandson). The person nearest is determined in the following way: for the first claimant, determine the nearest common ancestor for the claimant and the deceased. Count the number of *steps* from the claimant up to the common ancestor *and* down to the deceased. Proceed in a similar way with regard to the second (or other) claimant. The claimant who reaches the deceased in the fewest steps is his next-of-kin. If two or more claimants require the same number of steps, they share equally. The following diagram may assist the reader. Here X is the deceased and, while various relations are included for illustrative purposes, the only survivors on the diagram are the grand-nephew (GN_2) and the second cousin, $2C_2$.

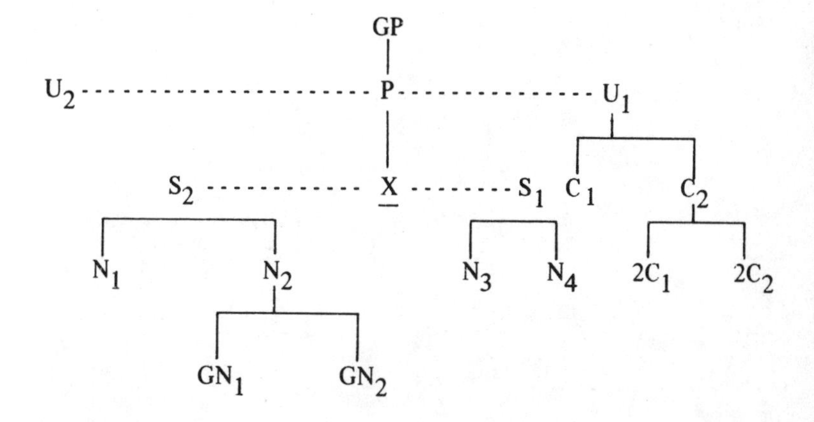

(Where there is no surviving next of kin, land may to the present day revert to the State.)

All persons in this diagram are described by the relationship to the deceased, X. Thus P refers to parents, GP to grandparents, U to uncles, S to sisters, N to nephews, C to cousins, GN to grand-nephew and 2C to second-cousins. The common ancestor shared by GN_2 and X is P; thus there are four steps in this relationship. The common ancestor shared by $2C_1$ and X is GP; thus there are five steps in this relationship. Accordingly, GN_2 takes to the exclusion of $2C_1$.

Finally, where a direct lineal ancestor and any other relatives are equal in 'steps', the direct lineal ancestor is postponed to the other relative, i.e. uncles and aunts would take before great-grandparents.

CONCLUSION

The rules of land law and, to a lesser extent, those of succession introduce the reader to new and difficult concepts. Parts of this chapter may have to be read more than once before being assimilated. A knowledge of the historical foundation of modern land law is a prerequisite to an understanding of many concepts such as tenures and estates. Other concepts are possible only because of the relative indestructibility of land. In the case of all rules and concepts presented in this chapter the reader should ask himself two questions: first, why did such a rule emerge? second, how far has its early form (if any) been modified to meet modern conditions? This will permit the reader to bring to bear upon the rules his own knowledge of history, sociology and even politics. As we have seen before, rules do not develop suddenly or by accident, nor do they operate in a vacuum. Land law and succession are important indicators of the kind of society in which we live.

Chapter 15*

COMPANY LAW[1]

In Chapter 3 we referred to the special status enjoyed by a company in our legal system. We indicated that a company has an identity or personality distinct and separate from that of its members. The practical importance of the company is highly significant in modern society in general and in the commercial world in particular. This chapter examines briefly the manner in which the law regulates companies in their formation, administration and dissolution.

Companies first developed under the Tudors in 16th-century England. The early practice, which may still be observed in the United Kingdom today, was to confer a royal charter upon a particular organisation. This company was

**See also 1988 Supplement pp. 327-332.*

permitted to do anything which was not prohibited by the charter. Chartered companies were looked upon as a gift of a set of rights from the Crown to certain people. These gifts were usually subject to certain conditions and if a condition was broken the gift might be revoked.[2]

Only people of wealth and influence could ever hope to obtain a royal charter. The ordinary trader could not expect such a privilege. From the 17th century, domestic trade within the State began to grow but the only form of organisation available to the small trader was a partnership which vested the property in trustees and gave powers of management to a committee or a board. But this method was not without its difficulties. First, at this time it was doubtful if a share (a chose in action) was capable of assignment. Secondly, it was not clear who should be sued, the firm or individual partners. In spite of these difficulties this form of business organisation became popular and it was from these large partnerships that the modern company developed. The earlier form was loosely referred to as a joint stock company.

In 1720 the 'South Sea Bubble' scandal helped to accelerate the rate of reform. This was a scheme to make money in the South Seas out of slave-trading. The Bank of England supported the venture. The company proposed to buy out the total State debt and pay for it by the issue of shares in their company. The directors of the Bank became alarmed and started bidding against the South Seas Company. Finally the Government introduced the Bubble Act, 1720, which outlawed the large partnerships and attempted to provide protection for investors in the South Seas Company. In spite of this, however, panic set in and the shares fell from 1000 to 150 in six months. This marked a considerable setback for the development of companies and, indeed, was followed by a growth in unincorporated associations formed by a deed of settlement. It was not until 1855 that limited liability, the corner-stone of modern company law, was finally introduced.[3] Since that time there have been many legislative efforts at regulating companies. Today, for the greater part, Irish law on the topic is consolidated in the Companies Acts, 1963 and 1977.

This legislation, often considered difficult and complex, can be more readily assimilated if the reader keeps one or two basic ideas in mind. Regulation of companies is essentially an attempt to balance a number of conflicting interests. For the entrepreneur it is essential that a mode of protection from unlimited liability be available. He will often wish to seek capital from the public to assist in the development and expansion of his business. The public, and creditors in particular, must be protected from fraud and unscrupulous promoters and directors. These are essentially the interests which are recognised and dealt with by the Companies Act, 1963, in which there are various rules aimed at protecting investors and/or creditors.

We will now deal with the rules as they relate to incorporation, administration and dissolution.

The incorporation of companies and matters incidental thereto are provided for in Part II of the Act. Section 5 deals with the distinction between public and private companies and between a company limited by shares, a company limited by guarantee and an unlimited company. These matters have already been discussed in Chapter 3, where it was noted that every company must have a Memorandum of Association and Articles of Association in order to be incorporated. These are the two main documents which make up the constitution and rules of the company. The memorandum must contain the following:

(i) The name of the company

(ii) The objects of the company

(iii) Unless it is an unlimited company it must state that the liability of its members is limited

(iv) In the case of a company limited by shares,

  (a) the amount of the share capital and the division thereof into shares of fixed amounts

  (b) the number of shares (at least one) taken by each person who subscribes his name to the memorandum.

The Name of the Company

Provided the last word in the name of a limited company is 'limited' or 'teoranta', there is no strict limitation on the choice of a name. Provided the name is not objectionable or so similar to that of another company as to lead to confusion, any name may be selected. Moreover a change in the name of a company has as little effect as the change in the name of a person. In order to change its name the company must pass a special resolution and obtain the consent of the Minister for Industry and Commerce. Certain companies may be permitted to dispense with the word 'limited'. These companies are of a charitable nature, with a purpose of general public utility. Such a company must provide that its income will be devoted to its objects and it must, by its articles, prohibit the payment of a dividend to its members.

Objects Clause

This clause has a twofold purpose: first, it defines and determines affirmatively the powers of the company; secondly, it restricts and limits these powers as the promoters of the company may think fit. As a general rule the objects clause will contain a number of paragraphs on the following lines:

(a) Main objects clause, e.g. to trade in a particular business.

(b) Power to enter into contracts with companies in the same business.

(c) Power to purchase, lease or otherwise deal with land.

(d) Power to borrow money.

(e) Power to guarantee payments and debts.

(f) Power to deal with bills of exchange, negotiable instruments (e.g. cheques), bills of lading, debentures, etc.

(g) Schemes for employees.

(h) Schemes for insurance.

(i) General clause empowering the company to do all other things incidental to the main objects.

Difficulties may arise where the company acts *ultra vires,* i.e. in excess of its powers. The matter is now governed by section 8 of the Act and S.I. No. 163 of 1973. In such a case the action is binding on the company provided that it would have been lawful for the company to so act had the appropriate provision been made in the memorandum. Accordingly, if the company enters into a contract which is *ultra vires,* the contract will nonetheless be binding on the company if it would have been lawful and effective but for the omission in the objects clause. In such a case, however, any director or officer who was responsible for the company acting *ultra vires* is liable to the company for any loss or damage suffered by it in consequence of his actions. A person who contracts with the company but who is, at that time, aware that the company is acting *ultra vires,* cannot rely on this provision.

The alteration of the objects clause can only be done by passing a special resolution. There is provision for shareholders of debenture-holders to object resolution. Generally speaking such persons must either hold 15% of the company's shares or debentures or, if the company is not limited by shares, represent 15% of the members.

Limited Liability

In a normal trading company the members' liability will be limited to the amount, if any, remaining unpaid on their shares. Likewise in the case of a company limited by guarantee the liability of members is limited to the amount they undertake to pay in the event of liquidation. Under Section 36, however, this protection may be lost. It provides that where the number of members of a public company falls below seven or, in the case of a private company, below two, and it carries on business for more than six months with its number so reduced, every member of the company who is aware of these facts is personally liable for *all* debts contracted on the expiration of six months.

Capital

The authorised or nominal share capital is the limit of capital the company proposes to issue. Issued or subscribed capital refers to the amount of shares actually bought. A shareholder may make full or partial payment. In the case of partial payment, e.g. 25p in every £1, he agrees to pay the balance when called upon by the company to do so. The following table may help to illustrate these and other points with regard to capital:

Authorised capital	–	£50,000
Issued capital	–	£30,000 (shares at £1 each)
Paid-up capital	–	£ 7,500
Unpaid capital	–	£22,500
Unissued capital	–	£20,000

The figure for unissued capital is purely a paper one and may quite easily be reduced. The figure for issued capital, however, is very real and is quite difficult to reduce though, of course, it may easily be increased either by calling in the unpaid capital or by selling more shares. In the same way the authorised or nominal capital is only a paper figure and, provided it does not fall below the issued capital figure, is quite easily reduced. In like manner it is very difficult for the company to release the shareholders from their liability to pay the balance, if any, due on their shares. The topic of shares and capital is more fully discussed later.

The articles of association are the rules for the internal regulation of the company. The management and administration of every company is, subject to the Act, governed by its own articles of association. The first schedule to the Act contains five tables which set out model articles of association and memoranda of association. Table A contains model articles for the management of a company limited by shares. Table B contains a form of memorandum of association for such a company. Table C provides a memorandum and articles of association for a company limited by guarantee and not having a share capital, while Table D contains the same for such a company which has a share capital. A model memorandum and articles of association for an unlimited company is contained in Table E. With the exception of the articles of association of a company limited by shares, it is provided by section 16 that the memorandum and articles of association of all companies shall, as far as circumstances permit, be in accordance with the appropriate model in the first schedule.

A company that is limited by shares does not have to file any articles of association. In that even Table A applies. Even if it does register articles, in so far as they do not exclude or modify Table A, that Table applies.

The combined effect of the memorandum and articles, when registered, is to bind the company and its members to the same extent as if they had been signed and sealed by each member and contained covenants (i.e. undertakings) by each member to observe all the provisions they contain.

In the case of some companies, e.g. private companies, all the shares might be taken up by the directors and this may provide the company with sufficient capital for its needs. More commonly, however, companies, even private companies, must look elsewhere in order to obtain sufficient capital to permit the enterprise to commence and develop. This will usually entail borrowing money from some quarter and a power to borrow is implied in the objects of a trading company, though in the case of a non-trading company such a power must be expressly reserved in the memorandum. There are two ways in which this might be achieved. First, through unsecured borrowing whereby the company manages to secure a loan without pledging any security by way of mortgage or otherwise. A person who advances such a loan runs a considerable risk since, should the company later go into liquidation, he will find himself at the end of the queue of creditors. Accordingly, a person advancing money to a company will usually require either participation rights in the company or else will require some security which he can realise to satisfy the debt should the company become insolvent. The former protection is achieved through the issue of shares while the latter is effected through the issue of debentures. By becoming a member of the company as a shareholder, a creditor will usually have a say and a vote in the management and administration of the company and, in some cases, can be placed very close to the head of the creditors' queue upon liquidation. As we shall see later, a debenture holder, though not a member of the company, can exercise considerable control over it and usually have a charge on definite or specific property of the company (known as a fixed charge) or on company property of a more *fluctuating type,* e.g. stock in trade (known as a floating charge). We now propose to examine the provisions relating to the issue of shares and debentures and then to discuss briefly the manner in which the company may deal with the debt so incurred.

The members of the company are the subscribers of the memorandum and every person who agrees to become a member and whose name is entered in its register of members. A public company once formed (indeed, on occasion, even prior to formation) will invite members of the public to subscribe for its shares. This invitation is known as a prospectus and sections 43 – 52 set out in considerable detail the manner in which it may be issued. The main interest here is to ensure that any such invitation is a fair, honest and accurate statement with regard to the company. Certain information must be provided as set out in the third schedule and any prospectus must, before issue, be registered with the companies' office. Section 49 renders directors, promoters and any person who has authorised the prospectus or permitted himself to be named as a director therein liable in damages for any loss or damage sustained as a result of any untrue statement contained in the prospectus. Moreover under section 50 a person is criminally liable (6 months months/£100 on summary conviction, 2 years / £500 on indictment) if he authorised the issue of a prospectus containing an untrue statement, unless he can prove that the statement was irrelevant or that he had reasonable grounds to believe and did, up to the time of the issue of the prospectus, believe that the statement was true. Private companies do not have to file a prospectus because their shares cannot be advertised to the public.

Once members of the public offer (for the prospectus is but an invitation to treat – see Chapter 12), the company may either accept or reject the offer. If the offer is accepted then shares are allotted. It is common for the prospectus to provide that unless there is at least a minimum amount of offers, no allotment will be made. The amount must be reached before any allotment can take place. Moreover while it is not necessary that the shares be fully paid-up, the amount payable upon application must not be less than 5% of the nominal amount of the share, i.e. the amount into which the issued share capital has been divided (see, for example, p. 278 *supra*). Provided these conditions are met, shares may be allotted three days after the issue of the prospectus and the company must, within one month thereafter, deliver a statement of the details of the allotment to the registrar.

Shares must be paid for and the company cannot give them away free. This rather simple statement conceals a number of important points. First, though shares must be paid for, this need not necessarily be done in cash. Consideration other than cash, such as property, goods or services, is sufficient. Here the general contractual principle that, while consideration must be real, it need not be adequate, applies. Secondly, section 59 permits the payment of commission in return for subscribing, agreeing to subscribe or the procuring of subscription for any shares in the company. The result of these two principles is, of course, that shares may be issued at a discount. In addition, the only other circumstances in which shares may be issued at a discount are set out in section 63. These are as follows:

(i) The shares are of a class already issued.

(ii) At least two years must have elapsed since the company became entitled to commence business, or, if a private company, since the date of incorporation.

(iii) The issue must be authorised by a special resolution of the company.

(iv) The resolution must specify the maximum rate of interest discount.

(v) The issue must be sanctioned by the court.

(vi) The issue must be made within six months of the sanction of the court, unless the time is extended by the court itself.

The main purpose of these conditions is to ensure that the discount is not excessive. Rule (i) ensures that the court can determine a market value for the shares. Rules (ii) and (vi) respectively ensure that the company has been in business long enough for the real market value to have been reached and that the issue takes place before any great change can occur. Rule (iii) ensures that the informed consent of the voting members of the company is also obtained.

Unlike the case of an issue at a discount there is nothing to restrict a company from issuing shares at a premium, i.e. above their nominal value. In such circumstances, however, the amount by which the price of the share (i.e. premium price) exceeds the nominal or par value must be transferred to a special account known as the 'share premium account'. To all intents and purposes it is then treated as issued or share capital and can only be reduced in cases which permit the reduction of share capital. Before dealing generally with the question of capital, however, a number of points with regard to shares must be mentioned.

The most widely quoted definition of a share is that which was provided by Farwell J. in *Borland's Trustee* v. *Steel.*

> A share is the interest of a shareholder in the company measured by a sum of money, for the purpose of liability in the first place, and of interest in the second, but also consisting of a series of mutual covenants entered into by all the shareholders *inter se* . . . . A share is not a sum of money . . . but is an interest measured by a sum of money and made up of various rights contained in the contract, including the right to a sum of money of a more or less amount.[4]

Thus the shareholder is, in the first instance, under a liability to pay for his shares. The 'covenants' mentioned refer to the conditions in the articles of association. The articles define the various rights which are not only rights *against* the company but also rights *in* the company. These rights accrue to the shareholder and the share certificate is merely evidence of the ownership of shares. As a chose in action, the share may be transferred (proper formalities must be complied with), mortgaged, surrendered and, in exceptional cases, even forfeited. This is, of course, subject to the provisions of the articles.

Finally, a word on share warrants: section 88 provides that, where articles permit, share warrants may be issued on fully paid-up shares. The advantage of a share warrant is that the shares it represents may be transferred by simply transferring the warrant. Accordingly, share warrants considerably facilitate the transfer of shares which otherwise must comply with the proper formalities.

We must now examine the rules relating to debentures, since this is the additional or alternative method through which the company can raise extra capital. The term 'debenture' is very widely defined in the following terms: ' "Debenture" includes debentures stock, bonds and any other securities of a company whether constituting a charge on the assets of the company or not.'[5]

The term 'securities' means any undertaking by a company to repay. Consequently an unsecured loan is, in this sense, a debenture. It is more common, however, to find that a debenture is accompanied by a charge for the reasons outlined earlier and, indeed, it is more usual to find that a debenture is one of a series of debentures issued to different lenders. When the debenture is not accompanied by a charge it is known as a 'naked debenture'.

The distinction between a share and a debenture should be kept in mind. A share is a chose in action, evidenced by a document called a share certificate. A debenture is a document which is evidence of a chose in action, i.e. a debt. A share certificate is to a share what a debenture is to a debt. There are a number of different forms of debenture. Registered debentures are subject to many of the rules which apply to shares. A transfer of such a debenture must comply with the proper formalities and, just as in the case of shares, a register of such debenture holders is kept at the company's offices. There are usually two parts to such a debenture, namely, the covenants by the company to pay interest and repay the principal, and the terms or conditions on which the loan has been made. Bearer debentures are similar to share warrants in that the debt may be transferred by delivery of the debenture without further formality. Perpetual debentures are debentures representing a debt which is only repayable upon winding up or after a long period of time. This is an exception to the general rule that debentures are repayable (redeemable) within a fixed period of time.

So far it has been assumed that all shares in a company will be exactly alike. While this may be the case it is more common to find different classes of shares. The rights (class rights) attached to different classes of shares will vary on such important matters as voting, dividends and by return of money upon liquidation. Some shares have a preferred fixed dividend. This means a dividend of a fixed amount payable on a certain day, and this dividend will be payable before the ordinary shareholders receive anything.

MANAGEMENT AND ADMINISTRATION

Though a company has a legal existence or personality of its own it clearly has no physical existence and its management and administration must be carried out by human persons. The persons appointed to perform this function are known as directors. Every company must have at least two directors and must also appoint a secretary who may, however, be one of the directors. As a general rule no particular qualifications are required of directors though certain persons, such as an undischarged bankrupt, and bodies corporate are excluded.

The manner in which directors may be appointed will be provided for in the articles, and these will usually name the first directors. Moreover section 178 provides that the acts of a director shall be valid notwithstanding any defect which may afterwards be discovered in his appointment or qualification. In spite of anything to the contrary in the articles or in any agreement between a director and the company, a director may be removed from office before the expiration of his term of office (if any) by merely passing an ordinary resolution to that effect. Such a director may be entitled, however, to sue for damages for breach of contract. Subject to this ultimate power of removal shareholders exercise very little control over directors who control the day-to-day affairs of the company. In exercising their powers, however, directors are required to act in the interests of the company and equity has developed some very strict rules regarding any personal profit accruing to directors by virtue of their office. At the company's annual general meeting, in addition to the financial statements such as the balance sheet and auditors' report, the directors must also report on the state of the company and section 158 lays down the matters which must be dealt with therein. Finally, section 194 imposes a duty on any director who is in any way, directly or indirectly, interested in a contract or proposed contract with the company to declare the nature of his interest at a meeting of directors of the company.

The control which members exercise over directors and the company generally is exercised at *meetings,* of which there are four types:

(i) *Annual General Meeting:* Every company is required to hold a general meeting each year as its annual general meeting, in addition to any other meetings which may be convened. So long as the company holds its first annual general meeting within 18 months of its incorporation, it need not hold it in the year of its incorporation or in the following year. Members must receive at least 21 days notice of an annual general meeting.

(ii) *Statutory Meeting:* Public companies limited by shares, or limited by guarantee but having a share capital, must hold a general meeting not less than one month and not more than three months from the date at which the company is entitled to commence business.[7] Such a meeting is called a statutory meeting and only one such meeting is held during the existence of any company. Members must be supplied with a statutory report usually at least 14 days before such a meeting. The report contains information on the issue of shares, the preliminary expenses, the names of the directors and secretary, and other matters. The members may, under s.130 (8), discuss any matter relating to the formation of the company, or arising out of the statutory report, or whether previous notice has been given in accordance with which the articles may be passed.

(iii) *Extraordinary General Meeting:* All general meetings, other than the annual general meeting or the statutory meeting, are known as extraordinary general meetings. Article 50 of Table A authorises the directors to convene an extraordinary general meeting whenever they think fit. Section 132 provides that, notwithstanding anything to the contrary in the articles, the directors *must* convene such a meeting upon a request from, in general terms, the holders of 10% of the paid-up share capital or, in the case of a company limited by guarantee *and* without a share capital, members representing not less than 10% of the voting rights. The requisition must state the object of the meeting and the directors must then, within 21 days, proceed to convene the meeting, which must be held within two months. If the directors fail to do this the requisitionists may themselves convene the meeting, but such a meeting cannot take place until the expiration of three months from the date of the request.

(iv) *Class Meeting:* This is the term used to describe a meeting of a particular class of shareholders or creditors. Generally speaking the provisions relating to general meetings are applied to class meetings by Article 3 of Table A.

The minimum period of notice for convening a general meeting is 21 days for the annual general meeting and 14 days for other meetings, except that in the case of a private or unlimited company, notice of the latter is reduced to 7 days.[8] A meeting may be called by shorter notice, however, if it is so agreed by the auditors and by all the members entitled to attend and vote.

In addition to being convened in the proper manner, meetings also must be conducted in a proper manner. General meetings must have a quorum, i.e. a minimum number of members present, usually at the commencement of the meeting. This matter is usually dealt with by the articles (see Table A, Article 54) but otherwise s.134 (c) provides that, in the case of a private company, two members, and in the case of other companies, three members, constitute a quorum.

Issues to be determined by the meeting are usually expressed in the form of resolutions. There are two kinds of resolution, ordinary and special. An ordinary resolution is one passed by a simple majority. Section 141 defines a special resolution as one which has been passed by not less than three-fourths of the votes cast (in person or, where permitted by the articles, by proxy) at a general meeting of which not less than 21 days notice, specifying the intention to propose the resolution as a special resolution, has been duly given. The Act is silent as to the notice required of an ordinary resolution so the matter is governed by the minimum period of notice of the meeting, described earlier. A special resolution is necessary only where the Act or the articles require it and in all other cases, an ordinary resolution will suffice. We have already dealt with issues which require a special resolution but, for convenience, these and some others may be listed here:

(i) To alter the objects clause (s.10).
(ii) To alter the articles (s.15).
(iii) To alter the company name (s.23).
(iv) To issue shares at a discount (s.72).
(v) To make the liability of directors unlimited (s.198).
(vi) To effect a voluntary winding up (s.251).
(vii) To effect a winding up by the court (s.213).

Unless otherwise provided by the articles, issues arising at meetings are decided after discussion by a show of hands, but the articles usually provide for a poll to be taken in certain circumstances.

While the necessary majority in favour of a resolution may be obtained, the minority may be entitled to relief. Since the passing of the Joint Stock Companies Act, 1858, company law has always attempted to protect minority shareholders and we must now briefly examine these protections.

The rights of a member may be divided into two categories: individual membership rights and corporate membership rights. In the case of the latter the member is generally bound by the decisions of the majority under the rule in *Foss* v. *Harbottle.*[9] In that case the minority shareholders alleged that the company had a claim in damages against some directors arising out of fraudulent acts committed by them. At the general meeting the majority had resolved not to pursue this action and two of the minority shareholders brought these proceedings to compel the directors to make good the loss occasioned by their alleged fraud. The court dismissed the action holding that the actions of the directors were capable of confirmation by the company and that it was for the company, through its majority, to determine the best course of action. Individual membership rights, however, entitle the shareholder to sue in his own name and he is not affected by any decision of the majority. Examples of individual rights are the right to object to his liability being increased without his consent, the right to vote and the right to object to a compulsory transfer of his shares.

In the case of corporate rights we have indicated that these are rights of the majority and accordingly any action must be brought as a representative action on behalf of the plaintiff and other shareholders, or on behalf of the company. But even in the case of corporate rights there are exceptions to the general rule that the decision of the majority prevails. First, the majority cannot confirm an act which is *ultra vires* or illegal, nor an act which constitutes a fraud against the minority and the wrongdoers are themselves in control of the company, nor a resolution which requires a qualified majority but has been passed by a simple majority. Secondly, if the majority acts in oppression of the minority, the minority may petition the court to dissolve the company on the grounds that it is just and equitable. This is not capable of precise or exhaustive definition but, by way of example, the courts have exercised this power where the company was formed for the purposes of fraud, where a shareholder, having a majority of the voting power, refused to produce accounts or to pay dividends, and where the petitioner was excluded from all participation in the company. Finally, what is generally referred to as *the alternative remedy* is provided by s.205.

If a member could not bring his case within the ambit of the exceptions to the rule in *Foss* v. *Harbottle,* he was faced, before 1963, with the alternative of seeking the rather drastic remedy of dissolution or accepting the conduct of the majority. It is now provided by s.205 that the court may intervene when the affairs of the company are being conducted, or when the powers of the directors are being exercised, in a manner oppressive to him or any of the members, or in disregard to his or their interests as members. Given the grounds for intervention the court may make such order as it thinks fit to bring the oppressive conduct to an end. This may involve prohibiting or cancelling any transaction, ordering the transfer of shares among members of the company or even an alteration to the Memorandum or Articles of Association.

The company may reach a stage where it desires either to reorganise its capital structure, amalgamate with another company or, if the company is in financial difficulties, to arrange compromises or settlements with its creditors. These are detailed and complicated provisions which will not be dealt with here beyond noting that such schemes usually require the support of 80% of those affected by the proposal (i.e. creditors and/or members) and the approval of the court. Provision is also made for dissenting members whose shares may be required by the company upon payment of a fair price.

DISSOLUTION OR WINDING UP

A company may be dissolved in any one of three ways:

(i) By the court.

(ii) Voluntarily, either as (a) members' voluntary winding up, or (b) creditors' voluntary winding up.

Of these, a voluntary winding up is the most commonly used but we will briefly examine each one. It should be noted, however, that some provisions apply with equal force to all three modes, while others apply in all cases of winding up, whether by members or creditors.

Winding Up by the Court

A petition for winding up by the court may be presented by a creditor, a contributory or, in limited circumstances, by the Minister.[10] The term 'contributory' refers to present and certain past members of the company. The court may order the winding up of the company on any of one of the following grounds under section 213:

(i) The company has by special resolution resolved that the company be wound up by the court.

(ii) Default is made in delivering the statutory report to the registrar or in holding the statutory meeting.

(iii) The company does not commence its business within a year from its incorporation or suspends its business for a whole year.

(iv) The number of members is reduced, in the case of a private company, below two, or in the case of any other company, below seven.

(v) The company is unable to pay its debts.

(vi) The court is of the opinion that it is just and equitable that the company should be wound up.

(vii) In the case of oppression of the minority (see p. 285 *supra*) the court, in spite of the existence of an alternative remedy, considers winding up justified and appropriate.

Section 216 provides that on hearing a winding-up petition, the court may dismiss it, or adjourn the hearing conditionally or unconditionally, or make any interim order or any other order it thinks fit. Where a petition is presented under (ii) above, the court may, instead of ordering a winding up, order the report to be delivered and the meeting held.

It is important to determine the moment of commencement of winding up which, in the case of winding up by the court, is either the time of passing the resolution, if the petition is brought under (i), or, in all other cases, the time of the presentation of the petition.[11] This rule applies to all modes of winding up: where the petition is based on a resolution the crucial time is the time of passing the resolution, and in all other cases the winding up is deemed to commence at the date of presentation of the petition.

It is also important to know the date of commencement because from that time certain consequences occur: all dispositions of the company's property after that date are void;[12] all actions against the company are stayed;[13] the powers of the directors cease and the servants of the company are dismissed, to mention but a few.

In order to effect the winding up, s.225 provides that the court may appoint a liquidator. The principal duties of the liquidation involve the collection and protection of the company's assets and the payment, in the order directed by the Act, of the company's debts. This may entail summoning meetings of members and creditors, the conduct of legal proceedings in the name of the company, the making of compromises and arrangements with creditors and the sale of the company's property.

When the affairs of the company have been fully wound up, the court will, on the application of the liquidator, make an order that the company be dissolved from the date of the order.

Voluntary Winding Up

A voluntary winding up is initiated by the members passing a special resolution to that effect. The directors, or a majority of them, may make and file a declaration that, having duly examined the affairs of the company, they are of the opinion that the company will be able to pay its debts in full within a period of 18 months from the commencement of the winding up. Such a declaration is known as a declaration of solvency. Provided such a declaration is made within 28 days preceding the date of the passing of the special resolution (and is delivered to the registry of companies before that latter date) and provided it contains a statement of the assets and liabilities of the company, then the winding up is a members' voluntary winding up.[14] In all other cases the voluntary winding up is a creditors' winding up.

The declaration of solvency is thus crucial to determining whether the members or the creditors have control over the subsequent stages of the winding up, e.g. the appointment of a liquidator. In the case of a members' winding up, as soon as he has wound up the affairs of the company the liquidator must report on his actions to a general meeting of members.[15] The liquidator then sends the account to the registrar who registers it. At the expiration of three months from the date of registration the company is automatically dissolved. The same rules apply in the case of a creditors' winding up, except a meeting of creditors must also be held.

CONCLUSION

The commercial importance of the company cannot be overstated. It is now the cornerstone upon which business in the Republic (and Western society in general) is based. This area of law, owing to its practical relevance, attracts a considerable amount of litigation, but that is more properly the topic for discussion in more specialised works elsewhere.

Chapter 16*

LABOUR LAW

The law of industrial relations encompasses many of the traditional or core subjects studied and practised in the Republic. As such, a working knowledge of basic legal principles is necessary in understanding the evolution and application of labour law. As will be shown the law has over the last two hundred years developed from a position of criminal and civil intolerance to a situation in which organised labour is now, in specified circumstances, expressly protected by law.

The contemporary relevance of labour law to Ireland, and its unique position in legal and social history, renders the subject of particular importance in a book of this nature. The structure of labour law is considered in this chapter in outline only, but the general principles of the study should become apparent. The reader will notice that the law on this topic has both a substantive and adjective weight. While laws regulating the relationship of capital and labour have been frequently litigated and pronounced in the courts, substantial changes have been introduced through legislation. The basis of this relationship lies in contract and tort, but increasingly statutes and regulations have intervened to provide, *inter alia,* minimum standards to which all relevant parties must comply. While substantive rules govern the extent of liabilities of employers and their employees, labour law is also concerned with distinct procedures. It has already been indicated that many industrial relations disputes are resolved by officers and tribunals, supplemental to the traditional court structure.

The law here falls under two broad headings. The first concerns the relationship between employer and employee. From the early days of the industrial revolution the law has dictated principles in accordance with an *individual* concept of accountability. This has to a large extent been preserved with both courts and tribunals resolving disputes on the basis of personal rights and duties. Thus the protection accorded to employees against unfair dismissal or dismissal without due notice (wrongful dismissal) is enforced on an individual level. Traditional legal principles have applied, however, since the early 19th century, when workers secured the right to combine, and the law thereby recognises certain *collective* rights. Associations may represent both sides of the industrial relations, i.e. capital and labour, but are popularly attributed to workers. With these dual concepts of individuality and collectivism in mind an outline of the law of industrial relations in Ireland can be described.

Finally, as has been stressed on many occasions in this text, the starting point for discussion of the relevant law must be the Constitution of 1937.

**See also 1988 Supplement pp. 327-332.*

This affects both individual and collective rights, but it suffices for the present to highlight Articles 40 and 45. Further details concerning the general provisions of the Constitution can be found in Chapter 9. Article 40 acknowledges, *inter alia,* the right of persons, subject to lawful regulation, to form associations and unions. This has been judicially interpreted as meaning a person has the right to join, or not to join, such an association. Article 45 contains a directive for social policy and indicates the desirability of non-discrimination in terms of employment on grounds of sex or marital status. It is also stressed that the distribution of wealth should not subserve the common good.

RIGHTS AND LIABILITIES OF THE INDIVIDUAL

This section is concerned with the law as it directly affects employers and employees in their individual capacity. While many aspects of this relationship are governed by law we will concentrate on the most important, namely, contractual obligations, unfair dismissal, redundancy, discrimination and safety at work. The importance of the collective and its overlap with these issues cannot be overstated.

Contractual Obligations

To discover the conditions of employment one must look initially to what is agreed between the parties. Such agreement may be express (written or oral), implied through the parties conduct, or implied through statutory intervention. In many cases the terms of the contract will be a combination of these sources. As much will depend on the contract and its construction, there is little point in discussing this subject in detail. Reference can, however, be made to the most important of the terms likely to be contained in the agreement. Hours of work, place of work, rate of pay, method of payment, benefits in kind, holiday allowances, modes of termination of the contract, grievance procedures and description of duties may well be listed. (If so, it is, subject to comments made below, a matter of interpretation as to the extent of the respective liabilities.) Certain common denominators can be found that apply to most contracts of employment. These are imposed by legislation and are mainly statutory minima which must be observed. Examples of these are numerous. Working hours are restricted for both young persons and adult workers.[1] Certain trades and industries have particular restrictions on hours of work.[2] Minimum paid holiday periods are preserved for most employees.[3]

In terms of law one of the most significant of the minimum standards required relates to the termination of employment. After 13 weeks service a person is entitled to such written terms. At common law a contract (thus employment) could be lawfully terminated by notice, it usually being sufficient to give a period of notice equivalent to the length of the time between pay-days (e.g. one week, if paid weekly). This is to say that the normal rules of contract law apply. Now most employees, who work at least 21 hours and have 13 weeks' continuous employment behind them, are entitled to minimum periods of notice. These periods increase in accordance with the length of service.[4] The relevant Act supplemented by the provisions of the Unfair Dismissals Act, 1977, also gives the employee the right to certain information concerning his or her conditions of employment. Likewise a minimum period of notice is required from the employee. This is a standard one-week period. These provisions relate only to the contract and do not apply if the contract is broken, and such breach entitles either party to rescind the contract without notice. In accordance with basic principles of contract the breach must be of sufficient weight to entitle the aggrieved party to rescind. In addition to this limited protection, ensuring proper notice is given, the employee may also have the right not to be unfairly dismissed. The contract, however, may provide for longer periods of notice.

Statute also provides that deductions should not be made from wages apart from statutory deductions (income tax, social welfare insurance, etc.), except in accordance with the wishes of the employee. These provisions are contained in the Truck Acts[5] that were originally devised to prevent payment of employee in kind. This protection, however, can be lost in certain instances, e.g. a right of a court to order maintenance payments to be deducted directly from wages.[6]

Unfair Dismissal

At common law a person could be dismissed from employment at will providing adequate notice was given or the employee was dismissed without notice for breach of contract (e.g. misconduct). The employee could establish no grounds for legal complaint if the employer complied with the minimum notice period. If adequate notice should have been but was not given, a claim for wrongful dismissal could be made.[7] This claim which is relevant today covers only compensation for the period of requisite notice. Since May 1977, however, certain employees have had the right not to be unfairly dismissed. In describing the extent and consequences of such a right two points should be noted. First, a separate and quasi-judicial administrative body was created to adjudicate in such disputes. This has already been explained.[8] The Rights Commissioner and Employment Appeals Tribunal adjudicate in matters of unfair dismissal. In limited circumstances reference can be made to the court structure *via* the circuit court. Secondly, contrary to traditional court procedure, the burden of proof for establishing the unfair dismissal does not lie with the applicant. The respondent (employer) in general is given the task of showing that the dismissal falls within the permitted grounds of the Act.[9] Failure to do so means that the dismissal is considered unfair. The employer will satisfy this burden of proof if, for example, misconduct has occurred on the part of the employee and the employer was entitled to dismiss the employee in these circumstances. Likewise a redundancy situation will amount to a satisfaction of this burden, as will incompetency. Examples of unsatisfactory grounds might include the personal circumstances of the employee which do not affect the job or the sex of the employee. Once a finding of an unfair dismissal has been reached, the officer or tribunal or court can make one of a number of directions: either reinstatement, re-engagement or compensation can be ordered. The compensation is limited to two-years remuneration. The conduct of the employee is also taken into account and any compensation awarded can be reduced by such proportion as fairly reflects any behaviour that contributed to the dismissal.

Who may make such a claim? The protection is open to all employees with 12 months' continuous service with the same employer and who do not fall within the exceptions mentioned in the Act.[10] Such exceptions include the Defence forces, pensioners and State employees. An application should be made within six months of dismissal, although the relevant authority has a discretion to allow late applications. If a person is dismissed for legitimate trade union activities the 12 month period of service is disregarded.

The Act therefore tries to redress past and future damages and goes far beyond the provisions of wrongful dismissal at common law.

Redundancy

One of the grounds that justify dismissal under the Unfair Dismissal Act, 1977, is redundancy. A person who is redundant cannot substantiate a claim for unfair dismissal. However, since 1967 a right has existed for persons made redundant, to fall within the terms of the Redundancy Payments Act, to claim compensation from the State and employer. As will shortly be seen regulations exist covering collective redundancy rights, but here mention will only be made of the individual right to redundancy payments. This right is an amalgamation of social insurance benefit (i.e. based on contributions paid to the Department of Social Welfare) and compensation paid by the employer. Both employer and employee contribute to a redundancy fund as a part of the Social Insurance Scheme. A person, in order to claim, must have been employed for two years by the same employer and must be insured under the Social Welfare Act, 1952 (as amended).[11] Those working for less than 21 hours a week are excluded. All employment is included unless the Minister for Labour excludes certain categories.

Redundancy is a legal term and arises where either a person is dismissed or put on short time or lay-off, and the principal reason for this state of affairs is:

(a) because the employer has ceased or intends to cease carrying on business, *or*

(b) that the reason for the employment of the person no longer exists (i.e. the job has ceased or less persons are required).

The entitlement is lost if a reasonable offer of re-employment is made or good reason existed for dismissal (e.g. misconduct).

The employer, however, is under a duty to conduct the redundancy in accordance with the established procedure and if due notice of the redundancy is not given or a person is made redundant on any other basis but last in and first out, the dismissal may be unfair.

The employer on creating the redundancy must make a lump sum payment to the employee in question, calculated by reference to the length of the employee's service and the normal weekly wage at the date of dismissal.[12] In addition, weekly payments are made to the employee from the redundancy fund in the form of social welfare benefits.

The employer is entitled to a rebate from the State of 60% of the lump sum.

The calculation of entitlement is made by the deciding officer of the Department of Social Welfare and an appeal lies to the Employment Appeals Tribunal and thence to the High Court on matters of the law. The legal provisions are to be found in the Redundancy Payments Acts, 1967/71/79. It should be noted that certain collective rights exist under the Protection of Employment Act, 1977, concerning liaison between employers and trade unions about proposed redundancies. Sanctions are applied for a failure to observe such regulations.

Discrimination

Recent legislative moves have been made to provide compensation and create criminal offences for acts of discrimination occurring prior to, during and after employment. These anti-discrimination provisions are aimed at ensuring parity of wages regardless of sex, and recruitment, employment and promotion of persons without regard to sex or marital status. Provisions for financial compensation and the creation of criminal offences exist in both fields. However, it should be noted that the efficacy of these laws is seriously qualified by the nature and number of the permitted exceptions and qualifications. The law is to be found in the Anti-Discrimination (Pay) Act, 1974, and the Employment Equality Act, 1977, operative since December 1975 and July 1977 respectively.

The first enactment provides that a person of one sex has the right to be paid the same rate of remuneration as a person of the opposite on like work by the same employer. Disparity in pay can exist for *any other reason.* Much litigation has been attracted, under similar legislation in the United Kingdom, by the definition of like work.[14] The Employment Equality Act extends this concept to conditions of employment other than pay. Further, the Act makes unlawful any attempt during pre-employment to practise discrimination. Thus advertisements for jobs, the selection of employees and discrimination during employment are all issues within the scope of the Act. Again significant exemptions exist, e.g. where sexual denomination is a *bona fide* qualification for the job or where statutory restrictions exist on the employment of women.[15]

Under both statutes complaint can be made by the person subject to dis-

nation or by the Employment Equality Agency to an equality officer. ither party may appeal to the Labour Court and thence on law to the High Court. The adjudicators will decide if discrimination exists, if action is to be taken and if compensation is payable. Criminal offences also exist under the Act and non-compliance with a Labour Court order is also an offence. An application for unfair dismissal may also lie in discriminatory circumstances but compensation for the same loss can only be claimed from the one source. This latter point is common to any field of law where a number of possible actions lie in defined circumstances.

The Employment Equality Agency also has considerable powers of investigation and recommendation regardless of complaint or application.

Safety at Work

There is considerable overlap in this area with collective rights, but it will suffice for the present to discuss the topic with reference to the individual employee. Several enactments apply to impose both civil and criminal liability on employers to ensure a safe working environment for both manual and clerical workers. The best-known and widest-reaching provisions are to be found in the Factories Act, 1955 (as amended). The statute imposes regulations aimed at minimising danger from equipment, providing safety equipment and providing welfare facilities for employees. Breaches of the Act may lead to civil or criminal proceedings through the established court structure.

RIGHTS AND LIABILITIES OF THE COLLECTIVE

It is the writers' opinion, well endorsed by current industrial practice, that the significant changes in labour relations occur in the collective sense. By this we mean that organised labour (unions) and capital (employers' federations) make the decisions affecting the majority of the working population. While individual rights and liabilities are highly significant in terms of compensation and job security, it is the collective unit that gives labour its muscle. Thus the law has intervened to provide obligations on and entitlement to collective representation. It will be recalled that as common law systems operate on the basis of res judicata, the law has treated disputes primarily in an individual rather than collective way. This is significant, for the regulations affecting collective activity have often been subject to individual application and interpretation. For this reason the rights and duties of individual members within the collective will be discussed.

First, the law concerning collective bodies in labour relations will be described, and this includes the status of such bodies, their immunities and liabilities, and the control over their activities. Secondly, the role of the individual within the collective will be looked at. This will cover strikes, lock outs and picketing. For convenience this will also include members of such collective organisations and non-members. Finally, the process of collective bargaining will be examined.

The Status of the Collective

Without diverting the course of the present discussion it should be appreciated that at the turn of the 19th century the organisation of labour (and, theoretically, capital) was prohibited. Severe sanctions were consequently administered against the combination of workmen on the basis that such was an illegal conspiracy. Liability was on the individual members. The legislation of 1824/25 recognised the right of combination yet effectively denied the means of bringing about the objectives of association. Once contracts of employment were broken, or trade interfered with, the combination and its members became subject to the law. This situation continued with some minor alteration until the Trade Union Act, 1871. This recognised the *prima facie* legality of the union (and for that matter of the employer's federation). The legislation expressly provided that the purpose of such association was neither illegal (criminal) nor unlawful (civil) merely because it was in restraint of trade. So, for example, a trade union demanding higher wages was not committing a breach of the criminal or civil law merely because of such an aim. The significance of this was to make the existence and objectives of the trade union *prima facie* lawful. This Act is still law in the Republic, with subsequent additions and amendments also to be considered. The Act provides for the registration of trade unions although such provisions are now incorporated in the more recent legislation.[16]

While the 1871 Act and its amendments form the 'charter' of trade unionism, events of the turn of the 20th century were to define the extent of the law's protection of such combinations.

Despite the apparent safeguards against civil and criminal actions a decision in 1901 known as the Taff Vale Railway Case[17] tore a gaping hole in the presumed immunities of trade unions from legal action. The details need not concern us here. It is enough to note that, following a rail strike and a resulting picket, the union concerned was found to have picketed without legal authority and was ordered to pay £23,000 compensation to the railway company. The powers of the union were thus rendered inoperative by way of judicial attack on union funds. This resulted in the passing of the Trade Disputes Act of 1906, which, with some minor amendments, forms the basis of Irish statutory labour law for the collective. While the courts have had much to say on the application of these statutory provisions, the Act itself can be described as the foundation of current industrial relations law. The Act covers four main issues:

(i) The abolition of conspiracy as a criminal and civil matter where two persons agree on a course of action that is not unlawful in the absence of such agreement (i.e. if perpetrated by an individual). This immunity from action only applies where the parties concerned are acting in contemplation or furtherance of a trade dispute.[18]

(ii) The immunity from legal action for persons picketing work or residential premises in contemplation or furtherance of a trade dispute, provided such picketing is peaceful.[19]

(iii) An immunity against civil legal action for persons acting in contemplation or furtherance of a trade dispute, regardless of whether they are union members and regardless of whether their action interferes with the business interests of another.

(iv) A general immunity for a trade union, its officials and members, for any civil action based in tort arising out of the activities of the union in contemplation or furtherance of a trade dispute.

These provisions are contained in sections 1, 2, 3 and 4 respectively of the Trade Disputes Act. It should be noted, however, that in the Trade Union Act of 1941, sections 2, 3 and 4 of the 1906 Act only extend protection to trade unions, their members and officials if the union holds a negotiating licence. The relevance of this and the extent of these immunities will be discussed shortly.

In a work of this scope there is insufficient space to explain how the courts have interpreted such provisions. It is sufficient for the present to note that the key phrase to all of these protections offered is 'in contemplation or furtherance of a trade dispute'. Legislative and judicial definitions exist and the reader must seek the relevant sources to which reference is given. The essence of this is that a dispute must exist concerning the terms and conditions of employment and the employment or non-employment of labour.

Registration under 1941 provisions involving the granting of a negotiating licence is, *inter alia,* proof of trade union existence. In order to obtain such a licence the trade union must satisfy the registrar created under the legislation of the lawful objectives of the union and must lodge a deposit with the High Court. The extent of the deposit increases in proportion to the size of the membership. It is unlawful for an association to negotiate conditions of employment without such a licence. Consequently the law can restrict associations who are able to negotiate conditions and in return for such control extend the above-mentioned immunities to such bodies. It should be remembered that none of these provisions prevent an individual negotiating for his or her own conditions of employment.

In any event these provisions must be read in light of the fundamental rights of association preserved by Article 40 of the 1937 Constitution.[20]

The Right to Strike and Picket

From the discussion above it can be seen that the immunity conferred under the 1906 Act as amended affects not only the union and its officials but also its members. Brief mention must therefore be made in this context of the individual liability of members or non-members in industrial action.

The law, rather than conferring a right to take industrial action, works in a negative sense and provides a limited immunity for persons involved in trade disputes. This has been covered in outline above, through the provisions of sections 1–4 of the Trade Disputes Act as amended by the 1941 Trade Union Act. This qualified protection will not be repeated here, except that the legal consequences of strike action and picketing can be set out.

If a person is on strike, unless notice has been given terminating the contract, that person is in breach of contract and therefore the employer can normally sack that person without notice. The employee has no cause for legal complaint unless others who were also on strike are not also dismissed. This is covered by the provisions of the Unfair Dismissals Act, 1977. Theoretically an action for damages could also lie by the employer against employee, but this is unlikely. An employee, however, cannot be compelled to work.[21]

For the duration of the strike the participants are not entitled to wages, but may, if the strike is official, receive strike pay from the union. The person on strike will be disqualified from recovering social welfare benefits, although their dependents may be entitled to them.[22]

Legal action will not lie, however, against a person on strike if that person falls within the provisions of the immunity sketched above. Thus strike action which may be interpreted as interfering with trade will not be actionable providing it is exercised by officials or members of a union holding a negotiation licence and the action is in contemplation or furtherance of a trade dispute.

Similarly the individual right to picket is available in the same terms, providing it is peacefully effected and is to collect or disseminate information or persuade persons to sympathise with the dispute in hand. This 'right', however, is also expressed negatively in terms of a civil immunity and is closely bounded by many restrictions, particularly the commission of criminal offences that result from the exercise of the picket. Criminal offences are created both at common law and by statute, the most important of which are contained in the Conspiracy and Protection of Property Act, 1875, the Offences Against the State Act, 1939 (as amended), and the common law offence of breach of the peace.

It is popularly understood that liability for individual industrial action means worker's liability. Clearly in this context the employer may be liable. The lock-out is the parallel to strike action, except that the employer controls the plant and the premises and as such is in an infinitely stronger position. A lock-out is certainly a breach of contract and may amount to a dismissal. Likewise any conduct following which an employee cannot be expected to work may be a dismissal in a constructive sense if the employee is so forced to leave the employment.[23]

COLLECTIVE BARGAINING

In realistic political terms the bulk of industrial relations is conducted at a collective level. Regardless of the fact that unions and employers' federations consist of individual membership, these collective entities occupy a unique position under the law. They are, subject to statute, empowered to negotiate conditions of employment and other matters of national importance. The point that requires emphasis is this: any agreement, local or national, entered into by such collectives is, in itself, not binding on those parties. Once, however, the negotiated issues become part of the individual member's (and non-member's) contract then normal contractual provisions apply. The law, however, provides in a number of ways the means by which such collective negotiations can be conducted.

The legalisation in the Combination Act of 1871 and the protection of its funds by the Acts of 1906 and 1941 gives the union a basis for lawful negotiation. Further statutory intervention provides a forum within which such negotiations can be conducted. Unions and employers are, providing the former holds a negotiation licence under the 1941 legislation, able to negotiate conditions of employment. Such conditions include pay, holidays, hours and facilities at work. These are not binding until they form part of each individual worker's contract. Remedies for breach of such agreement may include individual court actions and/or industrial action.

The Labour Court, established under the Industrial Relations Act, 1946, is empowered to conduct investigations in industrial disputes. The decision of the Labour Court is final but not enforceable. One significant power of the Labour Court is to maintain a register of employment agreements. These, when registered with consent of the employer and union, can become applicable to all workers in a particular trade, industry or group. This will bind employers even if they are not privy to the agreement, providing they fall within its boundaries.

The Labour Court also examines the agreement and publishes the proposals to enable all affected parties (including those not privy to the agreement) the opportunity to make representation. Once the agreement is registered a failure to observe its terms is, on a complaint to the Labour Court, liable to render the offending party open to prosecution in the ordinary criminal courts. This is an exception to the principle of non-enforceability of pre-contractual negotiated agreements and covers both parties privy to the agreement and within its scope.

Joint labour committees also exist representing trades and industries. These make representations with a view to registering agreements. Again interested parties may object. Such agreements are known as Employment Regulation Orders and contain similar provisions for non-compliance.

National Wage Agreements and understandings should be distinguished here, for such are guide-lines only for social and economic policy. The sanctions applied by the Government for non-compliance will be indirect, e.g. reduction of Government subsidies or increased taxation. The National Wage Agreements are not within the negotiations indicated above.

The nature and extent of the law of industrial relations is both complex and wide-ranging. Its political importance cannot be over-estimated. Its sources lie in common law contractual concepts, sprinkled liberally with statutory regulations. For those interested, reference can be made to a number of more detailed analyses.[24]

Finally, although the principal framework has been sketched above, contemporary legislation has been introduced that takes the State's role in industrial relations further.

The Industrial Training Act, 1967, sees the State taking a positive role in the provision of industrial and commercial education under the body known as AnCO. Facilities for training in industry and commerce in many trades and occupations are provided and encouraged. Grants, loans and levies also exist for the financing of such schemes.

The Worker Participation (State Enterprises) Act, 1977, sees an even wider concept of harmonising industrial relations being introduced, providing for the appointment of employees to the Board of Directors of certain enterprises. The Act only applies to State industry. Thus worker-directors are appointed.

The reader might be led to believe by now that the law has evolved in order to protect organised labour. While this is certainly the case it is not the only direction in which the law has turned; one should be aware, for example, of the restrictive judicial application of such protection. Also, at the other extreme, the law has given explicit powers to trade unions in the form of sole negotiation and representative rights. Indeed the delegating power of the trade union has not escaped recent comment both in and out of court. It is likely that organised labour will increasingly dominate the future growth of labour law.

The past two hundred years have seen a constant battle between capital and labour. How far this battle has been won or lost, or how far the conflict has been defused, is a matter for conjecture.

Chapter 17*

FAMILY LAW

CONSTITUTIONAL PROVISIONS RELATING TO THE FAMILY

Family law may be defined as that body of law which attempts to regulate the internal relationships within the family and the relationship of the family to the outside world. Since all members of the family are individuals in their own right they are, of course, affected by all the law set out in the other chapters of this text. This chapter is concerned with those special rules or principles which affect people because of their status within the family. In particular, those rules which deal with marriage and parenthood are of chief concern here.

The starting-point for any discussion of Irish family law is the Constitution of 1937.[1] Article 41 recognises the family as the natural, primary and fundamental unit group of society, and as a moral institution possessing inalienable and imprescriptible rights antecedent and superior to all positive law. The Article guarantees to protect the family, it recognises the role of women within the home and pledges the State to guard with special care the institution of marriage. To this latter end Article 41. 3.2 prohibits the enactment of any law which would provide for the grant of a dissolution of marriage.

There are a number of points to note about these provisions. First, the family protected by the Constitution is the family founded on marriage. Accordingly, the illegitimate child and its parents do not constitute a family for this purpose.[2] Secondly, in recent years Irish courts have been prepared to recognise a divorce granted by a foreign jurisdiction under certain limited conditions.[3]

Article 42 provides that the State acknowledges that the primary and natural educator of the child is the family and guarantees to respect the inalienable right and duty of parents to provide, according to their means, for the religious and moral, intellectual, physical and social education of their children. It should be noted that the right to provide for welare of the child does not imply the right to deny such provision. One of the main problems with Article 42, however, is that it appears to render legitimate children ineligible for adoption. Rights which are inalienable are, of course, incapable of being surrendered and thus the parent of a legitimate child could not, by virtue of Article 42, give a valid consent to the adoption of that child.

HUSBAND AND WIFE

Contracts to Marry

The marriage itself is usually preceded by a contract to marry or, as it is more

**See also 1988 Supplement pp. 327-332.*

commonly known, an engagement. All of the ordinary rules of contract apply to this contract to marry and thus if at a subsequent stage one of the parties seeks to withdraw from the contract without justification, the innocent party may recover damages. The Law Reform Commission of Ireland has recently recommended that such an innocent party should only be able to recover actual *economic* loss in these actions.[4]

Marriage Contracts – Formation of Marriage

Formalities: These are two main issues involved in the formation of marriage, (a) formalities and (b) capacity. The law relating to formalities (in other words the kind of ceremony or formalities with which the parties must comply in order to get married) is neither uniform nor consistent. There are essentially three ways in which the parties may marry:

(i) According to pre-Reformation Canon Law (known as a common law marriage).

(ii) According to the current regulations of the Catholic Church.[5]

(iii) According to the Marriages Acts, 1844 to 1972. These Acts provide for the celebration of marriages by religious groups other than Roman Catholics, and for the celebration of marriage in the office of the Registrar.

Capacity: In order to have capacity to marry the parties must comply with the following conditions:

(i) *Age:* Under the Marriages Act of 1972 both parties must be over the age of 16 years in order to have capacity to marry. However, in exceptional circumstances, a judge of the High Court may grant permission where one or both of the parties are under this age.

(ii) *Single status:* Both parties must be unmarried.

(iii) *Ability to consent:* A party to a marriage must be capable of understanding the nature of marriage. The level of understanding required is not very high and merely requires the party should understand the normal duties arising from marriage.

(iv) *Prohibited degrees of a relationship:* The parties may be too closely related because of their blood ties or because of a relationship based on another marriage.

(v) *Different sex:* Parties of the same sex cannot marry.

Nullity of Marriage: The Distinction between Void and Voidable Marriages
A void marriage is, in a sense, a contradiction in terms. It means that though the parties have attempted to go through a ceremony of marriage, they have never been married. In other words the marriage is of no effect whatsoever. A voidable marriage, on the other hand, will remain a valid marriage in all respects until a decree is obtained. The three main distinctions between a void and a voidable marriage are as follows:

(i) In a case of a void marriage no decree is necessary. As already noted, in the case of a voidable marriage the marriage remains valid until such a decree is obtained.

(ii) Only the parties to a voidable marriage may challenge its validity. In the case of a void marriage any person with an interest may do so.

(iii) A void marriage may be challenged at any time. In the case of a voidable marriage not only is the action confined to one of the parties, but such an action must be brought during their joint lives. In other words, once one of the parties dies, the marriage will be considered valid for all purposes and for all time.

Defects Which Render a Marriage Void
The following defects render a marriage void:

(i) A prior existing marriage.

(ii) Where the parties are of the same sex.

(iii) Where one party is under age.

(iv) Where the parties are within the prohibited degrees of relationship.

(v) Where the parties have not complied with the appropriate provisions under the Marriages Acts (it is only on very rare occasions that a failure to comply with the proper formalities will render a marriage void).

Defects Which Render a Marriage Voidable
The main ground upon which a marriage may be voidable under Irish law is that the marriage has not been consummated due to a permanent disability on the part of one of the parties. In such circumstances, however, the petitioner may have approbated the marriage by acts which show an intention to accept the marriage in spite of the non-consummation.

Consortium

The term 'consortium' is used by lawyers to refer to the various rights and duties which arise upon marriage. These rights include the right to be maintained, to share the matrimonial home, to sexual intercourse and generally to enjoy the companionship and comfort of the other spouse. Thse rights are reciprocal so that while a husband enjoys all of these rights with regard to his wife, he is also under a duty to permit his wife to exercise similar rights with regard to him. That said, the law continues, however, to restrict in a number of ways the right of a wife to enforce such rights. In particular the action known as criminal conversation is not available to a wife to enforce such rights and duties. The Law Reform Commission has recently recommended that the nature of such actions as criminal conversation and other related actions should be changed and that they should be known as family actions, available to both husband and wife.[6]

Matrimonial Breakdown and Reorganisation

Even though the relationship between the parties may have broken down, the rights and duties which arise upon marriage continue to exist. Accordingly, the functions of the law in the context of marital breakdown may be achieved in a number of ways:

Separation Agreements: This is the means employed when it is possible for the parties to reach agreement with regard to the reorganisation of their rights and duties. Such agreements usually involve the parties agreeing to live separate and apart, and for one (usually the husband) to provide maintenance for the other and any dependent children of the family. Such agreements usually attempt to deal with the question of custody of the children, and the parties may (and usually do) surrender their respective *succession* rights. It is no longer possible for *maintenance* rights to be surrendered in such agreements. The real advantage of a separation agreement is that it avoids the expense and delay of legal proceedings.

Divorce 'A Mensa Et Thoro' (Legal Separation): The term is misleading in the same sense that nowadays people associate the use of the word divorce with the dissolution of marriage. In our context divorce *a mensa et thoro* simply means that the parties are released, by virtue of a court order, from their mutual duty to cohabit. Such a decree usually provides for alimony (maintenance) to be paid. In addition to such a decree the parties will normally seek to resolve the question of custody and, often, the questions of ownership and possession of property acquired during the marriage. These proceedings are expensive and time-consuming and thus, if a separation agreement can be obtained, should be avoided.

Dissolution of Marriage: The Constitution of 1937 prohibits the enactment of any law which would provide for the grant of a dissolution of marriage.

Accordingly, our courts have no authority to dissolve (to grant a divorce) a marriage. In certain limited circumstances, however, our courts are prepared to recognise a decree of divorce granted by a court of another jurisdiction. Such a decree would be recognised where it has been granted by the court of the parties' common domicile.[7] The concept of domicile is different from that of nationality or citizenship and essentially entails residence, coupled with the intention to permanently reside in that place. All persons require a domicile of origin at birth. Once persons reach the age of 21 they may acquire a domicile of choice. The law of a person's domicile governs most questions of status in family law and is relevant to such issues as legitimacy and capacity to marry as well as divorce. Children (persons under 21) and married women have a domicile of dependency. In the case of a married woman this means that her domicile is dependent upon that of her husband. As a result a married woman is not free to acquire a domicile of choice. Consequently the crucial issue in the recognition of a foreign divorce decree would be the question of the husband's domicile. For example, if a husband is domiciled in England, then, irrespective of her residence or intention, a wife is considered to be domiciled there as well. In such circumstances a decree of divorce obtained by the husband would probably be recognised by an Irish court. It should be seen, however, that a divorce obtained by a wife while her husband is domiciled in Ireland will not be so recognised.

Proceedings under the Family Law (Maintenance of Spouses and Children) Act, 1976: As its title suggests, this Act is primarily concerned with the question of maintenance but it also confers upon the courts the power to make protection orders, i.e. orders excluding a spouse from the family home.

On the question of maintenance a spouse is obliged to provide such support for the other spouse and any dependent children of the family as is reasonable in the circumstances. The Act uses the term 'spouse' throughout so that in appropriate circumstances a wife could be obliged to support her husband. Whether the court will impose a duty to maintain and, if so, the extent or amount of that liability, will depend on all the circumstances of the case. Failure to comply with a maintenance order may result in the court making an attachment-of-earnings order.

The court will make a protection order wherever it believes that the safety or welfare of an applicant spouse or any dependent child of the family requires it. Such an order when made by the District Court expires after three months, but may be renewed.

Disputes as to Property: With some minor exceptions, there are no special rules relating to the question of property between husband and wife. In other words our system applies the doctrine of a separation of property. This means that any property purchased by a husband with his money belongs to him and, conversely, any property purchased by a wife with her money belongs to her. As a general rule this means the parties are free to deal with their own property as they see fit. In the case of the family home, however, these rights have recently been restricted by the Family Home Protection Act, 1976, which aims at preventing the sale of the family home by one spouse without the consent of the other. The Act does not affect the question of *ownership,* however, since essentially it seeks to prevent the sale or disposition of the home without the consent of the other spouse.

CHILDREN IN FAMILY LAW

The Status of Children

A child conceived or born in wedlock is presumed to be the legitimate child of the spouses. Such a presumption can only be rebutted by proof beyond reasonable doubt, which establishes that the husband could not be the father of the child. Where the presumption does not apply, or where it has been rebutted, the child is considered to be illegitimate. The status of the child (whether he is legitimate or illegitimate) has important consequences in the area of custody, maintenance and succession rights. It should also be noted that the Legitimacy Act, 1931, provides that a person who at the time of birth is illegitimate may be subsequently legitimated by the marriage of his parents, provided the father is domiciled in this country at the time of such marriage, and both he and the mother could have been lawfully married to each other at the time of the birth or sometime during the period of 10 months preceding the birth. With one very minor exception, the position of the legitimated child is identical in all respects to that of the legitimate child.

Guardianship and Custody of Children

Both parents have rights and duties with regard to the upbringing of their children. These rights are recognised in the Constitution of 1937 and by the Guardianship of Infants Act, 1964. The term 'guardianship' is used to refer to the collection of rights and duties which parents enjoy with respect to their children. One such right is the right to the custody of the child. This, in a strict sense, simply means the right to have the day-to-day control and upbringing of the child. If a parent is deprived of custody he nonetheless retains the other rights incidental to guardianship.

Disputes about the custody of a child are now to be resolved by section 3 of the Guardianship of Infants Act, 1964, which provides as follows:

> Where in any proceedings before any court the custody, guardianship or upbringing of an infant, or the administration of any property belonging to or held in trust for an infant, or the application of the Income thereof, is in question, the court in deciding that question, should regard the welfare of the infant as the first and paramount consideration.

The Act defines welfare as the religious and moral, intellectual physical and social welfare of the child. In reaching a decision the court must take into account all of the above factors. Matters which are frequently taken into account as well are the conduct of the parents, particularly with regard to immoral conduct or the expression or irreligious opinions. The decisions of the courts in previous custody cases are, at best, of marginal assistance to future litigants. Each case is, in the last resort, determined upon its own particular facts.

Adoption

Adoption in Ireland is governed by the Adoption Acts, 1952 to 1976. This includes four separate Acts, enacted in 1952, 1964, 1975 and 1976. The general administration of adoption in Ireland is governed by the Adoption Board.

Legitimate children are generally thought to be excluded from the adoption process by virtue of the Constitution of 1937. Formerly, children under the age of seven years were also excluded but since 1964 that is no longer the case. Where the child is over seven years, however, the Board must give due consideration, having regard to his age and understanding, to his wishes.

An application for an Adoption Order with respect to a child may be made by the following:

(i) A married couple.
(ii) A single parent or relative of the child.
(iii) A widow.
(iv) A widower.

With regard to the first three groups the only limitation is the minimum age which the parties must achieve at the time of their application for the Adoption Order. A widower may obtain an Adoption Order only in very special circumstances. Provision is made for such an application by section 5 of the 1974 Act and essentially deals with the situation where the application was originally made by a married couple but, since the time of the application, the wife has died. In these circumstances if the widower has another child in his custody and all persons whose consent is necessary know of the facts, then an Order may be made. The only other general requirement with regard to an applicant for an Adoption Order is that he or they should ordinarily be resident in the State during the year ending on the date of the Order.

The most crucial and controversial issue concerning adoption is the question of consent. The Acts set out the persons whose consent is required to the making of an Adoption Order. Only in very special circumstances can such a consent be dispensed with. By virtue of section 14 of the 1952 Act a mother's consent may be dispensed with when she cannot be found or cannot give such a consent by reason of mental infirmity. Section 3 of the 1974 Act extended the circumstances in which a consent might be dispensed with. The section provides that where a person applied for an Adoption Order and any person whose consent to the making of the Adoption Order relating to the child is necessary and who has agreed to the placing of the child for adoption either (a) fails, neglects or refuses to give his consent or (b) withdraws a consent already given, the applicant may apply to the High Court for an Order dispensing with the required consent. If the court is satisfied that it is in the best interest of the child to do so, it may award custody to the applicants and authorise the Board to dispense with the mother's consent.

If the consent of the mother is not dispensed with under either of these provisions then it must be obtained in the manner provided for by the Acts. The mother must be informed of her various rights (e.g. her right to withdraw her consent at any time before the Adoption Order is made) so that her consent must not only be a *voluntary* one but it must also be an *informed* consent. The Adoption Act, 1976, now provides for the case where an Adoption Order is subsequently challenged.

CONCLUSION

This chapter has concentrated on some of the special *rules* which deal with the family. It should not be overlooked that in other areas of the law special *provision* is made for the family or for the protection of familial interests. Examples of this are to be found in our laws relating to evidence (e.g. the compellability of a spouse in criminal proceedings), contract (the presumption against an intention to create legal relations in domestic agreements), property (special position of the surviving dependents of a deceased) and in many other areas of Irish law. Only when all these provisions are seen together can we have a clear idea of the position of the family in the Irish legal system.[8]

Chapter 18*

WELFARE LAW

INTRODUCTION

There is in the Republic a growing body of law that attempts to provide a minimum standard of living for the population. This standard affects many aspects of life including work, home, education and health. The history of welfare law makes interesting reading, and references to further information are given. In the course of its growth the welfare state, spanning barely a century, has altered so as to be almost unrecognisable. The law of the 19th century made little or no provision for the protection of the general standard of living. Poverty was, on the whole, seen as a personal failing. While charitable benevolence existed there was a dominant philosophy in these times that promoted a minimum of assistance. The essence of such a philosophy was aimed at preserving the work incentive, liberalised by charity. In a word the workhouse of the 19th century was punitive. This was known as the *poor law* and operated in true *laissez-faire* tradition.[1]

As so frequently experienced in the Republic, British legislation was introduced based largely on the political and social atmosphere of the dominant country. The first major step towards a primitive welfare system was taken in 1911, although British legislation before this date had given limited protection in the areas of employment, education and working conditions.

The National Insurance Act, 1911, provided for a system of insurance against contingencies such as sickness and unemployment. Pension provisions also existed by this time.

When the Irish Free State was formed in 1922, Ireland, therefore, inherited a piecemeal welfare system from the British. Although the principles of the 1911 legislation (i.e. paying a contributory sum during employment to provide for benefits when unable to work) have remained unchanged, the welfare state has now assumed a far more wide-reaching role. This recognises the social pressures of a modern, increasingly industrialised society.

This situation can be contrasted with the individual paternalism of the poor law. It is suggested, however, that such State intervention is both moralistic and severely restricting.

By way of introduction it should also be noted that welfare law, as it is found in Ireland, owes much of its origins to a British appraisal of the welfare state contained in the *Beveridge Report* of 1945. The Department of Social Welfare that handles the majority of financial claims in cases of inability or

**See also 1988 Supplement pp. 327-332.*

incapacity to work was formed in 1947, and the basic social welfare scheme as it now exists in the Republic was instituted some five years later.[2] It can be seen, therefore, that welfare law has its roots in 19th-century Christian paternalism, although the structure is more recent.

This chapter examines some of the most significant legal provisions of the welfare state, but before this the writers' own approach should be explained. We are of the opinion that law is not an objective and equalitarian tool. Law clearly represents the interests and concerns of particular classes within society. Its merits are not up for debate here. Such an opinion is important in this context because welfare law can, and ought to be, studied in the context within which it operates. This is to say that welfare law, with its respective rights and duties, is a topic worthy of study as a legal subject in its own right. Once entitlements are provided by law, material will be forthcoming on the enforcement of such provisions. However, the issues within the scope of welfare law clearly affect a particular class or group within the social order and, as such, welfare law can be justifiably studied as the new poor law. Equally, but by comparison, company law or commercial law can be taught as the old rich law.[3]

A study of this topic necessarily involves an understanding of the basic principles of law and its substantive topics. Contract, tort and land law stand to the fore, along with constitutional law, administrative law and the related procedures. It should also be appreciated that the law regulates both State and the individual interests (e.g. social welfare benefits), and the rights and duties of private individuals (e.g. private rented housing).

This chapter, for reasons indicated above, might equally be entitled 'Law and the Underprivileged'.[4] Its arrangement reveals the following key areas of concern: (i) Law of income; (ii) Law of accommodation.

The writers, while acknowledging the distinct, perhaps contentious, bias of this chapter, justify it in terms of the interests at stake. It is concerned with law for the poor. How far that law can in fact be implemented of course depends on issues already indicated in Chapter 8.

THE LAW OF INCOME

Three interrelated circumstances require examination:

(a) Employment
(b) Unemployment
(c) Non-employment

The first concerns the contract between employers and employees. This has been referred to elsewhere, as have other issues of employment protection including health and safety, conditions of employment, redundancy and unfair dismissal. It is not proposed to re-examine these topics but their importance in terms of entitlement must be appreciated.[5]

Unemployment and non-employment require further analysis within the present context. If a person is out of work and/or unable to work, income can be obtained from the *State* in the form of *social welfare benefits.* The law is contained in the Social Welfare Act, 1952 (as amended), with a plethora of statutory instruments imposing more detailed regulations.[6] The provisions are both many and complex, but the outline of the benefits can be noted.

A distinction is made in the Act between what are known as *contributory benefits* and *non-contributory benefits.* There is also a miscellaneous category of benefits to consider. Income, therefore, can be gained from the State social welfare system.

The structure of the system must now be explained. All persons in insurable employment (i.e. jobs) must pay a social insurance contribution (stamp) for each week of that employment. If a person suffers from unemployment or other incapacity or hardship benefits may be payable. These types of *contributory* benefits will be set out shortly.

If a person does not have any or sufficient contributions to be entitled to such benefits, a *means test* may be applied and the person may be entitled to certain non-contributory benefits.

In both cases, subject to the particular requirements for entitlement, the right of the individual to benefit is a positive and a legal one. Thus this entitlement can be legally enforced. The decision-making process in both instances falls within the quasi-judicial function of certain officers and tribunals. All benefits (contributory and non-contributory), with the exception of social welfare assistance and non-contributory old age pension, are determined by the Department of Social Welfare. A welfare officer examines eligibility (contribution or means test), a deciding officer gives a verdict on entitlement and an appeal lies to an appeals officer. This has been covered elsewhere.[7] The social welfare assistance is administered by similar officials of the Regional Health Board, and the non-contributory old age pension is processed by a special committee and an appeals officer.

Contributory Benefits

These are known as social insurance benefits. A person's entitlement to contributory benefits depends on the claimant satisfying two requirements. First, the claimant must have paid a minimum number of contributions during his or her working life and, in addition, must have paid or have had credited a similar number during the last contribution year.[8] This minimum number is 26, but for full entitlement 48 contributions must have been paid or credited.

The contribution year is the year before the period of claim and is now the same as the tax year. The benefit year runs from June to June and December to December, for men and women respectively. This means that if A, a man, claims a contributory benefit in September 1977, the contribution paid in and before the year April to April 1976-77 would be taken into account. This apparent time-lag allows for continuity of benefit, given the nature of the bureaucratic machine involved in processing such claims.

Secondly, any other requirements for individual benefits must be satisfied, e.g. to claim unemployment benefit a person must be unemployed etc.

The contribution payable is directly related to the amount of the weekly wage earned and is divisible between the employer and employee on roughly a 2:1 basis. This system is known as the pay-related social insurance.

Before setting out the basic contributory benefits reference must be made to the relevance of Ireland's membership of the E.E.C. In order to promote uniformity and encourage the mobility of labour, contributions paid in any country within the Common Market will be recognised by the Irish adjudicators in determining a claim. Thus if a person works in Germany, moves to Ireland, and is then made redundant, that person may claim Irish employment benefits and any contributions paid prior to entry into Irish employment will be taken into account. While contributions paid in another Common Market country will be acknowledged the claimant will only receive the benefit available in the country in which he or she is a resident.[9]

What, then, are the main benefits? Benefits are determined by four particular circumstances: (i) Unemployment; (ii) Incapacity; (iii) Old Age; (iv) Other hardship.

The first category is self-explanatory. If sufficient contributions are paid and the person is unemployed, that person would be entitled to unemployment benefit.

The incapacity benefit covers instances of sickness, disablement, injuries suffered while in employment and treatment benefits. The old age contributory benefits consist of retirement pensions in a number of forms. The final category of hardship includes benefits for orphans, widows and deserted wives.

Each individual benefit carries, in addition to the general contributory requirement, further conditions as referred to above. It is not proposed to examine the terms here but the Department of Social Welfare lists these conditions comprehensively in its published handbook.

In each case of entitlement a flat rate of benefit is payable, and where short-term benefits are concerned (e.g. that is not pensionable), a pay-related benefit is also given. This relates proportionally to gross earnings in the previous income tax year. Additions to benefits are made for dependents, e.g. spouse or children.

Contributory benefits, therefore, are calculated by reference to insurance principles and entitlement is adduced on this basis. These can be directly contrasted with the non-contributory benefits.

Non-Contributory Benefits

A person unable to satisfy the criteria for contributory entitlements may gain income from the *non-contributory* or *social assistance* scheme. Entitlement is calculated on the basis of the means test. The principle behind this is to balance the officially defined 'need' with actual income. Should a person's income fall short of such need it is supplemented, on qualification, with benefit. Thus if a person's income is nil and the need is £15 a week, a payment of £15 will be made. This figure will accordingly be reduced by any income received. Cash and capital (if any) are taken into account, with limited exceptions. In addition, other requirements will also exist in relation to the individual benefits. The benefits again relate to circumstance: (i) Unemployment; (ii) Old age; (iii) Other hardship. In addition, a benefit known as *supplementary welfare allowance* can be claimed. This is also calculated on the basis of a means test and supposedly acts as a safety net for those not falling within the categories of the individual benefits referred to above. An example should make this clear. To claim deserted wife's benefit a woman must show either the requisite contributory entitlement plus desertion for three months, or satisfy the means test and show desertion for three months. Up until the third month of desertion the applicant would not be eligible for either benefit but would be eligible for supplementary welfare allowance. This can also be granted to supplement any other benefit received on the needs/income basis, e.g. for special dietary requirements. Supplementary welfare allowance is also available in the form of an emergency payment, e.g. where a person suffers at the hands of a fire, flood, or loses a wage packet. This scheme is administered by the Regional Health Board.[10]

Miscellaneous Benefits

There are several important benefits that do not fall exclusively within the categories described above. The most important are benefits in kind and children's allowances.

Benefits in Kind: The benefits included here are not in the form of cash payment but consist of the provisions of goods or services. Some of these benefits apply to insured persons (e.g. treatment benefits covering dental, optical and aural care), while others are calculated on a means test (e.g. the provision of medical cards). All persons resident in the Republic (regardless of contributions) are entitled to hospital services although, for those earning above a certain income, doctor's fees must be paid by the patient. Insurance can be taken out in respect of this risk.[11] The conditions and requirements are stated in the relevant Department of Social Welfare handbook.

Other benefits in kind include free travel, electricity, gas, television licence, telephone rental, school meals, fuel allowances and footwear allowances. Entitlement depends on either status, e.g. pensioners, and/or a means test.

Children's Allowance: The children's allowance is a monthly cash payment, usually to the mother of a child. It is payable regardless of contributions or means test. It is payable in respect of all children who are residents in the State and who are under 16 years of age. Certain limitations exist and these are clearly documented elsewhere.

How to Make a Claim

Given the quasi-judicial process involved and the concept of legal entitlement (coupled with considerable discretion), it might be useful to note the application procedure. The following matters arise in connection with an application for social welfare benefits.

(i) The person must apply. There is no State monitoring of a person's need unless the person applies for benefit. This may appear to be stating the obvious but the situation can be contrasted with, for example, income tax liability. The likelihood of application depends, *inter alia,* on the extent of publicity of such rights.

(ii) The initial application is vetted by a welfare officer and considered by deciding office or officer of the Regional Health Board in the case of social welfare allowance. The decision is communicated to the applicant but no reasons are given. No formal procedure has yet been established for the determination of such applications.

(iii) An aggrieved applicant (bearing in mind no reasons are given other than whether the claim is admitted or not) may appeal to an appeals officer within 21 days of receipt of the decision. The appeals officer may determine the procedure, may include or exclude representation, may call witnesses, may ask for documents, and may take evidence on oath. No reasons again need be given for the decision.

(iv) No appeal on the determination of benefit lies to any other court or tribunal.[12] In limited circumstances an appeal may be made on law to the High Court but not where the issue is one of determination of benefit.

(v) Subject to this reservation the only powers of intervention on this decision-making process are vested in the ordinary court system in the guise of judicial review. This has been previously explained and is an attempt to regulate excess of jurisdiction.[13]

The social welfare system, therefore, in addition to employment rights, embodies a vital and essential area of law in so far as a determination of income is concerned. The relevance of such 'rights' cannot be overstated in the present political and economic climate. Its importance in terms of the number of people reliant on such benefits in the State must be made clear. As a topic for legal study the boundaries are, as yet, undefined and material, both judicial, academic and public, is scant. Suffice it to say that the law of social welfare will, one might speculate, rapidly form an important topic for both practising and non-practising lawyers. The advent of a comprehensive legal aid system could only complement such a development. Some measure of potential growth can be gleaned from the increased legislation in this area in the United Kingdom.[14] Its importance for the claimant is of course vital in maintaining an income.

THE LAW OF ACCOMMODATION

As the emphasis in this chapter is on law and the underprivileged, some attention must be given to housing rights. The welfare state has increasingly found itself involved in legislating in this field. Likewise the common law has had to concern itself with the rights and duties of land-owners and land users. While many people own their own homes (i.e. have purchased the house and land) a significant percentage live in rented property. This is perhaps not so true in Ireland as it is in Britain. It is the rights arising in this context that we are concerned with. This is known broadly as the law of landlord and tenant.

The regulations cover three principal areas: (i) Rent control; (ii) Security of tenure; (iii) Repair/improvement of property.

When considering these issues a distinction should be borne in mind. Rented property can be divided into public and private accommodation. The landlord of the former type of property will be the local authority (council), while the landlord of the latter will be a private individual or company. The law provides significantly different regulations in respect of each.

Private Sector Tenancies

The law here rests essentially on the contract between the landlord and tenant. If no written contract exists, an agreement and its terms may be implied. Statute now provides certain minimum standards. *Rent,* determined by the initial agreement, is the primary term of the contract and generally remains payable in any event.[15] The rent can only be altered by agreement. However, unless security of tenure exists (see below), failure, e.g. to agree to pay an increased rent, may result in eviction.

The principal regulation of rent is to be found in the Rent Restrictions Act, 1967. The former introduces the concept of controlled dwellings. The term must be borne in mind, as a number of 'rights' stem from such a definition. The meaning of this will be explained although it applies equally to security of tenure. Controlled dwellings are residential and self-contained dwellings. The Act, however, lists a number of exclusions, including houses built since 1941, premises where the landlord is in partial occupation, and flats that have been converted since 1960. All furnished property is also excluded from the protection of the Act. (These provisions were devised to encourage the availability of private accommodation and to provide tenants with protection from undue exploitation.) If a dwelling is within the definition, the rent may not exceed a statutory limit calculated with reference to a formula contained in the Act.[16] The contractual rent may lawfully be reduced or increased to such a level. Landlords may only increase the rent beyond this level under specified circumstances, e.g. to take account of repairs carried out on the premises.

Security of Tenure: At common law a tenancy agreement (a contract) can be ended with due notice.[17] This will usually relate to the period of the tenancy, e.g. weekly or monthly. However, if the premises fall within the definition of the 1960 legislation, additional protection or security is accorded to the tenant. Simply put, the landlord, to evict the tenant who has such protection, must obtain a court order for possession that will only be granted on proof of certain grounds (e.g. breach of a term of the agreement such as arrears of rent, or damage to property, or, alternatively, the landlord requires the premises for his own use).[18] If the landlord purports to end the contract by notice the tenancy will continue until determined by the court, or surrendered by the tenant. This is then known as a statutory tenancy. The tenancy continues on the same terms as before. The spouse or children of the tenant may also gain such protection. It should also be noted, regardless of statutory protection (e.g. in the case of a furnished tenancy), that the landlord cannot lawfully regain possession of the premises without the tenant's consent until first the tenancy is ended by notice. In any event a court order ought to be obtained as there are considerable restrictions at criminal law on the forcible entry on premises without the consent of the occupier. Technically once the tenancy is at an end the landlord may assume possession by using reasonable force, as the tenant is reduced to a trespasser, but a court order for possession will avoid any possible breach of criminal or civil obligation. The Prohibition of Forcible Entry and Occupation Act, 1971, and Article 40.5. of the 1937 Constitution provide protection against unlawful interference with property. Conversely it should be noted that if the landlord does regain possession that has been wrongfully withheld the tenant can in theory be charged double rent for the time of wrongful overholding.

Repair and Improvement: The law here is extremely complicated. The common law position provides no rights and duties appertaining to the repair or improvement of private property unless contractually stipulated, although statute has intervened to provide obligations in defined circumstances. The tenant should, however, at common law surrender the premises at the appropriate time in substantially the same condition as when the tenancy was taken, subject to fair wear and tear.

The implied obligations of the landlord are as follows:

(i) If the premises are let on a short-term basis (weekly/monthly) the landlord is under a duty to keep the structure and services in good repair.

(ii) If the premises are furnished they must be fit for human habitation at the commencement of the tenancy,[20] and under section 114 of the Housing Act, 1966, a landlord must *keep* a house let at a low rent (under £130 p.a.) fit for human habitation.

(iii) A tenant of a controlled tenancy may apply to the circuit court for a reduction in rent if the landlord fails to carry out repairs for which he or she is responsible.

In the absence of agreed terms, statutory standards or disrepair caused by action other than fair wear and tear, *neither* party is responsible for repairs and improvements.

It should be also noted that the local authority and Regional Health Board have considerable powers of intervention to ensure premises are not unsafe or unhygienic. Similar powers also lie with the Gas Board and the Electricity Supply Board. This process is instigated by serving notice to the 'person responsible' to rectify such. If this person fails to act the authority concerned can carry out the work and charge the person for the belated expenses. It is thus possible for a tenant to bring considerable pressure on the landlord through the local authority to carry out repairs and improvements.[21] It should be noted however that as the person responsible may be the tenant, this may be counterproductive.

Public Sector Tenancies

A tenant of local-authority-owned housing is in a very different legal position to the private tenant. Local-authority-owned houses are expressly excluded from the Rent Restriction legislation. Again, simply put, the tenant has no security of tenure, there is no real rent control and there are few repairing obligations. This statement requires some qualification. It should be pointed out here that much will depend on *policy* rather than law. While the public housing tenants are denied the protection contained in the relevant legislation, this does not mean that the tenant cannot rely on a preservation of certain standards. The important thing to stress is that such standards are not legally enforceable. Each local authority has a committee responsible for housing and policies are drawn up governing the administration and maintenance of publicly owned property. While a strong argument can be made for full legal rights in the form of 'A Tenant's Charter', the absence of such does not make the tenant's plight as bad as it might seem. This should be appreciated in the light of the presumed reluctance of a council to disregard its tenants (and electorate). The fact of the notional public accountability of the council renders their policies open to at least potential criticism. Although the local authorities in Ireland have no expressed duty to rehouse the homeless, it is difficult to imagine a housing policy geared to neglect of property and wholesale eviction of tenants.

The existing rights can be listed:

Rent: This is not subject to the Rent Restriction control but is calculated by reference to a statutory formula known as the *Differential Rent.* This is contained in regulations made under delegated power. If the rent is not so calculated, the abuse of decision-making can be checked by prerogative order. The rent is calculated by taking into account family size and income.[22]

Security of Tenure: While a council tenant enjoys no security as such, the council must determine the tenancy by notice and would be wise to obtain a court order before taking possession, as seen before. The important thing to stress is that the council need establish no grounds for possession except that the tenancy has been determined.[23]

Repair and Improvement: The Housing Act, 1966, a consolidating Act, provides for the general maintenance of local-authority-owned homes.[24] Unlike the provisions of the Rent Restrictions Act, however, there are few specific duties on the local authority. Housing policy may, especially through tenants' own organised action, be clarified and enforced but, except for the power of judicial review, the activities of the local authority cannot be regulated by legal enforcement.

Theoretically the Health Board and local authority themselves can compel repairs, though this is unlikely in respect of their own property. Also, statutory duties do exist on the local authority to maintain the sewage system, drains, roads, footpaths and similar structures. These duties can be legally enforced.

Overall, a classification and enactment of the law is necessary for public sector tenants and this, by way of example, has been eventually negotiated in Britain.[25]

Many persons, however, fall outside of the protection existing at present. Again, the provisions of the British legislation are more far-reaching in this field and one may speculate how long it will be before Ireland's welfare state follows a similar and necessary course.

CONCLUSION

Welfare law is as wide and undefined as it is recent. Its importance, both as a substantive legal topic and as indicator of an era of social history, has been clearly stated.[26]

It should be recalled that a number of other issues directly affect the implementation of welfare law. By the nature of the subject and the type of class and groups affected, the role of legal aid, law centres and advice groups must stand to the fore. This was clearly noted in the Pringle Report when it was stated:

> . . . staff at [law] centres very soon develop an expertise in dealing with the types of problems which particularly concern the underprivileged . . . Centres are better suited to deal with problems which have their roots in

the social conditions of deprived areas.[27]

Law for the poor is a somewhat hackneyed expression but a poor law with modern relevance exists, and it is of rising importance.

THE IDEOLOGY OF LAW

In the preceding chapters the reader has been introduced to the elementary principles of legal study. Reference has also been made to the process by which the law is administered. In addition, the most important of the substantive issues have been sketched, ranging from the traditional legal subjects of contract, tort and property to the more recent in the form of labour, welfare and family law. One question, however, has yet to be posed and answers suggested. In the introduction the problem of 'what is law?' was raised. An attempt to answer this has been avoided until now. The reason, one hopes, is that the reader, with a knowledge of law and the legal system, is better placed at this stage to appreciate its underlying philosophy. The fact that law has so far been described in a quasi-autonomous way can now be qualified. It has been suggested that the legal system does not operate independently of other sources.[1] It is by definition a tool for the regulation of the social structure. The following pages will attempt, in conclusion, to posit some of the most significant of the philosophies used to date in explaining both the law and its effect on the social order.

WHAT IS LAW?

This question can be approached in two ways. The first is to describe law as it appears, i.e. a series of rules affecting the lives of members of society. This level of analysis will not be pursued here except as appears below, for the wide ambit of regulations have already been discussed.

The second approach is to ask more fundamental questions about the basis of knowledge or truth. While these issues cannot be examined in detail, one can relate the ways in which these problems have been addressed and how this is relevant to the study of law. This approach is traditionally known as jurisprudence, or legal philosophy. We prefer to use the expression 'legal theory' as, for reasons that will become apparent, this breaks tradition with formal legal analysis and attempts to portray law in a theoretical and analytical framework, avoiding the historical presumptions of objectivity and autonomy.

The answer (such as there is) to the question therefore entails a wider appreciation of what has been termed law and ideology[2] and can be discussed as a particular example of a social institution within this overall framework.

Once a critical philosophical stance has been adopted many concepts current within the law (as an example of an important social institution) can be questioned. Thus cornerstones of legal philosophy, including justice, freedom and democracy, stand for examination. Without such a base a study of law, it is submitted, is necessarily artificial.

It has been said that contemporary legal philosophy is atheoretical. Lawyers seem to have expressed little concern in the past for the relevance of law within society. Consequently a body of rules has grown up that is accepted at face value because *it is law.* The following review of dominant philosophies over the centuries will reinforce this comment and indicates how law might be appreciated on any but atheoretical grounds.[3]

The philosophies expounded in these schools of thought are not exclusively attributed to one era, even though they arise in a particular period. Thus a strand of theoretical argument may span several centuries.

CLASSICAL THEORY

In historical terms the first persons to articulate the problems of philosophy appear to have been the ancient Greeks. Two themes are particularly relevant to our debate, *religion* and *science.* Early philosophy was concerned with a criticism of a religious belief based in a variety of omnipotent sources. How does this affect the law? The belief in the unquestionable authority of gods leads to a belief in the unquestionable authority of law. Those accepted as having religious powers could dictate the law which was divine and to be obeyed. Balanced with this view were other competing philosophies, which, while criticising unswerving obedience to the gods, were still unable to conceive a world that was not governed by principle or unalterable rules of nature.

Those who followed gods and idols thought law (and society) to be of divine origin. Others who tried to analyse this from a scientific base were to come to the conclusion that the law was a natural and unquestionable process. A qualification should be added here in that some philosophers felt human beings, through delegation to others, had the power to make internal regulations (laws) within this natural legal framework. The Greek philosophers include *Plato, Aristotle* and *Socrates,*[4] metaphysicians who explained world events and hence its laws by reference to a natural determinant. The strands of this argument can be found in their work on early scientific theory as well as comment on law and society. Mechanical rules, it was believed, once deduced, could be applied to life. In political terms these early thinkers were either idealists (theologians) or materialists (scientists), who both based their knowledge in nature – the first used divinity, and the latter experiment.

While originating in ancient Greece this view of the law and world still exists and is argued today. The common factor in the classical theory is ignorance of the mobile society. As we shall see, this was to be exposed later.

The classical or natural theory explained law quite clearly, namely, that law was unchanging and beyond human power to alter, except in so far as it could be supplemented by additional internal regulations.

While the natural theorists based their view either in religion or science, the balance lay heavily in the favour of the former during the Middle Ages, as the Christian Church gained greater influence over the conduct of its subjects. A useful example of the development of this theory can be found in the work of Thomas Acquinas. He wrote extensively on law, dividing it into law divinely given, law of natural reason, law of human intervention, etc. Law was seen to be God-given and natural, rather than of human origin, but this natural base did not obstruct man's ingenuity for creating intricate categories of laws and regulations.

All this is not to suggest, however, that the law (unlike the theory) was in itself undeveloped. We need to look no further than the Roman law codes of the 6th century A.D.[5] to see how far human intervention had gone in making law. The theory meanwhile was effectively stagnant. The pre-eminent classical theoreticians of more modern times include Rousseau, Hobbes, Locke and Hume.[6] The internal debate, religion versus science, continued but the philosophical groundwork remained unaltered. Law therefore was, and still is, for classical theorists, a matter of unalterable nature (divine or otherwise). We, however, do not have to look into ancient history to find the classical theory of law. The common law principle of 'natural justice' is still operational. The Constitutions of the United States and Ireland embody the *natural* rights of the individual.

POSITIVISM

The 18th and 19th centuries brought enormous changes in society.[7] The manifestations of industrialisation were slow to appear in Ireland, but the effect was widespread and nowhere more so than in the law. With such changes came a distinctively 19th-century philosophy, broadly known as *positivism.* The essence of this theory lies in the recognition of society as a product of human creation. Hence its laws, too, are man-made. Law here owes its validity to the head of the social order, i.e. the sovereign or head of State. Rather than thinking in terms of the supernatural, the positivists considered law from the point of utility. Law was to be found in the edicts of the law makers, whose authority stems from the head of State. Each law should stand the test of utility, beyond which the philosophy had no reference. This utilitarian philosophy is credited to Jeremy Bentham and is concerned with the law's form and content.[8] It also has its appearance in more modern times. Of the most famous contemporary legal positivists, Austin, Kelsen and Hart stand to the fore.[9]

The common failing of this presentation was its short-sightedness. The theory, such as it was, put forward a view of society and hence law, but was not explained in any terms other than its own validity. Just as the society made an implicit agreement to delegate authority to its governors (a social contract), law has gained its authority from such appointees. This is not, however, to be understood through democracy but rather by presumed and often forcibly achieved social control.

Some of the natural and classical philosophers had talked of a surrender of individual rights for the common good,[10] where law took its authority from beyond the social order, but the positivists look no further than the head of the social order itself.

As with classical theory, however, much research was conducted internally to give this approach weight and volume. Empiricism, especially in the light of the immense changes of the industrial society and its laws, reinforced the perceived values of the theory. In effect law was elevated to an unquestionable and seemingly objective pedestal. The importance of empirical research cannot be overstressed, for the stage was set for detailed work on the nature of the law through introverted scientific evaluation. The fundamental failing of positivism in its original or more contemporary form lies in the belief that there is a consensus in society and that law is a result of commands made to regulate such an implicit agreement. Thus an absolute and deterministic model of society and law is created, with legal authority thereby assumed.

Both the classical and positivist theorists, therefore, in their analysis of law and society, ignore the relevance of social relations. The first school of philosophers who attempted to place law in an operational context was the historical school.

HISTORICAL SCHOOL

During the 19th century, coexisting with elements of both positivist and classical theory, attention was also turned towards the fact that law operated in a social setting. While gods, kings or mother nature were seen to give law its validity, some thinkers also considered that the law did respond to social change and was not, therefore, a matter of metaphysics or royal edict. The historical school became concerned with the theory of evolution. Darwin himself caused great controversy by suggesting that human beings had evolved from more primitive animal forms.[11] Likewise law was explained by the historical school in a developing and changing form. Again we see a strong overlap between the contemporary physical sciences and more traditional philosophical approaches. First, comparative studies were made and differences in behaviour of law explained by reference to a variety of factors, including geography, climate and population density. Law was seen by this school as a growing body of rules that reacted to social demand. As yet, the *nature* of that society has not been revealed. Equity, law fictions, presumptions, case law and legislation were all the result of historical interaction. Law evolved in the same way as any other growth. Nature's role was thereby delimited. Again, the battle between religion and science reared its head. Evolutionary theory was in itself a radical departure from the previous work. However, despite the use of scientific tools of analysis, evolution was often seen as a process towards religious achievement. For example, Hegel, an influential German philosopher of the late 18th and early 19th centuries, recognised the process of social change and consequently legal change and explained this by reference to the ultimate goal: a State-run society in which maximum liberty could be attained.[12] Earlier, the French philosopher Montesquieu had pioneered openly discriminatory social systems (remembering slavery was widely practised until the late 19th century) were altered through such change by replacing them with a Christian model in which the State was in control. The theory had broken new ground, explaining laws in terms of historical evolution but not taking the analysis any further.

Law was an evolutionary product reflecting changing social norms. This break with the blinkered approach of the two previous schools is highly significant. The law could be explained, not in terms of unquestionable authority, but by reference to a mobile society. Today, as in the other instances, this school of thought attracts a following. Maine and Savigny are good examples of the historical philosopher.[13]

THE SOCIOLOGICAL SCHOOL

The sociological school is the most recent to attack the problem of the meaning of law. Again there is much diversity within this approach. Divine authority and metaphysics are, however, largely disregarded by this school, other than as issues highly relevant to particular social orders. The sociological approach generally speaking is one that attempts to analyse society and law from its ideological foundation. Two questions are posed: what is law? and how does law work? To a certain extent the attempts to provide satisfactory answers are self-reliant. By this we mean that how law works indicates what law is, and vice versa. The work of this school can be divided into two areas. The first is a purely empirical and/or a conventional, theoretical approach. Law is seen through the eyes of judges, defendants, witnesses and victims, and their picture of law is analysed and discussed. The anthropological approach current in some of the historical schools' work was taken further by the empiricists of the sociological school, and evidence of the meaning of law presented through studies of housing, education, population, etc. The results of such studies were used in the explanation of law. Law was seen in the historical sense of evolution, i.e. reflecting changing values, but in addition it was seen as a mobile concept that had a conscious growth. This means that there were identifiable reasons for change.

An early proponent of this approach was Roscoe Pound. His 'theory' of social engineering attempts to show the balance between stability and change as reflected by the law. Others taking this approach include Ehrlich Von Ihering and Hagerstrom.[14]

A modern extension of this approach can be found in the works of the U.S. legal 'realists'. This branch of the wider movement explains laws by reference to the behavioural sciences, e.g. psychology, modern technology (computers). The law is thus presented *as it is* through such media.[15]

The second and radically different approach can be found in the work of the critical theorists. Most of the work cited above operates either on the premise that the authority of law is objective and unquestionable or that it reflects a tacit consensus within society. These studies, including much of the sociological approach, starts from a non-critical level of analysis. Theories and explanations are made within a largely presumed ideological framework. The final approach to be mentioned here, by way of substance and contrast, is to be found in the non-acceptance of such a presumption. The critical theorist questions the very existence of this foundation. There is a very wide range of material available but we refer here only to the most outstanding contributions. Historically both the right and left of the political spectrum are represented.

Karl Marx speaking ironically, in the mid-19th century said: 'Society is not based on law, that is a legal fiction; rather law must be based on Society, it must be the expression of Society's common interests and needs';[16] and, more contentiously, 'Your jurisprudence is but the will of your class made into law for all.'[17]

The point to stress, regardless of whether one approves or disapproves of the interests which are preserved, is that law is a product of society and reflects that society's interests. The critical theorists stand to question the values inherent in the rules, thus revealing the nature of the law. That such studies historically have had little to say expressly about the law indicates the emphasis of the approach, i.e. law is but *one* social institution among many others.

Given that about one-third of the world's population practises Marxism and the remainder seems to argue about it, it is perhaps appropriate to consider briefly the way in which Marx and subsequent Marxist theoreticians have explained law.

Simply put, law is one of the processes by which class interests are created, preserved and maintained. To understand how such interests arise it is necessary to understand the evolution of classes within society. Some emphasis has been laid at the outset of this text on the political and economic relationship between lord and vassel (feudalism) and employer/ee (capitalism). Law has to service these relations for law, according to this approach, is created by the dominant party (lord, employer, etc.). For Marx the essence of class distinction lies in the existence of capital and labour and the relationship between these two concepts. Unlike previous theoreticians (e.g. Hegel) Marx recognises the irreconcilable and conflicting interests of these classes. The ruling class, i.e. the class in power, own the means and factors of production (raw material, land, factories, machines) while the rest own only their labour power. This is sold to the capitalist in return for wages. However, the profit (over and above wages paid and cost of production) lies in the hands of the ruling class. Law quite simply reflects this position, despite its more liberal form offering, for example, limited protection to the working populus, with the increase in the provisions of welfare benefits. To substantiate such a claim one need look no further than the law protecting private property interests and see in fact with whom those interests lie.

Again, we stress that the merits of this system are not being debated. Rather the way in which the law is seen by the critical theorists is described. In this context what should be appreciated is the predictive nature of such theory. Not only is law explained by reference to its past and present but also to how the social order is to change and how law will then fulfil a totally different role. For Marx this would be superficial and eventually, under socialism, redundant.

Of others within the wide-ranging interest of the critical theorists mention should be made of Engels and Lenin on the political left and, to the other extreme, of Franco and Hitler.[18]

CONCLUSION

What relevance, therefore, does an understanding of the meaning of law have to Ireland? Three points can be made. First, law has been for far too long considered atheoretical and autonomous. This point has been raised in some detail in the text and we hope that in studying the topic the reader realises that law has to operate in a social context. To ignore the purpose and meaning of law is to misunderstand its application. This can be more clearly illustrated by the law of industrial relations. A theory of the law, in the writers' opinion, is necessarily a theory about society, law being an institution of society.

Secondly we argue that Ireland's Constitutional history implicitly recognises equality before the law. While our own opinion may be critical of the realities of such a situation one matter can be stated, that access to the law *is* a basic right and the law should be both studied and publicised in this context.

Thirdly, and finally, one might speculate as to the future of the law in Ireland. Law will continue, obviously, to play an important, significant role in the well-fashioned common law tradition. More and more, however, one notices that greater dissatisfaction with the law is being expressed, and that the State is playing an increasing role as mediator in the provision of legal and social services. The concept of legal aid has been discussed at some length and this perhaps is a convenient concluding example of the point in question. Legal aid will be implemented in one form or another in Ireland, and the law may be open to more public criticism, but beyond this ameliorative facade, the substance of the law is unlikely to alter in principle.

At the very least an analytical study of the law provides the reader with the opportunity of predicting the likely interpretation of legal provisions – a task which has occupied practising lawyers wherever issues of law are mooted. The reader should now appreciate, at least in outline, the foundations, concepts and principles upon which the Irish legal system works and some of the rules that make up the system itself.

SUPPLEMENT TO THE 1988 REPRINT

It has not been possible to make corrections and additions to the text for the purposes of this reprint. However, the following summary texts provide a brief outline of the most significant developments in law since this book was first published.

Chapter 9
CONSTITUTIONAL LAW

The last decade has seen an increase in litigation and controversy on Constitutional issues. There have been four referenda, three of which resulted in Constitutional amendments. The first of these in 1983 incorporated a new Art. 40.3.3° protecting the right to life of the unborn. In 1984 the 9th amendment of the Constitution extended the Dáil Franchise to non-citizens. In 1985 a proposal to admit the introduction of divorce failed and in 1987 the 10th amendment of the Constitution was passed in order to authorise the ratification of the Single European Act by the Government.

Recent expansion in the field of unenumerated rights is also evident. The categories have been seen to incorporate a right to one's good name;[1] a right to bodily integrity;[2] a right not to have one's health endangered by the State;[3] a right to work and earn a livelihood;[4] a right to privacy between married couples;[5] a right to individual privacy;[6] a right to litigate or to have access to the courts;[7] a right to justice and fair procedures;[8] a right to travel outside the State;[9] a right to marry;[10] a right to communicate;[11] a right to beget children;[12] and possibly a right to take industrial action.[13]

Notes

1. State (O'Rourke and White) v Martin [1984] ILRM 331.
2. Hanrahan v Merck Sharp and Dohme (Irl.) Ltd. High Court 7/8/86.
3. Murray v Ireland [1985] I.R. 532.
4. A. G. v Paperlink [1984] ILRM 373.
5. Kennedy v Ireland. High Court 12/1/87.
6. Murphy v PMPA Insurance Co. Ltd. High Court 21/2/78.
7. State (M.C.) v Eastern Health Board. High Court 29/7/86.
8. S. v S. [1984) I.R. 68.
9. State (M) v Minister for Foreign Affairs [1979] I.R. 73.
10. Donovan v Minister for Justice 85 ILTR 134.
11. State (Murray) v Governor of Limerick Prison. High Court 23/8/78.
12. Murray v Ireland [1985] I.R. 532.
13. Talbot (Irl.) Ltd. v Merrigan, Supreme Court 30/4/81.

Chapter 10
EUROPEAN COMMUNITY LAW

The most important development in EEC law in the past decade is the controversial Single European Act for which a referendum was required in Ireland due to conflicts with the Irish Constitution. The Single European Act will streamline the Community decision-making process by providing for qualified majority voting in matters concerning the completion of the internal market. In addition, the role of the European Parliament in the decision-making process has been modified significantly by the establishment of a co-operation procedure involving a second reading of commission proposals. The Act also introduces into the EC Treaty new articles on monetary co-operation, social policy, regional policy, research and technological development and environment policy. The increased case load in the Court of Justice of the Communities has also been recognised by the Single European Act which allows for the establishment of inferior tribunals for the trial of certain categories of cases with a right of appeal on points of law to the Court of Justice. Finally, the practice of the member states with regard to European Political Cooperation had been put into treaty form and provision has been made for the establishment of a small administrative secretariat located at Brussels.

This is a development of major significance which is the culmination of a process of reform which had been in train for at least 15 years. Its aim is the establishment of an internal market before 1/1/1993 providing for free movement of goods, people and capital mainly.

Chapter 11
CRIMINAL LAW

The Criminal Law (Rape) Act 1981 defines rape as unlawful sexual intercourse committed with knowledge or recklessness as to whether the woman consented and it is up to the jury to decide on the presence of reasonable grounds for belief of consent.

The controversial Criminal Justice Act 1984 introduced widespread amendments to criminal law and procedure. The amendments include increased Garda powers in relation to the detention of certain suspects; the imposition of consecutive sentences for offences committed while on bail; increased penalties in relation to certain firearms offences and the taking of motor vehicles without authority; the drawing of inferences from the Defendant's failure to give explanations when questioned to account for objects or marks which may be attributable to his participation in the alleged offence. Trial procedures have also been amended: notice of particulars of an alibi must be given to the Prosecution; admissibility of written statements to like extent as oral evidence; proof by formal admission; abolition of the right to make an unsworn statement and the introduction of majority verdicts.

The Extradition (Suppression of Terrorism) Act 1987 was enacted to conform to the provisions of the Convention on the Suppression of Terrorism of 1977 and extending the Extradition Act 1965. The major change affected by the Act is the effective abolition of the 'political offence' exception contained in S.50 of the 1965 Act.

Chapter 12
THE LAW OF CONTRACT

The main change in the law of contract in the last decade occurred in 1980 with the enactment of the Sale of Goods and Supply of Services Act which has been called the most significant piece of consumer protection legislation since the founding of the State. The Act in part builds upon the 1893 Act and the various Hire-Purchase Acts from 1946 to 1960. It extends protection into commercial areas which had been ignored by the Legislature especially in the provision of services and especially if the practice was seen as unfair.

Another important facet of the Act is the implied terms which apply to contract with regard to skill, care and diligence and quality of merchandise or materials used or supplied. Also the right to contract out of the Act is curtailed by the terms of the Act itself and only allowed in certain circumstances whereby the consumer's interests are still protected.

Chapter 13
THE LAW OF TORT

As a result of the Stardust tragedy in 1979 the Fire Services Act 1981 was passed to make provision for the establishment of fire authorities and the organisation of fire services and for fire safety, fire fighting, the protection and the rescue of persons and property.

Due to concern regarding accidents caused by stray animals on roads the Animals Act 1985 placed a heavy onus of responsibility on animal owners and they are strictly liable for damage caused by the animals straying on to the public road.

A major change affecting the law of tort in its procedural aspect is the abolition of juries in personal injuries and certain other actions in the High Court brought in by the Courts Act 1988. This is intended to affect the amount of damages awarded in such actions and thereby lessen insurance premiums and also to improve the speed of processing civil actions in court.

Chapter 14
THE LAW OF PROPERTY

Legislation has been introduced to give existing tenants rights against their landlords to require the grant of a new tenancy or enabling them to acquire the landlord's interest in the property. The Landlord and Tenant (Amendment) Act 1980 also amended the law relating to compensation for improvements and for disturbance or loss of title. The rent restriction legislation in force in Ireland was held unconstitutional in 1982 and new laws protective of tenants were introduced by the Housing (Private Rented Dwellings) Act 1982 as amended in 1983.

The Land Act 1984 was passed with the main aim of encouraging leasing of agricultural land by excluding such leases from the application of certain nineteenth-century statutory provisions which tend to favour the lessee.

Chapter 15
COMPANY LAW

Regulations on Company Law have been updated on a number of occasions in the past decade in keeping with European Community Directives on Company Law. The main reforming Act was the Companies (Amendment) Act in 1983 which provides, inter alia, for the formation of Public Limited Companies and the re-registration of older companies as PLCs.

The Act also prohibits the issue of shares at a discount and the purchase by a company of its own shares. These restrictions are an attempt to prevent the company trafficking in its own shares and influencing the market value of the shares by artificial purchases. The restrictions also recognise the increased need for protection of investors and creditors by way of maintenance of capital rules.

Also in recent years strict compliance regarding financing and filing of company accounts and tax returns has become necessary to avoid penalties introduced to ensure protection of shareholders and to reflect increased awareness of the dangers of insider dealing.

Chapter 16
LABOUR LAW

The main developments in Labour Law in recent years have been (i) The introduction of legislation on hours of work and the protection of employees in the event of their employer's insolvency, both 1984 Acts, the latter being the implementation of an EEC Council Directive which became effective in 1983. (ii) An enormous increase in the number of cases coming before the

Employment Appeals Tribunal in the last two or three years. (iii) Rejection by the Labour Court of claims for paid paternity leave.[1] (iv) The first decision on sexual harassment in employment where compensation was ordered[2] and the harassment described as discrimination within the terms of the Employment Equality Act 1977.

Notes

1. Unifi Textures Yarns Europe Ltd. and ITGWU LCR 10,1932, and RTE and RTE Trade Union Group. LCR 10,440.
2. A Worker v Garage Proprietor EEO2/1985.

Chapter 17
FAMILY LAW

Family Law is the area which has been the subject of most reforms in the last decade, it being an area of law which is continually in need of reform.

The Family Law Act in 1981 dealt with the difficulties which arise when an engagement to marry is broken, the ensuing disputes regarding the couple's property and gifts between the parties.

Perhaps due to the unsuccessful attempt to introduce divorce in 1985 or perhaps due to advances in medicine there has also been an expansion of the grounds for nullity in recent years. A new category has evolved through the case law, namely an inability to enter into and sustain a normal marriage relationship. This improvement emphasises the relationship involved rather than the contractual aspect of the marriage and as such is a radical change in the nullity jurisdiction.

The Irish Nationality Citizenship Act 1986 places both men and women in a position of equality in relation to the acquisition of citizenship upon marriage.

The Status of Children Act 1982 was introduced to equalise the rights under the law of all children, whether born within or outside marriage. There is also a statutory procedure to enable any person to obtain a court declaration as to his parentage in civil proceedings. The Act also amends the law with regard to legal presumptions and other evidential matters and to the registration of the births of children whose parents have not married each other. Part III of the Act amends the provisions of the Guardianship of Infants Act 1964 so as to allow, by virtue of a statutory procedure, the father of an illegitimate child to be a guardian of his child jointly with the mother and if the father's application is opposed, the court must determine the issue with the welfare of the child as the paramount consideration.

The Domicile and Recognition of Foreign Divorces Act 1986 abolished the wife's dependent domicile and the dependent domicile of a minor may now be that of his mother if his home is with her and not with his father. Also a divorce shall be recognised if granted in the country where either spouse is domiciled i.e. it is no longer necessary for both spouses to be domiciled there.

The Adoption Act 1988 permits the adoption of any child, whether his parents are married or unmarried or have adopted him without requiring the consent of his parents or guardian, but only in certain strictly defined circumstances where authorised by the High Court. The Act also reduces from 21 to 18 years the maximum age at which a person may be adopted.

Chapter 18
WELFARE LAW

Many reforms of Social Welfare Law were canvassed in the Report of the Commission on Social Welfare (Pl. 2851) and are being put into effect through the Welfare Acts which are promulgated each year. The Social Welfare Act 1986 in particular provided for the introduction of a new child benefit scheme to replace the old children's allowance. The Act also provides for an increase in the ceiling on earnings used in the calculation of social insurance contributions.

The Social Welfare Act 1988 deals with new rates of social insurance benefits and social assistance payments, family income supplement, employment contributions, pay-related benefit, social insurance for the self-employed and other miscellaneous amendments.

NOTES AND REFERENCES

CHAPTER 1

1. D. A. Binchy, 'The Linguistic and Historical Value of the Irish Law Tracts' Sir John Rhys lecture p.109. This comment is derived from the 12th Century preface to *Senchas Már* and has been widely criticised for its double meaning.
2. ibid p. 210.
3. ibid p. 214.
4. Crith Gablach.
5. E. McNeill *Early Irish Law and Institutions,* p. 83.
6. See Ch. 2.
7. V. T. H. Delaney (ed. C. Lysaght), *Administration of Justice in Ireland* (I.P.A. 1975) p. 16.
8. Walker & Walker *The English Legal System* (4th ed. Butterworths 1976), p. 10.
9. The function of the magistrate can be seen by reference to the Riot Acts and ancillary legislation 1714/1886. Further information is available in L. Radzinowcz, *A History of English Criminal Law* (Sweet & Maxwell 1968), vol. 4.
10. Winsmore and Greenbank (1745) Willes 578.
11. See R. H. Maudsley *Hanbury's Modern Equity* (9th ed., Stephens 1969), p. 15.
12. P. S. James, *Introduction to English Law* (9th ed. Butterworths 1976), p. 25.
13. (1615) Cro. Jal. 343.
14. (1615) I Rep. Ch. I.
15. Delaney, op cit, pp. 16-17.
16. See Basil Chubb *The Government and Politics of Ireland,* Historical introduction by David Thornley (OUP 1970).
17. ibid p. 11.
18. Delaney, op cit, p. 18, 39 & 40 Geo. III c.67; 40 Geo. III c. 38 (Ir.).
19. W. J. Johnson, 'The First Adventure of the Common Law' L.Q.R. CXLI pp. 24-5.
20. Delaney, op cit, p. 19; 28 Hen. VIII c. 19; Eliz. I c. I.; 23 & 25 Geo. III c. 14 (Ir).
21. 33 Geo. III c. 36 (Ir).
22. 22 Geo. III, c. 53.
23. A. V. Dicey, *Law and Public Opinion in England* (Macmillan 1963) p. 111.
24 James, op cit, p. 27.
25. Administration of Justice Act, 1970.
26. See Royal Commission on Capital Punishment, 1827.
27. 6 & 7 Will. IV, c. 13.
28. Delaney, op cit, p. 36.

CHAPTER 2

1. Sir R. Cross, *Precedent in English Law* (Butterworths 1977) p. 155.
2. (1901) AC 495 at 506.
3. Professor Goodhart.
4. Asquith J.
5. (1965) I.R. 70 at 126.
6. (1952) I.R. 62.
7. ibid p. 126.
8. ibid p. 127.
9. (1965) I.R. 642 at 653.
10. ibid p. 645.
11. ibid at 653-4.
12. (1965) I.R. 1.
13. ibid.
14. [1932] AC 562.
15. [1929] AC 358.
16. [1972] 1 All E.R. 749.
17. Supreme Court (unreported) November 1975.
18. *Mogul v. Tipperary* (unreported) Supreme Ct.
19. [1978] 1 All E.R. 841.
20. Supreme Court (unreported) October 1978.
21. [1975] I.R. 230.
22. per O'Higgins C. J., *McDonnell v. Byrne* (unreported) Supreme Court (Oct. 1978).
23. (1944) KB 718.
24. See Dowrick, 'Precedent in Modern Irish Law', *Law Q. Rev.* 25 (1953).
25. ibid
26. High Court (unreported) March 1976.
27. ibid.
28. ibid.
29. per Gavan Duffy J. in *Exham v. Beamish* (1939) I.R. 336 at 384.
30. (1977) I.R. 24.
31. ibid. p. 29.
32. (1977) I.R. 129.
33. 'Statutory Interpretations' at 41.
34. (1958) 92 ILTR 59.
35. (1957) Ir. Jur. Rep. 8.
36. (1560) Plowd 199.
37. (1836) 7 C & P 446.
38. (1973) I.R. 33.
39. (1880) 5 App. Cas. 214.
40. (1947) 81 ILTR 130.
41. ibid, p. 131.
42. Ex Parte Cambell (1896) L.R. 5 Cl 763 at 766.
43. (1949) 2KB 417.
44. Sir R. Cross (op cit) p. 135.
45. (1898) AC 571 at 575.
46. [1935] AC 445.
47. (1972) I.R. 36.
48. ibid at p. 34.
49. [1931] AC 126.
50. (1874) L.R. 9 Exch. 125.
51. (1965) I.R. 217 at 239.
52. 1973 I.R. 121.

53. ibid p. 137.

54. (1974) I.R. 19.

55. ibid p. 22.

55a. Reference must be made to the Interpretation Act, 1937. Under the title 'Meaning and Construction of Parliamentary Words and Expressions', Part III of the Act contains a number of provisions relating to every Act of the Oireachtas. Thus, for example, every word importing the singular is to be construed as importing the plural, and *vice versa,* unless a contrary intention appears. A similar provision is made for words importing masculine and feminine gender. Finally, the schedule to the Act contains a list of thirty-seven words which are to bear the meaning ascribed to them in the schedule unless a contrary intention appears. The list includes such words as affidavit, land, month, swear, town, week, writing and year.

56. *Johnson v. Clarke* (1908) ch. 303 at 334.

57. (1872) L.R. 7QB 214.

CHAPTER 3

1. *Post* p. 90.

2. The relationship of importance here is between creditor and debtor. The rights and obligations of the shareholder and company is described post pp. 98-99, and in detail in Chapter 15.

3. A company can also be formed under the Industrial and Provident Society Act, 1852 (as amended). This legislation allows for the registration of societies that are bona fide co-operatives or are otherwise for the benefit of the community and there are special reasons why the Companies Acts are not used. This method of formation is attractive to co-operatives community initiatives and falls under the powers of the registrar for Friendly Societies.

4. (1897) A.C. 22.

5. Registration of Business Names Act, 1963.

6. The scope of judicial review is examined in Ch. 4 and has recently been surveyed by the Law Reform Commission in working paper No. 8 – 1979 'Judicial Review of Administrative Action: The Problem of Remedies'.

7. Unlimited liability within a partnership is permitted under defined circumstances by virtue of Limited Partnerships Act, 1907.

8. In particular *Taff Vale Rail Co. v Am Society of Railway Servants* (1901) A.C. 426.

9. The immunity is provided for by Trade Disputes Act, 1906.

10. For further details see Ch. 16.

11. In particular the 'Fundamental Rights' Articles, 40-44, Constitution of Ireland 1937.

12. This point was raised in the Supreme Court but not pursued in the *State (Nicolaou) v An Bórd Uchtála* [1966] I.R. 567.

13. The concept of domicile is exhaustively discussed in Alan Shatter *Family Law in the Republic of Ireland* (Wolfhound Press), pp. 102-5 of 1st edition 1977. Further mention appears in Ch. 17.

14. *Gaffney v. Gaffney* (1975) I.R. 133 *Per Walsh J.*

15. *List of age limits from the Law Reform Commission Working paper No. 2 1977, 'The Law Relating to the Age of Majority, the Age for Marriage and Some Connected Subjects:*

A person aged 5:

(i) It is an offence for any person to give intoxicating liquor (other than for medical purposes) to a child under 5 years. The Children Act 1908, s. 11(9).

(ii) A child under the age of 7 is entirely exempt from criminal responsibility. Common law.

A person aged 7:

For a child between the ages of 7 and 14, there is a rebuttable presumption that he is incapable of committing a crime.

A person aged 13:

A boy under 14 is conclusively presumed to be incapable of committing the crime of rape or any other crime of which sexual intercourse is an ingredient or buggery, though he may be convicted of aiding and abetting. Common law.

A person aged 14:

(i) Age of full criminal responsibility. Common law.

(ii) Children aged 14 and under are not allowed in a bar. 1908 Children's Act, ss. 13 and 120.

(iii) Unlawful carnal knowledge of a female under 15 is a felony. Criminal Law Amendment Act 1935, s. 1 (1). Consent is not a defence.

(iv) Consent is not a defence to a charge of indecent assault on a person under 15. Criminal Law Amendment Act 1935, s. 14.

(v) A child under the school-leaving age (15) may not be employed at a mine. Mines and Quarries Act 1965, ss. 5(1) and 108.

A person aged 15:

(i) Entitlement to children's allowances ceases when a child reaches the age of 16 unless the child is receiving full-time instruction, is an apprentice or is incapacitated, in which case it continues until the age of 18. Children's Allowances (Amendment) Act 1946, s. 4 and Social Welfare Act 1973, s. 2(1).

(ii) Under the Health Acts 1947 to 1970, a person under the age of 16 is treated as a child. Health Act 1957, s. 2 (1).

(iii) The obligation of a parent to maintain a child under the Family Law (Maintenance of Spouses and Children) Act 1976 ceases when the child attains the age of 16 unless the child is or will be, or, if a maintenance order were made for his support, would be, receiving full-time education or instruction at an educational establishment, in which case it may continue up to the age of 21. If the child is suffering from mental or physical disability to such extent that it is not reasonably possible for him to maintain himself fully, there is no upper age limit for the entitlement to maintenance. Ss. 3, 5 and 6(3) of the 1976 Act.

(iv) Every man must maintain his legitimate children and every child of his wife born before her marriage to him, until they reach 16. Every woman is liable to maintain those of her children who are under 16. The liability to maintain is *only* for the purposes of supplementary welfare allowances, so as to allow for the recovery of and contributions to such allowances. Social Welfare (Supplementary Welfare Allowances) Act 1975. ss. 16 and 17.

(v) It is an offence to sell cigarettes to children under the age of 16. The Children Act 1908, s. 39.

(vi) A person under the age of 16 may not be employed in a bar. Intoxicating Liquor Act 1924, s. 12.

A person aged 16:

(i) Minimum age for marriage. Marriages Act 1972, s. 1 (1). Marriages of persons below 16 need permission of the President of the High Court. Ss. 1(2) and 1(3) of 1972 Act.

(ii) Unlawful carnal knowledge of a girl under 17 is a misdemeanour. Criminal Law Amendment Act 1935, s. 2. Consent is not a defence.

(iii) Compulsory social insurance of workers commences at 16. Social Welfare Act 1952, s. 4.

(iv) Under the Health Acts 1947 to 1970 a person aged 16 and over is treated as an adult, i.e., he is free to choose his own doctor, obtain a medical card in his own right, give consent for an operation and apply for a disabled person's maintenance allowance. Health Act 1947, s. 2(1).

(v) A 16 year old may be a member of a friendly society or credit union, but he may not be a member of the committee or its manager or borrow money until he reaches 21. Industrial and Provident Society Act 1893, s. 32 and Credit Union Act 1966, ss. 3 and 4.

(vi) A 16 year old may hold a licence to ride a motor cycle with engine not exceeding 150 cc. Road Traffic Act 1961, s. 31; Road Traffic (Licensing of Drivers) Regulations 1964, Article 6 (S.I. 29 of 1964).

A person aged 17:

(i) A 17 year old may hold a licence to drive a private car, tractor or a vehicle for use by a person suffering from a physical disability. Road Traffic Act 1961, s. 31; Road Traffic (Licensing of Drivers) Regulations 1964, Articles 6 and 8 (S.I. 29 of 1964).

(ii) A "qualified child" for certain benefits under the Social Welfare Acts means a person who is either under the age of 18 or, if over 18, is under 21 and receiving full-time instruction. S. 2(1) of 1952 Act and s. 29(3) of 1970 Act.

(iii) It is an offence to sell alcohol to a person under the age of 18. Intoxicating Liquor (General) Act 1924, s. 10.

(iv) A girl aged 16 but under 18 may not be employed in, or permitted to sell drink for consumption on, licensed premises, unless she is a relative of the licence holder residing with him. Intoxicating Liquor (General) Act 1924, s. 12.

A person aged 18:

(i) May vote in Presidential, national and local elections and in referenda. Articles 12.2.2° and 16.1.2° of the Constitution; and Electoral (Amendment) Act 1973, ss. 2 and 3.

(ii) May stand as a candidate in local elections. Electoral (Amendment) Act 1973, s. 4.

(iii) May make a valid will. Succession Act 1965, s. 77(1) (a). (He or she may make a will under that age if he or she is or has been married: *id.*)

(iv) May serve on a jury. Juries Act 1976, s. 6.

(v) May be served alcohol in a bar. Intoxicating Liquor (General) Act 1924, s. 10.

(vi) May hold a licence to drive class D vehicles, i.e., heavy lorries and trucks, or motor bicycles with engines of more than 150 cc. Road Traffic Act 1961, s. 31; Road Traffic (Licensing of Drivers) Regulations 1964, Articles 6 and 8 (S.I. 29 of 1964).

(vii) May, if a male, qualify for unemployment assistance. Females aged 18 and over must have a certain number of social insurance stamps before they qualify. Unemployment Assistance Act 1933, s. 10; Social Welfare Acts 1952, s. 68, 1973, s. 9 and 1975, s. 10.

A person aged 21, 25, 30 and 35:

(i) The age of eligibility for membership of the Dail and Seanad is 21. Articles 16.1.1° and 18.2 of the Constitution. To be eligible for the Presidency a person must be at least 35. Article 14.1 of the Constitution.

(ii) Persons aged under 21 need parental consent to marry but the requirement to obtain such consent is directory and not mandatory. Marriages Act 1972, s. 7.

(iii) An illegitimate, legitimated or orphan child who has not attained the age of 21 may be adopted. Adoption Acts 1952, ss. 3 and 10, 1964, ss. 2 and 3, and 1974, s. 11.

(iv) An applicant for an adoption order, being the mother, natural father or a relative of the child must have attained the age of 21. If the applicants are a married couple and the wife is the mother of the child, she or her husband must have attained the age of 21. If the applicants are a married couple and one of them is the natural father or a relative of the child, each of them must have attained the age of 21. Normally, an applicant for an adoption order or, if the applicants are a married couple, each of them must have attained the age of 30. However, an adoption order may be made on the application of a married couple who have been married to each other for not less than 3 years and each of whom has attained the age of 25. Adoption Act 1952, s. 11 and Adoption Act 1964, s. 5.

16. ibid.

17. Married Women's Property Act, 1882, but now governed in the Republic by Married Women's Status Act, 1957. See Ch. 17 for further details.

18. Anti-Discrimination (Pay) Act, 1974: Employment Equality Act, 1977.

19. Since April 1979 some of the discriminatory provisions in the social welfare legislation have been repealed. There are, however, considerable differences in the treatment of men and women claimants, particularly if the woman is married. Further details are contained in Ch. 18.

20. Constitution of Ireland 1937 Article 41.2.2.

21. ibid. Articles 46-47.

22. For further discussion see Law Reform Commission working paper No. 5 – 1978 'The law relating to the criminal conversation and the enticement and harbouring of a spouse'. A bill is now before the Oireachtas to abolish the action of Criminal Conversation.

23. Social Welfare Act, 1973, s.17.

24. Although at the time of writing regulations for the introduction of such a

scheme lay before the Oireachtas. Further information is to be found in Ch. 8.

25. Sale of Goods Act, 1893, s.2.

26. The details of such actions are contained in Ch. 12.

27. A concise and well reasoned account of the mental aspect of criminal liability is contained in *Cross and Jones 'Introduction to Criminal Law'* Jones and Card (Butterworths 1976) pp. 30-45.

28. M'Naghten's case (1843) 10 C.L. & F.I.N. 200.

29. This procedure is specifically catered for in Article 40.4.2, which is available for any person alleging unlawful detention.

30. Unfair Dismissals Act, 1977.

31. Ch. 16 expands the legal obligations arising out of this relationship.

CHAPTER 4

1. A thorough description of court's role in controlling the scope of administrative decision-making (although judicial review is applicable to regulate the activities of other bodies, e.g. the lower courts) is contained in Law Reform Commission working paper No. 8 1979, op cit.

2. Constitution of Ireland 1937. Articles 26 and 34.

3. ibid. Articles 40-44.

4. For further discussion on Constitutional law in the U.K. see O. Hood Philips, *Constitutional and administrative Law* (6th ed. Sweet & Maxwell 1978).

5. This point was well argued in *Kiely v Minister of Social Welfare* (1977) I.R. 267. As stressed in Ch. 9, the Constitutional rights accorded to the citizen are not exhaustive and the inherent power of the superior courts (High Court and Supreme Court) to intervene on grounds of natural justice remains largely unaltered by the Constitution.

6. (1924) I.K.B. 256.

7. (1852) 3 H.L.C. 759.

8. *Moran v A.G.* (1976) I.R. 400.

9. The characteristics of civil law systems are well documented in David and Brierly *Major Legal Systems in the World Today* (Stevens 1968).

10. The legal definition of murder and the appropriate authorities are discussed in Ch. 11.

11. This will be allowed where, for example, facts not reasonably available at the time of trial are discovered.

12. See Ch. 2.

13. *Blackburn v A.G.* (1971) 2 All E.R. 1380. *Reg v G.L.C. exparte Blackburn* (1976) 3 All E.R. 184.

14. [1973] Q.B. 629.

15. But note the limitations expressed in *Weir v Fermanagh County Council* (1913) I. I.R. 193, and the arguments continued in the British case of *Gouriet v Union of Post Office Workers* (1977) 3 All E.R. 70. The recent case of *Martin v Dublin Corporation* (unreported) Dec. 1977, is a good example of the modern relevance of *locus standi.*

16. See Chapters 2 and 9.

17. The Padfield case (1968) A.C. 997; *A.G. v Wilts United Dairy* (1921) 37 T.L.R. 884.

18. Generally see Denning, M. R., *Discipline of the Law* (Butterworths 1979) pp. 61-108.

19. *R. v Northumberland Compensation Appeal Tribunal exparte Shaw* (1952), I.K.B. 338.

20. For more detailed analysis of the scope and application of the declaration see Law Reform Commission working paper No. 8 – 1979, op cit, pp. 29-34.

21. Sections *18 and 20* Offences Against the Person Act, 1861; see Ch. 11 for further authorities.

22. A child involved in the circumstances of the commission of a crime may be subject to care proceedings under the Children Act, 1908, and subsequent legislation, see Shatter *Family Law in the Republic of Ireland* Ch. 13.

23. *R. v Waite* (1892) 2 Q.B. 600.

24. See Ch. 16.

CHAPTER 5

1. The conditions under which the right to trial by jury is withdrawn are specified broadly under Article 38 of the Constitution (1937) and further amplified by Criminal Justice Act, 1951; Offences Against the State Act, 1939 (as amended) and Criminal Proceedings Act, 1967.

2. Prosecution of Offences Act, 1974.

3. For example under the Official Secrets Act, 1963.

4. Fisheries (Consolidation) Act, 1959. Although the constitutionality of such legislative power has been questioned.

5. Constitution of 1937, Article 38.2, op cit.

6. (1966) I.R. 379.

7. S. 25 Courts (Supplemental Provisions) Act, 1961 and Offences Against the State Act, 1939, Part V.

8. S. 62 Courts of Justice Act, 1936 as amended by the Criminal Procedure Act 1967.

9. The special form of oath is provided for in these cases by S. 19(2) of the Juries Act, 1976.

11. See generally Robinson, The Special Criminal Court (D.U.P. 1974).

12. See Ch. 1 and 4.

13. See Ch. 9 and Article 40.4.2°, 3°, 4°, 5°.

14. See Ch. 7.

15. Now principally governed by the Courts Act, 1971, but some jurisdiction is derived from enactments that relate to specific issues e.g. Rent Restriction Acts, 1960/67, and Family Law (Maintenance of Spouses and Children) Act, 1976.

16. Since Courts Act, 1971.

17. For example appeals on issues of law can, under the Unfair Dismissals Act 1977 be brought from the Employment Appeals Tribunal directly to the High Court.

18. With the constant expansion of the welfare state increasing decision-making functions are bestowed on officers and tribunals. Social welfare benefits, redundancy payments, and compensation for unfair dismissal are, as is noted, examples of this development. In each case an administrative machinery has been created, to a greater or lesser extent, to cater for the applications thereby arising.

19. For detailed discussions of the function of the institutions of the United Nations see D. W. Greig *International Law* (Butterworths 1976).

20. See, for example, the Lawless case; *Ireland v U.K.* (E.C.H.R.) as discussed in Boyle, 'Human Rights and the Northern Ireland Emergency', a paper prepared for U.K. National Committee of Comparative Law Colloquium, Sept. 1978, 'Human Rights in Criminal Law'.

21. Under Article 6 of the convention.

22. An interesting if incomplete account of the English Court of Appeals attitude to the exercise of this discretion is contained in Lord Denning M.R's Autobiography *Discipline of the Law* pp. 83-99.

23. 20 & 21 Vict. c. 79, and 23 & 24 Vict. c. 114.

CHAPTER 6

1. Act of Settlement, 1701.
2. Judicature (Ir.) Act, 1877, and 21 & 22 Geo. III c. 11.
3. The law affecting the conditions of a judge's office are now contained in The Courts (Establishment and Constitution) Act, 1961.
4. Courts of Justice (District Court) Act, 1946.
5. ibid s. 21.
6. A general and interesting, if controversial, account of the relationship between the judiciary and politics is contained in J. A. G. Griffith *The Politics of the Judiciary* (Fontana 1977). More specifically, Paul C. Bartholomew's *The Irish Judiciary* (Institute of Public Administration 1971) presents a valuable account of the features of the judges in Ireland.
7. Delaney, *Administration of Justice in Ireland,* pp. 79-83.
8. Court Officers Act, 1945.
9. See Ch. 7.
10. We do not intend the terms 'academics' and 'legal profession' to be mutually exclusive. Many lawyers both teach and practise, but each is a distinct aspect of the personnel of the law.
11. Delaney, op cit, pp. 89-92.
12. See Ch. 1.
13. See the British case of *Rondel v Worseley* (1967) 3 All E.R. 993, but recently a barrister has been held accountable in England for negligence in preparing paperwork. (*Saif Ali v Sydney Mitchell* [1978] 3 All E.R. 1033).
14. Courts Act, 1971.
15. Both solicitors and barristers, by virtue of the European Commission (services of lawyers) Order, 1978, have had the right of audience in all courts in the Member States of the E.E.C.
16. Delaney, op cit, pp. 89-92.
17. Royal Commission on Legal Services C.M.N.D. 7648, paras. 17 and 39.

CHAPTER 7

1. Wide-ranging powers are contained in Criminal Law Act, 1976, s. 18 in particular.
2. A very useful review of the law of search, seizure and arrest is contained in Declan Costello J. 'Rights of Accused Persons and the Irish Constitution of 1937'. Presented at the U.K. National Committee of Comparative Law Colloquium Sept. 1978, 'Human Rights in Criminal Procedure'.
3. This point has attracted much litigation, especially in Britain; see *Christie v Leachinsky* (1947) A.C. 573 and, more recently, *Kenlin v Gardiner* (1967) 2 Q.B. 510; but in Ireland must be read in close juncture with the 'Fundamental Rights', Articles 40-44 of the Constitution; see Costello (op cit), pp. 1-7 for further details.
4. An interesting account of this Act is contained in D. G. Morgan, 'The Emergency Powers Bill – Reference 1', *The Irish Jurist,* XIII (1978) p. 67.
5. This must be considered in the light of the case of *A.G. v O'Brian* (1965) I.R. 142, in which the Supreme Court laid down guide-lines for the courts to follow when dealing with evidence illegally obtained in general.
6. See *D.P.P. v Madden* (unreported).
7. See for example *Douglas v California* (1963) 9 L. Ed. 2d. 811.
8. This is discussed in greater detail in Cross, *Cross on Evidence,* (Butterworths 1979) Ch. 1, 17, 18, 19 and 20.
9. This would appear to be common law in origin, though its constitutionality might, if tested, be doubted (i.e. imposing a penalty regardless of conviction).

10. Under the Mental Treatment Acts, 1945/61.

11. The scheme under which compensation for damages suffered to property is contained in the Criminal or Malicious Injury Act.

12. This was discussed at great length in *A.G. v O'Callaghan* (1966) I.R. 501.

13. More detail on this Constitutional protection is contained in Ch. 9.

14. See Ch. 5 for the description of the civil courts.

15. The procedure in the civil courts is described in Delaney *Administration of Justice*, Ch. 7, pp. 57-64.

16. The rule against asking leading questions has been noted above, see reference 8.

17. These technical terms are explained in Osborne *A Concise Law Dictionary* (Sweet & Maxwell 1964). Also see Delaney, op cit, p. 63.

CHAPTER 8

1. Constitution of Ireland 1937, Article 40.1 and 40.3.1°.

2. This was discussed in the *State (Healy) v Donoghue* (1976) I.R. 325.

3. *Johanna Airey v Republic of Ireland.* European Court of Human Rights, 9th October 1979, 6289.

4. See Ch. 4.

5. Many alternative ways of solving a dispute may exist, including arbitration, or industrial action. Nowhere is this more clearly demonstrated than in the field of labour/management relations.

6. Adamsdown Community Trust 'Community Need and Law Centre Practice' (1978), available from Adamsdown Community Trust, Clifton St., Cardiff.

7. Note in particular Morris, Cooper and Byles 'Public Attitudes to Problem Definition and Problem Solving' British Journal of Social Work 3 (1973), p. 301; Morris, White and Lewis *Social Needs and Legal Action* (Martin Robertson 1973), Bankowski and Mungham *Images of Law* (Routledge and Kegan Paul 1976).

8. The role of the insurance company should be more fully explained. A contract of insurance is an agreement between an individual and the insurer to pay a certain figure by way of indemnity if damage is suffered by a third party (or the insured), depending on the terms of the agreement and the law. Thus if A is injured through B's careless driving, A might sue B for damage suffered. Theoretically if B denies liability A would have to sue B. The fact that B is insured against such a risk is generally of no concern to A. However, it is standard practice if liability is admitted for B's insurers to settle the damages without B having to pay (and consequently having to recoup from the insurance company) thus saving two claims for the one issue of damage.

9. In such a case a payment might be made into court in an attempt to settle. If the court awards the amount of the payment in, or less, the plaintiff A would not be likely to be awarded costs. The payment is therefore an attempt to show willingness to settle the dispute. At any stage prior to judgement A can accept the payment. This device puts considerable pressure on the parties to settle, for fear of losing costs.

10. 'Scheme of Civil Legal Aid and Advice' Dec. 1979 (Stationery Office, Dublin) Prl. 8543 (the Regulations).

11. Criminal Justice (Legal Aid) Act, 1962.

12. See the Regulations, op. cit, section 3.2.

13. With the exception of the rulings of the European Court of Human Rights, the only litigation on the point has been over the right to access to lawyers under the criminal law in the *State (Healy) v Donoghue* (1976), op cit.

14. This is currently available under the Family Law (Maintenance of Spouses and Children) Act, 1976, and the Enforcement of Court Orders Act, 1940.

15. There is in any case an inherent power for the State to agree to defray costs, but this is discretionary and cannot therefore be relied upon as by right.

16. The willingness and ability of centres to take on casework beyond advice-

giving is noted by the Pringle Report, op cit, para. 1.6.3, p. 31.

17. Report of Committee on Civil Legal Aid and Advice (Stationery Office Dublin) Prl. 6862. 1977. (The Pringle Report).

18. ibid, paras. 5.4 – 5.6, pp. 126-33.

19. ibid, paras. 2.3 – 4.11, pp. 39-104.

20. ibid, paras. 6.1 – 6.2, p. 134.

21. Regulations, op cit, paras 3.1 – 3.2, pp. 12-15.

22. ibid, paras A1.A4, p. 38.

23. ibid, paras. 5.1 – 5.3, and paras. B1-B6, pp. 25-8 and 39-48.

CHAPTER 9

1. Article 2.

2. Article 3.

3. Article 6.

4. Mansergh, *Survey of British Commonwealth Affairs (1931-1939)* p. 297, cited by Chubb, *The Constitution of Ireland* (I.P.A. 1963) at 21 (hereinafter referred to as Chubb).

5. After consultation with the Council of State.

6. The Offences Against the State (Amendment) Bill, 1940 (upheld), The School Attendance Bill 1942 (repugnant), The Electoral Amendment Bill, 1961 (upheld), The Criminal Law (Jurisdiction) Bill 1975 (upheld) and The Emergency Powers Bill 1976 (upheld).

7. Article 34.3.3.

8. See Chubb *The Constitution of Ireland* p. 23 and *The Government and Politics of Ireland* generally.

9. Article 28(11)(i).

10. Article 13(7)(i).

11. Article 13(7)(ii).

12. Article 13(7)(3).

13. Article 13(10).

14. Article 13(9).

15. Article 13(11).

16. Article 14(1).

17. Article 14(2).

18. Article 14(4).

19. Article 12(9).

20. Article 13(8)(i).

21. Article 12(10)(i).

22. Article 12(10)(iii).

23. Article 12(10)(v).

24. Article 12(10)(vi).

25. Article 15(1).

26. Article 15(2) as amended by the Fourth Amendment of the Constitution Act 1972 (E.E.C.).

27. Article 28(2).

28. Article 21(1).

29. Article 20(2).

30. Article 23(1)(i).

31. ibid.

32. Article 21(2).

33. Article 24.

34. Article 18(8).

35. Article 16(5). The article goes on to provide that a shorter period may be fixed by law. A shorter period of five years has been fixed by the Electoral Act, 1963, s. 10.

36. Article 28(i).

37. Article 28(5).

38. Article 28(6).

39. Article 28(7)(i).

40. Article 28(7)(ii).

41. ibid.

42. Article 34(4)(ii).

43. Article 34(3)(ii).

44. Kelly, *Fundamental Rights in Irish Law and Constitution,* 2nd ed. (Figgis & Co., Dublin, 1967) pp. 17-21 (hereinafter referred to as Kelly).

45. ibid, p. 19.

46. The Seanad passed a resolution in identical terms the same day.

47. Heuston, Personal Rights under the Irish Constitution, *Irish Jurist* (N.S.) XI (1976), 205 at 211.

48. [1965] I.R. 294.

49. The *State (Healy) v Donoghue,* [1976] I.R. 325, 347.

50. See *Landers v A.G.* (1975) 109 I.L.T.R., and *Murtagh Properties Ltd. v Cleary* [1972] I.R. 330.

51. Emphasis added.

52. Emphasis added.

53. Kelly at 73.

54. *McMahon v A.G.* (1972) I.R. 69.

55. *De Burca v A.G.* (1976) I.R. 38.

56. See Heuston, Personal Rights under the Constitution, *Irish Jurist* XI (1976) 205.

57. Chubb at 57.

58. Emphasis added.

59. See generally Barrington, Private Property under the Irish Constitution, *Irish Jurist* (N.S.) VII (1973) 1.

60. Barrington, at 3.

61. See *Buckley & Ors. v A.G. & Ors.* (Sinn Fein Funds Case) (1950) I.R. 67.

62. For a thorough and recent account of the Constitution see J. Kelly, 'The Irish Constitution', *Irish Jurist,* 1980.

CHAPTER 10

1. See generally Lasok and Bridges, *An Introduction to the Law and Institutions of the European Communities,* 2nd ed., (Butterworths 1976) (hereinafter referred to as Lasok).

2. See Lasok, pp. 293-301.

3. Lasok, p. 294.

4. Smit & Herzog, 'The Law of the European Economic Community', (Columbia Law School Project on European Legal Institutions, New York), (hereinafter referred to as Smit & Herzog).

5. *Frilli v Belgian State,* 1/72, [1973] C.M.L.R. 386, cited by Lasok at 306.

6. *Angelo Alaimo v Prefet du Rhone,* 68/74, [1975] E.C.R. 109, cited by Lasok at 307.

7. Smit & Herzog 2-461.

CHAPTER 11

1. See Ch. 7.
2. (1969) I.Q.B. 439.
3. *R. v Gibbons and Proctor* (1918) Cr. App. Rep. 134.
4. See Smith and Hogan, *Criminal Law* (4th ed. Butterworths 1978).
5. For a useful and concise account see Cross and Jones, *Introduction to Criminal Law* 8th ed. (Butterworths 1976) Ch. 3, pp. 30-37.
6. The relationship between intention to commit a crime and foreseeability of the damage caused was discussed at length in the British cases of *R v Mohan (1975)* 2 All E.R. 193, and *Hyam v D.P.P.* (1974) 2 All E.R. 41.
7. The unlawful act may be stealing or attempting to steal, inflicting or attempting to inflict grevious bodily harm, raping or unlawfully damaging the property in question. See Larceny Act, 1916 (as amended by Criminal Law (Jurisdiction) Act, 1976) s. 23 (a) and 23 (b).
8. In *People v Murray* 1977 I.L.T.R. the court accepted however, that an offence will only be one of strict liability where it is clear that the legislature intended to dispense with the requirement of mensrea.
9. *R v Waite* (1892) 2 Q.B. 600.
10. But a woman can be convicted of indecent assault.
11. For example certain offences relating to prostitution.
12. The British case of *Hill v Baxter* (1958) I.Q.B. 277 sets out the general proposition with automatism caused by an outside force but *R v Charlson* 1955 I All E.R. 859, which gave the concept a wider base, stands alone and has not been approved by the courts in Ireland or Britain. Clearly if automatism is caused by a non-mental condition (e.g. being rendered unconscious by a flying stone while driving) this defence may be pleaded. If the automatism is, however, caused by a mental condition the person is either guilty or legally insane. It would appear that in *People v Hayes* (1967) the concept of irresistible impulse is to be considered, but this would for all intents and purposes be tantamount to insanity.
13. (1843) 10 C.I. and Fin. 200. In the case of *Doyle v Wicklow County Council* (1971) I.R. 55 however, the Supreme Court said that the old principles contained in the *McNaghten Rules* were not to be considered the exclusive test for determining the question of insanity.
14. Thus it would seem that in this country a person is either insane or sane, with no middle ground to allow for acquittal where the mental state of mind is impaired but falls short of insanity.
15. For example manslaughter.
16. See the case of *A.G. for Northern Ireland v Gallagher* (1963) A.C. 349, and more generally *D.P.O. v Beard* (1920) A.C. 479.
17. *R v Tolson 1889* 23 Q.B.D. 168.
18. *Fagan v M.P.C.*, op cit.
19. *A.G. v Whelan* (1934) I.R.
20. (1884) 14 Q.B.D. 273.
21. The British authority of *R. v Donovan* (1934) 2 K.B. 498. would appear to be accepted in Ireland.
22. Generally see *People v Byrne* (1974) I.R. I as based on the British case of *Woolmintgon v D.P.P.* (1935) A.C. 462.
23. The topic of participation in crime was discussed by the Court of Criminal Appeal in *People v Madden* (1977) I.L.T.R.
24. The law in Ireland was developed somewhat further than the position at common law by the case of *People v Crosbie* (1966) I.R. where the culpable act/omission was described as unlawful and dangerous (voluntary manslaughter).
25. Contrast the British cases of *R v Smith* (1959) 2 Q.B. 35. with *R. v Jordan* (1956) 40 Cr. App. Rep. 152.

26. As in the British case of *D.P.P. v Smith* (1961) A.C. 290.
27. Criminal Justice Act, 1964, S.I.
28. It was thought that the test for provocation was an objective one. However, in the recent case of *McEoin* (1978) 112 I.L.T.R. 53 a subjective standpoint was adopted.
29. S.60 Offences Against the Person Act, 1861.
30. The principle of transferred malice is laid down in *R. v Latimer* (1886) 17 Q.B.D. 359. But note the limitations of this as shown by *R. v Pembliton* (1874) L.R. 2C.C.R. 119 (a qualitative rather than quantitative difference resulted).
31. For a thorough discussion of assault and battery see *Fagan v M.P.C.*, op cit.
32. Ss. 18 and 20 Offences Against the Person Act, 1861.
33. See *People v Messitt* (1974) 406.
34. Ss. 17-35 Offences Against the Persons Act, 1861.
35. Note the limitations of this as in *People v Keathley* (1954) I.R. 12.
36. Note the Criminal Law Amendment Act, 1935 has been amended by the Health (Family Planning) Act, 1979.
37. ibid., s.1.
38. See s. 55 Offences Against the Persons Act, 1861, and s. 7 Criminal Law Amendment Act, 1885 (as amended).
39. See McGee v A.G. (1975) 109 I.L.T.R. 29. *Quare* whether the test for reasonable access to contraceptives for married persons has been met.

40. See Ch. 2 (the rules of statutory interpretation).
41. The British case of *Billing v Pill* (1953) 2 All E.R. 1061 illustrates the point.
42. *R. v Foley* (1889) 17 Cox 142.
43. This complex aspect of larceny has attracted several significant cases in Britain including *D.P.P. v Ray* (1974) A.C. 370; *Lawrence v M.P.C.* (1972) A.C. 626 and *D.P.P. v Turner* (1974) A.C. 357, where the verdicts hinged upon the application of property rights as much as criminal law. But note the effect of s. 13 of Debtors (Ir.) Act, 1872, which may still be relevant.
44. For a more detailed analysis of these topics see P.A.O'Siochain, *The Criminal Law of Ireland*, Dubhlinn Foilsiúcháin, Chapter XI 1977.
45. *R. v Tomlinson* (1895) 18 Cox 75.
46. *A.G. v Kyle* (1933) I.R. 15.
47. This is clearly set out in the British case of *R. v Gambling* (1974) 3 All E.R. 479.
48. For example possession of forged documents (ss. 8-10).
49. S.6 Offences Against the Persons Act, 1939.
50. ibid, s.7.
51. ibid., s.8.
52. ibid, s.9.
53. ibid, s.16.
54. ibid, s.15.
55. ibid, s.17.
56. ibid, s.21 Part V and s.3 Offences Against the State (Am) Act, 1972.
57. Many offences of this nature that are either strict liability or require only negligence on the part of the defendant, are contained in Road Traffic Act, 1961 (as amended).
58. Coinage Act, 1861.
59. Generally see *R. v Robinson* (1915) K.B. 342.
60. See the judgement of *Haughton v Smith* (1973) 3 All E.R. 1109.
61. The problems appertaining to attempting the physically impossible examined in *D.P.P. v Nock* [1978] 2 All E.R. 654.
62. *R. v Jones* (1832) 4 B and Ad. 345.
63. S.1. Trade Disputes Act, 1906.
64. S.2 Criminal Law (Jurisdiction) Act, 1976.

CHAPTER 12

1. Constitution of 1937, Articles 43 (1)(i) and (ii), and see the judgement in *Meskell v C.I.E.* [1973] I.R. 121.

2. For a detailed account of these rules see Trietel, *The Law of Contract* (Stevens 1979) and Cheshire and Fifoot, *The Law of Contract* (Butterworths 1976) (although the post-1922 statutory and case references are British in origin, most of the provisions are relevant to Irish law).

3. (1932) 49 T.L.R. 369.

4. *Minister of Industry v Pim* (1965) I.R. 154.

5. *Carlill v Carbolic Smokeball Co.* (1893) Q.B. 256.

6. *Felthouse v Bindley* (1862) II C.B. (N.S.) 869.

7. *Household Fire Ins. v Grant* (1879) 4 Ex. D. 216, but note the limitations of this in *Arms v Lindsell* (1818) B & Aid 681.

8. *Harvey v Facey* [1893] A.C. 552, and *McQuaid v Lynam* [1965] I.R. 564.

9. *Hillos v Arcos* (1932) 147 L.T. 503, and *Kerns v Manning* [1935] I.R. 809.

10. Note the cases in Britain of *Jones v Paduation* [1969] 1 W.L.R. 328, *Balfour v Balfour* [1919] K.B. 571, *Simpkins v Pays* [1955] 1 W.L.R. 975.

11. This has been litigated in Britain in *Ford v AUEFW* [1969] 2 Q.B. 303, but it has been affected by statutory intervention reversing the presumption.

12. Again examples from Britain serve as illustrations of this point. See the case of *Hussey v Palmer* [1972] 3 All E.R. 744, with the court's use of the constructive or implied trust.

13. *Lampleigh v Braithwaite* (1615) H.O.B. 105.

14. (1884) 9 App. Cas. 605.

15. (1947) K.B. 130 approved in *Cullen v Cullen [1962]* I.R.

16. The contract need only be evidenced by memoranda) by writing and not be completely documented itself.

17. Note the British case of *Hillos v Arcos,* op cit.

18. *Robophone v Blank* [1966] 1 W.L.R. 1428.

19. The tendency for the courts to ensure the operation of commercial contract has been an increasing feature of modern litigation. The Privy Council in *New Zealand Shipping Co. v A.M. Satterwaite & Co.* [1975] A.C. 154 showed how they were willing to interpret a commercial contract for the benefit of all parties. Decisions that bring out the same point is the *Moorcock* (1889) 14 P.B. 64.

20. *Brown v Gailbraith* [1972] 3 All E.R. 31.

21. This important statute which implied conditions of quality and fitness for purpose has been significantly amended by the Sale of Goods & Supply of Services Act, 1980 (effective from 1.1.1981). References to the 1893 Act here refer to it as amended by the 1980 Act.

22. [1962] 2 Q.B. 26.

23. Ss. 12 and 15 imply conditions or warranties.

24. See *Hong Kong Fir Shipping Co. v Kawasaki* op. cit.

25. See *Wallis v Pratt* (1911) A.C. 394.

26. (1876) I. Q.B.D. 183.

27. See the Sale of Goods & Supply of Services Act, 1980, which considerably restricts the use of exemption clauses to avoid liability for shoddy goods or unsatisfactory services.

28. (1934) K.B. 394.

29. *Olley v Marlborough* [1949] 1 K.B. 532.

30. *Thornton v Shoelane Parking* [1971] 2 Q.B. 163.

31. [1951] Q.B. 805, and note *Miley v McKechnie Ltd.* (1950) 84 IL.T.R. 89, and *Alexander v Irish National Stud Farm* (1977).

32. op cit, see reference 19.

33. [1967] A.C. 361.

35. *Andrews v Hopkinson* [1957] 1 Q.B. 229.

36. *Delassale v Guildford* [1901] 2 K.B. 215.
37. *Tamplin v James* (1880) 15 Ch. 1 215.
38. *Raffles v Wichelhaus* (1864) 2 H & C 900, *Hardiman v Galway C.C.* (1966) I.R. 124.
39. *Couturier v Hastie* (1956) 5 H.L.C., 73.
40. *Cooper v Phipps* (1876) L.R. 2 H.L. 149.
41. See *Bell v Lever Bros.* [1932] A.C. 161 and *Leaf v International Galleries* (1950) 2 K.B. 86.
42. *Riverlate Properties v Paul* [1974] Ch. 133.
43. See *Nolan v Graves and Hamilton* (1946) I.R. 377.
44. *Cundy v Linsay* (1878) 3 App. Cas. 459.
45. *Kings Norton Metal v Eldridge Merrett & Co.* (1897) 14 T.L.R. 98.
46. *Phillips v Brooks* [1919] 2 K.B. 243.
47. [1972] I.Q.B. 198 and note *Anderson v Ryan* [1967] I.R. 34.
48. (186A) L.R., 4 C.P. 704.
49. See *Saunders v Anglia Building Society* [1971] A.C. 1004.
50. The role of equity was examined in *Solle v Butcher* [1950] I.K.B. 671.
51. See Trietel, op cit, pp. 302-06 and 830-2.
52. *Bissett v Wilkinson* [1927] A.C. 177.
53. *Pearson v Dublin Corporation* [1907] A.C. 357.
54. [1936] C.H. 575.
55. *Derry v Peek* (1889) 14 Cas. 337 and *Anderson v Ryan* (1967) I.R. 34.
56. [1964] A.C. 463 adopted by the High Court in *Securities Trust v Hugh Moore and Alexander* (1964) I.R.
57. *Wittington v Seal Hayne* (1900) 16 T.L.R. 181.
58. [1966] I.R. 661.
59. (1937) 2 K.B. 389. and note also *Headford v Brockett* [1966] I.R. 277.
60. [1887] 36 Ch. D. 145; see also *McMackin v Hibernian Bank* [1905] I.R. 296.
61. *Peters v Fleming* (1840) 6 M and W 42.
62. [1935] K.B. 110.
63. *Godley v Perry* [1960] 1 W.L.R. 9.
64. See *Leslie v Sheill* [1914] 3 K.B. 607, *Burnard v Haggis* (1863) 14 C.B. (N.S.) 45, *GRPE v Overton* (1833) 10 Bing. 252.
65. *Smith v Mawhood* (1845) 14 M and W 452.
66. [1924] 1 K.B. 138.
67. (1725) 9 L.Q.R. 197.
68. [1968] A.C. 269.
69. *Oates v Romano* (1950) 84 I.L.T.R. 161, and *Esso Petroleum v Fogarty* [1965] I.R. 531.
70. *Maxim-Nordenfelt v Nordenfelt* [1894] A.C. 535 and note *Lewis v Lewis* (1940) I.R. 42.
71. *Brittain v Rossiter* (1879) 11 Q.B.D. 123.
72. *Cheagh v Sheedy* (1955) Ir. Ju. 85.
73. op cit.
74. *Maritime Fishing Co. v Ocean Trawlers* [1935] A.C. 524.
75. (1863) 3 B and S 826.
76. Contrast the cases of *Krell v Henry* [1903] K.B. 740 with *Herne Bay Steamship Co. v Hutton* [1903] K.B. 683.
77. *Fibrosa v Fairbairn* [1943] A.C. 32.
78. (1854) 9 Ex 341.
79. See *Jarvis vs Swans Tours* (1973) 1 All E.R. 71 and *Johnson v Longleat* 19/5/76 (unreported).
80. *Brace v Calder* [1895] 2 Q.B. 253.
81. See Ch. 13 and in particular the cases of the*Wagonmound* No. 1 [1961]

A.C. 388 and No. 2 (1967) A.C. 617.

82. *Harsham v Zenab* (1960) A.C. 316.

83. *Hill v Parsons* [1972] Ch. 305.

84. See *Glynn v University of Keele* (1971) 1 W.L.R. 487.

85. S. 8 op cit.

86. Ss. 50-54.

CHAPTER 13

1. See generally Heuston, *Salmond. The Law of Torts* (17th ed., 1977) (hereafter cited as Salmond). The authors wish to acknowledge that this chapter draws heavily on Professor Houston's edition of Salmond.

2. Fleming. *An Introduction to the Law of Torts* (Oxford, 1967), at 4.

3. See Jordan C. J. in *Dougherty v Chandler* (1946) 46 S.R. (N.S.W.) 370 at 375 cited by Salmond (Houston ed.) 452.

4. See *Lister v Romerd Ice Co.* [1951] A.C. 555.

5. (1808) I. Camp. 493.

6. A license to enter land may be expressed or implied, gratuitously given or granted for consideration under a contract.

7. *Harrison v Duke of Rutland* [1893] I.Q.B. 142.

8. Salmond at 41.

9. *Simpson v Weber* (1925) T.L.R. 302 cited by Salmond at 42.

10. *St. Helens Smelting Co. v Tipping* (1865) 11 H.L. Cas. 642 at 650 (cited by Salmond at 57).

11. Knight Bruce V.C. in *Walter v Selfe* (1851) 4 De G. & Sm. 315 at 322 (cited by Salmond at 56).

12. Salmond at 57.

13. (1868) L.R. 3 H.L. 330.

14. Per Blackburn J. ibid at 279.

15. (1947) A.C. 156.

16. Salmond at 327.

16a. *Electricity Supply Board v Hastings* [1965] Ir. Ju. Rep. 51.

16b. *National Coal Board v Evans* [1951] 2 K.B. 861.

17. Per O'Keefe J. O'Dalaigh C. J. and Walsh J. concurring [1968] I.R. 305.

18. (1841) 8 M and W 540 cited by Salmond at 98.

19. [1937] 2 K.B. 242 cited by Salmond at 97.

20. See Salmond at 138.

21. The tort of negligence is discussed in this section even though it relates to other issues as well. Since many reported negligence actions involve claims for personal injuries we decided to deal with negligence here. The reader should not conclude, however, that the scope of this tort is confined to injuries to the person. It applies equally to damage negligently caused to property and may, in certain circumstances, be the appropriate cause of action for purely economic loss. And it should be stressed that negligence at least numerically, is the most important area of tort in practice, with the majority of civil tortious actions based on a claim of negligence.

22. [1932] A.C. 562 at 579.

23. *Dorset Yacht Co. Ltd. v Home Office* [1969] 2 Q.B. 412 at 426 cited by Salmond at 202.

24. See McMahon 'The Reactions of Tortious Liability to the Industrial Revolution' (Part II) III Ir. Ju. (Ms) 284 at 285 (1968).

25. [1963] 2 All E.R. 575.

26. Salmond at 202.

27. *Glasgow Corporation v Muir* [1943] A.C. 448 at 457 cited by Salmond at 222.

28. [1951] A.C. 850.

29. See McMahon study foı Report of Advisory Committee on Law Reform, 'Occupier's Liability in Ireland'., pr. I 4403 1975, pp. 21-22.

30. ibid, at 29-30.

31. [1972] I All E.R. 749.

32. [1974] I.R. I.

33. ibid, at 14.

34. ibid.

35. See Law Reform Commission Working Paper No. 1 1977, entitled 'The Law relating to the Liability of Builders, Vendors and Lessors for the Quality and Fitness of Premises'.

36. *Berry v The Irish Times* (1973) I.R. 368.

37. [1940] I.K.B. 377.

38. See Shatter *Family Law in the Republic of Ireland,* 1st ed., Ch. 6, pp. 88-90; and Ch. 17 (herein).

39. An interesting account of this aspect of tortious liability in Britain can be found in Perrin, *Labour Relations Law Now* (Butterworths 1975)) Ch. 5.

CHAPTER 14

1. For a detailed account of the law relating to personal property see James, *Introduction to English Law* 10th ed. (Butterworths 1979) pp. 480-495, although the post-1922 statutory references are not applicable to Ireland.

2. See Wylie, *Irish Land Law* (Professional Books 1975). This chapter draws heavily on Mr. Wylie's excellent book.

3. See Wylie.

4. The powers of the tenant-for-life were strictly limited at common law. Legislation enacted in the 19th century (known as the Settled Land Acts) has considerably enlarged these powers.

5. Seisin was a precondition to bring an action in the King's Courts. Hence the leaseholder could not bring such an action.

6. But see s. 95 of the Succession Act, 1965.

7. See Wylie at 146/147.

8. No. 27 of 1965 (hereinafter referred to as the Act).

CHAPTER 15

1. For a general discussion of company law with British statutory references see Topham and Ivamy, *Company Law* (Butterworths 1978).

2. For example the East India Company, incorporated by Elizabeth I in 1600.

3. Limited Liability Act, 1855.

4. (1901) I Ch. 278 at 288.

5. Companies Act, 1963, s.2(i).

6. ibid, s.31.

7. ibid., s.130.

8. ibid, s.133.

9. (1843) 2 HARE 461.

10. Companies Act, 1963, ss. 201-204.

11. ibid, s.215.

12. ibid, s.220.

13. ibid, s.218.

14. ibid, s.222.

15. ibid, s.256.

16. ibid, s.263.

CHAPTER 16

1. Conditions of Employment Act, 1936/44, and Protection of Young Persons (Employment) Act, 1977.
2. Shops (Condition of Employment) Act, 1938/42, and Night Work (Bakeries) Act, 1936.
3. Holidays (Employees) Act, 1973.
4. Minimum Notice and Terms of Employment Act, 1973.
5. Of 1831, 1887 and 1896.
6. Family Law (Maintenance of spouses and Children) Act, 1976.
7. The relevance of damages for wrongful (as opposed to unfair) dismissal can be seen in the case of *Glover v B.L.M.* [1973] I.R. 388.
8. See Ch. 5.
9. Strictly speaking, the employee (applicant) must establish that he or she was dismissed (this is usually admitted by the employer) and the onus then lies with the employer (respondent) to establish compliance with one of the grounds contained in s.6 of the 1977 Act, e.g. misconduct, incapability, redundancy, etc.
10. ibid, s.2.
11. See Ch. 18.
12. Redundancy Payment Acts, 1967/71/79, Sched. III 1967 (as amended).
13. The 1977 Act lays down minimum periods of notice that must be given when collective redundancies are planned. These notices relate to the notification of redundancy and not, as such, to the termination of the contract (which will be subject to contract and/or the Minimum Notice and Terms of Employment Act, 1973). The notice must be given to employees via their union and the Minister of Labour. This is an important piece of legislation aimed at conciliation.
14. See *Electrolux v Hutchinson* [1976] I.R.L.R. 410 and [1977] I'C.R. 252.
15. S.2 (3) Anti-Discrimination (pay) Act, 1974.
16. Trade Union Act, 1941, s.5.
17. [1901] A.C. 426.
18. Note in particular the scope this has given to judicial interpretation, especially in Britain. See *Sherard v A.U.E.W.* (1973) I.C.R. 421.
19. For further discussion on the 'right' to picket see Perrins, *Labour Relations Law Now* (1975) Ch. 5, and a now somewhat dated account in Shillman, *Trade Unions and Unionism in Ireland* 1960 Ch. 4 and 5.
20. See Shillman (op cit).
21. Generally see Ch. 12 and the availability of specific performance to enforce a contract.
22. See Ch. 18 and the entitlement to welfare benefit.
23. See Perrins, op cit, pp. 83-5.
24. See Bibliography below.

CHAPTER 17

1. On Constitutional law generally see Ch. 9.
2. See for example *State (Nicolaou) v An Bord Uchtala (Adoption Board)* [1966] I.R. 567.
3. See *Bank of Ireland v Caffin* [1971] I.R. 123; *Gaffney v Gaffney* [1975] I.R. 133.
4. Law Reform Commission Working Paper No. 4 – 1978 'The Law Relating to Breach of Promise of Marriage'.
5. As a result of certain early cases this has been interpreted to mean that the simple exchange of promises between the parties, in the presence of an episcopably

ordained priest, is sufficient. See *Ussher v Ussher* [1912] 2 I.R. 445.

6. Law Reform Commission Working Paper No. 5 (1978) 'The Law Relating to Criminal Conversation, and the Enticement and Harbouring of a Spouse'.

7. See note 3. *supra*.

8. Generally see Shatter *Family Law in the Republic of Ireland* 2nd ed. (Wolfhound Dublin 1981).

CHAPTER 18

1. See Ogus and Barendt, *The Law of Social Security* (Butterworths 1978) Ch. 1, pp. 1-7.

2. In the Social Welfare Act, 1952, which despite many amending and additional statutes is still the principal statutory base for social welfare benefits.

3. For an interesting account of the way in which law is thought and perceived see Maureen Cain, 'Rich Man's Law or Poor Man's Law', *Brit. Journal of Law and Society* (1975).

4. Indeed this is the title of a publication in Britain by C. Smith and D. Hoath (Routledge and Kegan Paul 1975).

5. See Ch. 16.

6. Statutory instruments 1952-79.

7. See Ch. 5.

8. The exact details of number of contributions, time periods and dates involved are described in a booklet issued free of charge from the Department of Social Welfare, entitled 'Summary of Social Insurance and Social Assistance Services'.

9. While European Regulations (principally 1408/71) attempt to ensure equality of access to benefits for all nationals of Member States, regardless of country of residence within the E.E.C., this does not as yet ensure parity of benefits throughout all States. Thus an Irish National resident in France will take the benefits available in *that* country, but may use contribution records paid in Ireland.

10. This was made available under the Social Welfare (Supplementary Welfare Allowance) Act, 1975, effective since 1st January, 1977, which replaced the home assistance allowances which were discretionary.

11. The scheme most frequently used in Ireland is the Voluntary Health Insurance Scheme.

12. Social Welfare Act, 1952, ss. 41-46, in particular s.45.

13. A thorough appraisal of the courts' powers to intervene in the decision-making process can be found in *Kiely v Minister for Social Welfare* (1977) I.R. 267 per Henchy J.

14. There is to date little material on social welfare law in the Republic. However, valuable material can be found in R. W. Clark, 'Social Welfare Insurance Appeals in the Republic of Ireland', *Ir. Jur.* XIII (1978) 265.

15. For somewhat bizarre results see *Whitehall Court v Ettlinger* [1920] 1 K.B. 680.

16. Part II Rent Restriction Act, 1960.

17. *Cole v Kelley* [1920] 2 K.B. 106.

18. Part IV Rent Restriction Act, 1960, op. cit. Note generally, an appeal on the Constitutionality of the Act lies to the Supreme Court.

19. Rent Restriction (Amendment) Act, 1967.

20. *Smith v Marrable* (1843) 11 M and N.S.

21. The main provisions are to be found in Public Health (I.) Act, 1878, and the Health Act, 1947 (as amended).

22. Regulations made under s. 58 of the Housing Act, 1966.

23. However, in Britain it has been held that the exercise of the decision to evict must be reasonably arrived at, see *Bristol D.C. v Clark* (1975) 3 All E.R. 1976.

24. Ss. 53-62, Housing Act, 1966.

25. Contained in the Housing Bill, 1980, currently before the British Parliament.

26. Further information can be gleaned on a regular basis by subscription to *Case* (Journal of Irish Social Welfare Law and Civil Rights), issued by the Coolock Community Law Centre, Dublin.

27. Pringle Report, op cit, para. 4.6.1 (b) and (c), pp. 90-91.

CONCLUSION

1. This has we hope been an underlying theme of this text even though the material has by and large been descriptive in nature.

2. Law and ideology is a field of comparatively recent study to both sociologists and more particularly lawyers. An interesting appraisal of the study of ideology generally is to be found in a useful 'reader' entitled *Ideology in Social Science.* Blackburn Ed. (Fontana 1972).

3. The traditional atheoretical approach of lawyers to their subject and indeed others to the topic of law is well exposed by Cain, 'Rich Man's Law or Poor Man's Law'.

4. For the uninitiated (and initiated perhaps) a colourful account of the Greek philosophers is contained in Rius, *Marx for Beginners* (Writers and Readers Publishing Co-operative 1976) pp. 36-53.

5. For further details see Allen *Law in the Making* (Oxford Univ. Press 7th ed.) pp. 262-4.

6. Note Dias, *Jurisprudence,* (Butterworths 1970) generally Part III and in particular Ch. 20.

7. See Ch. 1.

8. 1748-1832, see Dias, op cit, pp. 490-94, although we are not sure why this section appears in a chapter devoted to the sociological school as such.

9. This brief account is not satisfactory and the reader should familiarise him or herself with the main strands of these works. A general overview is available in Dias, op cit, Ch. 14 and 15.

10. Rousseau and his concept of a social contract.

11. Cesare Lombrosso; and for further details see the thorough account of this 'progress' as documented in *The New Criminology* (Routledge and Kegan Paul 1973), Taylor, Walton and Young.

12. An outline of Hegel's philosophy is contained in Dias, op cit, pp. 437-9.

13. ibid, Ch. 16.

14. ibid, Ch. 19.

15. In the last 25 years a new 'economic school' has been developing in the United States. This concentrates on an economic analysis of legal rights; the modern development generally represents the view that State intervention in the economy is at best useless, and at worst detrimental. Using economic concepts such as 'utility', 'efficiency', and theories of price, competition and markets (as derived from micro- and macro-economics), this analysis asserts that the market forces will ensure the most efficient use of scarce resources. While of value in anti-trust problems and in examining questions of liability in tort (two of its earliest contributions) this school has recently propounded a complete theory of law. This economic theory is known as the Coarse Theorem. The principal foundation of the economic school is that the initial assignment of rights (whether property rights in the traditional sense or as including for example, the right to bodily integrity) is immaterial to their ultimate ownership in a free market. From here it is a short step to general opposition to all State intervention.

16. K. Marx, 'Speech in his Defence' (Cologne Trial, 1849) in D. McLellan, *Karl Marx: His Life and Thought.* (Macmillan 1973).

17. K. Marx and F. Engels, *Manifesto of the Communist Party* (1848) in 'Marx-Engels Selected Works' (Lawrence and Wishart 1950).

18. Hitler's reliance upon the theories of Nietzsche is well documented in O. Kirchheimer *Political Justice* (Princetown Univ. Press 1961). For further reading on

conceptions of legality in fascist states note P. Q. Hirst, *On Law and Ideology* (Macmillan 1979).

BIBLIOGRAPHY

This bibliography is arranged in chapter order. It contains works referred to in the text and footnotes, together with additional material that might be of interest to the reader.

CHAPTER 1

Baker, J. H. *An Introduction to English Legal History* (Butterworths 1979).
Chubb, B. *The Government and Politics of Ireland* (Oxford Univ. Press 1970).
Delany, V. T. H. (Lysaght ed.) *The Administration of Justice in Ireland* (I.P.A. Dublin 1975).
Dicey, A. V. *Law and Public Opinion in England* (Macmillan 1963).
Hanbury, H. G. & Maudsley, R. H. *Modern Equity: The Principles of Equity* (Sweet & Maxwell 1976).
James, P. S. *Introduction to English Law* (Butterworths 1979).
McNeill, E. *Early Irish Laws and Institutions.*
Manchester, A. H. *Modern Legal History* (Butterworths 1980).
Radzinowcz, L. *A History of English Criminal Law* (Sweet & Maxwell 1968).
Walker, R. J. & M. G. *The English Legal System* (Butterworths 1976).
Zander, M. *Cases and Materials on the English Legal System* (Weidenfeld and Nicolson 1980).

CHAPTER 2

Allen, C. K. *Law in the Making* (Oxford Univ. Press, 7th ed.).
Cross, R. *Precedent in English Law* (Butterworths 1977).
Cross, R. *Statutory Interpretations* (Butterworths 1976).
Dias, R. W. M. *Dias on Jurisprudence* (Butterworths 1976).

CHAPTER 3

Chesterman, M. *Charities Trusts and Social Welfare* (Weidenfeld & Nicolson 1979).
Underhill *Principles of the Law of Partnership* (Butterworths 1975).
Wright, D. H. *Co-operatives and Community* (Bedford Square Press 1979).

CHAPTER 4

Denning, Lord *The Discipline of the Law* (Butterworths 1979).
Farrar, J. *Introduction to Legal Method* (Sweet & Maxwell 1977).
Harris, P. *An Introduction to Law* (Weidenfeld & Nicolson 1980).
Twining, W. & Miers D. *How to do Things with Rules* (Weidenfeld & Nicolson 1976).

CHAPTER 5

Delany, V. T. H. *Op-cit.*
Jackson, R. M. *The Machinery of Justice in England* (Cambridge Univ. Press 1977).
Zander, M. *The Law Making Process* (Weidenfeld & Nicolson 1980).

CHAPTER 6

Bartholomew, P. C. *The Irish Judiciary* (I.P.A. Dublin 1971).
Griffith, J. A. G. *The Politics of the Judiciary* (Fontana 1977).

CHAPTER 7

Cross, R. *Cross on Evidence* (Butterworths 1979).
James, P. S. *Op cit.*

CHAPTER 8

Bankowski, Z. & Mungham, G. *Images of Law* (Routledge and Kegan Paul 1976).
Byles A. & Morris, P. *Unmet Need* (Routledge and Kegan Paul 1977).
Grace, C. & Wilkinson, P. *Negotiating the Law* (Routledge and Kegan Paul 1978).
Morris, P., White, R. & Lewis, P. *Social Needs and Legal Action* (Martin Robertson 1973).

CHAPTER 9

Chubb, B. *The Constitution of Ireland* (I.P.A. Dublin 1963).
Greig, D. W. *International Law* (Butterworths 1976).
Hood, Philips, O. *Constitutional and Administrative Law* (Sweet & Maxwell 1978).
Kelley, J. M. *Fundamental rights in the Irish Law and Constitution* (Figgis: Dublin 1967).
Kelley, J. M. *The Irish Constitution* (Irish Jurist 1980).

CHAPTER 10

Lasok, D. & Bridge, J. W. *Introduction to the Law and Institutions of the European Communities* (Butterworths 1976).
Smit and Herzog. *The Law of the European Economic Community* (Columbia Law School).

CHAPTER 11

Jones, P. A. & Card, R. I. E. *Cross and Jones' Introduction to Criminal Law* (Butterworths 1976).
O'Siochain, P. A. *The Criminal Law of Ireland* (Dubhlinn Foilsiuchain Dli 1977).
Smith, J. C. & Hogan, B. *Criminal Law* (Butterworths 1978).

CHAPTER 12

Furmston, M. P. *Cheshire & Fifoot on the Law of Contract* (Butterworths 1976).
Lowe, R. & Woodroffe, G. *Consumer Law and Practice* (Sweet & Maxwell 1980).
Trietel, H. G. *The Law of Contract* (Sweet & Maxwell 1979).

CHAPTER 13

Atiyah, P. S. *Accidents, Compensation and the Law* (Weidenfeld & Nicolson 1980).
Fleming, *An Introduction to the Law of Torts* (Oxford Univ. Press 1967).
Heuston, R. F. V. *Salmond. The Law of Torts* (Sweet & Maxwell 1977).

CHAPTER 14

James, P. S. *Op-cit.*
Megarry, R. & Wade, H. W. R. *The Law of Real Property* (Sweet & Maxwell 1975).
Wylie, J. C. W. *Irish Land Law* (Professional Books 1975 London).

CHAPTER 15

Hadden, T. *Company Law and Capitalism* (Weidenfeld & Nicolson 1977).
Ivamy, E. R. *Topnam and Ivamy's Company Law* (Butterworths 1978).

CHAPTER 16

Boyd, A. *The Rise of the Irish Trade Unions* (Anvil Dublin 1976).
Davis, P. & Freedland, M. *Labour Law: Text and Materials* (Weidenfeld & Nicolson 1979).
Kahn-Freund, O. *Labour and the Law* (Stevens 1977).
McMullen, M. *Rights at Work* (Pluto Press 1978).
Perrins, B. *Labour Relations Law Now* (Butterworths 1975).
Shillman, B. *Trade Unions and Unionism in Ireland* (Dublin Press 1960).

CHAPTER 17

Cretney *Principles of Family Law* (Sweet & Maxwell 1979).
Eekelaas, J. *Family Law and Social Policy* (Weidenfeld & Nicolson 1978).
Shatter, A. *Family Law in the Republic of Ireland (2nd Ed.)* (Wolfhound Dublin 1981).

CHAPTER 18

Calvert, H. *Social Security Law* (Swett & Maxwell 1978).
Hoath, D. *Council Housing* (Sweet & Maxwell 1978).
Ogus, A. & Barenot, G. M. *Law of Social Security* (Butterworths 1978).
Partington, M. *Landlord and Tenant* (Weidenfeld & Nicolson 1980).
Smith, C. & Hoath, D. *Law and the Underprivileged* (Routledge and Kegan Paul 1975).

CONCLUSION

Blackburn, Ed. *Ideology in Social Science* (Fontana 1972).
Hirst, P. Q. *Law and Ideology* (Macmillan 1979).
Kirchheimer, O. *Political Justice* (Princetown Univ. Press 1961).
McLellan, D. *Karl Marx: His Life and Thought* (Macmillan 1973).
Marx, K. *Manifesto of the Communist Party in Marx-Engels Selected Works* (Lawrence and Wishart 1950).
Rius, E. *Marx for Beginners* (Writers & Readers Pub. Co-op. 1976).
Taylor, I., Walton, P. and Young, J. *The New Criminology* (Routledge & Kegan Paul 1973).
Taylor, I., Walton, P. and Young, J. *Critical Criminology* (Routledge & Kegan Paul, 1975).

ADDITIONAL MATERIAL

Aubert, V. *Sociology of Law* (Penguin 1972).
Carlen, P. *Sociology of Law* (Univ. of Keele 1977).
Hartley, T. C. & Griffith, J. A. G. *Government and Law* (Weidenfeld & Nicolson 1975).
Wade, H. W. R. *Administrative Law* (Oxford Univ. Press 1979).
Osborn, P. G. *Concise Law Dictionary* (Sweet & Maxwell 1976).

The following periodals are recommended:

Case (Journal of Civil Rights, Social and Welfare Law) (Coolock Law Centre, Dublin.)
FLAC File: Free Legal Advice Centres (Flac Ltd., Dublin.).
The Irish Jurist (University College, Dublin).
Journal of Social Welfare Law (Sweet & Maxwell).

Table of Statutes

I Articles of the Constitution

II Statutes

Table of Cases

Index